T0134980

Springer Series on Cultural Computing

Founding Editor

Ernest Edmonds

Series Editor

Craig Vear, De Montfort University, Leicester, UK

Editorial Board

More information about this series at http://www.springer.com/series/10481

Vladimir Geroimenko

Editor

Augmented Reality in Tourism, Museums and Heritage

A New Technology to Inform and Entertain

 Springer

Editor
Vladimir Geroimenko
Faculty of Informatics & Computer Science
British University in Egypt
Cairo, Egypt

ISSN 2195-9056   ISSN 2195-9064   (electronic)
Springer Series on Cultural Computing
ISBN 978-3-030-70200-7   ISBN 978-3-030-70198-7   (eBook)
https://doi.org/10.1007/978-3-030-70198-7

This Springer imprint is published by the registered company Springer Nature Switzerland AG
The registered company address is: Gewerbestrasse 11, 6330 Cham, Switzerland

This research monograph is dedicated to future generations of heritage tourists and museum visitors.

With sincere gratitude to the British University in Egypt (BUE), a great place to work and edit books.

Preface

This book presents an extensive body of research into the use of augmented reality (AR) in the three interconnected and overlapping fields of the tourism industry, museum exhibitions, and cultural heritage. It explores the opportunities and challenges of augmented reality applications, their current status and future trends, informal learning and heritage preservation, mixed reality environments and immersive installations, cultural heritage education and tourism promotion, problems of special needs visitors and emerging post-COVID-19 museums and heritage sites, and aims to be essential reading for researchers, application developers, educators, museum curators, tourism and cultural heritage promoters, graduate and undergraduate students, and anyone else who is interested in the efficient and practical use of augmented reality technology.

It has been written by a virtual team of 50 leading researchers and practitioners, who are effectively and innovatively employing augmented reality as a new technology to both inform and entertain tourists and visitors. The book's contributors—distinguished by their specialist expertise, significant publications, and ongoing projects—have been chosen from 16 countries around the world: Brazil, Canada, Cyprus, Egypt, Germany, Greece, Indonesia, Italy, Malaysia, Mauritius, Portugal, Romania, Slovenia, Spain, Turkey, and USA.

It can also be considered as part of a series of six pioneering monographs published by Springer on the same subject of augmented reality and with the same editor:

- Augmented Reality Art: From an Emerging Technology to a Novel Creative Medium. Geroimenko V (Ed), Springer, 2014—314 p
- Augmented Reality Art: From an Emerging Technology to a Novel Creative Medium. Geroimenko V (Ed), 2nd Edition, Revised and Updated, Springer, 2018—384 p
- Augmented Reality Games I: Understanding the Phenomenon of Pokémon GO. Geroimenko V (Ed), Springer, 2019—256 p
- Augmented Reality Games II: The Gamification of Education, Medicine and Art. Geroimenko V (Ed.), Springer, 2019—306 p
- Augmented Reality in Education: A New Technology for Teaching and Learning. Geroimenko V (Ed), Springer, 2020—414 p

- Augmented Reality in Tourism, Museums and Heritage: A New Technology to Inform and Entertain. Geroimenko V (Ed), Springer, 2021—322 p

The book's 17 chapters, which can be read in sequence or randomly, are arranged in 3 parts as follows.

Part I "General Aspects and Augmented Reality in the Tourism Industry" includes 6 chapters (Chaps. 1 to 6).

Chapter 1 "Informal Learning with Extended Reality Environments: Current Trends in Museums, Heritage, and Tourism" discusses the capabilities of extended reality technology in informal learning environments, such as museums and cultural heritage sites. Recent developments in extended reality technologies have led to increased integration into these informal learning spaces and have heightened the need for a systematic investigation into the affordances of modern multimedia representations spanning tangible to virtual mediums. These affordances vary across settings, ranging from personalizing learning experiences, increasing engagement through interactive activities, and augmenting exhibits with rich multimedia content. The chapter critically appraises several affordances of extended reality technologies while expanding on these notions by outlining the cognitive theory of multimedia learning to inform practical instructional design principles. Drawing on case examples from their own research with tangible and virtual museum objects in these settings, the authors explore and discuss how extended reality technologies can serve to both collect and analyse ambient data in real time. The authors claim that ambient data will become increasingly prevalent in such settings and critical to gain insights into visitor experience and promote meaningful and engaging learning experiences. They discuss the implications of their findings for practice and suggest directions for future research.

In Chap. 2 "Collaborative Augmented Reality for Cultural Heritage, Tourist Sites and Museums: Sharing Visitors' Experiences and Interactions", synergies between augmented reality (AR) and shared experiences are explored. The shared experiences (such as visiting a cultural site or a museum) can benefit from computer-supported collaborative work done in the context of maintenance, training, and simulation. With the wide availability and use of AR-enabled smartphones, it is now possible to create collaborative experiences built upon knowledge gained from such industry-oriented training applications. This novel approach allows for a greater user engagement fostered by the collaborative nature of an AR shared space. Recent AR works allow for many users to observe the same superimposed object as the group and interact collaboratively with it, as users can see not only the other users but their actions and effects in the virtual elements. This methodology allows for group interaction around tangible cultural points of interest at different scales (such as ruins or buildings but also statues and paintings).

Chapter 3 "Augmented Reality Systems and their Future in Tourism: Before, During and After the Journey" describes Mixed Reality (MR) systems and applications in tourism from the perspective of when they support tourists: before, during, or after the journey. MR technologies have been around for five decades and have seen many developmental stages and breakthroughs. However, only in the past two decades have the technologies been available to the wider public. As such, they provided a platform to be used in tourism as well. The authors present a review following the PRISM methodology by which they uncovered 108 relevant applications, prototypes, and services. The authors labelled them based on the time when the provided functionalities would normally be used, e.g., before, during, and/or after the journey. The review highlights that the majority of prototypes and applications support the travel as it happens (105 out of 108 systems), whereas functionalities that support users before and after the visit only start to emerge later on as the field matures (9 and 10 out of 108, respectively). Therefore, MR applications that support tourist applications before and after the journey offer an untapped potential for future MR applications, prototypes, and services. Within the discussion, the authors also provide possible directions in which this domain could evolve in the future.

Chapter 4 "Augmented Reality and Intelligent Packaging for Smart Tourism: A Systematic Review and Analysis" addresses the systematic review and analysis of AR's convergence with intelligent packaging, specifying this interaction inside the touristic environment. The interchange of the real with the digital world gives importance to Internet of Things, Fifth Generation Mobile Phone Network (5G), Radio Frequency Identification (RFID), and Near Field Communication (NFC), which elicit this "intelligence" for the smart tourism. The review is focused on the components of tourism (tourist attractions, accommodation, catering, and transportation) that can be enhanced by the simultaneous redefinition of intelligent packaging with AR features and presenting possible perspectives of personalized and multisensorial attributes.

Chapter 5 "The New Normal Tourism in Indonesia: The Expansion of the Wonosari AR Project to Enhance Holiday Experience" examines the expansion of Wonosari AR, an augmented reality application in Agrowisata Wonosari, Malang, Indonesia. Digital reality applications have been widely used in the tourism industry of developed countries. The advancement of augmented reality technology in the tourism field is proven to increase people's interest, which has barely been done in developing countries, such as Indonesia. During the COVID-19 pandemic, most tourist attractions were closed for a few months to prevent the virus's spread. This phenomenon causes a reduction in the number of tourists. Focuses on its three markers' development process, the project aims to raise tourist affection during The New Normal Tourism in agricultural tourism with a digital approach. This chapter comprises the introduction of the research problem, the previous Wonosari AR project, the Wonosari AR project during The New Normal Tourism, and the development of this new application. The authors designed three AR markers in play cards, face masks, and tea packaging using the design thinking methodology. The combination of three different shapes of the AR marker fitted perfectly to promote future digital tourism. The chapter's discussion explores the prototyping and trial experiences, including the opportunity for future research in the use of AR for agrotourism.

Chapter 6 "Augmented Reality in Spain: Heritage Education, Cultural Tourism and Museums" analyses how Spanish institutions, archaeological sites, and publishers in the field of formal education are using augmented reality as an educational tool. After a decade since its arrival in the cultural world of Spain, augmented reality has undergone a process of implementation and settlement characterized by being in the background of activities, exhibitions, and by apps with such short life cycles that only a few specific studies have been conducted. The use of AR in some Roman sites in Spain, the Sorolla Museum in Madrid and the Alhambra in Granada, are examples that are analysed in this chapter based on significant educational theories within the field of Heritage Education.

Part II "Augmented Reality for Museums" comprises 5 chapters (Chaps. 7 to 11).

Chapter 7 "Immersive Installations in Museum Spaces: Staging the Past" reflects on museums' use of immersive media (IM) as a specific form of presentation. Augmented reality and virtual reality have long since found their way into museums. Considering that the museum itself is effectively a stage on which objects are displayed to the public in a way intended to convey meaning, one can assume that immersive installations build on an already semiotically complex reality. By drawing on the concept of theatricality, as defined in cultural studies, as well as contributions made by micro-sociology, a conceptual framework is proposed to understand and analyse IM in the museum. Against this background, two theses are discussed: First, to create a meaningful experience, curators have to manage a specific form of perspectivity to integrate physical space, and the rules applied to it, into its augmentation. Second, like every form of media, IM must develop strategies to cope with technical imperfection by creating a sense of immediacy.

Chapter 8 "The Use of Augmented Reality to Expand the Experience of Museum Visitors" is devoted to augmented reality in the museum context. Augmented reality has been regarded as a way to enhance the real-world environment using computer-generated perceptual information. It is a tool that museums should explore more to enhance the visitor experience. The aim of this chapter is to go further in understanding the use of augmented reality technology in museums. The objectives are (1) to give an overview of the meaning of augmented reality in tourism, (2) to provide examples of the use of augmented reality in museums, and (3) to offer suggestions for future research in the field. The results are the suggestions for future research and the contributions for academics and practitioners.

Chapter 9 "Gestures and Re-enactments in a Hybrid Museum of Archaeology: Animating Ancient Life" studies the interrelationship between a traditional archaeological museum and some digital ways of creating complex virtual cultural contexts. It is well known that the traditional archaeological museum has separated the objects from the viewer and has decontextualized them, thus greatly reducing the degree to which they can be understood. Lately, especially during a time of quarantine and lockdowns, museums are starting to become digital, and this renders possible a broad range of display options. However, the transformation is not a total one, the museums acting as hybrid organisms, with both real and virtual presences. This study describes the making of a virtual cultural context in which the shape of virtually reconstructed objects, gestures, and re-enactments, positioned both in the real and virtual worlds, animate ancient life and create a museum of hybrid archaeology.

Chapter 10 "Supporting Spontaneous Museum Visits by Deaf People: An Augmented Reality Application and a Case Study" presents research that aims to identify accessibility characteristics necessary for a satisfactory interaction of prelingual deaf users with the contents of a museum exhibition. To achieve this goal an application was developed and a case study carried out at the UFRJ (Federal University of Rio de Janeiro) Geodiversity Museum. Augmented reality was chosen in order to provide different types of information about one of the museum's exhibition rooms. The application was submitted to an accessibility evaluation with experts and, subsequently, to tests with users, involving five prelingual deaf volunteers. The users' observations occurred in the real context and identified the demands of the deaf and the effects of providing accessibility with the help of augmented reality.

Chapter 11 "Ensuring Resilience Using Augmented Reality: How Museums Can Respond During and Post COVID-19?" explores how cultural and heritage sites such as museums can weather the unpredictable storm of the COVID-19 pandemic by quickly adapting to the unprecedented situation to continue serving their communities in new innovative ways. The museums are awakening to the need for proactive and innovative measures for mitigating the impacts of the pandemic in order to ensure survival. These include offering online educational resources, showcasing museum collections, and engaging its communities with art-related discussions on social media. Powered by the key enabling technologies of the Fourth Industrial Revolution, many popular museums create virtual tours using mixed reality technologies to improve visitors' discovery in an interactive, engaging, and enjoyable way. This chapter also highlights the challenges of the innovative applications. What might be introduced as temporary measures to address the current situation, could become paradigm shifts that lead to higher and more impactful engagement between the museums and the society, ensuring museums' resilience and irreplaceable status in the people's minds. Also, during such times of high stress in society, culture can play an important healing role as it can offer rallying beacons of solidarity leading to emotional resilience and overall well-being.

Part III "Augmented Reality and Cultural Heritage" consists of 6 chapters (Chaps. 12 to 17).

Chapter 12 "Augmented Reality and New Opportunities for Cultural Heritage" considers the potential for Augmented Reality (AR) in cultural heritage, based on a literature review and the authors' previous work. Firstly, AR technology is briefly presented and explained. Then, the cultural heritage applications of AR are examined in both the Visualization and Gamification sections. Visualization includes applications that enhance the visitor's experience by blending it with text, sound, or 3D models in a museum or heritage site. Gamification engages AR games about cultural heritage and is aimed at attracting the visitor's attention to inform the visitor about the site in a more entertaining way. Finally, Future Work is discussed within the context of the Total Augmentation Paradigm.

Chapter 13 "User Experience and Engagement in Augmented Reality Systems for Cultural Heritage Domain" reviews the different models of user experience (UX) and user engagement (UE) proposed for augmented reality systems and discusses their applicability to the Cultural Heritage (CH). Traditional models of UX and UE are not totally adaptable to the current trends in the AR continuum for the CH domain. Thus, an important HCI research area that requires investigation is the evaluation of UX and UE factors for AR systems in the CH field. This chapter proposes a conceptual framework model for assessing UX and UE in AR systems. Initially, the UX categories (such as instrumental, cognitive, emotional, sensory, social, and motivational) are investigated thoroughly to have a deep understanding of all the related components. Further, the UE factors (such as aesthetics, interest, goal, novelty, interactivity, gamification, and learning) are identified and categorized. Twenty AR systems in the CH domain (AR-CH) have been selected based on predefined criteria and evaluated against a list of derived AR characteristics. The gaps in current literature have been considered to formulate a comprehensive framework for the assessment of UX and UE factors in AR-CH systems. Metrics and methods are investigated and identified for the measurement of the UX and UE factors. This chapter lays a solid foundation for the assessment of UX and UE factors in AR-CH systems, which has the potential to help AR system developers with identifying and improving the most UX and UE influential factors in their systems.

Chapter 14 "The Transhuman Docent: Persistent Human Interaction in Digital Heritage Sites" looks at the way mobile augmented reality has evolved since 2008, based on implementation, development, obsolescence, and the persistent necessity of human docents to preserve its usage in heritage places such as museums and historical sites. Works examined include the various augmented reality festivals put on by members of the Manifest.AR group and others, including the Virtual Public Art Project and the (Un)Seen Sculptures in Australia. The usage of the term "artist-as-docent" explores the intersections between various notions proffered from transhumanist philosophers from the 20th century, such as Timothy Leary, FM 2030 and Buckminster Fuller. Concepts such as fifth circuitry, telespheres, info-space, psychogeography and the infinitesimal are applied to the augmented reality artist as docent. Ultimately, the transhuman docents are necessary for mobile augmented reality to be used by a general audience in our contemporary setting. This is changing due to the new mediafication of all things due to the COVID-19 crisis, but ultimately the need for human interaction is what is driving the usage of augmented reality technology.

Chapter 15 "Literature-Based Augmented Reality: Integrating Urban Novels with Context-Aware Augmented Environments" investigates the ways in which the dialogism and unfinalizability of cultural heritage experiences redefine place attachment, so that inhabitants and visitors of cities can recognize and process the urban multivariate collective cultural and aesthetic distinctiveness. The suggested approach is founded on the amalgamation of novels with mobile/context-aware augmented reality. Urban novels play a threefold role. First, they reveal a multiplicity of embodied situations as spatiotemporal representations of the surrounding built environment. Second, they create socially mediated memories related to groups and places. Third, the reading of novels offers strong bodily enactment, opening up the minds of readers to the vivid collective, social and cultural potential, surprise, and aesthetic awareness of the urban environment. Augmented reality integrated with novels can render possible the exploration of such characteristics; as a result, a mutated, transformed urbanscape emerges as a multilayered experience capable of defining durable relationships with the city's hidden collective, cultural, and aesthetic memories.

Chapter 16 "Applying Augmented Reality in the Italian Food and Dining Industry: Cultural Heritage Perspectives" researches the intention to use augmented reality technology within dining experiences and activities in the Italian food and dining industry by focusing on cultural heritage perspectives. Six case studies are presented drawing on state of art within the industry, catching insights and highlighting limits and opportunities for the future. From the results, it emerges that AR is considered as a potential means able to increase the opportunity for the food and dining industry. At the same time, the industry is not quite culturally ready for the technology improvement of customer contacts. From the analysis emerges the intention of entrepreneurs to consider AR as a potential element of business improvement to enhance the connection between food value proposition and cultural heritage.

Chapter 17 "Reintroducing Indonesian Folk Songs to Children Using Augmented Reality Books" deals with a new approach to reintroduce Indonesian folk songs to children using augmented reality children's books. Indonesian folk songs' existence as intangible cultural heritage is declining nowadays because children prefer popular music with exciting visuals and presentations. At the same time, augmented reality technology assimilation to conventional media has started to emerge. Previous studies show the great potential of AR-based books for children and indicate that this technology enhances their learning experience. This project adapts Bruce Archer's design methodology, including programming, data collection, analysis, synthesis, development, and communication. There were two phases for testing the AR book: the alpha testing phase used a digital book as a marker, then a printed book was used for the beta testing phase. The AR book is expected to provide a tangible experience for children to enjoy and preserve Indonesian folk songs.

Lastly, we hope that the reader will not judge the book's editor and contributors too harshly. We have accepted the challenge of researching the three interconnected and overlapping areas, and we have done our best to bring out this comprehensive work on the use of augmented reality technology in tourism, museums, and heritage. Please go ahead and read the monograph. We hope sincerely that you will enjoy it.

Cairo, Egypt   Vladimir Geroimenko

Contents

Part II   Augmented Reality for Museums

Part III   Augmented Reality and Cultural Heritage

Contributors

Kamarulzaman Ab. Aziz Faculty of Management, Multimedia University, Cyberjaya, Selangor, Malaysia

Zauwiyah Ahmad Faculty of Business, Multimedia University, Melaka, Malaysia

Patricia Amorim Graduate Program in Informatics (PPGI), Federal University of the State of Rio de Janeiro (UNIRIO), Rio de Janeiro, Brazil

Borja Aso University Institute for Research in Environmental Sciences of Aragón (IUCA), University of Zaragoza, Zaragoza, Spain

Dhia Asfa Awliya Faculty of Letters, Art and Design Department, Universitas Negeri Malang, Malang, Indonesia

Priscyla Barbosa Graduate Program in Informatics (PPGI), Federal University of the State of Rio de Janeiro (UNIRIO), Rio de Janeiro, Brazil

Erkan Bostanci Computer Engineering Department, Ankara University, Ankara, Turkey

Roberto Bruni Department of Economic and Law, University of Cassino and Southern Lazio, Cassino, Italy

Kirsten R. Butcher Department of Educational Psychology, University of Utah, Salt Lake City, UT, USA

Federica Caboni Department of Economic and Business Science, University of Cagliari, Cagliari, Italy

Aline Castro Museum of Geodiversity, Institute of Geosciences (IGEO), Federal University of the State of Rio de Janeiro (UNIRIO), Rio de Janeiro, Brazil

M. Christodoulou Digital Humanities and Digital Knowledge, Department of Classical Philology and Italian Studies, University of Bologna, Bologna, Italy

Annarita Colamatteo Department of Economic and Law, University of Cassino and Southern Lazio, Cassino, Italy

Klen Čopič Pucihar Faculty of Mathematics, Natural Sciences and Information Technologies, University of Primorska, Koper, Slovenia;
Faculty of Information Studies, Novo mesto, Slovenia

Khairul Azhar Bin Mat Daud Fakulti Teknologi Kreatif Dan Warisan, Universiti Malaysia Kelantan, Kelantan, Malaysia

Simone Bacellar Leal Ferreira Graduate Program in Informatics (PPGI), Federal University of the State of Rio de Janeiro (UNIRIO), Rio de Janeiro, Brazil

Silvia García-Ceballos University Institute for Research in Environmental Sciences of Aragón (IUCA), University of Zaragoza, Zaragoza, Spain

Dragoş Gheorghiu Doctoral School, National University of Arts, Bucharest, Romania;
Instituto Terra e Memória, Centro de Geociências de Universidade de Coimbra, Mação, Portugal

Mehmet Serdar Guzel Computer Engineering Department, Ankara University, Ankara, Turkey

Ima Kusumawati Hidayat Faculty of Letters, Art and Design Department, Universitas Negeri Malang, Malang, Indonesia

Marius Hodea National University of Arts, Bucharest, Romania

João Jacob LIACC, DEI, Faculdade de Engenharia, Universidade do Porto, Porto, Portugal

Kavi Kumar Khedo University of Mauritius, Reduit, Mauritius

Matjaž Kljun Faculty of Mathematics, Natural Sciences and Information Technologies, University of Primorska, Koper, Slovenia;
Faculty of Information Studies, Novo mesto, Slovenia

P. Konstantinou Department of Graphic Design and Visual Communication, Faculty of Applied Arts and Culture, University of West Attica, Aigaleo, Greece

Sandra Maria Correia Loureiro Business Research Unit (BRU), Intituto Universitário de Lisboa (ISCTE), Lisbon, Portugal

Dimitrios Makris Faculty of Applied Arts and Culture, Department of Conservation of Antiquities and Works of Art, University of West Attica, Athens, Greece

R. Metzitakos Department of Graphic Design and Visual Communication, Faculty of Applied Arts and Culture, University of West Attica, Aigaleo, Greece

Maria Moira Faculty of Applied Arts and Culture, Department of Interior Architecture, University of West Attica, Athens, Greece

A. Mountzouri Department of Graphic Design and Visual Communication, Faculty of Applied Arts and Culture, University of West Attica, Aigaleo, Greece

Iñaki Navarro-Neri University Institute for Research in Environmental Sciences of Aragón (IUCA), University of Zaragoza, Zaragoza, Spain

Rui Nóbrega NOVA-LINCS, DI, Faculdade de Ciências e Tecnologia, Universidade Nova de Lisboa, Lisbon, Portugal

M. G. Nomikou Department of Wine, Vine and Beverage Sciences, Faculty of Food Sciences, University of West Attica, Aigaleo, Greece

Dimas Rifqi Novica Faculty of Letters, Art and Design Department, Universitas Negeri Malang, Malang, Indonesia

Matthew Orr Department of Educational Psychology, University of Utah, Salt Lake City, UT, USA

Dimitrios Panagiotakopoulos Department of Graphic Design and Visual Communication, Faculty of Applied Arts and Culture, University of West Attica, Aigaleo, Greece

A. Papapostolou Department of Graphic Design and Visual Communication, Faculty of Applied Arts and Culture, University of West Attica, Aigaleo, Greece

Eric Poitras Faculty of Computer Science, Dalhousie University, Halifax, NS, Canada

Sebastian Pranz Faculty of Media, Macromedia University of Applied Sciences, Munich, Germany

Dwi Nikmah Puspitasari Faculty of Letters, Art and Design Department, Universitas Negeri Malang, Malang, Indonesia;
Faculty of Psychology Education, Universitas Negeri Malang, Malang, Indonesia

Arvind Ramtohul University of Mauritius, Reduit, Mauritius

Denik Ristya Rini Faculty of Letters, Art and Design Department, Universitas Negeri Malang, Malang, Indonesia

Pilar Rivero University Institute for Research in Environmental Sciences of Aragón (IUCA), University of Zaragoza, Zaragoza, Spain

Nathan Shafer Structured Learning Classrooms, Anchorage School District, Anchorage, AK, USA;
N-Collective Media/Shared Universe, Anchorage, AK, USA

G. Stathakis Open University of Cyprus, Nicosia, Cyprus

Livia Ştefan EasyDO Digital Technologies, Bucharest, Romania

Gek-Siang Tan Faculty of Business, Multimedia University, Melaka, Malaysia

Metehan Unal Computer Engineering Department, Ankara University, Ankara, Turkey

Fatima Zehra Unal Computer Engineering Department, Ankara University, Ankara, Turkey

Part I
General Aspects and Augmented Reality in the Tourism Industry

Chapter 1
Informal Learning with Extended Reality Environments: Current Trends in Museums, Heritage, and Tourism

Matthew Orr, Eric Poitras, and Kirsten R. Butcher

Abstract This chapter discusses the capabilities of extended reality technology in informal learning environments, such as museums and cultural heritage sites. Recent developments in extended reality technologies have led to increased integration into these informal learning spaces and have heightened the need for a systematic investigation into the affordances of modern multimedia representations spanning tangible to virtual mediums. These affordances vary across settings, ranging from personalizing learning experiences, increasing engagement through interactive activities, and augmenting exhibits with rich multimedia content. The chapter critically appraises several affordances of extended reality technologies while expanding on these notions by outlining the cognitive theory of multimedia learning to inform practical instructional design principles. Drawing on case examples from their own research with tangible and virtual museum objects in these settings, the authors explore and discuss how extended reality technologies can serve to both collect and analyze ambient data in real time. The authors claim that ambient data will become increasingly prevalent in such settings and critical to gain insights into visitor experience and promote meaningful and engaging learning experiences. They discuss the implications of their findings for practice and suggest directions for future research.

M. Orr · K. R. Butcher
Department of Educational Psychology, University of Utah, Salt Lake City, UT, USA
e-mail: matt.p.orr@utah.edu

K. R. Butcher
e-mail: kirsten.butcher@utah.edu

E. Poitras (✉)
Faculty of Computer Science, Dalhousie University, Halifax, NS, Canada
e-mail: eric.poitras@dal.ca

1.1 Introduction

Extended reality (XR) experiences refer to experiences in which technology is used to enhance, support, improve, or change the affordances of reality. Varied technologies are combined to create situations in which components of virtual and real-world environments are combined or integrated in various ways. The result is a spectrum of technologically mediated experiences that include virtual reality (VR), mixed reality (MR), and augmented reality (AR) approaches. On one end of this spectrum, virtual reality places the learner in a fully immersive virtual environment that largely excludes their current physical surroundings. Virtual reality often requires extensive hardware that includes handheld controllers and a head-mounted display that immerses the learner in the virtual environment. On the opposite end of the spectrum, augmented reality combines the learner's current surroundings and virtual objects by overlaying virtual content onto the learner's physical surroundings. Augmented reality often uses the camera of handheld digital devices, such as a smartphone, to overlay (nonpresent) virtual content onto the learner's physical surroundings. Near the middle of the spectrum, mixed reality blends the learner's physical world with virtual content fairly seamlessly. Mixed reality hardware often includes head-mounted displays that respond in real time to learners' interactions with their physical surroundings. But it also can be used to describe situations where virtual content has been integrated into the physical environment, such as when 3D scans of objects are enlarged and printed to created hands-on experiences that would not otherwise be possible in the real world. Although the opposite ends of the extended reality spectrum (VR vs. AR) traditionally have been used to characterize the extent to which virtual representations are utilized in a display and the ways in which the virtual components are controlled, recent advances in device processing capabilities have contributed a great deal to rethinking previous definitions and boundaries between "real" and "virtual" content.

The blurring boundaries between virtual and real content have been increasingly evident within informal learning environments, where digital and virtual advances have been enthusiastically adopted as a means to promote engaging and meaningful visitor experiences. Museums, historical sites, and cultural institutions face a significant challenge—how best to create highly engaging instructional experiences by emphasizing and highlighting particular aspects of an exhibit (Bressler 2013). Extended reality experiences provide unique affordances related to this challenge—particularly, the ability to focus attention and provide interactive experience with objects, specimens, or artifacts that otherwise may be overlooked by or unavailable to learners. However, there are numerous challenges of designing and developing extended reality exhibits in informal contexts; these challenges call for data-driven methods to inform design approaches and decisions by providing useful insights into multiple aspects of visitor experiences. Such insights include (but are not limited to) visitor enjoyment and engagement, perceived utility and authenticity of the digitized content, the quality and quantity of visitors' subjective learning, and the quality and quantity of objective learning outcomes for those same visitors.

Existing data from research on learning with extended reality exhibits in informal spaces are sparse and inconclusive; it is not even clear the extent to which visitors find extended reality labels to be engaging or informative in modern museums (Davis 2020). The lack of robust and rigorous studies concerning augmented reality experiences in informal contexts likely reflects the complexity of these environments, rather than a lack of appetite for research on visitors' learning processes, outcomes, and perceptions. While there are studies that investigate the impact of extended reality experiences on visitor enjoyment and engagement (e.g., He et al. 2018; Leopardi et al. 2020), there are few studies that focus on understanding the impact of extended reality experiences on visitors' learning processes and outcomes. Learning activities in informal environments usually are low-structured and open-ended combinations of interactions with objects and (potentially) other learners. People may or may not interact for significant periods of time (or with intentional purpose) with the technologies that are being offered for a specific exhibit within the larger informal environment. In this chapter, we assert that extended reality technology, in various forms, can support not only learning goals in informal contexts, but also provide a mechanism for conducting research and collecting authentic usage data that spur new insights. A particular emphasis is placed on ways of utilizing objects to support unobtrusive collection of ambient data that does not interfere with visitors' activities or require direct interactions between a researcher and the learner.

In the first section of this chapter, we briefly review relevant research background and discuss some fundamental shortcomings in current investigations within informal learning contexts. We then present a theoretical perspective to design multimedia content within extended reality technology and discuss, in general, its application to inform instructional design moving forward. In the second section, we consider two detailed case examples that exemplify aspects of unobtrusive methods to collect ambient data that lead to insights on informal learning experiences and the teaching of reasoning skills involved within the domain of archeology. In doing so, we draw on examples from our own research with tangible and digital representations of objects and the use of theory and methodology to understand how students interact with these objects in a museum environment. Finally, we discuss implications for both practitioners and researchers in accordance with several instructional design principles that pertain to personalizing and augmenting informal learning through extended reality experiences.

1.2 Affordances of Extended Reality

Extended reality visitor experiences in informal learning environments offer many (diverse) affordances that would be difficult or impossible to achieve without technology. One of the most important characteristics of such experiences is the personalization of learning in informal spaces. For example, a digital guide could provide a glossary for a visitor who indicates that terminology is unfamiliar to them or suggest a

Fig. 1.1 Superior (left), lateral (middle), and zoomed (right) views of an *Allosaurus fragilis* jaw in a virtual environment

deep dive into cultural origins of an exhibit for visitors interested in that area. Personalization scaffolding offers educational support to those who want (or need) it and can enhance learner control over their experience—allowing visitors to make decisions about what they see and how they explore (Pujol et al. 2013). Museums are interested in the potential of personalized learning experiences as a mechanism to meet the needs of a wide range of visitors with diverse experiences, interests, personalities, and profiles (Merritt 2016), with some researchers arguing that personalization, choice, and control are crucial factors in determining the potential of museums to impact visitors' lives (Rennie and Johnston 2004). The personalized options offered by extended reality experiences support the andragogical model of learning, which posits that adult learners have strong needs to self-direct their learning experiences and align learning opportunities to their experiences and interests (Conaway and Zorn-Arnold 2015; Knowles et al. 2015). In informal environments—where visitors decide what to learn and how long to engage—providing control and customization may be particularly important to ensuring opportunities for deep and meaningful learning experiences.

In many cases, visitors can use extended reality technologies to choose the type of experience they want during a visit. We can describe these learner-controlled decisions as "active control" over context and goals, particularly when extended reality is available to promote autonomy. For example, learners may choose how they want to explore objects or what views interest them (Fig. 1.1). Active control over learning experiences can be enhanced by automatic forms of extended reality that are triggered by some aspect of the learning context. For example, geolocated experiences offer visitors materials or experiences that are customized to specific and changing environments as learners progress through an informal space in real time. This type of affordance is particularly useful in large, outdoor sites where it is difficult for site attendants to reach each visitor (Harley et al. 2016). For example, in a historic park, extended reality experiences would be customized to specific locations as the visitor moves through each exhibit in the space. These could provide further information, interesting narratives, or engaging multimedia assets in a nonlinear manner that transport visitors to different times in the site's history and enhance their experiences. Although automatic extended reality can act as a smart guide during learner exploration, combining automatic and active customization may be optimal for visitor-directed experiences that engage highly varied audiences. In this "combined" case, extended reality options are automatically customized to the learner's location but the choice of personalized support or extended reality materials actively is selected by the visitor according to their needs and/or preferences (Keil et al. 2013). Thus, combined approaches to personalization allow the learner to direct their extended reality experiences according to diverse individual interests and self-determined learning needs, but within a relevant set of customized options that directly align to the learner's surrounding (physical) context.

The aforementioned examples are easy to imagine as individual experiences supported by personal devices. But collaborative experiences are prevalent in informal settings where visitors often arrive in small groups (Lukosch et al. 2015). There has been concern that extended reality experiences may isolate visitors from rich, collaborative experiences—the result being "heads-down" interactions with devices rather than the "heads-up" social and discourse-based learning associated deep inquiry in authentic contexts (Cahill et al. 2011). However, Cahill et al. (2011) found that concerns about "heads-down" work associated with technology-based learning may be overstated; digital devices were no more likely to direct attention away from exhibit content than when analog learning materials were used. In fact, some research has shown that extended reality can enhance and expand collaboration by providing visitors with the opportunity to create synchronous and asynchronous annotations (e.g., verbal recordings) for other visitors (Bartie and Mackaness 2006; Lukosch et al. 2015). With limited physical space for a museum to annotate each object's features in a collection, the amount of information that can be provided to visitors (in that physical space) also is limited. As a result, visitors who do not have the opportunity to engage with extended reality experiences may leave an exhibit with questions about unidentified aspects of an exhibit. By using technology to overlay diagrams, definitions, and other scaffolds onto a physical exhibit, visitors using the extended reality materials have the opportunity to engage in more directed exploration and observation of objects within a collection (Sugiura et al. 2019). While not all visitors may choose to take advantage of these extended reality materials, it allows learners to engage in the ways they prefer and to the depth they desire. Accordingly, extended reality experience in informal spaces can create numerous learner experience options poised to serve a wide variety of visitors. In the following sections, we explore how extended reality is creating specific experiential options in museums and in cultural heritage and historical sites.

1.3 Museum Exhibits

In a museum, visual representations, collection objects and specimens, and narratives are essential components of conveying information to visitors and creating an engaging visitor experience (Hammady et al. 2020). Until recently, "technology-enhanced" experiences with museum collections largely were limited to viewing physical objects and specimens on display in conjunction with available audio tours (Bell and Smith 2020). In addition, museum digitization efforts were focused mainly on 2D photography or creation of digital metadata records (Primary Research 2015).

But recent advances in the availability of technologies to support extended reality experiences have drastically increased the range of materials and experiences that can be made available to visitors. Some extended reality experiences (e.g., exploration of 3D printed scans) make museum objects accessible to learners with visual impairments (Hewitt 2015) in addition to expanding the forms of sensory input that can form the basis of a learning opportunity (Christidou and Pierroux 2018; Neely and Langer 2013). Visitors are enthusiastic about the ways that 3D prints enhance opportunities for interacting with collections during their museum trip (Wilson et al. 2017), with visitors readily accepting digitized objects as meaningful substitutes for rare or sensitive museum objects (Schwan and Dutz 2020). However, extended reality experiences available in modern museums can go far beyond tangible input. Experiences now may include fully immersive virtual reality simulations of historical events or objects (Carrozzino and Bergamasco 2010), blended virtual and real-world environments that bring additional context to the museum collection (Hughes et al. 2004), or mobile applications that expand relevant information available to visitors (Sugiura et al. 2019). Extended reality experiences can offer kinetic (movement-based) input, enhanced visual input (including details, views, and scale), and new approaches to temporal input (allowing learners different experiences over time).

Overall, public acceptance of these new experiences seems to be positive and visitors report that they value the role that technology can play in their museum experiences. For example, in a recent study that used Microsoft's HoloLens to recreate ancient Egyptian battle scenes, Hammady et al. (2020) found that visitors' ratings of enjoyment, usefulness, and willingness to use similar technology in the future were quite positive. In a study of 3D printed replicas in a museum setting, Wilson et al. (2017) found that 93% of visitors believed that being able to handle these materials would enhance their museum experience, by increasing their understanding and enjoyment of collections, providing multisensory experiences, and making the objects more accessible for examination and close observation. In a study that compared tangible 3D prints and immersive virtual experiences with digitized objects in a museum, Di Franco and colleagues (Di Franco et al. 2015) found that visitors agreed that 3D prints and immersive virtual experiences supported their understanding of objects and strongly agreed that both types of experiences were engaging. Similar trends are evident in the context of cultural heritage sites, a less structured type of informal learning environment.

1.4 Cultural Heritage and Historical Sites

There are several augmented reality systems for mobile devices that have been developed for use at cultural heritage sites that provide narration and digital reconstruction of important features, objects, and artifacts (Kretschmer et al. 2001; Kyriakou and Hermon 2019; Vlahakis et al. 2001). Extended reality experiences at cultural heritage sites can enhance visitor experiences using multiple approaches that include reconstructing heritage sites to their previous states in history, documenting data collection, excavating heritage sites (Bekele et al. 2018; Schofield et al. 2018), and making protected objects available for virtual handling and interaction (Kyriakou and Hermon 2019). In doing so, technology-based extensions of the visitor experience can change both the visual information available (allowing enhanced viewing experiences) and the degree to which interactive experiences can be enabled (allowing enhanced sensory input during a visit).

With modern virtual reality technology, visitors can be immersed in a complete reconstruction of a site that they then can explore for themselves (Carrozzino and Bergamasco 2010). These options support improved personalization and control with a larger set of meaningful experiential content. Additional features in extended reality technologies may provide personalized scaffolding for visitors (e.g., suggestions of what to visit next or recommendations about how to explore their current location), a significant benefit to visitors who have not received individualized attention in the past due to the typical size of these sites and the number of daily visitors (Plecher et al. 2019). Thus, there is enthusiasm that extended reality experiences can improve the learning processes and outcomes for individuals and small groups during their visits.

1.5 Issues and Challenges

To date, much of the research on extended reality technology in museums and cultural sites has focused on either technical aspects of system design, object digitization, or experience implementation (e.g., Fau et al. 2016; Fiorenza et al. 2018; Hudson et al. 2015; Rahaman et al. 2019). Other research has focused on the measurement of visitor perceptions, particularly engagement (Bekele and Champion 2019; Di Franco et al. 2015; Wilson et al. 2017). However, few studies have focused on visitors' learning *processes* with these technology-enhanced experiences or on measuring the quality and quantity of learning *outcomes*. The nature of informal education environments makes it difficult to measure traditional learning gains without obtrusive pre- and post-visit assessments that are long and detailed enough to be sensitive to conceptual changes or modest additions to prior knowledge. As such, we first must consider issues and challenges that arise with extended reality technologies from a cognitive perspective grounded in multimedia learning theory and then apply theoretical considerations to the development of unobtrusive learning research in these environments, with an eye toward how ambient data can inform and advance our understanding of learning with extended reality.

Research shows multiple competing considerations when designing extended reality educational experiences. While some research suggests heightened engagement when mixed reality experiences are available in a learning environment (Kyriakou and Hermon 2019; Venigalla and Chimalakonda 2019), engagement does not guarantee more effective or efficient learning. Indeed, research evidence has demonstrated a potential disconnect between engagement and learning. Findings from research on immersive technologies have shown that these extended reality experiences can enhance learner engagement without corresponding benefits to observable—or even perceived—learning. In a study on immersive, virtual reality lab simulations with high school students, students enjoyed the immersive labs more than simple instructional videos, but the immersive simulations did not improve their observed learning outcomes (Makransky et al. 2020, 2019). Similarly, research on elementary students' virtual field trips showed that students were highly engaged by immersive virtual visits but did not perceive learning benefits beyond those offered by traditional (non-immersive) technology (Han 2019). These results suggest that explicit and clearly focused learning scaffolds may be needed to facilitate meaningful cognitive processes (i.e., high-level cognitive processes necessary to facilitate deep learning outcomes) when students are engaged in immersive environments. However, the nature of extended reality experiences may entail barriers to learning via increased processing demands.

Increased cognitive demands associated with extended reality necessitate that designers and researchers alike should seek to simplify, support, and offload unnecessary decisions, interactions, or controls for visitors whenever possible. Cognitive demands are heightened in the context of extended reality experiences when the materials require instructions or include extraneous information (Richards 2015). Dunleavy et al. (2008) also have demonstrated that in location-based augmented reality experiences, there is a need for explicit scaffolding of interpersonal skills to facilitate learning during collaborative activity. By scaffolding collaborative skills—and thereby freeing up associated cognitive resources—learners were better able to dedicate sufficient processing capacity to the extended reality component of the experience. These findings suggest that there are multiple avenues to designing supports and scaffolds that enhance learning with extended reality experiences. While it may be helpful to design supports for using and analyzing the extended reality materials themselves, it also may be helpful to design scaffolds that reduce demands of other aspects of the experience (e.g., collaboration, monitoring, navigation), so that learners can devote more attentional resources to processing the (potentially complex) extended reality experience and the information it presents.

Extended reality materials often include visual and verbal components; as such, they can be considered a complex, modern form of multimedia materials for learning. In the following section, we discuss how the cognitive theory of multimedia learning (Mayer 2014) can serve as a strong foundation for anticipating potential issues in learning with extended reality materials and in guiding designs that can promote successful informal learning experiences with these technologies.

1.6 Multimedia Learning Theory

The cognitive theory of multimedia learning (CTML) (Mayer 2014) describes a theoretical model of the cognitive processes that combine to predict when and how individuals learn with visual and verbal materials. CTML serves as a framework for understanding how learning occurs with multimedia content as well as a predictive model that suggests effective design principles that should promote effective outcomes when an individual is engaged in multimedia learning. CTML is based on several assumptions about human learning and information processing. A critical assumption is that learners have limited cognitive resources for processing incoming auditory and visual information due to inherent limitations in working memory capacity. Limited capacity of working memory has been well-established for some time (Baddeley 1986), leading CTML to assume that to-be-processed content must be selected from among all available information as processing begins. While limited processing capacity applies to learning of all materials, it may be particularly relevant for extended reality experiences with complex representations. Research has found that learners with low spatial ability can be overloaded by the processing requirements of 3D visualizations (Huk 2006). For extended reality experiences, limited cognitive processing capacity means that learners often will need support in focusing on relevant content and focusing their attention on a subset of available inputs.

A second critical assumption of CTML is that visual and verbal information are (initially) processed via separate channels—a visual and a verbal channel. This assumption is based on dual-coding theory (Paivio 1986), as well as modern models of working memory where individuals demonstrate separate capacities for verbal and spatial processing (Shah and Miyake 1996). According to dual-coding theory, visual and verbal information is encoded as separate representations during learning. When information is represented both visually and verbally during learning (as is the case with multimedia materials), learners encode both a visual representation and a verbal representation. These two representations are likely to support enhanced recall over verbal-only materials (since two separate representations can be activated), suggesting that multimedia materials should support improved recall. This suggestion is supported by multiple studies of multimedia materials, showing improved memory for to-be-learned content with multimedia materials (Butcher 2006; Mayer 1989; Mayer and Gallini 1990). By virtue of extended reality experiences being both visual and verbal in nature, these materials should support enhanced memory for content and objects in informal environments over verbal-only supports like audio tours. According to CTML, separate visual and verbal channels are maintained as individuals select and organize incoming information. But, in order to achieve meaningful learning that can transfer to multiple contexts, visual and verbal information must be integrated into a single representation.

According to CTML, after visual and verbal information is selected and organized, further processing integrates the separate (visual and verbal) representations into a single mental representation (Schüler et al. 2015). But the integration process can be demanding, as has been shown by research demonstrating that integration of visual and verbal materials requires more working memory resources than learning with a single form of input (Dutke and Rinck 2006). Research on multimedia learning has suggested that design decisions during media development can have significant impact on active processing and integration of visual and verbal content, leading to a collection of principles that guide developers to create effective multimedia materials.

For example, the *contiguity principle* asserts that designers should present relevant visual and verbal information at the same time and in close physical proximity, the *coherence principle* suggests that designers should remove extraneous details from learning materials, the *redundancy principle* suggests that optimal materials combine visual content with spoken narration, the *signaling principle* asserts that essential material should be highlighted in learning materials, and the *segmentation principle* advises designers to break down complex materials into more digestible segments (Mayer 2014, 2017). These design principles are derived mainly from laboratory and applied research focused on conceptual learning with visual representations combined with text or audio explanations (e.g., multimedia presentations, videos, slides).

Research on traditional multimedia learning materials generally has reported findings that are consistent with the multimedia effect (Butcher 2014) and in line with the predictions of CTML (Mayer 2014). Combinations of visual and verbal content are shown to improve factual retention as well as the transfer of knowledge (Mayer 1989; Mayer and Gallini 1990). These findings highlight that multimedia benefits can include both lower-level encoding benefits (e.g., recall) and support for higher-level cognitive processes (e.g., integration and inference generation). Although relatively simple forms of multimedia materials still are prevalent in many formal educational contexts, recent research has been directed at exploring the impact of more complex forms of multimedia that encompass extended reality experiences in informal contexts. Some researchers have argued that learning with dynamic and interactive forms of multimedia can be understood by combining CTML and models of comprehension processing (Butcher 2014; Butcher and Davies 2015). However, relatively little is known about how extended reality environments both engage learners and promote effective cognitive processing. Further, investigating best practices for the design of extended reality experiences to support informal learning and the development of a coherent, integrated representation is a considerable challenge due to the inherent technical difficulty of accurately rendering the environment and enabling intuitive interactions and controls.

Complex multimedia materials for extended reality contexts include a wide variety of dynamic visualizations and videos (Ainsworth and Vanlabeke 2004; Card 1999; Hari Narayanan and Hegarty 2002; Hegarty 2004), haptic simulations with feedback (Han and Black 2011; Jones et al. 2014), virtual reality and augmented reality (Sampaio et al. 2010), and tangible and digital 3D representations (Barrett and Hegarty 2014; Hegarty et al. 2012; Padalkar and Hegarty 2015; Stull, Barrett et al. 2012). Studies on complex forms of multimedia particularly have shown some benefits of 3D representations during learning. When the to-be-learned content is inherently 3-dimensional (e.g., anatomy), learning with 3D representations has been shown to enhance learner understanding of spatial structure, spatial relationships, and spatial transformations (Hoyek et al. 2014; Stull, Hegarty et al. 2012), possibly by offloading the cognitive demands of mentally representing and rotating structures to an external model that can be manipulated physically (Hutchins et al. 1985; Padalkar and Hegarty 2015; Wu et al. 2005). However, much of this research has been conducted in formal classrooms or research laboratories where the learning environment is easily controlled and manipulated. As 3D materials are integrated into a variety of learning contexts, it is essential that we understand how 3D materials can support meaningful experiences for learners.

Within informal contexts like museums and historical sites, extended reality often is used to create visitor opportunities that enhance opportunities for observation of and interaction with objects and artifacts. Accordingly, the multimedia materials found in these settings often go beyond simple diagrams or images, gravitating instead toward three-dimensional (3D) representations or models. These 3D representations can take the form of tangible 3D reproductions of important objects (e.g., a 3D printed fossil) that can be physically manipulated as well as virtual 3D reproductions of objects that are presented on and manipulated via a digital device (e.g., touch screen or smartphone). Over the past two decades, museums and academic institutions have made it a priority to digitize their extensive collections of historical, artistic, scientific, and culturally-significant objects (Clough 2013; Magnani et al. 2018). These efforts have resulted in a number of large online repositories (e.g., Morphosource.org) that provide access to high-quality 3D representations of authentic objects. In addition to accessing virtual 3D reproductions, these online repositories often allow users to 3D print digital files for educational purposes. We consider these 3D printed objects to be an interesting case of extended reality for informal learning environments because these materials are a tangible version of a 3D digitization and because learners are aware that they are interacting with the result of a digital representation rather than the "real" historical or scientific object. While there is great enthusiasm surrounding the integration of modern tangible (3D prints) and digital 3D representations into informal learning environments (Wilson et al. 2017), it is yet poorly understood how visitors utilize these extended reality materials in informal learning environments and how instructional supports within these loosely structured environments can maximize their learning.

Research in informal learning environments often has focused on learner satisfaction with technology integration (Tesoriero et al. 2014) or broad and holistic observation protocols or category-based rubrics of educational activities (Holtrop and Downey 2019). However, we are most interested in understanding real-time cognitive learning processes as associated with meaningful learning outcomes. Accordingly, we must find methods to measure learning unobtrusively, in ways that do not impact the quality or coherence of visitor experiences. Our research has explored methodological and practical approaches in these areas, using tangible and digital 3D representations of museum objects; this work has demonstrated that learners' physical interactions with digitized objects are predictive of the depth of cognitive processing in which they engage during a learning episode. Our goal is to use these findings to inform the development of scaffolds and supports that promote interactive behaviors leading to meaningful, long-term learning outcomes. The first step of this vision is to identify and demonstrate a link between interactions with extended reality materials and depth of learners' cognitive processes. The second step is to develop insights into visitor experiences by conceptualizing varied constructs and operationally defining them as a means to measure their different properties (e.g., frequency, temporal duration, valence). The third step is to model their relationship to desirable and undesirable outcomes (e.g., average time-on-site, satisfaction, rate of visits). And the challenge is to do all three steps without reducing the quality, consistency, or enjoyment of the informal learning experience. How might this be done? Through the use of unobtrusive data collection and analysis during extended reality experiences.

The following section describes our unobtrusive data collection methods, using ambient data from learner interactions with tangible and digital 3D representations of museum specimens. We explain how these data were used to investigate the effects of extended reality technologies on cognitive learning processes and learner engagement.

1.7 Informal Learning with Tangible Museum Objects

When looking to understand the impact of extended reality objects on cognitive processes and learner engagement in informal environments, it is helpful first to look into formal learning environments where considerably more research has addressed learning with 3D materials. Tangible 3D representations, in the form of learning objects, have been used as learning aids in science, technology, engineering, and mathematics (STEM) classrooms for many years. Several STEM domains such as medicine (Preece et al. 2013), mathematics (McNeil and Uttal 2009), and chemistry (Stull, Hegarty et al. 2012) use 3D representations to physically represent concepts. Example uses include Cuisenaire rods to represent mathematics concepts, scaled representations of objects that are too large or small to see without aid (e.g., 3D printed double helix of DNA), and direct representations of objects and structural relationships (e.g., 3D printed bones and tendons of the hand). Tangible representations enable students to identify and understand the multidimensional structure of objects, systems, and functions in ways that may be difficult to convey without multimedia materials and in more depth than supported by traditional 2-dimensional (2D) visuals.

Given the importance of objects and artifacts to museums and cultural sites—as well as the finding that virtual extended reality environments can overtax cognitive resources during a learning experience (Richards 2015)—an important extended reality format for these contexts may be 3D prints that allow learners to handle materials previously inaccessible to them. In the context of museum learning, these include 3D printed representations of original museum collections objects or specimens that closely resemble the original (Adams et al. 2015; Hatz et al. 2020; Li et al. 2012; McMenamin et al. 2014). These 3D prints are manipulated via direct, physical manipulation (i.e., the learners' hands). Physical manipulation frees up valuable cognitive resources by offloading complicated mental operations (e.g., mental rotation) to physical operations (Hutchins et al. 1985; Padalkar and Hegarty 2015; Wu et al. 2005). Available research supports the assertion that direct, physical manipulation impacts how learners attend to information and subsequently learn with objects—when there are incongruencies in shape, action, and location of digital 3D representations and interaction methods (e.g., using a computer mouse to manipulate and rotate a 3D molecule), subsequent learning may be negatively impacted (Arsenault and Ware 2004; Patterson and Silzars 2009; Ware and Rose 1999). A learner who interacts with a tangible 3D representation may have more cognitive resources available to encode information and generate inferences.

The potential impact of 3D prints in informal settings can be inferred from preliminary findings of research conducted with museum objects in authentic classroom settings (Butcher and Orr in preparation) and under controlled conditions in the laboratory (Orr and Butcher in preparation). These studies used 3D printed (tangible) and digital 3D (virtual) representations of museum objects for inquiry-based science exploration. Students worked with the tangible and virtual 3D representations of dinosaur fossils to answer scientific questions, including what kind of dinosaur had been found (see Fig. 1.2). Detailed analysis of video and audio recordings of students' learning behaviors showed that they used tangible and digital fossils differently. A key finding was that learners more often used the 3D printed fossils to simulate functional behaviors relevant to the scientific questions (Butcher and Orr in preparation)—for example, the opening and closing of a jaw. These behaviors occurred only rarely when learners worked with virtual 3D representations; instead, students using the virtual 3D representations were more likely to rotate the fossil and direct fellow students' attention to specific features (e.g., point using the cursor). Thus, informal environments may choose the form of extended reality material that is provided to visitors

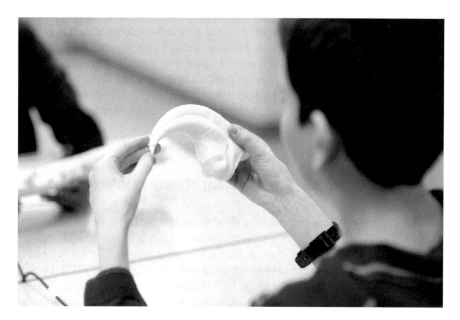

Fig. 1.2 Student participating in a scientific inquiry classroom activity with a tangible 3D representation of a dinosaur fossil

based on whether they want to see individuals engage in functional exploration (3D prints) or close, collaborative observation (virtual 3D representations).

Orr and Butcher's (in preparation) laboratory study followed up on this result by assessing whether simple prompts—similar to those that could be provided in informal contexts via signage or other methods—would be sufficient to change or enhance spontaneous interactions with the 3D fossils. That is, could simple usage prompts influence interactions with tangible and virtual materials? Or does the nature of the extended reality material (tangible vs. virtual) continue to exert strong influence on how it is used? In a study of hands-on chemistry models for formal education, oral prompts directing learners to use the models increased rates of interaction with the models and subsequent learning (Stull, Hegarty et al. 2012). But it is unclear to what extent prompts can impact varied forms of interaction with the kinds of highly engaging and real-world objects available via extended reality in informal environments. Orr and Butcher's (in preparation) study explored this by examining the impact of "functional prompts" (i.e., prompts that asked learners to use the tangible or digital representation in ways that show how the fossil functioned in real life) on learner behaviors. These prompts increased the rate of functional interactions with tangible 3D fossils but not virtual 3D fossils, suggesting that on-screen virtual models are nonoptimal for functional exploration, even when learners are prompted to use them this way. This has important potential implications for informal environments where there has been interest in using large-screen touch displays for virtual interaction. It is possible that on-screen virtual fossils do not engender the same feeling of reality as tangible 3D prints; moreover, on-screen virtual models must be manipulated using interactions that are somewhat less intuitive than physical manipulation (by hand). It may be the case that it will be necessary to use a virtual reality approach to support functional exploration of museum and cultural heritage objects provided in a virtual format. But this requires understanding if visitors can interact with virtual objects more naturally in immersive environments and whether we could detect varied forms of interaction to support meaningful personalization. In the following section, we outline analytical approaches that have been applied to model how learners interact with digital fossils.

1.8   Informal Learning with Virtual Museum Objects

Virtual 3D representations in immersive displays have affordances that are similar to tangible objects. The potential of virtual reality to facilitate interactions and reactions that are consistent with real-world situations has been recognized for many years in domains such as medicine and aviation (for a review see, Singh et al. 2013). Despite the affordances of such representations for the general public and young learners, few studies have investigated methods for student modeling in any systematic way in the context of virtual learning environments (Desmarais and Baker 2012). Past research in student modeling has been largely focused on 2D interfaces, whereas virtual objects enable rich, complex interactions and naturalistic motions.

Student interactions with 3D virtual materials have fundamental differences to traditional desktop user interfaces (Bowman et al. 2008). Interactive systems that display 3D graphics do not necessarily involve 3D interaction, as would be the case when tangible materials are physically manipulated. For example, if a user explores a 3D digital representation of a fossil on her desktop computer by choosing viewpoints from a traditional menu, no 3D interaction has taken place. On the other hand, 3D interaction does not necessarily mean that 3D input devices are used; for example, in the same application, if the user clicks on a 3D digital representation to change its orientation, then the 2D mouse input has been directly translated into a 3D interaction (Bowman et al. 2004). Compared to these standard input devices, 3D input devices (i.e., head-tracked view specification and six-degree-of-freedom hand tracking), enable rich interactions through point and click events, bounding boxes for orienting and scaling virtual objects, as well as voice commands and gesture recognition (Kalantari and Rauschnabel 2018). Figure 1.3 shows an example of both types of user interfaces using a digitized fossil (an *Allosaurus fragilis* claw) from the Natural History Museum of Utah; on the left, students interact with 3D digital representations using traditional input devices (i.e., mouse input), and on the right, the fossil is manipulated using remote controllers and a head-mounted display. Ambient data that describe student gestures and movement with virtual objects are characterized by changes over time along multiple dimensions. In the case of 2D mouse input interactions, the time-series data captures changes in the position and orientation of a perspective camera that orbits around the learning object (Fig. 1.3, left). While 3D input devices themselves include position and orientation data to track each motion controller, the perspective camera often consists of the viewport of the head-mounted display of the learner.

For this reason, virtual reality technology with head-mounted display and dual hand controls provides opportunities for 3D input that more closely resembles the direct physical manipulation enabled by tangible objects. At the same time, the virtual technology enables ambient data collection to gain insights into learners' cognitive processes during a learning episode—a process that ultimately should support personalization and scaffolding in informal environments. But this requires that the ambient

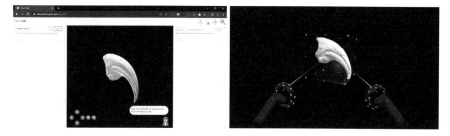

Fig. 1.3 FossilLab learning environment showing views of an *Allosaurus fragilis* claw in the 2D, screen-based display (left) vs. the 3D, immersive display (right)

data can be used to distinguish between different learner interactions with the virtual objects.

Preliminary data suggests that ambient data has potential to support tracking and identification of learners' interactions with virtual objects in real time. Figure 1.4 shows an example time-series sequence for the camera's position relative to the 3D virtual object in the case of two different gestures as users examined a virtual dinosaur claw in an immersive environment: either a clawing motion or typical movements involved in observing physical characteristics of the fossil. In this example, each data channel's sampling frequency is set to 1 Hz or 1 sample per second. A time-series sequence of log interactions with 3D digital representations consists of an ordered list of real numbers that capture the perspective camera position, projection, and orientation. Position is measured via the perspective camera as a reference point in the form of absolute coordinates (i.e., X, Y, Z) relative to a fixed reference point in the virtual space. Rotation can be measured by tracking changes in rotation using quaternions, a four-element vector where three points represent an axis about which rotation should be performed (i.e., X, Y, Z), and one point that specifies the amount or angle of rotation (i.e., W).

Preliminary findings obtained from synthetic data generated in controlled laboratory experiments suggest that ambient data allows for automated detection of not only distinct types of gestures (Poitras et al. 2020), but also differentiate between distinct profiles of movements within gestures (Orr et al. 2021). Synthetic data were generated in controlled conditions to obtain time-series data from different channels (i.e., orientation from the virtual model and remote controllers) and modalities

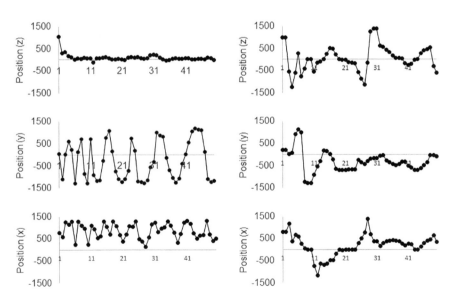

Fig. 1.4 Time-series data for changes in perspective camera position in virtual space for clawing motion (left) and observational behaviors (right)

(i.e., orientation in the form of Euler angles and quaternions). Results suggest that accurate detection of interaction behaviors with 3D virtual models requires smaller moving windows to segment the time-series data as well as features that characterize orientation of virtual models in the form of quaternions (Poitras et al. 2020).

Orr et al. (2021) further outlined an analytical framework that involves three consecutive steps. First, K-Means c derives a set of clusters in the time series that characterize distinct patterns in changes in orientation, position, and scale of virtual objects. Second, K-Nearest Neighbor is used to assign each time series to the corresponding cluster as a means to validate these gesture profiles. Third, Linear Regression is used to forecast time series and simulate each profile using the corresponding centroid as seed values. As a case example, analysis of changes in quaternion orientation collected over a 11-second duration at 10 Hz sampling rate for 160 clawing motions, where experimenters simulated the function of an *Allosaurus fragilis* claw, revealed six distinct gesture profiles that were accurately validated and forecasted. The benefit of this approach is to analyze time-series data of visitor interactions with virtual objects in an iterative manner, allowing for increasingly sophisticated representations of different gesture profiles. We now turn to a discussion of the broader significance of these findings for the use of ambient data to study informal learning processes with tangible and virtual objects.

1.9 Discussion

Novel methods are needed to reveal meaningful insights into dynamic actions with 3D digital representations, supporting the eventual development of extended reality experiences in informal environments that are meaningful and personalized. Because ambient data are gathered in real time without interfering with visitors' behaviors or interactions, it has strong potential to serve as a foundation for enhancing informal experiences when drawn from interactions with extended reality materials. Our work has shown that these ambient data are a promising avenue for pursuing learning research and for developing foundations upon which personalized support in informal environments can be built. However, there will be important challenges in gathering and interpreting temporal characteristics of visitor interactions with digital 3D representations in order to develop personalized experiences. In informal spaces, interactions with extended reality materials unfold dynamically throughout the course of learning and are characterized by varying frequencies and time durations in addition to contextual (i.e., informational, antecedent, and consequent events) and situational factors (i.e., learning domain, age, tasks, activities; see Merchant et al. 2014). Further, in addition to the potential reconstruction and abstraction of 2D and 3D objects (i.e., soils, terrains), there is the potential for extended reality materials to consist of dynamic processes (i.e., water flow) that promote learning not simply through object interaction but also through exploration of causal models and simulations (Ramasundaram et al. 2005). Further work can (and should) extend to immersive, narrative contexts—for example, game-based learning environments with 3D graphics where student affective states can be effectively modeled in multi-agent systems through knowledge-engineered rules based on analysis of student actions related to typing, mouse movements, and elapsed time between actions in addition to errors (Katsionis and Virvou 2008). Student interactions with virtual agents also can be constrained through response choices for the purposes of tracing and detecting learning events (Lester et al. 2014). These are but a few of the potential sources of ambient data from extended reality experiences in informal settings.

While the sheer number and variability of potential extended reality experiences (and associated ambient data) may make the challenge feel overwhelming, our research has shown promising solutions to personalizing instruction and—by modeling distinct interactions using unobtrusive methods to collect ambient data— has demonstrated the first step toward feasibility of real-time, adaptive systems for learning with extended reality. Over the last decade, an increasing body of literature acknowledges the importance of adaptive instruction to promote positive student learning and engagement (Kay and McCalla 2012; Shute and Zapata-Rivera 2012; Winne and Baker 2013). Personalized instruction involves four basic steps: (1) events are captured by the system; (2) student states are inferred as learning events and the system analyzes them; (3) instructional strategies are selected by the system based on observed learning; and (4) instructional content is delivered to the students through the user interface. Past research has outlined several approaches to design the requisite computational processes for student modeling (Desmarais and Baker 2012). Student models allow for automated detection of behaviors and often rely on machine learning algorithms to classify different types of behaviors on the basis of the log trace data of student interactions in the learning environment (Baker 2016). These entail data acquisition (i.e., sample rate), preprocessing (i.e., data segmentation and windowing), feature extraction (i.e., engineering and distilling discriminative features), and data processing models (predictive modeling algorithm; for review, see Siemens and Baker 2012). The timeliness and accuracy of these detectors are essential; identifying these behaviors enable adaptive systems to intervene in cases when students are off-task, exploiting properties of the system to perform a task, being careless, or performing any other behaviors unrelated to the learning task (Baker and Rossi 2013). The current work extends these findings to demonstrate when and how modeling is feasible for exploratory, interactive behaviors with museum objects.

1.10   Conclusion

Taken together, the research and findings in this chapter suggest that visitor learning with extended reality technologies in the context of informal environments (e.g., museums, heritage sites, and historical landmarks) can be informed through the collection of unobtrusive and nuanced data collected during exploration and interaction. The analysis of ambient data to distinguish between real-time interactions with museum objects represents a methodological approach with potential to advance the understanding of informal learning with extended reality devices within informal learning environments. Furthermore, these methodological advances have significant implications for the understanding of how informal learning processes unfold during visits and suggest that researchers should carefully consider the use of computational techniques to gain useful and actionable insights from complex ambient data. Preliminary findings from our own investigations—as reviewed in this chapter—illustrate how theory can be used to inform the design of extended reality experiences, and also demonstrate the benefits of studying phenomena under both controlled conditions in the laboratory and real-world situations. For practitioners, we must remember that the design of engaging and meaningful experiences not only leverages the affordances of extended reality, but also mitigates the potential difficulties and barriers to implementation. As extended reality technologies become increasingly commonplace in informal learning settings, and data-driven decision-making arises to meet the needs of visitors and site stakeholders, the wealth of available ambient data and the myriad of interesting problems to explore will require empirically driven approaches informed by theories of multimedia learning and instruction.

References

Adams JW, Paxton L et al (2015) 3d printed reproductions of orbital dissections: A novel mode of visualising anatomy for trainees in ophthalmology or optometry. Br J Ophthalmol 99(9):1162–1167. https://doi.org/10.1136/bjophthalmol-2014-306189

Ainsworth S, Vanlabeke N (2004) Multiple forms of dynamic representation. Learn Instr 14(3):241–255. https://doi.org/10.1016/j.learninstruc.2004.06.002

Arsenault R, Ware C (2004) The importance of stereo and eye-coupled perspective for eye-hand coordination in fish tank vr. Presence Teleop Virt Environ 13(5):549–559. https://doi.org/10.1162/1054746042545300

Baddeley AD (1986) Working memory. Oxford University Press, New York, NY

Baker R (2016) Stupid tutoring systems, intelligent humans. Int J Artif Int Educ 26(2):600–614. https://doi.org/10.1007/s40593-016-0105-0

Baker R, Rossi L (2013) Assessing the disengaged behaviors of learners. Des Rec Tut Sys 1:153

Barrett T, Hegarty M (2014) Interaction design and the role of spatial ability in moderating virtual molecule manipulation performance. Paper presented at the Proceedings of the Annual Meeting of the Cognitive Science Society.

Bartie PJ, Mackaness WA (2006) Development of a speech-based augmented reality system to support exploration of cityscape. Transactions in GIS 10(1):63–86. https://doi.org/10.1111/j.1467-9671.2006.00244.x

Bekele M, Champion E (2019) A comparison of immersive realities and interaction methods: cultural learning in virtual heritage. Front Rob Ai 6:1–14. https://doi.org/10.3389/frobt.2019.00091

Bekele M, Pierdicca R et al (2018) A survey of augmented, virtual, and mixed reality for cultural heritage. J Comp Cult Herit 11(2):1–36. https://doi.org/10.1145/3145534

Bell DR, Smith JK (2020) Inside the digital learning laboratory: new directions in museum education. Curator 63(3):371–386. https://doi.org/10.1111/cura.12376

Bowman D, Coquillart S et al (2008) 3d user interfaces: new directions and perspectives. IEEE Comput Graphics Appl 28(6):20–36

Bowman D, Kruijff E, et al (2004) 3d user interfaces: theory and practice, coursesmart etextbook, Addison-Wesley

Bressler DM (2013) Gateways to mobile learning. In: ZL Berge, L Muilenburg (eds) Handbook of Mobile Learning. New York, NY, pp 224–234

Butcher KR (2006) Learning from text with diagrams: promoting mental model development and inference generation. J Educ Psychol 98(1):182–197. https://doi.org/10.1037/0022-0663.98.1.182

Butcher KR (2014) The multimedia principle. In: Mayer R (ed) Cambridge Handbook of Multimedia Learning. Cambridge, UK, pp 174–205

Butcher KR, Davies S (2015) Inference generation during online study and multimedia learning. In: EJ O'Brien, AE Cook, RF Lorch (eds) Inferences During Reading. New York, p 321

Butcher KR, Orr MP (in preparation) The impact of physicality on model-based learning

Cahill C, Kuhn A, et al (2011) Mobile learning in museums: how mobile supports for learning influence student behavior. Paper presented at the Proceedings of the 10th International Conference on International Design and Children

Card SK (1999) Readings in information visualization: using vision to think. San Fransisco, Morgan Kaufmann Publishers

Carrozzino M, Bergamasco M (2010) Beyond virtual museums: experiencing immersive virtual reality in real museums. J Cult Herit 11(4):452–458. https://doi.org/10.1016/j.culher.2010.04.001

Christidou D (1990) Pierroux P (2018) Art, touch and meaning making: an analysis of multisensory interpretation in the museum. Museum Mgmt Cur 34(1):96–115. https://doi.org/10.1080/09647775.2018.1516561

Clough GW (2013) Best of both worlds: museums, libraries, and archives in a digital age. Smithsonian Institution, Washington, DC

Conaway W, Zorn-Arnold B (2015) The keys to online learning for adults: the six principles of andragogy. Distance Learning 12(4):37

Davis M (2020) Towards frictionless augmented reality (Date Accessed: Oct 12, 2020). https://www.aam-us.org/2020/06/15/towards-frictionless-augmented-reality/

Desmarais M, Baker R (2012) A review of recent advances in learner and skill modeling in intelligent learning environments. User Model User-Adap Inter 22(1–2):9–38

Di Franco PDG, Camporesi C et al (2015) 3d printing and immersive visualization for improved perception of ancient artifacts. Presence 24(3):243–264. https://doi.org/10.1162/PRES_a_00229

Dunleavy M, Dede C et al (2008) Affordances and limitations of immersive participatory augmented reality simulations for teaching and learning. JSEdT 18(1):7–22. https://doi.org/10.1007/s10956-008-9119-1

Dutke S, Rinck M (2006) Multimedia learning: working memory and the learning of word and picture diagrams. Learn Instr 16(6):526–537. https://doi.org/10.1016/j.learninstruc.2006.10.002

Fau M, Cornette R et al (2016) Photogrammetry for 3d digitizing bones of mounted skeletons: potential and limits. CR Palevol 15(8):968–977. https://doi.org/10.1016/j.crpv.2016.08.003

Fiorenza L, Yong R et al (2018) Technical note: the use of 3d printing in dental anthropology collections. Am. J. Phys. Anthropol. 167(2):400–406. https://doi.org/10.1002/ajpa.23640

Hammady R, Ma M et al (2020) Ambient information visualization and visitors' technology acceptance of mixed reality in museums. J Comput Cult Herit 13(2):1–22. https://doi.org/10.1145/3359590

Han I (2019) Immersive virtual field trips in education: a mixed-methods study on elementary students' presence and perceived learning. Br J Educat Tech 51(2):420–435. https://doi.org/10.1111/bjet.12842

Han I, Black JB (2011) Incorporating haptic feedback in simulation for learning physics. Comp Ed 57(4):2281–2290. https://doi.org/10.1016/j.compedu.2011.06.012

Hari Narayanan N, Hegarty M (2002) Multimedia design for communication of dynamic information. Int J Hum Comp Stud 57(4):279–315. https://doi.org/10.1006/ijhc.2002.1019

Harley JM, Poitras EG et al (2016) Comparing virtual and location-based augmented reality mobile learning: emotions and learning outcomes. Educational Tech Dev 64(3):359–388. https://doi.org/10.1007/s11423-015-9420-7

Hatz CR, Msallem B et al (2020) Can an entry-level 3d printer create high-quality anatomical models? accuracy assessment of mandibular models printed by a desktop 3d printer and a professional device. Int J Oral Maxillofac Surg 49(1):143–148. https://doi.org/10.1016/j.ijom.2019.03.962

He Z, Wu L et al (2018) When art meets tech: the role of augmented reality in enhancing museum experiences and purchase intentions. Tourism Management 68:127–139

Hegarty M (2004) Dynamic visualizations and learning: getting to the difficult questions. Learn Instr 14(3):343–351. https://doi.org/10.1016/j.learninstruc.2004.06.007

Hegarty M, Smallman HS et al (2012) Choosing and using geospatial displays: effects of design on performance and metacognition. J Exp Psychol Appl 18(1):1–17. https://doi.org/10.1037/a0026625

Hewitt D (2015) Please touch the art: 3-d printing helps visually impaired appreciate paintings (Date Accessed: Oct 12, 2020). https://www.smithsonianmag.com/innovation/please-touch-art-3-d-printing-helps-visually-impaired-appreciate-paintings-180954420/

Holtrop E, Downey S (2019) Taking a museum education study from research to practice (Date Accessed: Oct 12, 2020). https://www.aam-us.org/2019/07/24/taking-a-museum-education-study-from-research-to-practice/

Hoyek N, Collet C et al (2014) Effectiveness of three—dimensional digital animation in teaching human anatomy in an authentic classroom context. Anat Sci Educ 7(6):430–437. https://doi.org/10.1002/ase.1446

Hudson LN, Blagoderov V et al (2015) Inselect: automating the digitization of natural history collections. PLoS ONE 10(11):e0143402. https://doi.org/10.1371/journal.pone.0143402

Hughes CE, Smith E, et al (2004) Augmenting museum experiences with mixed reality. Paper presented at the Proceedings of KSCE 2004

Huk T (2006) Who benefits from learning with 3d models? the case of spatial ability. J Comput Assisted Learn 22(6):392–404. https://doi.org/10.1111/j.1365-2729.2006.00180.x

Hutchins EL, Hollan JD et al (1985) Direct manipulation interfaces. Human-Computer Interaction 1(4):311–338. https://doi.org/10.1207/s15327051hci0104_2

Jones MG, Childers G, et al (2014) The efficacy of haptic simulations to teach students with visual impairments about temperature and pressure. (research reports). J Visual Imp, 108(1):55

Kalantari M, Rauschnabel P (2018) Exploring the early adopters of augmented reality smart glasses: the case of microsoft hololens. In: Augmented reality and virtual reality, pp 229–245

Katsionis G, Virvou M (2008) Personalised e-learning through an educational virtual reality game using web services. Multimed. Tools App 39(1):47–71

Kay J, McCalla G (2012) Coming of age: Celebrating a quarter century of user modeling and personalization: Guest editors' introduction. User Model User-Adap Inter 22(1–2):1–7

Keil J, Pujol L, et al (2013) A digital look at physical museum exhibits: Designing personalized stories with handheld augmented reality in museums. Paper presented at the 2013 Digital Heritage International Congress

Knowles MS, Holton EFIII, et al (2015) Andragogy: A theory of adult learning. In The adult learner (8th ed.) (pp. 312–320). New York, NY

Kretschmer U, Coors V, et al (2001) Meeting the spirit of history. Paper presented at the Proceedings of the 2001 conference on Virtual reality, archeology, and cultural heritage

Kyriakou P, Hermon S (2019) Can i touch this? Using natural interaction in a museum augmented reality system. Digital App Arch Cult Herit 12:00088. https://doi.org/10.1016/j.daach.2018.e00088

Leopardi A, Ceccacci S et al (2020) X-reality technologies for museums: A comparative evaluation based on presence and visitors experience through user studies. In Press, J Cult Herit

Lester J, Lobene E et al (2014) Serious games with gift: Instructional strategies, game design, and natural language in the generalized intelligent framework for tutoring. Design Rec Tutuor Sys 2:205–215

Li J, Nie L et al (2012) Maximizing modern distribution of complex anatomical spatial information: 3d reconstruction and rapid prototype production of anatomical corrosion casts of human
specimens. Anat Sci Educ 5(6):330–339. https://doi.org/10.1002/ase.1287
Lukosch S, Billinghurst M et al (2015) Collaboration in augmented reality. Comput Support Coop
Work 24(6):515–525. https://doi.org/10.1007/s10606-015-9239-0
Magnani M, Guttorm A, et al (2018) Three-dimensional, community-based heritage management
of indigenous museum collections: archaeological ethnography, revitalization and repatriation at
the sami museum siida. (report). J Cult Herit, 31, 162. doi:https://doi.org/10.1016/j.culher.2017.
12.001
Makransky G, Andreasen NK, et al (2020) Immersive virtual reality increases liking but not learning
with a science simulation and generative learning strategies promote learning in immersive virtual
reality. J Educ Psychol (March 19, 2020), 1–17. doi:https://doi.org/10.1037/edu0000473
Makransky G, Terkildsen TS et al (2019) Adding immersive virtual reality to a science lab simulation
causes more presence but less learning. Learn Instr 60:225–236. https://doi.org/10.1016/j.learni
nstruc.2017.12.007
Mayer RE (1989) Systematic thinking fostered by illustrations in scientific text. J Educ Psychol
81(2):240–246. https://doi.org/10.1037/0022-0663.81.2.240
Mayer RE (2014) The cambridge handbook of multimedia learning (Second Edition ed.). New
York, Cambridge University Press
Mayer RE (2017) Using multimedia for e-learning. J Comput Assisted Learn 33(5):403–423. https://
doi.org/10.1111/jcal.12197
Mayer RE, Gallini J (1990) When is an illustration worth ten thousand words? J Educ Psychol
82(4):715–726. https://doi.org/10.1037/0022-0663.82.4.715
McMenamin P, Quayle M et al (2014) The production of anatomical teaching resources using three-
dimensional (3d) printing technology. Anat Sci Educ 7(6):479–486. https://doi.org/10.1002/ase.
1475
McNeil NM, Uttal DH (2009) Rethinking the use of concrete materials in learning: perspectives
from development and education. Child Dev Persp 3(3):137–139. https://doi.org/10.1111/j.1750-
8606.2009.00093.x
Merchant ZG, Ernest T, Cifuentes L, Keeney-Kennicutt W, Davis TJ (2014) Effectiveness of virtual
reality- based instruction on students' learning outcomes in k-12 and higher education: a meta-
analysis. Comp Ed 70:29–40. https://doi.org/10.1016/j.compedu.2013.07.033
Merritt E (2016) Museums and personalized learning (Date Accessed: Oct 12, 2020). https://www.
aam-us.org/2016/03/22/museums-and-personalized-learning/
Neely L, Langer M (2013) Please feel the museum. the emergence of 3d printing and scanning. In:
N Proctor, R e Cherry (eds) Museums and the Web. Silver Spring, MD
Orr M, Aina D, et al (2021) Embodied learning with virtual reality: gesture clustering and fore-
casting. Paper presented at the American Educational Research Association (AERA), Orlando,
Florida
Orr M, Butcher KR (in preparation) The impact of tangible materials and functional prompts on
learning with 3d models
Padalkar S, Hegarty M (2015) Models as feedback: developing representational competence in
chemistry. J Educ Psychol 107(2):451–467. https://doi.org/10.1037/a0037516
Paivio A (1986) Mental representations: a dual coding approach. Oxford University Press, New
York
Patterson R, Silzars A (2009) Immersive stereo displays, intuitive reasoning, and cognitive engi-
neering. J Soci Inf Disp 17(5):443–448. https://onlinelibrary.wiley.com/doi/abs/10.1889/1.182
8693
Plecher DA, Wandinger M, et al (2019) Mixed reality for cultural heritage. Paper presented at the
2019 IEEE Conference on Virtual Reality and 3D User Interfaces
Poitras E, Butcher KR, et al (2020) Modeling interactive behaviors while learning with digitized
objects in virtual reality environments. In: Cognitive and Affective Perspectives on Immersive
Technology in Education, pp 215–234

Preece D, Williams S et al (2013) "Let's get physical": advantages of a physical model over 3d computer models and textbooks in learning imaging anatomy. Anat Sci Educ 6(4):216–224. https://doi.org/10.1002/ase.1345

Primary Research G (2015) Survey of library & museum digitization projects (2016 edition ed.). New York, Primary Research Group Inc

Pujol L, Katifori A, et al (2013) From personalization to adaptivity: creating immersive visits through interactive digital storytelling at the acropolis museum. Paper presented at the Workshop Proceedings of the 9th International Conference on Intelligent Environments, Athens, Greece

Rahaman H, Champion E et al (2019) From photo to 3d to mixed reality: a complete workflow for cultural heritage visualisation and experience. Digit Appl Archaeol Cult Herit 13:e00102. https://doi.org/10.1016/j.daach.2019.e00102

Ramasundaram V, Grunwald S et al (2005) Development of an environmental virtual field laboratory. Comp Ed 45(1):21–34. https://doi.org/10.1016/j.compedu.2004.03.002

Rennie LJ, Johnston DJ (2004) The nature of learning and its implications for research on learning from museums. Sci Educ 88(S1):S4–S16. https://doi.org/10.1002/sce.20017

Richards DT, Meredith, (2015) A comparison of learning gains when using a 2d simulation tool versus a 3d virtual world: An experiment to find the right representation involving the marginal value theorem. Comp Ed 86:157–171. https://doi.org/10.1016/j.compedu.2015.03.009

Sampaio AZ, Ferreira MM et al (2010) 3d and vr models in civil engineering education: construction, rehabilitation and maintenance. Autom Constr 19(7):819–828. https://doi.org/10.1016/j.autcon.2010.05.006

Schofield G, Beale G, et al (2018) Viking vr: designing a virtual reality experience for a museum. Paper presented at the Proceedings of the 2018 Designing Interactive Systems Conference

Schüler A, Arndt J et al (2015) Processing multimedia material: dsoes integration of text and pictures result in a single or two interconnected mental representations? Learn Instr 35:62–72. https://doi.org/10.1016/j.learninstruc.2014.09.005

Schwan S, Dutz S (2020) How do visitors perceive the role of authentic objects in museums? Curator (New York, NY), 63(2), 217–237. https://doi.org/10.1111/cura.12365

Shah P, Miyake A (1996) The separability of working memory resources for spatial thinking and language processing: an individual differences approach. J Exp Psychol Gen 125(1):4–27. https://doi.org/10.1037/0096-3445.125.1.4

Shute VJ, Zapata-Rivera D (2012) Adaptive Educational Systems. Adaptive Tech 7(27):1–35

Siemens, G, Baker, R S d (2012) Learning analytics and educational data mining: towards communication and collaboration. Paper presented at the Proceedings of the 2nd international conference on learning analytics and knowledge

Singh H, Kalani M et al (2013) History of simulation in medicine: from resusci annie to the ann myers medical center. Neurosurgery 73(Suppl 1):S9–S14. https://doi.org/10.1227/NEU.0000000000000093

Stull A, Barrett T, et al (2012) Design of a virtual reality system for the study of diagram use in organic chemistry. Paper presented at the Workshop on technology enhanced diagrams research

Stull A, Hegarty M et al (2012) Representational translation with concrete models in organic chemistry. Cogn Instr 30(4):404–434. https://doi.org/10.1080/07370008.2012.719956

Sugiura A, Kitama T et al (2019) The use of augmented reality technology in medical specimen museum tours. Anat Sci Educ 12(5):561–571. https://doi.org/10.1002/ase.1822

Tesoriero R, Gallud JA et al (2014) Enhancing visitors' experience in art museums using mobile technologies. Inf Sys Front 16(2):303–327. https://doi.org/10.1007/s10796-012-9345-1

Venigalla AS M, Chimalakonda S (2019) Towards enhancing user experience through a web-based augmented reality museum. Paper presented at the 2019 IEEE 19th ICALT

Vlahakis V, Karigiannis J, et al (2001) Archeoguide: first results of an augmented reality, mobile computing system in cultural heritage sites. VR, Arch, Cult Herit, 9(10.1145), 584993–585015

Ware C, Rose J (1999) Rotating virtual objects with real handles. TOCHI 6(2):162–180. https://doi.org/10.1145/319091.319102

Wilson PF, Stott J, et al (2017) Evaluation of touchable 3d-printed replicas in museums. Curator: Mus.M J. 60(4): 445–465. https://doi.org/10.1111/cura.12244

Winne PH, Baker RS (2013) The potentials of educational data mining for researching metacognition, motivation and self-regulated learning. JEDM 5(1):1–8

Wu B, Klatzky RL et al (2005) Psychophysical evaluation of in-situ ultrasound visualization. IEEE Trans Visual Comput Graph 11(6):684–693. https://doi.org/10.1109/TVCG.2005.104

Chapter 2
Collaborative Augmented Reality for Cultural Heritage, Tourist Sites and Museums: Sharing Visitors' Experiences and Interactions

João Jacob and Rui Nóbrega

Abstract In this chapter, synergies between augmented reality (AR) and shared experiences are explored. The shared experiences (such as visiting a cultural site or a museum) can benefit from computer-supported collaborative work done in the context of maintenance, training, and simulation. With the wide availability and use of AR-enabled smartphones, it is now possible to create collaborative experiences built upon the knowledge gained from such industry-oriented training applications. This novel approach allows for a greater user engagement fostered by the collaborative nature of an AR shared space. Recent AR works allow for many users to observe the same superimposed object as the group and interact collaboratively with it, as users can see not only the other users but their actions and effects in the virtual elements. This methodology allows for group interaction around tangible cultural points of interest at different scales (such as ruins or buildings but also statues and paintings).

2.1 Introduction

The application of information technologies to museums is not a recent phenomenon. In fact, the earliest references to the process of using information technology as means to catalogue and index archives in the context of museums dates to the late 80s (Bearman 1987). A search on the Web of Science with the keywords "museum informatics" shows a growing number of entries, starting from said period. This is further corroborated by other works, such as that of Mamrayeva and Aikambetova, highlighting the current importance that information technology has been used on not only the collection management of museums, but also for communication, preservation and presentation of works (Mamrayeva and Aikambetova 2014). With museums

J. Jacob
LIACC, DEI, Faculdade de Engenharia, Universidade do Porto, Porto, Portugal
e-mail: joao.jacob@fe.up.pt

R. Nóbrega (✉)
NOVA-LINCS, DI, Faculdade de Ciências e Tecnologia,
Universidade Nova de Lisboa, Lisbon, Portugal
e-mail: rui.nobrega@fct.unl.pt

and art galleries entering this digital era, their roles and offers to their visitors have also expanded significantly. The active participation of these spaces in raising awareness of current issues has been improved with this advent, with online learning, community communication and the existence of virtual versions of museums democratizing the access to information (Perera and Chandra 2010). However, as noted by Griffin, the surge in the number of visitors to museums has presented several opportunities, but also several problems such as what some describe as the "Disneyfication" of museums and the marketability of gift shops (Griffin 2008). This ties with the general trend of profiting from tourism of tangible heritage sites, as discussed by Nuryanti (1996). What these trends indicate is that not only is there now a larger base of potential visitors for museums but also that these visitors have certain expectations from these spaces as well. Conversely, there are now many museums that feature a digital archive that has content that can be used not only for conservation and research purposes, but for enriching, extending or transcending the visit as well (Foo et al. 2009).

The tourism industry has also seen great growth, globally. However, while historically it has been associated with economic development, particularly for developing countries, recent studies argue that the expected "trickle down" effect is not necessarily true, and that it may not reduce poverty (Mahadevan and Suardi 2019). Additionally, there are authors that claim that mass tourism has the potential of creating negative effects for tourism itself and for the local population. Commonly known effects are "overtourism", common in major tourist attractions and cities where hot tourist spots are overcrowded, and "tourismphobia", where local residents become underrepresented and blame tourism for a loss of quality of life (Milano et al. 2019). One possible solution to mitigate these problems, while also capitalizing on the importance of the industry itself, is Digital Tourism. Benyon et al. define it as the application of digital means to support the tourists' activity, be it before, during or after (Benyon et al. 2014). This means that the use of Virtual Reality, Augmented Reality and Mixed Reality technologies can be used to build upon the foundations that museums, art galleries and tourist attractions provide to their visitors, allowing people to have an enhanced or alternative experience.

In this chapter, we explore how Augmented Reality and Collaborative Augmented Reality, as technologies, can be used to feasibly and potentially improve the visitors' experience, or even create a sense of a shared experience even if people are not necessarily sharing the same physical space.

2.2   Co-Located AR in Outdoor Sites

The wide availability of smartphones with location capabilities in the 2010s gave birth to new augmented reality tourism exploration applications. These outdoor applications used Location-Based Services (LBS) to explore a certain area guiding the user through several real-life Points of Interest (POI) (Tahyudin and Saputra 2016).

These techniques were first widely adopted and tested in games before being widely adopted for outdoor tourism or sparse museums. In the early 2000s, Geocaching[1] appeared worldwide presenting a collaborative platform where users participate in a GPS-enabled treasure hunt. This game enabled the activation and promotion of Cultural Heritage remote sites, landscapes or urban centers. By placing a certain cache, a hidden box, in one location, the players following the pre-known GPS position were instructed to find the box and check-in in a physical notebook that they passed through that location. This low-tech approach is actually the basis of any LBS for tourism. Current modern location-based games are able to make use of other sensors and third-party data sources and services to have greater knowledge of the player's context, providing a custom tailored experience (Jacob et al. 2018), even though issues regarding the availability of this data, its reliability and applicability are old problems that still persist (Jacob and Coelho 2011).

Still, the engagement cycle provided by Geocaching is important to study. The system redirects the user to a place that you want to promote. There is a small collection reward from getting there, the user can register itself in another location, collecting locations. Usually the user would leave an object inside the box and take another from it. There is a group memory and sense of collectiveness.

Using these concepts from LBSs, Niantic[2] expanded the technology stack around 2013 to include Augmented Reality with games such as Ingress or Pokémon GO. In Ingress, the world has a digital twin where actions in the real world affect the digital map. In Pokémon GO, this is taken a bit further with the game prompting the players to go to certain physical locations called gyms to engage in Augmented Reality battles where we can see virtual characters superimposed in real-life POI.

These pervasive or augmented reality games highlight the possibilities of creating mobile applications to explore a certain outdoor site using LBSs and Augmented Reality (Tahyudin and Saputra 2016) and can be used for purposes other than entertainment (Coelho et al. 2020). One important aspect of these applications is that, like in Ingress or Geocaching, there is a natural collaborative nature that can be studied.

Han et al. (2018) defined a user experience model for AR applications in urban heritage tourism. In it, they define the main features an application must have to enable a good touristic experience in terms of Content, Presentation, Functionality and Interaction. Some of the most important characteristics are the interaction using AR overlays, make use of offline modes, convenient (not obtruding the real-world attraction), and naturally, easy to use and playful.

Nóbrega et al. (2017) present a fast prototyping game model designed to enhance the exploration experience of a tourist using several steps in the following areas:

- Economy: Evaluate the tourist needs, what is he looking for? Who is the tourist? What can the business plan be?

---

[1] Geocaching, https://www.geocaching.com/, last access: October 2020.

[2] Niantic, https://nianticlabs.com/, last access: October 2020.

- Storytelling: What stories can potentiate the value and interest of the application? Background research on the tourism destination, creating a line of thought to drive the story.
- UX design/Game designer: What will the experience, the interface and the game mechanics be? Interface and User Experience design.
- Art design: Collection and creation of media elements to display in the application.
- Sound Design: Engage the player through sound.
- Game Development: Implementation of the game's design.
- System and Mobile Technologies: Gathering external information sources, creating a server and enabling a multimedia framework. Enabling location-based technologies. Logic and game mechanics implementation.

An example of the creation of a game to explore an outdoor location can be seen in Fig. 2.1. In this mobile app, the GPS position of the tourist is drawn in a stylized map. This is a common type of map available in touristic locations and can be easily adapted to provide the user's location even if the map includes exaggerated features and drawings. The importance is that the continuity of the contiguous space is preserved. In this application (Silva 2019; Santos et al. 2020) several events are automatically triggered by the location of the user. Sometimes these events present additional information, other times it switches to an AR mode where information or games are presented in an AR overlay, as seen in Fig. 2.2.

Using AR in tourism presents several advantages and challenges. The advantages include presenting the information *in-loco*, superimposing objects and buildings with different historical or ethnographic data, presenting a virtual tour to the tourist and engaging in a multimedia experience. The main challenge is how to make technology

Fig. 2.1 Outdoor park exploration in mobile application. The stylized touristic map is used and presented on the smartphone screen (Silva 2019)

Fig. 2.2 AR mode in Outdoor park exploration in mobile application. In this in-app game the user must identify certain birds of prey

invisible and pervasive enough so as to not hinder the experience of visiting a touristic site. Technology should improve the experience and not replace it or compete with it.

In this section, we presented the use of AR in wide outdoor spaces in the context of tourism. In the next section we describe several different AR techniques that are important to present multimedia content in Museums and Cultural and Heritage sites.

2.3   AR Techniques for Cultural Heritage and Tourism

The initial wave of applications for tourism used location-based systems with the addition of Augmented Reality using the smartphone's inertial system to place virtual objects at a certain GPS-location. This allowed the introduction of in-place tags and overlays such as LayAR (Tahyudin and Saputra 2016) and Junaio. Additionally, in closed spaces where satellite location was not an option several museums explored the use of augmented reality and multimedia content using fiducial markers (Bekele et al. 2018) to activate and locate the AR content, or other location techniques such as Bluetooth beacon triangulation (Fernandes and Jacob 2011). This was mainly executed using toolkits such as ARToolkit or more recently Vuforia.[3]

Currently there are two main techniques for AR:

Outdoor: It uses GPS coordinates for location and smartphone inertial measurement unit (IMU) to insert AR content superimposed to a fixed position. This is a good alternative for tourism, outdoor site exploration and map-based navigation, even though it accumulates error from both the GPS and the IMU.

Indoor: It uses markers (visible or disguised as a common image as in Fenu et al. (2018)) to activate and provide a reference point for the AR content. Most suitable for museums or to present details in a cultural heritage site. It has the inconvenience of requiring the user to point the device's camera at the marker. Bluetooth beacons can also be used but may require additional setup and calibration (Fernandes and Jacob 2011).

There are different techniques that require the use of computer vision methods paired with a clever user interface that leads the user to unknowingly calibrate the system. In the previous example of the outdoor park (Silva 2019; Santos et al. 2020), presented in Figs. 2.1 and 2.2, there was an AR method to explore hidden animals, fungus or small plants present in the park's stone walls. This method presented in Fig. 2.3 requires the user to follow specific instructions to align guidelines with a certain wall. Of course, the AR mode is still activated using the device location, but the AR content location is achieved by scanning a specific surface. This allows for much more stable AR without jitters, enabling the presentation of more detailed content in a touristic or cultural heritage site.

Another interesting technique is to take advantage of tangible items. Most heritage venues provide information pamphlets or maps with important locations. Tourism offices often provide city maps with POI. Nóbrega et al. (2016) present a solution to use physical maps and informational pamphlets as markers for AR content. In this example seen in Figs. 2.4 and 2.5, the visitor is holding a common city map in one hand and pointing the smartphone with the AR application with the other. This technique increases the value of objects, papers and pamphlets given to tourists by providing additional information and multimedia content.

Augmented reality in smartphone apps has widely been used in museums. Using images as markers (Fenu and Pittarello 2018), it is possible to display additional content. Although technology is important to achieve the desired effect, it is important to have a coherent storytelling narrative that is compelling for the visitor. AR by itself will be nothing but a gimmick if not used carefully and may become detrimental to the experience. The *Svevo tour* is an example of the use of a design process to create an engaging augmented reality application for a literary museum (Fenu and Pittarello 2018). This work highlights the importance of an iterative process where the position of the activation AR images is tested and evaluated with users several times in order to maximize the engagement level.

---

[3] Vuforia, AR platform, https://www.ptc.com/en/products/vuforia, last Access: October 2020.

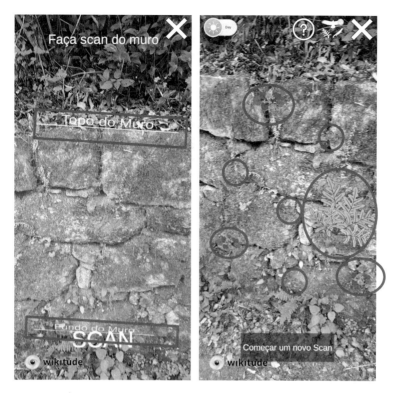

Fig. 2.3 AR method to explore hidden animals, fungus or small plants present in the park's stone walls. On the left, the user aligns the lines with the real wall. On the right, the AR botanical content is presented. AR overlays are shown with red enclosures

Fig. 2.4 Mobile tourism app exploring porto, Portugal and a nineteenth-century map it uses

There are several ways to activate and present AR content. Audio Augmented Reality is a novel form of AR that is gaining track. With this technique the visitor can explore a city or museum through sound where the current audio is transformed to include additional sounds. These can be a location-based explanation (Boletsis and

Fig. 2.5 Exploring the history of porto using a nineteenth-century map that is superimposed in AR onto the real map behind. Additionally, several wine barrels present different POI

Chasanidou 2018) or can take the visitor to another place in time, hearing sounds from the past.

There are more complex techniques that produce the AR effect but that are not so robust or depend on additional hardware. Computer vision algorithms can be used to create more advanced visualizations (Mata and Claramunt 2013; Nóbrega and Correia 2011) but many of them depend on lightning conditions and good camera pointing skills from the user. Mixed Reality headsets have a large potential to create immersive multimedia AR (Pietroszek and Moore 2019; Pietroszek et al. 2019) but the cost and maintenance of the headsets is a major drawback. One alternative is using tangible AR, where the superimposed content is projected into objects and reacts according to changes in the real world (Petrelli and O'Brien 2018). These projection techniques can even be used to foster collaborative behavior where several users interact with objects and projectors to change the displayed AR content (Willis et al. 2011).

In this section, we discussed the main techniques currently in use to show AR content. This is important to highlight that there are new possibilities that can arise from using smartphones differently or how to equip a space with sensors to enable tangible AR. In the next sections, we will explore the engagement advantages of pushing for collaboration between museum and heritage researchers, visitors and tourists in order to enable the concept of shared experiences.

2.4   Industry-Oriented AR Training Applications

The use of AR for tourist sites or museums has many times a pedagogical and a history learning factor. Several research studies point out that mobile augmented reality systems (MARS), as is the case of smartphones, enhance the learning process (Arth et al. 2015) and increase the interest and attention of the students (Coulby et al. 2011; Rambli et al. 2007). Educational content has a vast potential for future use in mobile devices, as they work virtually anywhere (Arth et al. 2015).

Evolving from educational applications, AR for maintenance or assembly tasks has been proposed in several applications (Kim and Moon 2013; Zhu et al. 2014). As the complexity of maintenance and assembly procedures can be huge, the training of professionals to perform these tasks has been the focus of several research groups (Webel et al. 2013). The use of an optimal AR system (low latency, high-quality see-through calibration, devices integrated into work clothes, optimize interaction, weight-reduced HMD) decreases the overall strain, compared to common work assistance systems (Tumler et al. 2008).

Webel et al. (2013) analyzes the use of augmented reality for training purposes. It states that a big advantage of AR for training is that the trainee can interact with the real-world objects and simultaneously access the virtual information for guidance. This way, the trainee learns how to perform the tasks by observing the augmented instructions, without the need of any physical training material (e.g. a user manual).

However, as pointed out by Webel et al. (2013), in the context of training applications, a potential danger is that users may not be able to perform the tasks without the AR instructions or when the technology fails. Therefore, the training programs should include phases in which the amount of AR features is reduced (e.g. less virtual components and instructions), in order to teach the user and not only guide him through the task. To summarize, AR-based training applications can be used as an example for collaborative apps for museums and cultural heritage sites where the person explores the space and occasionally is prompted to interact in AR with a center piece or collaborating with others.

As an example, Henderson and Feiner (2009) implemented a prototype AR application to support military mechanics conducting routine maintenance tasks inside an armored vehicle turret.

A maintenance task can be decomposed into several sub-tasks. For each sub-task, the application provides five forms of augmented reality content to assist the mechanic:

- arrows to redirect the attention of the user to a specific component (e.g. when the component is not in line of sight);
- text instructions that provide a description of the task, as well as notes and warnings;
- labels that show the location of the target component and surrounding context;
- a close-up view depicting a 3D virtual scene on the target component at close range;

- 3D models of tools and components at target locations, to assist in more ambiguous or complex tasks.

Conversely, these interface elements could be also applied in a museum application.

Many times, we want to engage several visitors at the same time in a museum. This interaction can be between the tour guide and the visitors or between the visitors themselves in a collaborative fashion.

Using the mentor-apprentice model (Maia 2017), several studies can be used to replicate the tour-guide–visitor relation either locally or remotely. Zhu et al. (2014) developed an AR mentoring system (AR-Mentor) to assist in maintenance and repair tasks of complex machinery, such as vehicles and industrial machinery. In this system, the user wears a helmet-based sensor head package that includes one pair of stereo cameras, one *inertial measurement unit* (IMU) and one *head-mounted monocular display* (monocular HMD). The IMU and the stereo cameras allow a pose estimation module to calculate the 3D location and rotation of the user's head, with respect to the target equipment, with high precision.

The AR-Mentor also features a virtual personal assistant that allows the user to interact with it, by asking questions and get specific guidance for the task at hand.

In this case, all the 33-step maintenance tasks on a vehicle are done with a virtual assistant that guides the user in all cases, answering asked questions and displaying virtual content useful for the task at hand. These concepts could be transferred to a collaborative application in which, instead of a virtual assistant, a remote user guided all the process by supervising the process and generating virtual instructions to guide the local user.

Using the mentor-apprentice model, Maia (2017) proposed Coop AR, an AR framework that encompasses two subsystems that communicate with each other. This system can be used to insert Augmented Reality content around a certain piece or artwork. The visitor can then explore different aspects of it following instructions from a mentor that can be in-site directing a large group or remotely.

The mentor prepares instructions that are sent to the apprentice. These instructions are presented using augmented reality that guide the apprentice performing the task. The virtual environment which the mentor interacts with has key similarities with the apprentice's real environment. Specifically, the objects that are being used to perform the task by the apprentice are in some way represented in the virtual scene of the mentor. These objects can be created by the mentor itself using tools provided by the application.

The mentor's subsystem seen in Fig. 2.6 offers several sample instructions, such as arrows and geometric primitives. The creation of custom instructions should also be supported. New instructions may be created by the mentor, by importing custom images and meshes.

The apprentice AR module, shown in Fig. 2.7, can send feedback to the mentor, either by interacting with the interface or by sending a video stream, depending on the implementation. The interface should provide visual cues to guide the user if

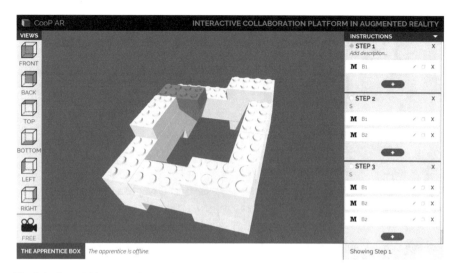

Fig. 2.6 Coop AR's mentor/tour guide application, where it is possible to build a set of instructions that can be used by the apprentice/visitor to explore a physical piece

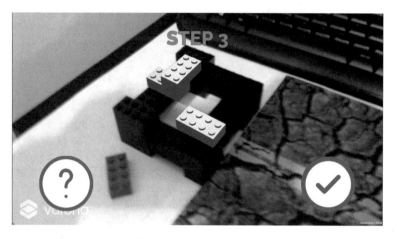

Fig. 2.7 Coop AR's augmented reality view, where the apprentice/visitor can see the physical piece and explore it using a set of instructions. In this example, the physical lego are augmented with virtual legos

there are instructions that are out of the field of view. Both modules can be seen in the diagram in Fig. 2.8.

Before beginning a collaboration session with the apprentice/visitor, the mentor/tour-guide should prepare the task around the chosen piece, define its steps and, for each step, create the corresponding instructions. The piece should be small enough to help the AR tracking and the several steps should be included in a general narrative on why it makes sense to use AR in the context of the museum/cultural

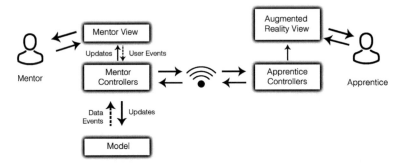

Fig. 2.8 Diagram depicting how collaborative augmented reality may be achieved using a mentor-apprentice approach

heritage site. In our experiments (Maia 2017), using this AR step-by-step approach, users took less than 59% of time completing a task than if they were explained what to do via Skype connection.

Visitors should be able to explore an object in a museum while having the option of asking for more information from an expert using an AR cooperation tool such as Coop AR. In the next section, we will explore how collaboration between users can enhance the overall experience of several visitors.

2.5 Collaborative AR Applied to Museums

Collaborative Augmented Reality allows multiple users to interact in a shared augmented reality instance. It has its roots in the field of Computer Supported Cooperative Work (CSCW), which is a popular research field, among others, in Human–Computer Interaction, dating to the 1980s (Grudin 1994). Traditionally, it focuses highly on the interactions of multiple users with a device, rather than a single one. However, when dealing with collaborative augmented reality, each user is usually equipped with an augmented reality capable device, be it a mobile phone, tablet, headset or custom hardware (Ahlers et al. 1995; Billinghurst and Kato 2002). These concepts of enabling or fostering cooperation and collaboration through digital systems have already been applied to tangible and intangible heritage and museums via game design and gamification (Lu et al. 2011; Nofal et al. 2020; Boschloos et al. 2017) and as the basis for shared experiences (Arroyo et al. 2011). There are still several lingering issues, however, such as context awareness, which relates to the understanding of every other collaborating user's actions in the context at hand, or the clear separation between collaborative and individual tasks, which consists of separating tasks that should be done by a single user or a restricted group from tasks where everyone should be able to cooperate, possibly even preventing users from doing tasks not associated with their roles (Thanyadit et al. 2018).

Fig. 2.9 Multiple augmented reality users sharing the same scenario and referential. Note how the system identifies each unique user in their real-life position

Figure 2.9 demonstrates an Augmented Reality Collaborative system, where users are able to see the virtual world but also their own avatars. This allows users to understand the intents and tasks that each user is tackling, even without any sort of verbal communication (Duque 2019).

Some usages for Collaborative AR have already been tested, for example, with police and military personnel. In this work by Kim et al. (2018), a collaborative tool was developed to be used in joint planning for disaster response. The results suggest improved task performance when comparing the tool's results with traditional approaches.

However, like in general AR, there are certain key attributes that are recommended as general guidelines, so as to achieve a better collaborative AR experience. This attractive User Experience (UX) is not always easy to achieve, as it can be challenging to allow interaction and modifications of the scene for multiple users simultaneously. The following 5 attributes have been identified as important for these experiences (Szalavári et al. 1998; Billinghurst and Kato 2002):

- **Virtuality**. Objects that don't exist in the real world can be viewed and examined.
- **Augmentation**. Real objects can be augmented with virtual annotations.
- **Cooperation**. Multiple users can see each other and cooperate in natural ways.
- **Independence**. Individual users control their own independent viewpoints.
- **Individuality**. Displayed data can appear in different forms for individual viewers depending on their personal needs and interests.

These can be applied to the context of tangible heritage via many forms. The following is not an exhaustive list as to how these concepts may be practically explored:

Virtuality: Digital Archivism, where researchers may study and examine objects and their details without having to be physically present in the same space. Visitors and Tourists are allowed to interact with artifacts and structures without the risk of degradation or self-harm as they are digital representations;

Augmentation: Digital Archivism, in a scenario where researchers may annotate certain features of interest of the object. This can also be extended to visitors, allowing them to focus on the parts that are of cultural interest;

Cooperation: Digital Archivism and Restoration, allowing scholars and researchers to explore the digital representation of an object or structure concomitantly and adding and sharing extra layers of information via multimedia annotations but also by transforming or editing the object (of particular relevance for restoration of works, such as a broken artifact that was laser scanned and in need of assembly, or a painting that needs maintenance, as this approach removes the risk of forever damaging the real object). For visitors it can be used as the basis for cooperative activities that allow them to engage with other visitors and the museum (usually through games or game-like activities), contributing to a better experience.

Independence: As users are in control of their point of view and scale of objects, they may experience viewing the representation of an object at a size or point of view that would be impractical or even impossible in real life. For instance, showing the inner workings of a pocket clock, or how the human digestive system works, or a diorama-sized representation of a large building;

Individuality: This concept can be explored through the personalization of the museum tour and the digital contents there-in. This concept has already been explored in digital museums and could also be applied in this context (Wang et al. 2009).

Visitors may prefer AR rather than immersive virtual environments (IVE) and do perform better on some collaborative tasks because they can interpret each other's nonverbal cues, as they can see each other and the environment around them (Billinghurst and Kato 2002). This makes the visualization of other collaborating users, though not mandatory, extremely useful and as something worth taking into consideration. So, face-to-face AR collaboration tries to get the most out of these communication cues, while enabling several users to experience a shared augmented physical space, hopefully intuitively, in order to enhance collaboration efficacy, lead to a greater sense of presence and, overall, enrich the experience.

Another important challenge in collaborative AR is how to handle the physical absence of a user in the local collaboration space (Kim et al. 2018). This could be useful in allowing researchers, both local and remote, to interact and collaborate with each other in a meaningful way. According to Billinghurst and Kato (2002), it was difficult for technology of that time to provide remote participants with the exact same experience as if they were physically present in the collaborative space.

This may also be nearly impossible to achieve, not only due to technical or logistical constraints, but also due to the "qualia" problem (Tye 2014). For instance, even when multiple cameras were used to capture and reconstruct avatars for all users involved, the use of a screen deeply hindered the efforts at enhancing collaboration. Though the field of remote AR collaboration has seen several advances since then, mainly its democratization and ease of use from a technology implementation point of view, this statement still holds. The matter of transmitting the nonverbal cues and limitations to the sense of presence and agency are still present challenges. However, for tasks such as researchers or museum curators to experience and collaborate on a given task remotely, these issues are not as impacting.

The project Painter (Pereira et al. 2019; Duque 2019) aims to bridge the gap between local and remote collaboration through the use of mixed reality. Figures 2.10 and 2.11 show how a given virtual scene is represented for the users that are present in the real-world location (above), and how the same scene may be viewed by those

Fig. 2.10 The same environment being explored by two users concomitantly: one in AR (above) and another in VR (bellow)

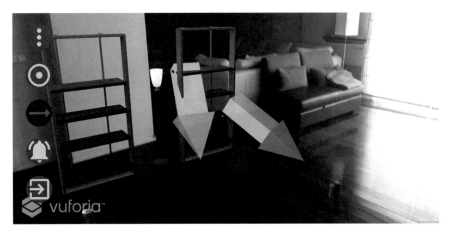

Fig. 2.11 Arrows and labels in augmented reality can be used to improve the museum space

users that are not there. This allows for users that are in the actual location to retain context through augmented reality and provides this context, now fully virtual, to remote users. As previously mentioned, this solution could be applied to visitors, with real (present) and virtual (absent) visitors interacting with each other and the representation of objects themselves, but also for researchers that may need to collaborate in a mixed fashion (remotely and face-to-face). While such a solution can be applied to museums easily, as lighting conditions are usually controlled, it is a difficult concept to adapt to outdoor museums or places of cultural or touristic interest correctly, as it relies on the identification of reference points to serve as a shared anchor or referential between the users. However, as technology improves, and other hardware solutions and techniques are further developed (such as simultaneous location and mapping) it may well be possible for future visitors to accompany friends and colleagues without being physically by their side.

2.6 Discussion

There are several techniques that can be used to convey AR content in a tourism-enabled setting. Some techniques are more experimental than others, some require more advanced devices or more effort from the user. From the examples presented in the previous section we can summarize the types of AR by content registration technology as belonging to the following categories:

1. **GPS**—Ideal for outdoor interaction in touristic locations, such as cities or parks.
2. **GPS/marker-based**—Ideal for outdoor interaction in touristic locations such as cities or parks but with attention to specific details, such as cultural heritage ruins or detailed small statues, monuments or ruins, as seen in Sect. 2.3.

3. **marker-based**—This technique should be used in indoor spaces such as museums. Markers can be images or specific shapes.
4. **AR headset-based**—this is a more expensive technique to be used in limited indoor spaces. Requires additional costs and maintenance.
5. **marker-based/mentor-apprentice (proposed)**—this technique is proposed in Sect. 2.4 and is ideal for detail pieces indoor or outdoor. Requires training as mentor for the staff.
6. **marker-based collaborative (proposed)**—collaborative-based interaction is ideal for an indoor space or small space with no extra cost apart from the app development, as seen in Sect. 2.5.

These categories have been exemplified in the previous sections with projects such as PAINTER (Sect. 2.5), Coop AR (Sect. 2.4), INVICTA (Sect. 2.3) or the AR park app described in Sect. 2.2.

One important aspect to discuss is how many people should be engaged in the tourism/museum AR application. As always this all depends on the story that needs to be conveyed but some clues can be extracted according to the type of event or experience that it is being promoted.

City or natural park exploration is usually a lone app experience. People have a certain objective to get to some place. Even though they are together with more people, the AR app is usually a navigational helper with occasional trivia or mini games. The visitor needs freedom from the app to deviate and interact with others (not necessarily through the app). This means that the AR application should be directed to a single user with sporadic interaction.

As was discussed in Sect. 2.5, collaboration may not be an important feature for visitors (unless used in a gamified application or as a means of socially extending the visiting experience), but for researchers and museum workers it may be a useful feature to support in situ or through remote collaboration. Ultimately it can lead to enable shared experiences and foster cooperation and socialization.

In a closed event or in a museum, visitors expect to be immersed in a controlled experience. This controlled experience can be the layout of the rooms, the order of the exhibition or the use of AR-guided technology. In this setting, people are much more receptive to technology and are more willing to participate in group collaboration. This gives opportunities to explore the mentor-apprentice method (Sect. 2.4) or collaborate with other users using smartphone-based applications (Sect. 2.5). Table 2.1 summarizes the best technologies for each space, and describes where our application proposals fit in terms of interaction area, AR method and number of users that interact together.

2.7 Conclusions

The use of augmented reality for tourism and cultural heritage has had mixed results. There are several successful examples where cities and museums have been able to

Table 2.1 AR methods versus ideal number of users using it

	GPS	IMU	Marker	SLAM	Single-user	Apprentice-mentor	Collaborative
Outdoor—wide	●	●	●		INVICTA		
Outdoor—patio	●	●	●	●	AR PARK		
Indoor—building			●	●		COOP AR	
Indoor—room			●	●		COOP AR	PAINTER
Indoor—detail			●				PAINTER

create interesting content for users to virtually explore real objects or building using AR. Many of these successful stories are local museums with very specific setup environments that many times do not scale properly. The risk of having the visitors more engaged with the technology itself *in lieu* of the visit itself is real and may lead to a slow or cautious adoption of Augmented Reality as a technology to support or extend a visit. The creation of AR content is still also a big problem since most content has to be created individually for each venue.

Another important aspect is that AR devices and AR content usually favors single-user applications. We believe that collaborative interaction is key for engaging users and groups around a center piece. One object that could be seen by visitors in one minute, can now tell a story that interacts with all the users in the room. Small museums can expand their experience showing more content in a more multimedia fashion. Visiting groups could have a joint experience.

In this work, we described the current AR state-of-the-art in how to present AR content, especially in tourism or museum setting. We proposed two multi-user techniques that should be used in museums and discussed the advantages and disadvantages of each method (Nóbrega et al. 2018). With the wide availability of more advanced smartphones with better cameras and satellite positioning systems we believed that AR-enabled systems will be more available, and at some point, visitors will expect that museums, parks or cities have a phone app with an AR layer in it.

Acknowledgements Th is work is financed by the ERDF—European Regional Development Fund through the Operational Programme for Competitiveness and Internationalisation—COMPETE 2020 Programme and by National Funds through the Portuguese funding agency, FCT—Fundação para a Ciência e a Tecnologia within project POCI-01-0145-FEDER-030740—PTDC/CCI-COM/30740/2017. We would also like to thank the researchers and our students at FEUP and INESC TEC that contributed to the works presented in this chapter.

References

Ahlers KH, Kramer A, Breen DE, Chevalier PY, Crampton C, Rose E, Tuceryan M, Whitaker R, RT, Greer D (1995) Distributed Augmented Reality for Collaborative Design Applications, Comput. Graph. Forum 14(3):3–14

Arroyo E, Righi V, Tarrago R, Blat J (2011) A remote multi-touch experience to support collaboration between remote Museum visitors. In: Lecture Notes in Computer Science, volume 6949 LNCS, pp 462–465

Arth C, Grasset R, Gruber L, Langlotz T, Mulloni A, Wagner D (2015) The history of mobile augmented reality (June)

Bearman D (1987) Archival informatics newsletter

Bekele M, Town C, Pierdicca R, Frontoni E, Malinverni E (2018) A survey of augmented, virtual, mixed reality. J Comput Cult Herit 11(2):36

Benyon D, Quigley A, O'Keefe B, Riva G (2014) Presence and digital tourism. AI & Soc 29(4):521–529

Billinghurst M, Kato H (2002) Collaborative augmented reality. Commun ACM 45(7):64–70

Boletsis C, Chasanidou D (2018) Smart tourism in cities: exploring urban destinations with audio augmented reality. ACM International Conference Proceeding Series, pp 515–521

Boschloos V, Nofal E, Ramakers R, Hameeuw H, Moere AV (2017) Collaborative tangible gamification of built heritage for young museum visitors. Digit Herit Conf 2017(August):1–3

Coelho A, Rodrigues R, Nóbrega R, Jacob J, Morgado L, Cardoso P, van Zeller M, Santos L, Sousa AA (2020) Serious pervasive games. Frontiers in Computer Science, 2(August)

Coulby C, Hennessey S, Davies N, Fuller R (2011) The use of mobile technology for work-based assessment: the student experience. Br J Edu Technol 42(2):251–265

Duque D (2019) AR interaction and collaboration in interchangeable reality. Master thesis, Faculdade de Engenharia da Universidade do Porto

Fenu C, Pittarello F (2018) Svevo tour: the design and the experimentation of an augmented reality application for engaging visitors of a literary museum. Int J Hum Comput Stud 114(January):20–35

Fernandes T, Jacob J (2011) Virtual location-based indoor guide. In: Serious Games Development and Applications, pp 36–48

Foo S, Theng YL, Goh, DHL, Na, JC (2009) From digital archives to virtual exhibitions. In: Handbook of Research on Digital Libraries, number January, pp 88–100. IGI Global

Griffin D (2008) Advancing museums. Mus.M Manag. Curatorship 23(1):43–61

Grudin J (1994) Computer-supported cooperative work: history and focus. Computer 27(5):19–26

Han DI, tom Dieck MC, Jung T (2018) User experience model for augmented reality applications in urban heritage tourism. J Herit Tour 13(1):46–61

Henderson SJ, Feiner S (2009) Evaluating the benefits of augmented reality for task localization in maintenance of an armored personnel carrier turret. Science and Technology Proceedings—IEEE 2009 International Symposium on Mixed and Augmented Reality, ISMAR 2009, pp 135–144

Jacob J, Lopes A, Nóbrega R, Rodrigues R, Coelho A (2018) Towards player adaptivity in mobile exergames. In: Lecture Notes in Computer Science (including subseries Lecture Notes in Artificial Intelligence and Lecture Notes in Bioinformatics), pp 278–292

Jacob JTPN, Coelho AF (2011) Issues in the development of location-based games. International Journal of Computer Games Technology 2011:1–7

Kim K, Billinghurst M, Bruder G, Duh HBL, Welch GF (2018) Revisiting trends in augmented reality research: a review of the 2nd decade of ismar (2008–2017) IEEE Trans Vis Comput Graph 24(11):2947–2962

Kim YD, Moon IY (2013) E-training content delivery networking system for augmented reality car maintenance training application. Int J Multimed Ubiquitous Eng 8(2):69–80

Lu F, Tian F, Jiang Y, Cao X, Luo W, Li G, Zhang X, Dai G, Wang H (2011) Shadowstory. In: Proceedings of the 2011 Annual Conference on Human Factors in Computing Systems—CHI '11, page 1919, New York, New York, USA. ACM Press

Mahadevan R, Suardi S (2019) Panel evidence on the impact of tourism growth on poverty, poverty gap and income inequality. Curr Issues Tour 22(3):253–264

Maia J (2017) Interactive collaboration platform in augmented reality. Master thesis, Faculdade de Engenharia Universidade do Porto

Mamrayeva DG, Aikambetova AE (2014) Information technology in museums, volume 5. Education & Science Without Borders

Mata F, Claramunt C (2013) Augmented navigation in outdoor environments. GIS: Proceedings of the ACM International Symposium on Advances in Geographic Information Systems, pp 514–517

Milano C, Novelli M, Cheer JM (2019) Overtourism and tourismphobia: a journey through four decades of tourism development, planning and local concerns. Tour Plan Dev 16(4):353–357

Nóbrega R, Correia N (2011) Design your room: adding virtual objects to a real indoor scenario. In: Extended Abstracts of the 2011 annual ACM SIGCHI Conference on Human Factors in Computing Systems (CHI'11), pp 2143–2148, Vancouver, BC, Canada. ACM

Nóbrega R, Jacob J, Coelho A, Ribeiro J, Weber J, Ferreira S (2018) Leveraging pervasive games for tourism: an augmented reality perspective. Int J Creat Interfaces Comput Graph 9(1):1–14

Nóbrega R, Jacob J, Coelho A, Weber J, Ribeiro J, Ferreira S (2017) Mobile location-based augmented reality applications for urban tourism storytelling. In: 2017 24° Encontro Português de Computação Gráfica e Interação (EPCGI), pp 1–8. IEEE

Nóbrega R, Jacob J, Rodrigues R, Coelho A, Sousa AA (2016) Augmenting physical maps: an ar platform for geographical information visualization. In: Magalhaes LG, Mantiuk R (eds), EG 2016—Posters, pp 1017–4656. The Eurographics Association

Nofal E, Panagiotidou G, Reffat RM, Hameeuw H, Boschloos V, Moere AV (2020) Situated tangible gamification of heritage for supporting collaborative learning of young museum visitors. J Comput Cult Herit 13(1):1–24

Nuryanti W (1996) Heritage and postmodern tourism. Ann Tour Res 23(2):249–260

Pereira V, Matos T, Rodrigues R, Nóbrega R, Jacob J (2019) Extended reality framework for remote collaborative interactions in virtual environments. ICGI 2019—Proceedings of the International Conference on Graphics and Interaction, pp 17–24

Perera K, Chandra D (2010) How museums in the digital age become more dynamic, visitor oriented? International Conference on Qualitative and Quantitative Methods in Libraries (QQML), (May):25–28

Petrelli D, O'Brien S (2018) Phone vs. tangible in museums, pp 1–12

Pietroszek K, Moore C (2019) AHMED: toolset for ad-hoc mixed-reality exhibition design. Proceedings of the ACM Symposium on Virtual Reality Software and Technology, VRST, pp 3–4

Pietroszek K, Tyson A, Magalhaes FS, Barcenas CEMH, WandP (2019) Museum in your living room: recreating the peace corps experience in mixed reality. 2019 IEEE Games, Entertainment, Media Conference, GEM 2019, pp 9–12

Rambli A, Sulaiman S, Nayan M (2007) A portable augmented reality lab. In: 1st International Malaysian Educational Technology Convention (IMETC 2007)

Santos L, Silva N, Nóbrega R, Almeida R, Coelho A (2020) An interactive application framework for natural parks using serious location-based games with augmented reality. In: Proceedings of the 15th International Joint Conference on Computer Vision, Imaging and Computer Graphics Theory and Applications—Volume 1, GRAPP, pp 247–254

Silva N (2019) Outdoor park exploration using augmented reality and mobile computing. PhD thesis, Faculdade de Engenharia Universidade do Porto

Szalavári Z, Schmalstieg D, Fuhrmann A, Gervautz M (1998) "Studierstube": an environment for collaboration in augmented reality. Virtual Rity 3(1):37–48

Tahyudin I, Saputra DIS (2016) Implementation of a mobile augmented reality application with location based service for exploring tourism objects. ACM International Conference Proceeding Series

Thanyadit S, Punpongsanon P, Pong TC (2018) Efficient information sharing techniques between workers of heterogeneous tasks in 3D CVE. Proceedings of the ACM on Human-Computer Interaction, 2(CSCW):1–19

Tumler J, Doil F, Mecke R, Paul G, Schenk M, Pfister EA, Huckauf A, Bockelmann I, Roggentin A (2008) Mobile augmented reality in industrial applications: approaches for solution of user-related issues. In: 2008 7th IEEE/ACM International Symposium on Mixed and Augmented Reality, pp 87–90, Cambridge. IEEE Computer Society

Tye M (2014) Transparency, qualia realism and representationalism. Philos Stud 170(1):39–57

Wang Y, Stash N, Sambeek R, Schuurmans Y, Aroyo L, Schreiber G, Gorgels P (2009) Cultivating personalized museum tours online and on-site. Interdisc Sci Rev 34(2–3):139–153

Webel S, Bockholt U, Engelke T, Gavish N, Olbrich M, Preusche C (2013) An augmented reality training platform for assembly and maintenance skills. Robot Auton Syst 61(4):398–403

Willis KD, Poupyrev I, Hudson SE, Mahler M (2011) SideBySide: Ad-hoc multi-user interaction with handheld projectors. UIST'11—Proceedings of the 24th Annual ACM Symposium on User Interface Software and Technology, pp 431–440

Zhu Z, Branzoi V, Wolverton M, Murray G, Vitovitch N, Yarnall L, Acharya G, Samarasekera S, Kumar R (2014) AR-mentor: augmented reality based mentoring system. In: ISMAR 2014—IEEE International Symposium on Mixed and Augmented Reality—Science and Technology 2014, Proceedings, number November, pp 17–22

Chapter 3
Augmented Reality Systems and Their Future in Tourism: Before, During and After the Journey

Klen Čopič Pucihar and Matjaž Kljun

Abstract In this chapter, we describe Mixed Reality (MR) systems and applications in tourism from the perspective of when they support tourists: before, during or after the journey. MR technologies have been around for five decades and have seen many developmental stages and breakthroughs. However, only in the past two decades have the technologies been available to the wider public. As such, they provided a platform to be used in tourism as well. We present a review following the PRISM methodology by which we uncovered 92 relevant applications, prototypes, and services. These were labelled based on the time when the provided functionalities would normally be used, e.g. before, during and/or after the journey. The review highlights that the majority of prototypes and applications support the travel as it happens (89 out of 92 systems) whereas functionalities that support users before and after the visit only start to emerge later on as the field matures (9 and 11 out of 92, respectively). Therefore, MR applications that support tourist applications before and after the journey offer an untapped potential for future MR applications, prototypes and services. We provide possible directions in which this domain could evolve in the future.

3.1 Introduction

Tourism is described by major dictionaries as an activity or practice of travelling for the sole purpose of pleasure (see, for example, www.thefreedictionary.com/tourism). A broader view taken by people who work in the tourism sector and by the United Nations World Tourism Organization (UNWTO) includes any type of travel

K. Čopič Pucihar · M. Kljun (✉)
Faculty of Mathematics, Natural Sciences and Information Technologies, University of Primorska, Koper, Slovenia
e-mail: matjaz.kljun@upr.si

Faculty of Information Studies, Novo mesto, Slovenia

K. Čopič Pucihar
e-mail: klen.copic@famnit.upr.si

V. Geroimenko (ed.), *Augmented Reality in Tourism, Museums and Heritage*, Springer Series on Cultural Computing,
https://doi.org/10.1007/978-3-030-70198-7_3

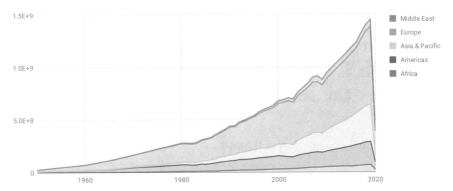

Fig. 3.1 International tourist arrivals in numbers from 1950 to October 2020 by United Nations World Tourism Organization (UNWTO)
UNWTO eLibrary https://www.e-unwto.org/

that involves consumption of tourism products and services be it for leisure, business, or other purposes. Another more encompassing definition was provided by Medlik (2012) with tourism explained as a "temporary short-term movement of people outside their normal environment and their activities". Tourism is also defined as a business of furnishing products and services, which provide a living to a variety of occupations in the tourism sector. It is nowadays a trillion-dollar industry with a steadily rising number of tourists over the past 70 years (excluding 2020). UNWTO reports that international tourist arrivals have increased more than 50-folds in the past seven decades with 25 million arrivals in 1950 to over 1.45 billion arrivals in 2019 (UNWTO World Tourism Organisation 2019) disrupted only by the epidemic in 2020 when numbers of international arrivals fell globally by 72% (data up to October 2020) as shown in Fig. 3.1.

Depicting a typical traveller equally consuming all tourism products and services is not possible as it is not possible to compare tourism to other types of consumption. The attitude towards environment, subjective norms, self-identity, prices, perceived value of a service, economic conditions, marital status, education, previous experiences and a variety of other factors all play an important role in choosing a travelling destination (Boto-García 2020). Today's tourism sector is highly influenced by the heterogeneity of the demand and consumption with constantly evolving tourism offerings in the form of new emerging destinations, withering of existing ones (Butler 1980) and by following specific trends, expectations and user groups with diverse set of offerings in the forms of eco, sport (Tütünkov-Hrisztov et al. 2020), wedding (Johnston 2006), medical (Gan and Frederick 2013), wildlife (Reynolds and Braithwaite 2001), cultural (Richards 2018) and other specific forms of tourism catering to special needs and aiming at providing peak experiences to tourists.

Besides being an important driver of economic growth in both developed and developing countries (Parrilla et al. 2007; Faber and Gaubert 2019) with billions of people depending on it, tourism is at the same time rapidly and negatively transforming societies (Dyer et al. 2003), their cultures (Greenwood et al. 1989) and

Table 3.1 Mixed reality (MR) prototypes and applications supporting tourists *before* (B), *during* (D) and *after* (A) the travel

Ref	Picture	B	D	A	Ref	Picture	B	D	A	Ref	Picture	B	D	A	Ref	Picture	B	D	A
Tsotros (2002)		-	D	-	Qosmo (2010)		-	D	-	Lochrie et al (2013)		B	D	A	MOSA (2016)		-	D	-
Val-buena (2004)		-	D	-	Smau (2010)		-	D	-	Madsen and Madsen (2013)		-	D	-	Střelák et al (2016)		-	D	-
Woj-ciechowski et al (2004)		-	D	-	van Eck and Kolstee (2010)		-	D	-	Van Eck and Kallergi (2013)		-	D	-	Kas-apakis et al (2016)		-	D	-
Kennedy et al (2005)		-	D	-	Bationo-tillon et al (2010)		-	D	-	Yoon and Wang (2014)		-	D		Dugulean et al (2016)		-	D	-
Dow et al (2005)		-	D	-	Kim et al (2010)		-	D	-	Wei-quan Lu et al (2014)		-	D	-	Can-ciani et al (2016)		-	D	A
Bimber et al (2005)		-	D	-	Jean-Michel et al (2011b)		-	D	-	Gian-nis Drossis (2014)		-	D	-	Kei et al (2017)		-	D	-
Wagner et al (2006)		-	D	-	Jean-Michel et al (2011a)		-	D	-	Papa-gian-nakis et al (2005)		-	D	-	Nóbrega and Correia (2017)		-	D	A
Schmal-stieg and Wagner (2007)		-	D	-	Jean-Michel et al (2011b)		-	D	A	Jean-Michel et al (2015c)		-	D	-	Gimeno et al (2017)		-	D	-
Bruns et al (2007)		-	D	-	Keil et al (2011)		-	D	-	Jean-Michel et al (2015a)		-	D	-	Sauter et al (2018)		-	D	-
Miyashita et al (2008)		-	D	-	Tillon et al (2011)		-	D	-	Jean-Michel et al (2015b)		-	D	-	Ham-mady et al (2018)		B	D	-
Zoellner et al (2008)		-	D	-	Keil et al (2011)		-	D	A	Jean-Michel et al (2015d)		-	D	-	Vosi-nakis and Ekonomou (2018)		B	D	-
Herbst et al (2008)		-	D	-	Blum et al (2012)		B	D	-	Jean-Michel et al (2015e)		-	D	-	Pittarello (2019)		-	D	-
Damala et al (2008)		-	D	-	Tanasi et al (2012)		-	D	-	Bostanci et al (2015)		-	D	-	Berlino et al (2019)		-	D	-
Scheible and Ojala (2009)		-	D	-	Thian (2012)		-	D	A	Kourouthanas-sis et al (2015)		-	D	-	Banfi et al (2019)		-	-	A
Future-lab (2009)		-	D	-	Lee et al (2012)		B	D	-	Chal-vatzaras et al (2014)		-	D	-	Barrile et al (2019)		-	-	A
Caarls et al (2009)		-	D	-	Wither et al (2010)		B	D	-	Scopigno et al (2015)		-	D	A	Blanco-Pons et al (2019)		-	D	A
Zöllner et al (2009)		-	D	-	Madsen et al (2012)		-	D	-	Roberto et al (2015)		-	D	-	Carrión-Ruiz et al (2019)		-	D	-
Choudary et al (2009)		-	D	-	Damala et al (2012)		-	D	-	van der Vaart and Damala (2015)		-	D	-	Garro et al (2019)		-	D	A
Val-buena (2010a)		-	D	-	Bal-duini et al (2012)		B	D	-	D'Agnano et al (2015)		-	D	-	Shabani et al (2019)		B	-	-
Val-buena (2014)		-	D	-	Jean-Michel et al (2013)		-	D	-	Jung et al (2015)		B	D	-	Zerman et al (2020)		-	D	-
Val-buena (2010b)		-	D	-	Jean-Michel et al (2013)		-	D	-	Jean-Michel et al (2016b)		-	D	-	Čejka et al (2020)		-	D	-
Val-buena (2010c)		-	D	-	Val-buena (2013)		-	D	-	Jean-Michel et al (2016a)		-	D	-	Paliokas et al (2020)		-	D	-
Val-buena (2014)		-	D	-	Han et al (2013)		-	D	-	Peddie (2017)		-	D	-	Litvak and Kuflik (2020)		-	D	-

environments (Green and Giese 2004). It has direct social (changing cultural identity, traditions, regional character, affecting rights of residents, disrupting local life, increasing alcoholism, delinquent behaviour, exploiting local residents), economic (affecting cost and standard of living) and environment impacts (changing an area's appearance, increasing litter, noise pollution, and using of the natural resource base by tourists previously available only to residents) (Tovar and Lockwood 2008).

In the last two decades, tourism has also been hit by financial and economic crisis in 2008 (Smeral 2009) and by the pandemic in 2020. In the former crisis the tourism was directly influenced by travelling capabilities of the world population due to economic recession, but the drop has not been dramatic as the numbers fell only to the levels of three years earlier as seen in Fig. 3.1. While in the latter crisis the numbers fell to the levels of 30 years back. Tourism even greatly contributed to the spreading of the virus throughout the world (Correa-Martínez et al. 2020) and exacerbated the problem even further with governments imposing strict confinement measures to ease the pressure on health services. It is these measures that contributed to another economic recession as well as prevented international and also national travelling.

Technology can play an important role in alleviating negative impacts as well as supporting positive impacts of tourism. Packer and Ballantyne (2016) have stressed that "the tourism industry has the responsibility to engage visitors in powerful and transformative learning experiences, both during and after their visit". Besides, the technology can engage tourists also before travelling even commences. Immersive technologies in the form of augmented reality and augmented virtuality (both also referred to as Mixed Reality or MR) are very suitable for the purpose as they can provide immersive experiences that can come close to experiences emerging from physically visiting the place.

To better understand the evolution and role of MR applications in the context of tourism and identify possible future directions based on positive and negative aspects of tourism this book chapter provides a systematic literature review following the Preferred Reporting Items for Systematic Reviews and Meta-Analyses (PRISMA) technique (Moher et al. 2009). The classification of the review is done based on classification of prototypes reported in the literature into three domains, namely: prototypes that support visitors *before* the experience by providing a set of tools to plan and prepare for the trip, *during* the experience with a set of tools that enable a more meaningful and enjoyable journeys, and *after* the experience by supporting reflection and help users reminiscing about the journey and experiences lived. The chapter is structured as follows: the first section describes the method used to compile the list of prototypes. The following three sections focus on these applications divided in supporting either *before*, *during* or *after* activities. The chapter concludes with a discussion revealing trends and opportunities.

3.2 Method

To understand the space of MR technologies for tourists, we did the literature review following the Preferred Reporting Items for Systematic Reviews and Meta-Analyses (PRISMA) technique by Moher et al. (2009) between October and December 2020. In Google Scholar we used a combination of the following keywords/phrases: "augmented reality", "AR", "mixed reality", "MR" and "tourism", "case studies", "cultural heritage". We included scientific articles and design project reports written in English only. In the next step, we reviewed first 200 search results for each search query and filtered the prototypes by this set of criteria:

1. The paper discusses a prototype used in tourism.
2. The prototype supports or could support visitors before, during or after the visit.
3. The prototype must include at least one element of AR or MR content.

We ended up with 92 relevant MR prototypes and applications used in tourism. These final 92 prototypes served as the corpus for an in-depth analysis. To enable easy recognition of common trends among the prototypes we classified them by identifying the type of the system, type of activity they support (before, during and after activities) and sort all articles by year of publication. The results of this classification are presented in Table 3.1.

3.3 A System to Support Preparation Before the Journey

One example of AR application that includes also functionalities to support tourists prior to their journey is TARX (Lochrie et al. 2013). This is a mobile AR application with components of location-based game mechanics. It lets users explore a city with a map (see Fig. 3.2 left) and decide where to go or how to traverse the city upfront. Upon arrival at the warp destination, users have the ability to warp back in time by clicking on the window marker to reveal the historic photo (see Fig. 3.2 centre). Users can also view details such as a brief description, information relating to the warp, and have the ability to store photos and data in their own sticker album enabling them to revisit the warp. Players can share these stickers by posting them to several social networking service sites. The application also included information of the tracked journey and achievements, which can be taken as a digital souvenir by users.

In TARX application a map functionality allows one to selectively choose augmented points of interest (POI). This is an example of a tool that supports users in planning their journeys. Additionally, the application includes a feature that allows individuals to track their journeys. This enables users to revisit the same journey or invite other people to follow their footsteps. This feature also supports the activity of preparing for the AR visit of the area in advance.

Our systematic literature review revealed that only 9/92 applications included functionalities that could be used before the actual journey takes place. Most of

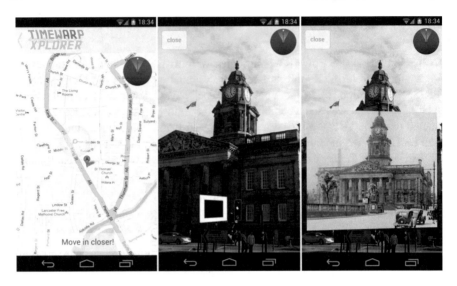

Fig. 3.2 TARX application: map, AR and warp view

these applications include map functionalities that enable some sort of planning. However, there are also other prototypes, applications and services that focus on marketing and try to convince visitors with the use of MR technologies to come and visit the attraction (Shabani et al. 2019).

There are also other types of MR interventions one could envision in order to address several problems commonly affecting tourism industry. One such problem is overcrowding at tourist destinations, which has immediate (negative) impact on the tourists' experience and local communities. In this respect, technology can be used to change decisions such as the time of travel to avoid overcrowded times of the year. Immersive technologies can, for example, prior to travelling present to the tourist how visiting a place in different times of the year changes the experience and persuade them to explore the destination in less crowded months. This can even contribute to the more balanced flow of tourists throughout the year and as such decrease the pressure on the environment, local population and people working in tourism.

Furthermore, immersive experience using MR systems can also support intrinsic desires to learn about particular aspects of culture at the destination by educating tourists before they even start their journey. As a consequence, immersiveness of the experience can help them better appreciate and respect local cultures once the journey happens.

By providing immersive experience about the impact of tourism on a certain destination (e.g. how mass tourism affects the coral reefs and how these degraded in the past decades) we can even discourage travelling while still provide a possibility of immersing oneself in the current or even past remote environments.

Immersive technologies could even ameliorate lives of the currently confined world population and enable novel business models offering personalised hours-long immersive tours to different world places, destinations, museums and other points of interest while being guided by, for example, a prominent actor (e.g. imagine having a two-hours-long immersive walk through the Škocjan cave with Sir David Attenborough[1] explaining all the details about it).

3.4 A System to Support Exploration During the Journey

One example of AR application that includes functionalities to support users during the journey is the prototype *The House of Olbrich*. This is a mobile augmented reality tour guide through architectural history (Keil et al. 2011). The application visualises the history of Darmstadt's unique Jugendstil (Art Nouveau) quarter and supports individuals in their journey through architecture, design and history of the buildings. The application integrates historical media, such as old photographs and blueprints on buildings, depicting the lost history of the famous House of Olbrich that was destroyed during World War II and has been only rudimentary restored. An illustrative example of how the application works is shown in Fig. 3.3—users can see how the original building looked like and reveal various descriptions of architectural details.

The application complements the journey with interesting insights through real-time augmentation with relevant information. This is likely to make experiences more educational and meaningful.

The literature review revealed that almost all applications to some extent support users during the journey (89/92). However, only one application considered personalisation in a form of personalised recommendations to users (Jung et al. 2015).

Researchers have already attempted to track tourists' movements (Edwards et al. 2010) and prototypes using augmented reality have already been explored for modelling users' movement throughout the city or museums (Hürst et al. 2019). These technologies offer a possibility to direct tourists from crowded areas in real time based on observed tourist saturation and measuring their mood. By encouraging tourists to explore less frequented points of interest we can also broaden their knowledge about a certain area. Furthermore, immersive technologies can be used to provide contextually relevant and personalised information to visitors that make such trips more meaningful and provide excellent opportunities for experiential learning, which has not been spotted in our review. Although the MR technologies provide a perfect platform for "anywhere" experiential learning by immersing the user with objects and activities relevant to the subject being learned, the actual physical presence during the journey can make it even more meaningful. Immersing users in historical events on the spot, showing them possible future effects of, e.g. global

---

[1] Sir David Attenborough Wikipedia page https://en.wikipedia.org/wiki/David_Attenborough.

Fig. 3.3 An illustrative representation of the application The House of Olbrich. Depicted house in the image is not originally from Olbrich and the image is schematic. For original application refer to Keil et al. (2011). In the figure we see the new house and overlaid old house that stood there before. The overlaid house has different clickable information circles explaining different architecturally interesting points

warming on a particular area they are visiting, or just provide MR game-like jour-neys throughout the city are just some of the capabilities that have not been thoroughly explored.

3.5   A System to Support Reflection After the Journey

Technology interventions after the visit has taken place are as important as the inter-ventions focusing on activities before and during the visit. Immersive technologies can support a long-term impact of tourism experience by keeping social relationship between tourists and the local population, informing about the developments and changes (even the impact of the tourism) through providing news about visited desti-nations as well as supporting individual and group immersive reminiscing about the experience long after the trip. The difference of immersing oneself in the environment compared to sliding through photos can be immense.

One example of an MR application that includes functionalities to support users also after the journey is a mobile application prototype of Parliament Buildings National Historic Site in Ottawa, Canada. The application includes an AR experience that enables simulated photo merging of a historic and present content (Blanco-Pons et al. 2019). The realistic photo merging enables one to create snapshots of the journey to this historic monument, which can serve as an anchor for reflection and later reminiscing about the visit (for an illustrative example, see Fig. 3.4).

Only 11/92 applications in our review included functionalities that relate to after the journey activities. Most of the applications included only simple tools for capturing moments or tools that enable one to revisit some parts of the journey through 3D visualisations within their current environments. There remains a great potential for tourism-related MR systems of the future.

3.6   Discussion and Trends

Despite the extensive set of reviewed MR prototypes, applications and services as well as AR/VR technology maturity researchers believe that the potential of these technologies has only now started to be explored in full (Wiltshier and Clarke 2017).

The evolution of MR systems and services in tourism presented in Table 3.1 clearly indicates that majority of them developed between 2004 and 2010 concentrated on functionalities that solely relate to augmenting the journey as it happens (i.e. during the activity). In the period after 2011, applications and prototypes included also func-tionalities that support planning and reflection activities. These two activities usually happen before and after the journey. Nevertheless, the vast majority of applications continue to focus on supporting the journey as it happens. To some extent this is understandable as AR is best suited for visualising information where the environ-ment provides the context. The majority of technological interventions presented

Fig. 3.4 An illustrative example of simulated photo merging of a historic and present content

in this review focus on preserving tangible and intangible cultural heritage for two reasons:

(**1**) to preserve original artefacts with digital replicas (e.g. Zoellner et al. 2008; Thian 2012; Scopigno et al. 2015; Banfi et al. 2019), and (**2**) to make them available to broader public (e.g. Lee et al. 2012; Lochrie et al. 2013; Keil et al. 2011). Nevertheless, we believe that there are still plenty of under-explored or under-utilised areas in MR technology for tourism, in particular within functionalities that support users before and after the journey and the functionalities that ameliorate the problems tourism brings to tourist destinations.

Moving beyond these two aims opens up numerous opportunities for local creative industry that could participate in content production not only in creating digital counterparts of physical artefacts but also to create encompassing immersive experiences including storytelling, elements of gamification (Mortara et al. 2014) and similar approaches in order to provide travellers (as well as remote tourists) a more enriching participation. Korea has, for example, taken this path through government-sponsored programmes supporting the development of creative experiences and applications focusing on tourism (Richards and Cooper 2018). The ingenuity of local inhabitants offering unique experiences to tourists on platforms such as Airbnb[2] is a great example of what kind of potential there is in every part of the globe. Combining this with MR can prove a winning combination.

To summarise, we list some key points from the chapter about how immersive technologies (such as MR) could support tourism in the future:

Before

- The use of MR technologies as persuasive technology to prevent overcrowding of tourist destinations by persuading tourists to visit at a different time of the year.
- The use of MR technologies to support intrinsic desires to learn about particular aspects of a culture at the travelling destination by educating tourists before they even start their journey in order for them to better appreciate the visited culture.
- The use of technologies to enable novel business models offering personalised hours-long immersive tours to different world places, destinations, museums and other points of interest while being guided by for example a prominent actor.
- The use of MR technologies as persuasive technology to prevent travelling to places where nature balance is very delicate (e.g. coral reefs) and at the same time provide an attractive immersive experience as explained in the previous bullet.

During

- The use of MR technologies for modelling users' movement throughout the city or museums to avoid overcrowding. By encouraging tourists to explore less frequented points of interest we can also broaden their knowledge about a certain area.
- The use of MR technologies for experiential learning by immersing users on the spot and for example (1) raise awareness about different issues such as showing users possible future effects of for example global warming or overcrowding on the area they are visiting, or (2) provide MR game-like journeys throughout an area by combining digital elements (historic, artistic, imaginative, etc.) and the physical environment.

After

- The use of MR technologies to support a long-term impact of tourist experience by keeping a social relationship between tourists and the local population by providing immersive meeting spaces rather than simple text or video chat.
- The use of MR technologies to inform past visitors about the status, development and changes (even the impact of the tourism) that are happening at the visited destination to further increase awareness of certain issues.
- The use of MR technologies to support individual and group immersive reminiscing about the experience long after the trip.

---

[2]https://www.airbnb.com/.

- The use of MR technologies to let users re-experience what they have already experienced during their trip.

Another important aspect of MR in tourism is user experience. The design of future MR experiences could benefit by including UX designers in the process of creation. In addition to offering these technologies to tourists, there is a particular need to explore user acceptance, how tourists experience such technologies and if these increase their level of engagement. The models such as the influential Technology Acceptance Model (TAM) can be used for explaining individuals' acceptance of technology and its usage. Other models such as Theory of Reasoned Action (TRA) have also been explored in technology acceptance context (Davis 1989) and it has been noted that the perception of usefulness and the ease of use of technologies are crucial factors in their acceptance as well as their usage. The influence of MR technologies can be also researched in the long run. Richards (2018) notes that "new technologies are now making it possible to study the behaviour of crowds and the interactions of groups via social media to gauge their reactions to cultural phenomena and their fellow tourists" and that this offers "new opportunities in future to study group dynamics and the interactions between individual tourists, residents and other actors".

The above-mentioned tentative list of future aspiration for MR applications in tourism and inclusion of local communities and creative industry in the process provide directions in which this domain could evolve in the future.

3.7 Conclusions

In this chapter, we present a review of Mixed Reality (MR) applications, prototypes and services aimed at the tourism sector. The systematic review uncovered 92 relevant applications, prototypes and services. The corpus of literature was labelled based on the time when the provided functionalities would normally be used, e.g. *before*, *during* and/or *after* the journey.

The review clearly highlighted that the majority of applications, prototypes and services offer functionalities that support the touristic journey as it happens (i.e. 89 out of 92). As the field matures we start to see also functionalities that (to some extent) support users before and after the visit (e.g. 9 and 11 out of 92, respectively). However, the vast majority continue supporting users solely in the *during* side of the journey. We identify this as the untapped potential for future MR applications, prototypes and services. In the discussion, we generate a tentative list of future aspirations for MR tourism applications.

Acknowledgements The authors acknowledge the European Commission for funding the InnoRenew CoE project (Grant Agreement 739574) under the Horizon2020 Widespread-Teaming programme and the Republic of Slovenia (Investment funding of the Republic of Slovenia and the European Union of the European Regional Development Fund). The research was also supported by Slovenian research agency ARRS (P1-0383, J1-9186, J1-1715, J5-1796 and J1-1692).

References

Balduini M, Celino I, Dell'Aglio D, Della Valle E, Huang Y, Lee T, Kim SHH, Tresp V (2012) BOTTARI: an augmented reality mobile application to deliver personalized and location-based recommendations by continuous analysis of social media streams. Web Semant: Sci, Serv Agents World Wide Web 16:33–41. https://doi.org/10.1016/j.websem.2012.06.004, http://dx.doi.org/10.1016/j.websem.2012.06.004, http://linkinghub.elsevier.com/retrieve/pii/S157082681200073X

Banfi F, Brumana R, Stanga C (2019) Extended reality and informative models for the architectural heritage: From scan-to-bim process to virtual and augmented reality. Virtual Archaeol Rev 10(21):14–30. https://doi.org/10.4995/var.2019.11923

Barrile V, Fotia A, Bilotta G, De Carlo D (2019) Integration of geomatics methodologies and creation of a cultural heritage app using augmented reality. Virtual Archaeol Rev 10(20):40. https://doi.org/10.4995/var.2019.10361, https://polipapers.upv.es/index.php/var/article/view/10361

Bationo-tillon A, Marchand E, Laneurit J, Servant F, Houlier P, Bationo-tillon A, Marchand E, Laneurit J, Servant F, Marchal I, Tillon AB, Marchand E, Laneurit J, Servant F, Marchal I, Houlier P (2010) A day at the museum: an augmented fine-art exhibit

Berlino A, Caroprese L, La Marca A, Vocaturo E, Zumpano E (2019) Augmented reality for the enhancement of archaeological heritage: a Calabrian experience. CEUR Workshop Proceedings 2320:86–94

Bimber O, Coriand F, Kleppe A, Bruns E, Zollmann S, Langlotz T (2005) Superimposing pictorial artwork with projected imagery. IEEE Multimed 12(1):16–26. https://doi.org/10.1109/mmul.2005.9, http://ieeexplore.ieee.org/document/1377099/

Blanco-Pons S, Carrión-Ruiz B, Duong M, Chartrand J, Fai S, Lerma JL (2019) Augmented reality markerless multi-image outdoor tracking system for the historical buildings on Parliament Hill. Sustain 11(16):4268. https://doi.org/10.3390/su11164268, https://www.mdpi.com/2071-1050/11/16/4268

Blum L, Wetzel R, McCall R, Oppermann L, Broll W (2012) The final TimeWarp. In: Proceedings of the designing interactive systems conference on—DIS '12, ACM Press, New York, USA, p 711. https://doi.org/10.1145/2317956.2318064, http://dl.acm.org/citation.cfm?doid=2317956.2318064

Bostanci E, Kanwal N, Clark AF (2015) Augmented reality applications for cultural heritage using Kinect. Hum-Centric Comput Inf Sci 5(1):20. https://doi.org/10.1186/s13673-015-0040-3, http://www.hcis-journal.com/content/5/1/20

Boto-García D (2020) Habit formation in tourism traveling. J Travel Res p 0047287520964597

Bruns E, Brombach B, Zeidler T, Bimber O, Weimar Bu (2007) Enabling mobile phones to support large-scale Museum guidance, pp 16–25

Butler RW (1980) The concept of a tourist area cycle of evolution: implications for management of resources. Canadian Geographer/Le Géographe canadien 24(1):5–12

Caarls J, Jonker P, Kolstee Y, Rotteveel J, van Eck W (2009) Augmented reality for art, design and cultural heritage—System design and evaluation. EURASIP J Image Video Process:1–16. https://doi.org/10.1155/2009/716160, http://jivp.eurasipjournals.com/content/2009/1/716160

Canciani M, Conigliaro E, Del Grasso M, Papalini P, Saccone M (2016) 3D Survey and augmented reality for cultural heritage. The case study of Aurelian wall at castra praetoria in Rome. ISPRS—International Archives of the Photogrammetry, Remote Sensing and Spatial Information Sciences XLI-B5 (July):931–937, https://doi.org/10.5194/isprsarchives-xli-B5-931-2016, http://www.int-arch-photogramm-remote-sens-spatial-inf-sci.net/XLI-B5/931/2016/isprs-archives-XLI-B5-931-2016.pdf

Carrión-Ruiz B, Blanco-Pons S, Weigert A, Fai S, Lerma JL (2019) Merging photogrammetry and augmented reality: The Canadian library of parliament. ISPRS—International Archives of the Photogrammetry, Remote Sensing and Spatial In- formation Sciences XLII-2/W11(2/W11):367–371. https://doi.org/10.5194/isprs-archives-XLII-2-W11-367-2019, https://www.int-arch-photogramm-remote-sens-spatial-inf-sci.net/XLII-2-W11/367/2019/

Čejka J, Zsíros A, Liarokapis F (2020) A hybrid augmented reality guide for underwater cultural heritage sites. Pers Ubiquitous Comput 24(6):815–828. https://doi.org/10.1007/s00779-019-013 54-6, http://link.springer.com/10.1007/s00779-019-01354-6

Chalvatzaras D, Yiannoutsou N, Sintoris C, Avouris N (2014) Do you remember that building? Exploring old Zakynthos through an augmented reality mobile game. In: 2014 international conference on interactive mobile communication technologies and learning (IMCL2014), IEEE, November, pp 222–225. https://doi.org/10.1109/imctl.2014.7011136, http://ieeexplore.ieee.org/document/7011136/

Choudary O, Charvillat V, Grigoras R, Gurdjos P (2009) MARCH: mobile augmented reality for cultural heritage. Proceedings of the seven- teen ACM international conference on Multimedia—MM '09 3:1023. https://doi.org/10.1145/1631272.1631500, http://dl.acm.org/citation.cfm?id=1631500 http://portal.acm.org/citation.cfm?doid=1631272.1631500

Correa-Martínez CL, Kampmeier S, Kümpers P, Schwierzeck V, Hennies M, Hafezi W, Kühn J, Pavenstädt H, Ludwig S, Mellmann A (2020) A pandemic in times of global tourism: super-spreading and exportation of covid-19 cases from a ski area in Austria. J Clin Microbiol 58(6)

D'Agnano F, Balletti C, Guerra F, Vernier P (2015) Tooteko: A case study of augmented reality for an accessible cultural heritage. Digitization, 3D printing and sensors for an audio-tactile experience. ISPRS—International Archives of the Photogrammetry, Remote Sensing and Spatial Information Sciences XL-5/W4(5W4):207–213, https://doi.org/10.5194/isprsarchives-xl-5-w4-207-2015, http://www.int-arch-photogramm-remote-sens-spatial-inf-sci.net/XL-5-W4/207/2015/

Damala A, Cubaud P, Bationo A, Houlier P, Marchal I (2008) Bridging the Gap be- tween the digital and the physical: design and evaluation of a mobile augmented reality guide for the Museum visit. In: Proceedings of the 3rd international conference on Digital Interactive Media in Entertainment and Arts - DIMEA '08, ACM Press, New York, USA, p 120. https://doi.org/10.1145/1413634.1413660, http://dl.acm.org/citation.cfm?doid=1413634.1413660

Damala A, Stojanovic N, Schuchert T, Moragues J, Cabrera A, Gilleade K (2012) Adaptive augmented reality for cultural heritage: ARtSENSE project. In: Euro-mediterranean conference EuroMed 2012: progress in cultural heritage preservation, vol 7616 LNCS, pp 746–755. https://doi.org/10.1007/978-3-642-34234-979, http://link.springer.com/10.1007/978−3−642−34234−9_79

Davis FD (1989) Perceived usefulness, perceived ease of use, and user acceptance of information technology. MIS quarterly, pp 319–340

Dow S, Lee J, Oezbek C, Maclntyre B, Bolter JD, Gandy M (2005) Exploring spatial narratives and mixed reality experiences in Oakland Cemetery. In: Proceedings of the 2005 ACM SIGCHI international conference on advances in computer entertainment technology—ACE '05, ACM Press, New York, USA, pp 51–60. https://doi.org/10.1145/1178477.1178484, http://portal.acm.org/citation.cfm?doid=1178477.1178484

Duguleana M, Brodi R, Girbacia F, Postelnicu C, Machidon O, Carrozzino M (2016) Time-travelling with Mobile augmented reality: a case study on the piazza dei Miracoli. In: Lecture notes in computer science (including subseries Lecture notes in artificial intelligence and lecture notes in bioinformatics), vol 10058 LNCS, pp 902–912. https://doi.org/10.1007/978-3-319-48496-973, http://link.springer.com/10.1007/978−3−319−48496−9_73

Dyer P, Aberdeen L, Schuler S (2003) Tourism impacts on an Australian indigenous community: A Djabugay case study. Tour Manag 24(1):83–95

van Eck W, Kolstee Y (2010) The augmented painting: playful interaction with multi-spectral images, pp 65–69

Edwards D, Dickson T, Griffin T, Hayllar B, et al (2010) Tracking the urban visitor: methods for examining tourists' spatial behaviour and visual representations. Cultural tourism research methods, pp 104–114

Faber B, Gaubert C (2019) Tourism and economic development: evidence from Mexico's coastline. Am Econ Rev 109(6):2245–2293

Futurelab AE (2009) Holoman. https://www.aec.at/futurelab/en/project/holoman/

Gan LL, Frederick JR (2013) Medical tourists: who goes and what motivates them? Health Mark Q 30(2):177–194

Garro V, Sundstedt V, Putta A, Sandahl C (2019) Possibilities and challenges of portraying cultural heritage artefacts using augmented reality: llby Crucifix Case Study the Mj a p 2019. DOI https://doi.org/10.2312/gch.20201296

Giannis Drossis DGXZ Antonios Ntelidakis (2014) Distributed, ambient, and pervasive interactions, lecture notes in computer science, vol 8530. Springer International Publishing, Cham, https://doi.org/10.1007/978-3-319-07788-8, http://www.scopus.com/inward/record.url?eid=2-s2.0-84901599558&partnerID=tZOtx3y1, http://www.scopus.com/inward/record.url?eid=2-s2.0-84901599558%7B%5C&%7DpartnerID=tZOtx3y1, http://link.springer.com/10.1007/978-3-319-07788-8

Gimeno J, Portalés C, Coma I, Fernández M, Martínez B (2017) Combining traditional and indirect augmented reality for indoor crowded environments. A case study on the Casa Batlló museum. Comput & Graph 69:92–103. https://doi.org/10.1016/j.cag.2017.09.001, https://linkinghub.elsevier.com/retrieve/pii/S009784931730153X

Green R, Giese M (2004) Negative effects of wildlife tourism on wildlife. Wildlife tourism: Impacts, management and planning. pp 81–97

Greenwood DJ, et al (1989) Culture by the pound: an anthropological perspective on tourism as cultural commoditization. Culture by the pound: an anthropological perspective on tourism as cultural commoditization (Ed. 2):171–185

Hammady R, Ma M, Powell A (2018) User experience of markerless augmented reality applications in cultural heritage museums: 'MuseumEye' as a case study. In: Lecture notes in computer science (including subseries Lecture Notes in Artificial Intelligence and Lecture Notes in Bioinformatics) 10851 LNCS:349–369. https://doi.org/10.1007/978-3-319-95282-626

Han JG, Park KW, Ban KJ, Kim EK (2013) Cultural heritage sites visualization system based on outdoor augmented reality. AASRI Procedia 4:64–71. https://doi.org/10.1016/j.aasri.2013.10.011, http://dx.doi.org/10.1016/j.aasri.2013.10.011, http://linkinghub.elsevier.com/retrieve/pii/S2212671613000127, https://linkinghub.elsevier.com/retrieve/pii/S2212671613000127

Herbst TITTwaMMRG, IrisIris, Braun AK, McCall R, Broll W (2008) Time- warp: interactive Time travel with a Mobile mixed reality game iris. In: Proceedings of the 10th international conference on Human computer interaction with mobile devices and services—MobileHCI '08, ACM Press, New York, USA, p 235, https://doi.org/10.1145/1409240.1409266, http://portal.acm.org/citation.cfm?doid=1409240.1409266

Hürst W, Geraerts R, Zhao Y (2019) CrowdAR table-an AR table for interactive crowd simulation. In: 2019 IEEE international conference on artificial intelligence and virtual reality (AIVR), IEEE, pp 302–3023

Jean-Michel S, Julien R, Bernard B, Motot T, Charmoillaux A, Lamy E, Nachtman G, Chambriat A, Sirot T (2011a) on-situ: La Rade. In: on-situ.com, on-situ.com, www.on-situ.com

Jean-Michel S, Julien R, Bernard B, Motot T, Charmoillaux A, Lamy E, Nachtman G, Chambriat A, Sirot T (2011b) on-situ: une guerre photoraphique. In: on-situ.com, on-situ.com, www.on-situ.com

Jean-Michel S, Julien R, Bernard B, Motot T, Charmoillaux A, Lamy E, Nachtman G, Chambriat A, Sirot T (2013) on-situ: Site archeologique de Bibracte. In: on-situ.com, on-situ.com, www.on-situ.com

Jean-Michel S, Julien R, Bernard B, Motot T, Charmoillaux A, Lamy E, Nachtman G, Chambriat A, Sirot T (2015a) on-situ: GE 200. In: on-situ.com, on-situ.com, www.on-situ.com

Jean-Michel S, Julien R, Bernard B, Motot T, Charmoillaux A, Lamy E, Nachtman G, Chambriat A, Sirot T (2015b) on-situ: Le Narbonnaise, entre terre et eau. In: on-situ.com, on-situ.com, www.on-situ.com

Jean-Michel S, Julien R, Bernard B, Motot T, Charmoillaux A, Lamy E, Nachtman G, Chambriat A, Sirot T (2015c) on-situ: Masion des projets. In: on-situ.com, on- situ.com, www.on-situ.com

Jean-Michel S, Julien R, Bernard B, Motot T, Charmoillaux A, Lamy E, Nachtman G, Chambriat A, Sirot T (2015d) on-situ: Panoramas. In: on-situ.com, on-situ.com, www.on-situ.com

Jean-Michel S, Julien R, Bernard B, Motot T, Charmoillaux A, Lamy E, Nachtman G, Chambriat A, Sirot T (2015e) on-situ: Site archeologique de Bibracte. In: on- situ.com, on-situ.com, www. on-situ.com

Jean-Michel S, Julien R, Bernard B, Motot T, Charmoillaux A, Lamy E, Nachtman G, Chambriat A, Sirot T (2016a) on-situ: Memorial de Dun les Places. In: on-situ.com, on-situ.com, www.on-situ.com

Jean-Michel S, Julien R, Bernard B, Motot T, Charmoillaux A, Lamy E, Nachtman G, Chambriat A, Sirot T (2016b) on-situ: Memorial de Verdun. In: on-situ.com, on-situ.com, www.on-situ.com

Johnston L (2006) 'i do down-under': naturalizing landscapes and love through wed- ding tourism in New Zealand. ACME: Int J CritAl Geogr 5(2):191–208

Jung T, Chung N, Leue MC (2015) The determinants of recommendations to use augmented reality technologies: the case of a Korean theme park. Tour Manag 49:75–86. https://doi.org/10.1016/j.tourman.2015.02.013, http://dx.doi.org/10.1016/j.tourman.2015.02.013, https://linkinghub.elsevier.com/retrieve/pii/S0261517715000576

Kasapakis V, Gavalas D, Galatis P (2016) Augmented reality in cultural heritage: Field of view awareness in an archaeological site mobile guide. J Ambient Intell Smart Environs 8(5):501–514. https://doi.org/10.3233/ais-160394, http://www.medra.org/servlet/aliasResolver?alias=iospress&doi=10.3233/AIS, https://www.medra.org/servlet/aliasResolver?alias=iospress&doi=10.3233/AIS-160394

Kei S, Takeshi M, Junpei W, Masayuki A, Younghyo B, Kitamura Y, Kim I, Yamakawa K, Shiratori K (2017) ARART. http://arart.info/en/

Keil J, Zollner M, Becker M, Wientapper F, Engelke T, Wuest H (2011) The house of Olbrich: an augmented reality tour through architectural history. In: 2011 IEEE international symposium on mixed and augmented reality—Arts, Media, and Humanities, IEEE, pp 15–18. https://doi.org/10.1109/ismar-amh.2011.6093651, http://ieeexplore.ieee.org/document/6093651/

Kennedy BO, Arevalo-Poizat M, Magnenat-thalmann N, Stoddart A, Thalmann D, Papagiannakis G, Schertenleib S, O'Kennedy B, Arevalo-Poizat M, Magnena-thalmann N, Stoddart A, Thalmann D (2005) Mixing virtual and real scenes in the site of ancient Pompeii. Comput Animat Virtual Worlds 16(1):11–24. https://doi.org/10.1002/cav.53, http://doi.wiley.com/10.1002/cav.53

Kim K, Seo BK, Kim K, Park JI (2010) Augmented reality-based on-site tour guide: A study in Gyeongbokgung. Asian Conference on Computer Vision ACCV 2010: Computer Vision—ACCV 2010 Workshops (November), https://doi.org/10.1007/978-3-642-22819-3

Kourouthanassis P, Boletsis C, Bardaki C, Chasanidou D (2015) Tourists responses to mobile augmented reality travel guides: the role of emotions on adoption behavior. Pervasive Mob Comput 18:71–87. https://doi.org/10.1016/j.pmcj.2014.08.009, http://dx.doi.org/10.1016/j.pmcj.2014.08.009, http://linkinghub.elsevier.com/retrieve/pii/S1574119214001527. https://linkinghub.elsevier.com/retrieve/pii/S1574119214001527

Lee GA, Dunser A, Kim S, Billinghurst M (2012) CityViewAR: A mobile outdoor AR application for city visualization. In: 11th IEEE international symposium on mixed and augmented reality 2012—Arts, media, and humanities papers, ISMAR-AMH, pp 57–64, https://doi.org/10.1109/ismar-amh.2012.6483989

Litvak E, Kuflik T (2020) Enhancing cultural heritage outdoor experience with augmented-reality smart glasses. Pers Ubiquitous Comput 24(6):873–886. https://doi.org/10.1007/s00779-020-01366-7, https://www.tandfonline.com/doi/full/10.1080/1743873X.2020.1719116, http://link.springer.com/10.1007/s00779-020-01366-7

Lochrie M, Čopič Pucihar K, Gradinar A, Coulton P (2013) Designing seamless mobile augmented reality location-based game interfaces. In: MOMM, ACM, New York, USA, pp 412–416. https://doi.org/10.1145/2536853.2536914, http://dl.acm.org/citation.cfm?id=2536914, http://dl.acm.org/citation.cfm?doid=2536853.2536914

Madsen CB, Madsen JB, Morrison A (2012) Aspects of what makes or breaks a museum AR experience. In: 2012 IEEE international symposium on mixed and augmented reality—Arts, media, and humanities (ISMAR-AMH), IEEE, pp 91–92. https://doi.org/10.1109/ismar-amh.2012.6483996, http://ieeexplore.ieee.org/document/6483996/

Madsen JB, Madsen CB (2013) An interactive visualization of the past using a situated simulation approach. In: 2013 digital heritage international congress (DigitalHeritage), IEEE, vol 1, pp 307–314. https://doi.org/10.1109/digitalheritage.2013.6743754, http://ieeexplore.ieee.org/document/6743754/

Medlik S (2012) Dictionary of travel, tourism and hospitality. Routledge, London

Miyashita T, Meier P, Tachikawa T, Orlic S, Eble T, Scholz V, Gapel A, Gerl O, Arnaudov S, Lieberknecht S (2008) An augmented reality museum guide. In: 2008 7th IEEE/ACM international symposium on mixed and augmented reality, IEEE, pp 103–106. https://doi.org/10.1109/ismar.2008.4637334, http://ieeexplore.ieee.org/document/4637334/

Moher D, Liberati A, Tetzlaff J, Altman DG (2009) Preferred reporting items for systematic reviews and meta-analyses: The PRISMA statement. PLoS Medicine 6(7):e1000097. https://doi.org/10.1371/journal.pmed.1000097, https://dx.plos.org/10.1371/journal.pmed.1000097

Mortara M, Catalano CE, Bellotti F, Fiucci G, Houry-Panchetti M, Petridis P (2014) Learning cultural heritage by serious games. J Cult Herit 15(3):318–325

MOSA (2016) The Museum of stolen art. http://mosa.ziv.bz/

Nóbrega R, Correia N (2017) Interactive 3D content insertion in images for multimedia applications. Multimed Tools Appl 76(1):163–197. https://doi.org/10.1007/s11042-015-3031-5, http://link.springer.com/10.1007/s11042-015-3031-5

Packer J, Ballantyne R (2016) Conceptualizing the visitor experience: a review of literature and development of a multifaceted model. Visit Stud 19(2):128–143

Paliokas I, Patenidis AT, Mitsopoulou EE, Tsita C, Pehlivanides G, Karyati E, Tsafaras S, Stathopoulos EA, Kokkalas A, Diplaris S, Meditskos G, Vrochidis S, Tasiopoulou E, Riggas C, Votis K, Kompatsiaris I, Tzovaras D (2020) A Gamified augmented reality application for digital heritage and tourism. Appl Sci 10(21):7868. https://doi.org/10.3390/app10217868, https://www.mdpi.com/2076-3417/10/21/7868

Papagiannakis G, Schertenleib S, O'Kennedy B, Arevalo-Poizat M, Magnenat- Thalmann N, Stoddart A, Thalmann D (2005) Mixing virtual and real scenes in the site of ancient Pompeii. Comput Animat Virtual Worlds 16(1):11–24. https://doi.org/10.1002/cav.53, http://dl.acm.org/citation.cfm?doid=2635823.2614567, http://doi.wiley.com/10.1002/cav.53

Parrilla JC, Font AR, Nadal JR (2007) Tourism and long-term growth a Spanish perspective. Ann Tour Res 34(3):709–726

Peddie J (2017) Augmented reality: where we will all live. Springer International Publishing, Cham, https://doi.org/10.1007/978-3-319-54502-8, http://link.springer.com/10.1007/978-3-319-54502-8

Pittarello F (2019) Designing AR enhanced Art exhibitions: a methodology and a case study. In: Proceedings of the 13th biannual conference of the Italian SIGCHI chapter on designing the next interaction—CHItaly '19, ACM Press, New York, USA, pp 1–5. https://doi.org/10.1145/3351995.3352052, http://dl.acm.org/citation.cfm?doid=3351995.3352052

Qosmo T (2010) N building.app—iPhone meets architecture. http://www.sonasphere.com/blog/?p=1288

Reynolds PC, Braithwaite D (2001) Towards a conceptual framework for wildlife tourism. Tour Manag 22(1):31–42

Richards G (2018) Cultural tourism: a review of recent research and trends. J Hosp Tour Manag 36:12–21

Richards G, Cooper C (2018) The creative economy, entertainment and performance. SAGE handbook of tourism management: Applications of theories and concepts to tourism, pp 315–327

Roberto P, Emanuele F, Primo Z, Mirco S, Paolo C, Ramona Q (2015) Advanced interaction with paintings by augmented reality and high resolution visualization: a real case exhibition conference, Lecture Notes in Computer Science, vol 9254. Springer International Publishing, Cham. https://doi.org/10.1007/978-3-319-22888-4, http://link.springer.com/10.1007/978-3-319-22888-4

Sauter L, Rossetto L, Schuldt H (2018) Exploring cultural heritage in augmented reality with GoFind! In: 2018 IEEE international conference on artificial Intelligence and virtual reality

(AIVR), IEEE, pp 187–188. https://doi.org/10.1109/aivr.2018.00041, https://ieeexplore.ieee.org/document/8613660/

Scheible J, Ojala T (2009) MobiSpray: Mobile phone as virtual spray can for painting BIG anytime anywhere on Any- thing. Leonardo 42(4):332–341. https://doi.org/10.1162/leon.2009.42.4.332, http://www.mitpressjournals.org/doi/10.1162/leon.2009.42.4.332, https://www.mitpressjournals.org/doi/abs/10.1162/leon.2009.42.4.332

Schmalstieg D, Wagner D (2007) Experiences with handheld augmented reality. In: 2007 6th IEEE and ACM international symposium on mixed and augmented reality, IEEE, pp 1–13. https://doi.org/10.1109/ismar.2007.4538819, http://ieeexplore.ieee.org/document/4538819/, http://ieeexplore.ieee.org/lpdocs/epic03/wrapper.htm?arnumber=4538819

Scopigno R, Gabellone F, Malomo L, Banterle F, Pingi P, Amato G, Cardillo FA (2015) LecceAR: An augmented reality App. digital presentation and preservation of cultural and scientific heritage, pp 99–108

Shabani N, Munir A, Hassan A (2019) E-Marketing via augmented reality: a case study in the tourism and hospitality industry. IEEE Potentials 38(1):43–47. https://doi.org/10.1109/MPOT.2018.2850598

Tovar C, Lockwood M (2008) Social impacts of tourism: an Australian regional case study. Int J Tour Res 10(4):365–378

Tsotros M (2002) Archeoguide: an augmented reality guide for (October):52–60

Tütünkov-Hrisztov J, Müller A, Molnár A (2020) The appearance of sport as a travel motivation in traveling habits. Geosport Soc 12(1):31–43

UNWTO World Tourism Organisation (2019) International tourist arrivals reach 1.4 billion two years ahead of forecasts. In: unwto.org. https://www.unwto.org/global/press-release/2019-01-21/international-tourist-arrivals-reach-14-billion-two-years-ahead-forecasts, [Published: 2019-01-21, Accessed: 2020-12-22]

van der Vaart M, Damala A (2015) Through the Loupe: Visitor engagement with a primarily text-based handheld AR application. In: 2015 Digital Heritage, IEEE, pp 565–572. https://doi.org/10.1109/digitalheritage.2015.7419574, http://ieeexplore.ieee.org/document/7419574/

Valbuena P (2004) Energy Passages—media art installation. http://energie-passagen.de/presse_engl.html

Valbuena P (2010a) Augmented spaces. http://www.flickr.com/photos/todaysart/3284513762/in/photostream/

Valbuena P (2010b) Quadratura. http://www.pablovalbuena.com/selectedwork/quadratura/

Valbuena P (2010c) Time tiling. http://www.pablovalbuena.com/selectedwork/time-tiling-stuk/

Valbuena P (2013) Chronography. http://www.pablovalbuena.com/selectedwork/chronography/

Valbuena P (2014) 6-columns. http://www.pablovalbuena.com/selectedwork/parasite-6-columns/

Van Eck W, Kallergi A (2013) Trees as time capsules: extending airborne museum Hartenstein to the forest. In: Cleland K, Fisher L, Harley R (eds) Proceedings of the 19th International Symposium on Electronic Art, ISEA2013, ISEA International Australian Network for Art & Technology University of Sydney, Sydney, pp 1–4. http://hdl.handle.net/2123/9693

Vosinakis S, Ekonomou T (2018) Mobile augmented reality games as an engaging tool for cultural heritage dissemination: a case study 4(May):97–107. https://doi.org/10.5281/zenodo.1214569.

Wagner D, Schmalstieg D, Billinghurst M (2006) Handheld AR for collaborative edutainment. In: Advances in artificial reality and Tele-existence, pp 85–96. https://doi.org/10.1007/1194135410, http://h畺畺畐://찓찧찧찧찤.푶푺푶畺찧찤찖푦畐/, https://doi.org/10.1007/11941354_10

Weiquan Lu, Linh-Chi Nguyen, Teong Leong Chuah, Ellen Yi-Luen Do (2014) Effects of mobile AR-enabled interactions on retention and transfer for learning in art museum contexts. In: 2014 IEEE international symposium on mixed and augmented reality—media, art, social science, humanities and design (IMSAR-MASH'D), IEEE, pp 3–11. https://doi.org/10.1109/ismar-amh.2014.6935432, http://ieeexplore.ieee.org/document/6935432/

Wiltshier P, Clarke A (2017) Virtual cultural tourism: Six pillars of vct using c creation, value exchange and exchange value. Tour Hosp Res 17(4):372–383

Smau (2010) Smau, international exhibition of information communications technology in Milan. https://www.smau.it/company/pages/home/

Smeral E (2009) The impact of the financial and economic crisis on European tourism. J Travel Res 48(1):3–13

Střelák D, Škola F, Liarokapis F (2016) Examining User Experiences in a Mobile Augmented Reality Tourist Guide. In: Proceedings of the 9th ACM International Conference on PErvasive Technologies Related to Assistive Environments, ACM, New York, NY, USA, pp 1–8. https://doi.org/10.1145/2910674.2935835, http://dl.acm.org/citation.cfm?doid=2910674.2935835, https://dl.acm.org/doi/10.1145/2910674.2935835

Tanasi D, Stanco F, Tanasi D, Buffa M, Basile B (2012) Augmented perception of the past: the case of the telamon from the Greek theater of syracuse, communications in computer and information science, vol 247. Springer Berlin Heidelberg, Berlin, Heidelberg. https://doi.org/10.1007/978-3-642-27978-2, http://link.springer.com/10.1007/978-3-642-27978-2

Thian C (2012) Augmented reality—What Reality can we learn from it? https://www.museumsandtheweb.com/mw2012/papers/augmented_reality_what_reality_can_we_learn_fr

Tillon AB, Marchal I, Houlier P (2011) Mobile augmented reality in the museum: Can a lace-like technology take you closer to works of art? In: 2011 IEEE international symposium on mixed and augmented reality—Arts, media, and humanities, IEEE, Figure 1, pp 41–47. https://doi.org/10.1109/ismar-amh.2011.6093655, http://ieeexplore.ieee.org/document/6093655/

Wither J, Allen R, Samanta V, Hemanus J, Tsai Yt, Azuma R, Carter W, Hinman R, Korah T (2010) The westwood experience: connecting story to locations via Mixed Reality. In: 2010 IEEE international symposium on mixed and augmented Reality—Arts, media, and humanities, IEEE, pp 39–46. https://doi.org/10.1109/ismar-AMH.2010.5643295, http://ieeexplore.ieee.org/document/5643295/

Wojciechowski R, Walczak K, White M, Cellary W (2004) Building Virtual and Augmented Reality museum exhibitions. In: Proceedings of the ninth international conference on 3D Web technology - Web3D '04, ACM Press, New York, New York, USA, vol 1, p 135. https://doi.org/10.1145/985040.985060, http://portal.acm.org/citation.cfm?doid=985040.985060

Yoon SA, Wang J (2014) Making the invisible visible in Science Museums through augmented reality devices. TechTrends 58(1):49–55. https://doi.org/10.1007/s11528-013-0720-7, http://link.springer.com/10.1007/s11528-013-0720-7

Zerman E, O'Dwyer N, Young GW, Smolic A (2020) A case study on the use of volumetric video in augmented reality for cultural heritage. In: Proceedings of the 11th Nordic conference on human-computer interaction: shaping experiences, Shaping Society, ACM, New York, NY, USA, pp 1–5. https://doi.org/10.1145/3419249.3420115, https://dl.acm.org/doi/10.1145/3419249.3420115

Zoellner M, Pagani A, Pastarmov Y, Wuest H, Stricker D (2008) Reality filtering: a visual time machine in augmented reality. In: Proceedings of international symposium on virtual reality, archaeology and cultural heritage (VAST). http://av.dfki.de/pagani/doc/papers/ZoellnerVAST2008.pdf

Zöllner M, Keil J, Wüst H, Pletinckx D (2009) An augmented reality presentation system for remote cultural heritage sites. In: the 10th international symposium on virtual reality, archaeology and cultural heritage VAST (2009)

Chapter 4
Augmented Reality and Intelligent Packaging for Smart Tourism: A Systematic Review and Analysis

Dimitrios Panagiotakopoulos, M. Christodoulou, A. Mountzouri, P. Konstantinou, M. G. Nomikou, R. Metzitakos, G. Stathakis, and A. Papapostolou

Abstract The tourism sector is one of the largest and fastest-growing financial industries developed and redefined through technology. Information Communication Technology (ICT) and immersive imaging technologies, such as Virtual Reality (VR), Augmented Reality (AR), and Mixed Reality (MR), develop a digital environment where smart tourism aims at improving travellers' experience through interactive and adaptive applications. Additionally, intelligent packaging's emerging trend enters the tourism market dynamically, benefiting manufacturers, and buyers-users. This chapter addresses the systematic review and analysis of AR's convergence with intelligent packaging, specifying this interaction inside the touristic environment.

D. Panagiotakopoulos (✉) · A. Mountzouri · P. Konstantinou · R. Metzitakos · A. Papapostolou
Department of Graphic Design and Visual Communication, Faculty of Applied Arts and Culture, University of West Attica, Aigaleo, Greece
e-mail: dpanagiotakopoulos@uniwa.gr

A. Mountzouri
e-mail: a.mountzouri@uniwa.gr

P. Konstantinou
e-mail: pkonstantinou@uniwa.gr

R. Metzitakos
e-mail: rossetosm@uniwa.gr

A. Papapostolou
e-mail: pap@uniwa.gr

M. Christodoulou
Digital Humanities and Digital Knowledge, Department of Classical Philology and Italian Studies, University of Bologna, Bologna, Italy
e-mail: marina.christodoulou@studio.unibo.it

M. G. Nomikou
Department of Wine, Vine and Beverage Sciences, Faculty of Food Sciences, University of West Attica, Aigaleo, Greece
e-mail: mnomikou@uniwa.gr

G. Stathakis
Open University of Cyprus, Nicosia, Cyprus
e-mail: georgios.stathakis@ouc.ac.cy

© The Author(s), under exclusive license to Springer Nature Switzerland AG 2021   69
V. Geroimenko (ed.), *Augmented Reality in Tourism, Museums and Heritage*, Springer Series on Cultural Computing,
https://doi.org/10.1007/978-3-030-70198-7_4

The interchange of the real with the digital world gives importance to Internet of Things, Fifth Generation Mobile Phone Network (5G), Radio Frequency Identification (RFID), and Near Field Communication (NFC), which elicit the "intelligence" for the smart tourism. The review is focused on the components of tourism (tourist attractions, accommodation, catering, and transportation) that can be enhanced by the simultaneous redefinition of intelligent packaging with AR features and presenting possible perspectives of personalized and multisensorial attributes.

4.1   Introduction

While traveling keeps its constant value as a leading reference in the tourism industry, the ICT (Information Communication Technology) applications become a challenging exploration for modern technology (Han and Jung 2017). The digital "reconstruction" of tourism using ICT, e-commerce, VR (Virtual Reality), and AR (Augmented Reality) creates an adaptive public culture. The tourism sector needs interactive entertainment technologies, such as AR, to personalize augmented digital layers of environmental information (Genç 2017), based on the user-generated content of social media users that allow them to navigate independently.

This challenging environment uses the immersive, Human-Computer Interaction (HCI) and Extended Reality (XR) technologies of VR, AR, and MR as means to produce satisfactory consumer experiences (Alcañiz et al. 2019) and to increase tourism, immersing users in computer-generated environments (Loureiro et al. 2020). During the last decades, VR touristic experiences have extensive use and the non-thoroughly studied role of AR in touristic applications are being researched recently (Han et al. 2013; Han and Jung 2017). AR, along with other technologies (Internet of Things, the Internet of Everything, the 5G, RFID, NFC, and Gamification), enhance the physical and digital interactions of Ambient Intelligence (AmI) in the tourism industry (Buhalis 2019).

Between $5 trillion and $10 trillion in consumables are sold worldwide each year, and the vast majority are somehow packaged. In that way, it created a $424 billion packaging market in 2016. However, packaging remains a minor consideration for many manufacturers. Traditional business models could be shaken as new technologies, materials, and careful design could add value to the packaging (Fazio et al. 2018; Konstantinou 2020). Thus, intelligent packaging is considered a new trend that could generate beneficial aspects for both sides of the tourism market. "Smartness" and "intelligence" in this kind of operating systems seem to share some similarities referring to material sensitivity, as well as the technical appliance for digital applications (Nomikos 2008). Intelligent packaging with modern technological developments in printed electronics, conductive printed materials, and wireless communication devices has connected to the network, enhancing the user experience (Lydekaityte 2019). Specifically, intelligence in packaging characterizes a capable system that

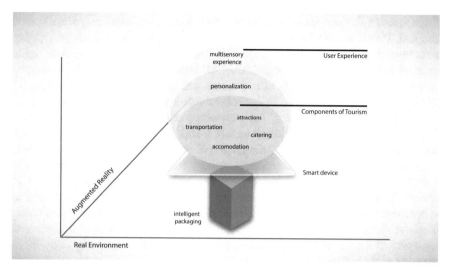

Fig. 4.1 Visual representation of intelligent packaging on the components of tourisms with the properties of personalization and multisensory experiences in reality—augmentation spectrum

stores and processes data for the exchange of information, while such smart functions as detecting, recording, tracking, and communicating for decision-making, take place (Yam et al. 2005).

This chapter presents the convergence of AR with intelligent packaging in a tourist environment. At the first level, referring to the tourist environment, we consider any environment that a traveler can visit and stay. In this kind of environment, the interaction of the real with the digital world is analysed, giving importance to the packaging technology's function that elicits and summarizes this "intelligent" collaboration in what is characterized as smart tourism. Consequently, background definitions (smart tourism, communication technologies, etc.) necessary for understanding the framework are given. Afterward, the applications of packaging technology, in the spectrum of reality and augmentation, in the context of the personalization of digital content, are presented. As the last element of this chapter, a perspective that concerns a "whole sense" augmentation packaging is summarized as the review gives multiple views for the user experience (see Fig. 4.1).

4.2 Background

4.2.1 Augmented Reality

The noticeable difference between VR and AR lies in the surrounding environment. VR's surrounding space is virtual, and according to Arthur (2000), it is an illusory visual state of the present immersed in a simulated, three-dimensional (3D) environment. This virtual environment (digital, virtual computer-generated reality, telepresence) removes and disconnects the user from the real environment with digital audio-visual stimuli (Loureiro et al. 2020). AR is implemented in a real environment by adding or removing objects in real space, enhancing the user's perception and interaction with the real world. AR displays virtual elements that the users cannot directly detect with their senses. The technology combines reality and virtuality in a real environment with real-time interaction and the recording of virtual and real two-dimensional (2D) or even 3D digital graphic objects in 3D space (Azuma 1997).

The augmentation can be experienced through handheld, smart AR devices with a camera (Android smartphones and Apple's ARKit), Head-Mounted Display (HMD[1]) headsets (such as *Microsoft HoloLens*[2] and *Meta 2*[3]), optical HMD (Smart Glasses with a see-through display like *Google Glass*[4]), 3D video mapping techniques named *Spatial Augmented Reality* (SAR), overlapping virtuality on large surfaces, and environmental AR (Kiosk Systems, interactive AR-Installations) (Wang et al. 2018; Loureiro et al. 2020).

Both technologies (VR and AR) are used in multiple fields, such as medical care, education, entertainment, and smart mobile applications (Park et al. 2014). However, VR is a mainstream term that does not currently cover the full range of virtuality. With technological advancement, the possibility of creating MR was achieved, extending between the real environment and the virtual environment, incorporating virtual and physical elements within the real world (Eve 2012; Kasapakis et al. 2018). Virtuality Continuum includes mixing real and virtual elements in a single environment, with the two most popular MR examples being AR and Augmented Virtuality (Kasapakis et al. 2018).

4.2.2 Smart Cities and Smart Tourism

The term "smart cities" was introduced in 2000 and refers to a city type that invests in advanced ICT, integrating complex information systems into urban infrastructure and home appliances to be automated by sensors. Such cities aim to adopt innovative solutions to improve the quality of life in various areas such as environmental protection, active participation of citizens, improving transport, etc. (Panagiotakopoulos 2020; Konstantinou et al. 2018).

---

[1]HMD are the most popular desktop imaging devices, as well as the computer-controlled Head Worn Displays (HWD) devices, that are placed on the user's head, displaying elements of combined images or video icons in the real or in the entire virtual world.

[2]Microsoft HoloLens—Project Baraboo. Issued March 30, 2016. https://www.microsoft.com/en-us/hololens.

[3]The Meta 2 Development Kit is an AR HMD. https://www.schenker-tech.de/en/meta-2/.

[4]Google Glass or Glass belongs to the smart glasses category as an AR wearable computer and optical HMD with a transparent display.

Today's views on urban functioning use to parallelize cities to biological systems, which the main feature is adaptability (Batty 2008). Cities are continuously developing to meet their citizens' needs to enroll a positive impact without either destroying the environment or endangering life over time (Girardet 2008). Smart cities' technologies will transform cities into autonomous, self-controlled systems that collect information and process them to organize communication between different devices (Khorov et al. 2015; Konstantinou et al. 2019).

The term "smart tourism" was coined in 2010 and is an essential element of smart cities describing the evolving progress of traditional tourism influenced by smart technology, including smart devices, smart cards, gamification, AR, personalized experiences, etc., to upgrade the visitor's experience. The phenomenon relies almost entirely on cloud computing, the Internet of Things, and sensor technology for real-time data collection and management, modeling and visualizing functions for the city, residents, businesses, and attractions (Harrison et al. 2010; Wang et al. 2016; Liu and Wei 2015; Gretzel et al. 2015, 2016).

4.2.3 The Nature of Intelligent Packaging

The packaging can be divided into traditional or conventional packaging, active packaging, smart packaging, and intelligent packaging. The primary functions of conventional packaging are protecting the product from the harmful effects of the external environment and the communication with the consumer as a marketing tool with various sizes and shapes (Yam et al. 2005). In the tourism industry, the term packaging describes the dynamic systems that function to display conventional information to the tourism community (Mountzouri et al. 2020).

Furthermore, the term *active packaging* is not synonymous with smart packaging or intelligent packaging. It refers to specific materials, elements, and indicators[5] into the packaging to detect and provide information about the function and properties of uniquely packaged foods[6] (Vigneshwaran et al. 2019). *Smart packaging* has been a trending topic referring to a system including mechanical, chemical, and electrical functions to improve the packaging with the four fundamental concepts of communication, content, protection, and usability (Vigneshwaran et al. 2019; Nomikos 2019).

Intelligent packaging makes use of the elements of the active packaging (Gregor-Svetec 2018), while it is considered as the evolution of smart packaging, formed in

---

[5]Active packaging systems may contain hardware components to detect chemicals, pathogens, and toxins in food, such as *TTI* (Time Temperature Indicators), indicating the temperature during storage and transportation, gas detectors/oxygen indicators, but even more thermochromic inks which change color in different temperatures (Schaefer and Cheung 2018; Kuswandi et al. 2011; Roya and Elham 2016).

[6]According to the European regulation (EC) No. 450/2009 active packaging systems are designed to "*deliberately incorporate components that would release or absorb substances into or from the packaged food or the environment surrounding the food*" (Yildirim et al. 2017).

an interactive, physical, and electronic environment. It can also be digitally enhanced as a hybrid digital-physical object consisting of Cyber-Physical Systems, cloud computing, the Internet of Things, sensors, actuators, and the new 5G that interacts with other everyday objects. It can detect and provide information on the operation and properties of packaged products, ensuring integrity, breaches, safety, security, quality, and lifespan extension (Lydekaityte 2019; Dobrucka 2013; Yam et al. 2005; Mountzouri et al. 2020). According to Vigneshwaran et al. (2019), intelligent packaging can include: barcodes, RFID, electronic article surveillance (EAS), digital watermark, quality indicators, as aforementioned on the active packaging, digital sensors, and other organic light-emitting diodes (OLED) and hologram.

4.2.3.1   RFID and NFC

The RFID's (Radio Frequency Identification) commercial use began more than 20 years ago and can benefit tourism globally by interacting with people and objects for electronic communication and visitor-tourist management (Nomikos et al. 2014; Mountzouri et al. 2020). It is an automated identification and tracking long-range wireless communication technology, recognizable as a capable technology of carrying out a complete ubiquitous computer network. RFID uses radio frequencies through electronic tags/labels (antenna) and a reader to wirelessly identify animate or inanimate objects in real-time (Goshey 2008; Debouzy and Perrin 2012; Yang et al. 2008; Mountzouri et al. 2020). RFID covers a wide range of frequencies, classified into Low Frequency (125 kHz ~ 134 kHz), the High Frequency (typically 13.56 MHz), the Ultra-High Frequency (860−960 MHz), and the Microwave Frequency (> 1 GHz) (Panagiotakopoulos 2020; Debouzy and Perrin 2012).

RFID systems include remote electronic chip components, the tags, where they memorize data and transmit them, and a reader that sends continuous radiofrequency waves to identify objects. Tags can be "active" using a transmitter and a battery as a power source for communicating with the reader, "passive" when they need the power source by the reader for powering themselves (as mainly used in the packaging industry), and "semi-passive" when the tags need an on-board battery to reflect radio waves to the reader without transmitting their message broadcasts. Multiple items can be monitored at every stage in the supply chains, increasing the speed and efficiency of distribution (Debouzy and Perrin 2012; Panagiotakopoulos 2020; Yang et al. 2008; Goshey 2008; Kuswandi et al. 2011).

NFC (Near Field Communication) is a subset of RFID and standardizing short-range, wireless, peer-to-peer communication technology between devices, tags/smart labels, operating typically within about 8 cm in the 13.56 MHz band, allowing data transfer up to 424 Kbit/s (Vauclair 2011; Panagiotakopoulos and Dimitrantzou 2020; Aristova et al. 2018). NFC communication can occur either between two active devices, where both the reader and the tag produce the radiofrequency signal for the data transmission, or an active and a passive where the radio frequency signal is generated only by the reader, and the tag communicates it back. Additionally, the peer-to-peer mode achieves the information exchange between two NFC devices with the tag using more power than the reader due to its supply (Panagiotakopoulos 2020).

The technology has many benefits for the industry and the user, such as ease of use, simple communication adjustment, and extremely low energy consumption, tag invisibility through the objects, a unique tag ID number verified by a server, safest way to transfer data, avoiding data monitoring (Dutot 2015; Panagiotakopoulos and Dimitrantzou 2020, Harrop et al. 2020). The interconnection of NFC in the Internet of Things network is gaining more ground, providing specific functions in the smart tourism sector (Pesonen and Horster 2012).

4.2.3.2   Communication Technologies

The Internet of Things (IoT) is a recent example of communication that envisions a future in which everyday objects will be equipped with microcontrollers, digital communication transceivers, and appropriate protocol stacks that will allow them to communicate with each other and could be an integral part of the new age Internet (Atzori et al. 2010). The Internet of Things aims to make the Internet more significant, more imposing, and pervasive with many new applications and services to citizens, companies, and public administrations (Bellavista et al. 2013; Konstantinou et al. 2018).

Objects with highly sophisticated built-in systems are connected in a smart city, providing seamless communication and services. Evolutionarily, the Internet of Things coincides with RFID sensor technology, which is its cornerstone. Gradually, this relationship became a popular achievement through the connectivity of RFID/NFC tags with real and physical objects as hyperlinks with extensive network systems of accessible information through the internet for the collection, processing, and simultaneous production of data in the real environment, with typical examples of supply-chain helpers, vertical-market applications to ubiquitous positioning (Greer et al. 2019; Abbas and Marwat 2020; Muguira et al. 2009; Jia et al. 2012).

Intelligent packaging, as an interconnected smart object, is equipped with a sensor or actuator, a tiny microprocessor, a communication device, and sometimes with a power source, interacting with the physical world. The microprocessor allows the conversion of the sensors' data, albeit with limited speed and limited complexity. The communication device activates the smart object to transmit the sensor measurements to the outside world and receive information from other smart objects (Konstantinou et al. 2018). Applicable to packaging and production, inventory traceability can be achieved through the Internet of Things. It is possible to minimize inventory loss and enhance environmental monitoring by using the Internet of Things and RFID, such as *UFlex* having achieved almost 80% accurate tracking using both technologies (Ramakrishnan and Gaur 2016), combining Geographic Information System (GIS) technologies in the analysis of spatial and temporal data (Shirowzhan et al. 2020).

Smart objects' connectivity is also supported by 5G networks affecting the development of smart city infrastructure with faster transmission capabilities, with *mobile*

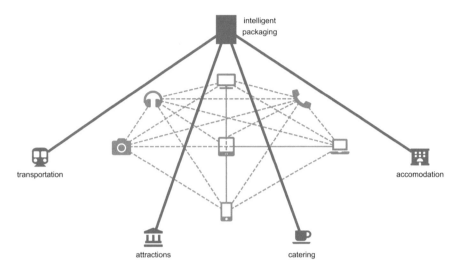

Fig. 4.2 Intelligent packaging combinatorial process within the components of tourism

edge computing and *cloud computing* being the most promising approach for delivering 5G content to smart cities. The Internet of Things is one of the major ICT's enabling smart cities, along with connectivity, data analytics, and Artificial Intelligence (AI) (Milovanovic et al. 2019). AI has significantly improved the efficiency of production and service systems by learning to solve complex problems (Naik 2016), and it is another technology that can be used for the packaging industry. AI tools can be used as knowledge-based expert systems, fuzzy logic, inductive learning, and neural networks to model microbial growth, process, and control food maturation (Yam et al. 2005). All the technologies mentioned above are included in the intelligent packaging creating a combinatorial approach within the societal and technological network (see Fig. 4.2).

4.3   Intelligent Packaging and Augmented Reality

AR has invaded many areas such as logistics and, more specifically, the packaging element. The process of interaction and synchronization in a multiscopic process environment becomes more efficient (Cirulis and Ginters 2013). AR is commonly performed on packaging through visuals: videos, logos, interaction buttons messages, animated graphs, 2D or 3D promotions for communicating information and augmented representation of the packaging and its content, while the user can interact with the visuals (Siakas 2018).

Introductory, the main access point for activating the augmentation in the package is initially the one dimension (1D) or 2D barcodes, the more comprehensive used Quick Response codes (QR) in the field of packaging. QR motives are printed in 2D on the package's surface, while a smart device camera is needed to read and identify their content (Panagiotakopoulos and Dimitrantzou 2020). In conjunction with AR technology, the codes achieve AR image recognition by retaining QR text information, using standard scan code software, or through an AR-recognized application (Li and Si 2019). Barcodes, QR, and NFC tags can encode GS1 identifiers[7] to make products detectable in the universal product codes (Vigneshwaran et al. 2019).

It should be noted that there is no interaction between QR code and AR content, as the additional information operates in digital space and is not included organically in the package, as shown in its physical space. Moreover, QR codes were considered the next big thing, the disadvantages to their usefulness and usability (such as: the camera's properly adjusted, poor lighting (light glare, light angle), camera rotation, vibration, video camera quality, environmental obstructions, the non-rewritable mode, the limited amount of information, the inability to be hidden behind layers, the easily distorted and destroyed) made industry professionals to replace them with NFC tags (Panagiotakopoulos and Dimitrantzou 2020; Cirulis and Ginters 2013). Using NFC labels, the above problems are ignored due to the NFC tags' ability to remain hidden behind the layers, with an outcome of a touchless and remote interaction between packaging and mobile devices, giving users the ability to personalize the package by storing information on its chip.

The development of interactive intelligent packaging, utilizing NFC is compatible and straightforward with NFC readers, thanks to the new smart device generation. Taping the smart device to the attached NFC tags of the intelligent packaging, the NFC tags' detection and identification are processed. While the NFC tag will be detected, then the application's automatic start is being carried out, providing almost simultaneously the downloaded from the database the AR contents (corresponding to the unique detected ID tag) (Joo et al. 2012). The user experience is realized through a multimedia device interface in combination with NFC communication.

4.4 A New Marketing Strategy in Tourism

The AR packaging can be used in various implementations of tourism components with several AR applications, including mainly interactive tours. Applicable gadgets have been promoted to improve the communications of visitors in real space through their smart devices. For example, AR packaging as a tool can enhance the tourist market by offering travelers interactive content, providing services, and making them feel familiar with the destination. AR can guide destination discovery by navigating visitors to restaurants, cafes, markets, and tourist attractions, with maximum independence.

---

[7]GS1 Application Identifiers (AIs) was developed in response to the growing use of AIs in the various industry sectors to include batch/lot number, serial number, best before date, and expiration date. It also allows users, solution providers, and GS1 Member Organisations to easily view, search, and share details about individual AIs through web-browsers or on a mobile device. https://www.gs1.org/standards/barcodes/application-identifiers.

AR marketing focuses on interactive and gamified digital customer experiences adaptively in the natural decision-making environment. This is achieved by shared digital content (images, information, or instructions) with mobile or wearable technology (Chylinski et al. 2020). Furthermore, except the conventional AR functionalities, it is observed that in a tourist context AR is associated with the creation of games, providing opportunities for interactive and engrossing games (Javornik 2016), while Goldman Sachs documents that AR has the potential to "become the next big computing platform."

Packaging marketing strategies deliver immersive brand experiences, such as the *Cadbury Quack Smack* and the McDonald's *Track My Maccas*, in which a package is augmented with an interactive game (Sterling 2011; Thrasher 2013). Subsequently, AR games can be played outdoors, like the recent and "biggest mobile game in U.S. history" Pokémon GO[8] (Lovelace 2016), where players are asked to locate and catch virtual creatures hidden in real-world locations with their smart devices, requiring physical activity. Research on *Game Transfer Phenomena* has shown that AR games can enhance sensory perception, which is usually evidenced by automatic correlations between physical and virtual stimuli (Ortiz de Gortari 2019). All the prior could be beneficial on AR marketing, promoting local products, while the tourist is moving and observing in the visited area.

AR marketing strategies can include transmedia techniques with narrative dimensions of the main story transmitted through a specific channel. In contrast, external narratives enrich the story through various channels that users can collect on their experience in the city, contributing to user-generated content to the whole story. *Transmedia Gaming* campaigns through AR game platforms can make visitors contribute to the destination's digital world by creating gaps that force tourists to find and buy packaging products around the game area's specified hotspots and act as protagonists in storytelling. This combination of intelligent packaging, AR marketing, and Transmedia Gaming can enrich the "Transmedia in Tourism" that has already been recognized as a primary tool for promoting sites and cultural heritage (Panagiotakopoulos 2020). However, today's AR campaigns are in a broader context through younger populations than in elders who are often excluded from user experience design (Lee et al. 2019).

4.4.1 Intelligent Packaging and Tourist Attractions

AR can be applied as an "Outdoor augmentation" for cultural, historical, and archaeological tourist sites, interacting with virtual content such as "On-site augmentation" or "Off-site augmentation" with the ability to expand and transform into different mixed environments. Museums and archeological sites are ideal environments for developing technologies such as "Gamification" and "Edutainment" (Educational

---

[8]Pokémon GO is a location-based mobile AR game developed and released by Niantic in 2016. https://www.pokemon.com/us/.

entertainment) to engage visitors in a non-game context using the game thinking as a reference to interactive experience and dedication to cultural exhibits of recreational value (Panagiotakopoulos and Dimitrantzou 2020).

During the travel experience, Information Technology (IT) systems use dynamic packaging with AR and Global Positioning System (GPS) to supplement or replace the traditional tour guide with commercial and historical information, including adaptive landscape and environmental details (Hunter et al. 2015). Mobile AR in culture and specifically in archaeology can be mostly applied through multi-character story games, virtual guides-tours, 3D computer reconstruction representations, providing reproducibility and experimentation with archaeological phenomenological experience (Gheorghiu and Ştefan 2019). An application example that shows the AR-centric future is the *BBC's Civilisations AR* app that gives the ability to admire various historical artifacts through tutorial guides, locating, rotating, and resizing them in everyone's physical space (Jansen and Beaton 2020).

4.4.2 Intelligent Packaging and Accommodation

Accommodation is a significant component of tourism. Smart technology helps tourists decide rationally and optimize the profit of their stay. Accommodation providers receive foreign guests from all over the world who may not communicate in a local or international language. Providers configure translator and AR interpreting applications so that their services can be understood. Another common AR use in accommodation is the interactive elements on hotels and other similar businesses, providing lodging information, such as *The Hub Hotel* from Premier Inn, which used wall maps to enhance them via smart devices as a tourist information tool, like the Italian AR *Florence Travel Guide*. Packaging can be integrated into the whole experience as a promotional product of the accommodation that provides useful information about the hotel's services or the partner companies of the business in the destination. Similarly, *LIFEWTR*, by Pepsi with customized tags on bottles, creates in-room experiences for Marriott Hotels, customizing their rooms virtually with an AR art gallery featuring (Butler 2019). Alongside ambient AR systems can work as "calm technologies," assisting peoples' overall well-being affecting their stress level projecting environmental scenes, and playing natural sounds into the visitor's room (Ducasse et al. 2019).

4.4.3 Intelligent Packaging and Catering

AR technology has several advantages in experiential marketing, shaping a future food and beverage industry, immersing the consumer in a branded experience. *AR for Catering* refers to the application of the technology in the field of catering, with businesses supported by the technology, for instance with AR the visitor by scanning the package can watch the process of its creation and its content with all the relevant information. Additionally, these functionalities provide a more specific and personalized service as informing visitors of food allergies that may result from the ingredients of the package's contents without reading its printed ingredients-specifications. A great example of using AR packaging is the booking of meals electronically and displaying digital 3D food menus of a realistic representation of the dishes, drinks, and desserts in all variations and sizes, showcasing customers to their future table, thus ensuring better reviews (Poghos 2018; Cassar and Inguanez 2018).

Moreover, through specific applications, the possibility of the *Diminished Reality*, where the augmentation removes objects or packaging parts from real space for the interior product to be presented (Azuma 1997; Đurđević et al. 2018), is being given. Välkkynen et al. (2011) refer to a "peeking in the box" illusion-like near-field AR X-ray allowed to be revealed. Nespresso, for example, has added AR content through the *Nespresso Essenza Mini AR App* to show what the product looks like when ready to eat and how the coffee machine can be used (Lucio 2018). The AR content can be created by advertising companies where digitally AR ads (coupons or other complementary-like products) enhance commercial competition (Zhu et al. 2004). Even more, AR can be used through packaging and help a buyer to assemble a product by guiding him with moving 2D or 3D images in his real environment instead of the static ones in the manual book (Widiyanto and Rifa 2014).

4.4.4 Intelligent Packaging and Transportation

Massive growth in transport has recently caused various problems such as the dramatic increase in traffic congestion, transport overload, and safety. Simultaneously, in opposition, mobile location services offer an accessible and more comfortable experience in several urban destinations (Boletsis and Chasanidou 2018). Subsequently, the integration of the Internet of Things to the transportation systems has already been achieved to offer several solutions to the above problems providing peripheral commute information, paving the way for a smarter and more informed travel, giving birth to Intelligent Transport Systems (Bhardwaj et al. 2019). Often intelligent packaging is a component of Intelligent Transport Systems such as smart tickets that include NFC. In the transportation process, package sensors can be tapped by multiple smart devices enabling the functionality of the Internet of Things to stabilize safety, improve traffic flow, and provide a more pleasant experience for drivers and passengers (Milovanovic et al. 2019).

Mobile AR "comes into play" by informing travelers about the exact locations and arrival times of vehicles, providing exploration of urban destinations, easily obtaining useful cultural information, strengthening the transport network with value-added services, alleviating congestion (Boletsis and Chasanidou 2018). Even more, the smart device captures the scene and is being identified for a visual element to be embedded or removed from the scene. The identification can also be supported also by virtual markers or tracking technologies such as sensors, NFC tags, laser, infrared, or GPS. The captured and identified scene needs to be processed with the visual elements requested from a database via the internet. From now on, the generated AR scene is visualized and ready to guide the visitor's visual field (Mahmood et al. 2018).

4.5 Personalization in Intelligent Packaging

Tourism's personalization concerns the visitor's entire journey so that he can be helped in various situations while his unfulfilled needs emerge. It is considered to be related to personal data (learning style, disabilities, age groups, starting level, time available to visit) scheduling offline visits or bookmarking to be explored and used extensively in the future (Čopič Pucihar and Kljun 2018). Personalization is aimed at consumers to create customized experiences in multiple kinds of products with advanced digital technologies (Abraham et al. 2017).

Smart tourism applications enable the customization of services and interaction with cultural objects, creating data, and sharing (Chianese and Piccialli 2016; Nguyen et al. 2016). Quality and personalized tourism of internet users push the development of Big Data and AI technology, providing a better tourism experience: image translators, instant AR translation, voice recognition, fast check-in with face recognition, smart guides, quality experimental services VR and AR, and even robots to interact with inanimate objects (Wei and Lin 2020).

Regarding the individualization of conventional packaging, there is a dual distinction, such as in the field of food and ingredient customization (functional customization) or even the personalization of the packaging itself as design, modifying its visual appearance (cosmetic customization) (Kolb et al. 2014). However, in the case of intelligent packaging that converges with the digital world and specifically with the spectrum of digital augmentation, there is a third distinction concerning the adaptability of digital content.

Package's NFC tags allow the customization of user information in multimedia devices, focusing on populations and special groups' convenience. Access to a destination's attractions is achieved through spatial visualization through AR with interactive guided features (Panagiotakopoulos and Dimitrantzou 2020). These tools offer the users the feeling of unique access to information mainly through an entertaining experience (Edutainment). Many visitors will more easily choose to visit a destination with special features, such as accessibility, enhancement, and supporting personalization activity, allowing tourists to utilize their products or the smart destination's benefits by digitally modifiable content through AR practice.

The personalized experience is not the only goal offered through the AR application. An alteration in buying and requesting merchandise is creating a personal company-consumer relationship at the market level. Thus a realistic depiction of the components of the product or the enhanced assistance in its assembly forms a relationship of trust and confidence in the purchase process, which can now be further strengthened by the immediate statement of satisfaction of the customer through the mass media and the consolidation of a constructive dialogue. The transformation of technology contributes to developing scalable technology platforms that support existing and future personalization technologies in any channel (Abraham et al. 2017).

4.6 Intelligent Packaging and Multisensory Experiences

This section presents a new form of multisensory enhanced experiences to the intelligent packaging in the context of smart tourism and its already aforementioned components. The augmentation of all the senses so that the product's experience makes the destination and the interaction with its products more attractive. In this case, the term "augmentation" is used in a dual sense, metaphorically to describe the ability of the conventional packaging itself to enhance the senses, as an active packaging which enables the consumer to interact (read, see, feel, smell) with the features of the package (absorbing and releasing materials, embedded scents, content) that can provide additional data and facilitate the purchase selection process, typically used on food and cosmetics packaging. However, we want to focus on the "augmentation" of the technical meaning of AR, which currently enables only the usage of audio-visual stimuli.

To pursue the next stage of the Internet, humans should not only communicate emotions with visual, audio, and tactile stimuli but also communicating all as a digital experience and sharing these incentives collectively (Cheok and Karunanayaka 2018b; Wang et al. 2018). It is about an intelligent and automated augmentation that will characterize the convergence of the physical and digital world (Wang et al. 2018).

The science of psychology and neuroscience has shown that the human brain in interacting with the outside world incorporates information from different sensory methods. The final experience results a mixture of many sensory pieces of information rather than a collection of independent senses (Bordegoni et al. 2019). However, today's digital communication is based only on text, audio, and video. The sense of smell (olfactory perception) and taste (gustatory perception) is currently little considered, while it is believed that it is going to be the real future innovation that will change the way digital experiences are communicated (Cheok and Karunanayaka 2018a).

Placing human senses and interactivity at the center of the commerciality is the primary trend of market renewal. Through technological restitution, innovative techniques, and in combination with intelligent packaging, a rehabilitated multisensory experience is offered to the consumer-visitor. This brings a new field of "Multisensory Marketing," which researches not only the visual aspects of the packaging design but also all senses (Velasco and Spence 2018). Differentiation in the branding process is no longer just the design of conventional packaging. The purpose of packaging is to realize an emotional connection between the consumer and the packaging through a multisensory approach (Joutsela 2010).

AR is being considered a virtual imagery technology, and this is something that is observed in most AR packaging projects, mainly relied on audio-visual content to deliver a multimedia experience. However, Azuma and different researchers believe in AR's multimodality and ability to augment information for all senses in the real environment (Wang et al. 2018). Thus, the senses of smell, touch, and taste could also be used to augment the package's content to make the user experience with the product more immersive.

The "Multisensory Branding" has emerged to create unforgettable experiences for consumers, including all five senses (Castillo-Villar and Villasante-Arellano 2020). Despite the enthusiasm for digitizing the chemical senses and their multisensory implications, commercialization efforts have failed (Spence et al. 2017). There is no substantial *Virtual Experience in Marketing* research using XR technologies to stimulate sensory channels other than audio-visual. However, several solutions for the tactile senses (power and touch), the olfactory system, and the taste have been proposed with great technical difficulties in the application (Alcañiz et al. 2019).

4.6.1 Smell Interfaces

The olfactory stimulation is a chemical sense that uses the neuron system to detect thousands of different chemical molecules in the air (Wang et al. 2018), while researchers claim that memories, experiences, and visual-spatial memories can be recovered through odors, though there are also correlations between smell and mood—emotional state (Gutiérrez et al. 2008).

Historically the olfactory stimulation was introduced as a fascinating trend to the audience of cinemas with the *Smell-O-Vision*[9] in VR systems (Spence et al. 2017) and with the *Sensorama*[10] (Gutiérrez et al. 2008). Digital perfume/scent applications are an evolving technology that is gradually being supported by the virtual world (Viswanathan and Rajan 2020). There have been different smell machines that can deliver the smell stimulus differently with multiple aromas and odors in real-time to provide the user with a truly immersive experience, such as the device *SmX-4DS* by SencoryCo (Martins et al. 2017), or "Scent synthesizers" (i.e., *iSmell* by DigiScents), that generate odors into the RE through digitized files (Viswanathan and Rajan 2020).

Digital smell interfaces could be incorporated with packaging to deliver an AR experience enhancing the audio-visual stimuli through electronic Odor Olfactory

---

[9]Smell-O-Vision under the patented name "MOTON PICTURES WITH SYNCHRONIZED ODOR EMISSION" was an invention (First Patent No. 2,813,452 issued November 19, 1957, and second Patent No. 2,905,049 issued September 22, 1959) related particularly to apparatus for distributing odors in timed sequence concerning a motion picture film.

[10]Sensorama Simulator was an invention of Morton Leonard Heilig that was patented in 1962 (Patent No. 3,050,870) and relates to a simulator to stimulate the senses of a user giving him an actual and realistic experience.

Displays (OOD) producing aroma, as has been researched to augment book reading experiences (Campos et al. 2019) or with external devices as already aforementioned. Odor devices, through packaging novel mechanisms, such as RFID tags and digital product codes, can activate the delivery and regulation of volatile flavors and aromas (Majid et al. 2018).

4.6.2 Taste Interfaces

Digital flavor synthesizers can evoke a sense of taste through the electrical stimulation of the tongue. To achieve the "Digital Taste - Electric Taste," the HCI experimentally develops interactive systems with chemical or non-chemical simulation methodologies as it is possible to use non-chemical stimulation methods to simulate the taste senses digitally (Cheok and Karunanayaka 2018b). Ranasinghe et al. proposed a Bluetooth device in a small capsule that can digitally enhance flavors (Campos et al. 2019). Multiple research attempts to create interface-devices as "food simulators" such as the one by Iwata et al. as a "food texture display." The device simulates chewing with different foods, releasing aromatic chemicals on the tongue, and chewing sounds are reproduced, while a sensor records the force of the resistance bite (Gutiérrez et al. 2008). Another example is the device developed by Hashimoto et al. simulating with a moderate success between 55 and 72% the stimuli of drinking to the mouth and lips, reproducing through a straw-like user interface pressure, vibration, and sound (pre-recorded sounds of different kinds of food; liquids, solids, gels). The interface has been presented in the ARS Electronica[11] 2005 exhibition with possibilities for interactive arts and entertainment (Gutiérrez et al. 2008).

A possible scenario is being developed to understand the system that is being considered around the development of this multisensory experience. Suppose a visitor is at a food and beverage exhibition with multiple packages. However, the visitor, due to mobility disabilities, cannot come in contact with the full gastronomic experience. Through an external and digital smell-taste interface, the degustation experience can be developed to such an extent that there will be no fair content loss. Extra functions could be supported by RFID/NFC technology, so such an interface can personalize the ingredient content according to the user's tastes, supported additionally by an audio-visual augmentation stimulus on the screen of his smart device (see Fig. 4.3).

4.6.3 Sonic Packaging

The sound can be transmitted with headphones or properly calibrated volumes and settings to ensure a 360-degree 3D experience in a virtual or real environment. People can receive important non-auditory information, such as temperature, from the sound.

---

[11] https://ars.electronica.art/news/.

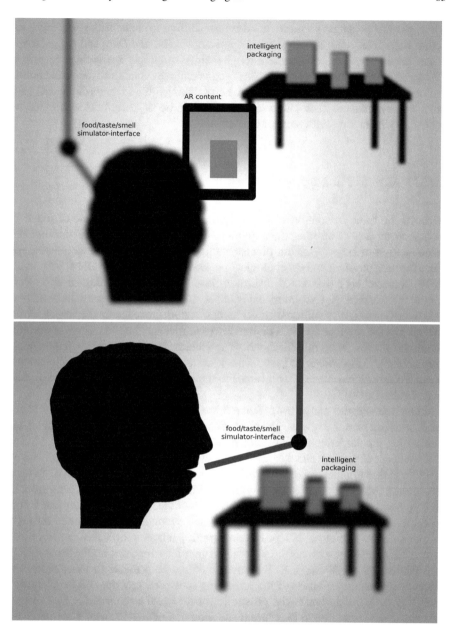

Fig. 4.3 Digital and mechanical taste/smell interfaces can deliver olfactory and gustatory perception combined with an audio-visual AR content

Thus, product packaging's future trend is also shifting to sonic packaging, incorporating augmented sounds with sensory applications. *Häagen-Dazs* and *Krug Champagne* have embraced music tracks through their AR products' marketing campaigns (Wang and Spence 2018). Audio packages can combine sounds and music in combination with other visual graphics so that when touching different parts of the package, sounds are produced. This sound reproduction can be supported through RFID or NFC tags' interaction with parts of the package.

4.6.4 Haptic Packaging

Most of the time, to complete the perception of a product, the sense of touch is an important aspect offering the exploration of the real environment through the manipulation of objects, giving precise, subjective, and individual tactile perceptions through physical and psychological phenomena (Albert et al. 2018; Thai et al. 2020). Researchers have created electronic gloves to reproduce tactile sensation with vibration motors in VR (Ashimori and Igarashi 2019). Haptic gloves can be classified into three types. The "traditional gloves" where a cloth glove leaves the fingers while the sensors are sewn or attached to the glove's fabric, such as the *Gloveone* and the *AvatarVR* gloves. The "thimbles" where an electromagnetic actuator applies pressure on the attached fingertip such as the *VRtouch* device. And the "exoskeletons," wearable articulated devices with forces to the fingers like the *CyberGrasp* (Perret and Poorten 2018).

Industrial logistics makes use of smart or scanning gloves mostly to make workers work with free hands, while the gloves scan and record quickly and comfortably data, confirming the performed action through sound or vibration (Jurenka et al. 2020). These advanced reading and wearable, computation, and wireless devices consist of RFID tags through their integration with RFID readers to improve the activity's user experience (Muguira et al. 2009). Another application of the RFID reader gloves is to help blind people locate and be informed about the type of food they are going to eat, with RFID tags placed on the plates and keeps the user informed through output sounds (Lee et al. 2010). In this regard, packaging as a real-world object with RFID/NFC sensors can be a potential interface for AmI applications (Zaiţi and Pentiuc 2013). Through RFID gloves, it could be possible to transfer from a distance the haptic sensation of the packaging (pressure, motion, and temperature) (see Fig. 4.4). For instance, the possibility of having the opportunity to feel and interact in real-time due to the current situation of COVID-19, where the touch of packaging in crowded places is highly dangerous.

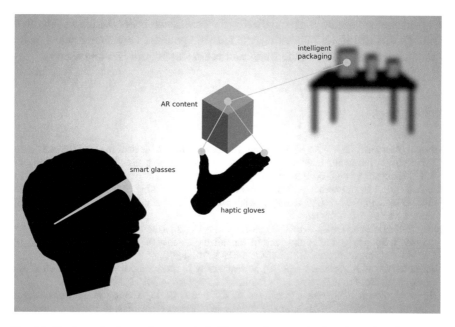

Fig. 4.4 Haptic packaging can be connected with smart gloves to simulate the package's pressure, temperature, etc

4.7   Conclusions

Overall, it may be said that the alteration of conventional packaging into intelligent packaging brings renewal and revision of many factors that determine the market. The combination of conventional and electronic elements results in the creation of a new packaging that identifies data and, at the same time, is self-identified, having the "ability" of reacting with information systems by creating a completely different correspondence condition, combining communication at multiple levels. In other words, the packaging becomes a hyperconnected, smart object, with the support of computer power, which can be used in everyday life, interact with other smart devices and with different software, receives and transmits information and data, thus contributing to the strengthening of the 5G and Internet of Things network.

The integration of intelligent packaging in the tourism sector brings a new breath to the management and promotion of tourism options, enhancing the components of tourism. Due to the upsurge of the offered services and products, the demands of the consumer-tourist have increased. In this context, the adaptability that intelligent packaging can provide covers with all levels of supply. Contributing to the consolidation and expansion of the destination business network, it provides experiences that the consumer could not have in the case of conventional packaging, and creates greater security at all levels of the system. Adaptability, however, is not limited to these contexts. The tourist could interact multi sensually through AR, with the package and create a personalized user experience based on his background. Through this multilevel interaction, the touristic potentials are strengthened, and a new "purchasing" reality in the smart tourist context of AmI is established.

References

Abbas A, Marwat S (2020) Scalable emulated framework for IoT devices in smart logistics based cyber-physical systems: bonded coverage and connectivity analysis. IEEE Access 8:138350–138372. https://doi.org/10.1109/access.2020.3012458

Abraham M, Mitchelmore S, Collins S et al. (2017) Profiting from personalization. In: BCG Global. https://www.bcg.com/publications/2017/retail-marketing-sales-profiting-personalization. Accessed 13 Jul 2020

Albert B, De Bertrand De Beuvron F, Zanni-Merk C et al. (2018) A smart system for haptic quality control: a knowledge-based approach to formalize the sense of touch. Commun Comput Inf Sci:173–190. https://doi.org/10.1007/978-3-319-99701-8_8

Alcañiz M, Bigné E, Guixeres J (2019) Virtual reality in marketing: a framework, review, and research agenda. Front Psychol. https://doi.org/10.3389/fpsyg.2019.01530

Aristova U, Rolich A, Staruseva-Persheeva A, Zaitseva A (2018) The use of internet of things technologies within the frames of the cultural industry: opportunities, restrictions, prospects. Commun Comput Inf Sci:146–161. https://doi.org/10.1007/978-3-030-02846-6_12

Arthur K (2000) Effects of field of view on performance with head-mounted displays. Ph.D, The University of North Carolina at Chapel Hill

Ashimori K, Igarashi H (2019) Development of an individual joint controllable haptic glove (crl-glove) and apply for CLASS. Adv Intell Syst Comput:895–901. https://doi.org/10.1007/978-3-030-11051-2_137

Atzori L, Iera A, Morabito G (2010) The internet of things: a survey. Comput Netw 54:2787–2805. https://doi.org/10.1016/j.comnet.2010.05.010

Azuma R (1997) A survey of augmented reality. Presence 6:355–385

Batty M (2008) The size, scale, and shape of cities. Science 319:769–771. https://doi.org/10.1126/science.1151419

Bellavista P, Cardone G, Corradi A, Foschini L (2013) Convergence of MANET and WSN in IoT urban scenarios. IEEE Sens J 13:3558–3567. https://doi.org/10.1109/jsen.2013.2272099

Bhardwaj K, Khanna A, Sharma D, Chhabra A (2019) Designing energy-efficient IoT-based intelligent transport system: need, Architecture, characteristics, challenges, and applications. Energy Conserv IoT Devices:209–233. https://doi.org/10.1007/978-981-13-7399-2_9

Boletsis C, Chasanidou D (2018) Audio augmented reality in public transport for exploring tourist sites. In: Proceedings of the 10th Nordic Conference on Human-Computer Interaction—NordiCHI '18. https://doi.org/10.1145/3240167.3240243

Bordegoni M, Carulli M, Ferrise F (2019) Improving multisensory user experience through olfactory stimuli. Emot Eng 7:201–231. https://doi.org/10.1007/978-3-030-02209-9_13

Buhalis D (2019) Technology in tourism-from information communication technologies to eTourism and smart tourism towards ambient intelligence tourism: a perspective article. Tour Rev 75:267–272. https://doi.org/10.1108/tr-06-2019-0258

Butler M (2019) Augmented reality for hotels—The future is here I Carmelon Digital Marketing. In: Carmelon. https://www.carmelon-digital.com/articles/ar-for-hotels/. Accessed 22 Sep 2020

Campos C, Ducasse J, Čopič Pucihar K et al. (2019) Augmented imagination: creating immersive and playful reading experiences. Augment Rity Games II:57–81. https://doi.org/10.1007/978-3-030-15620-6_3

Cassar L, Inguanez F (2018) ARC: Augmented reality for catering. In: 2018 IEEE 8th International Conference on Consumer Electronics—Berlin (ICCE-Berlin). https://doi.org/10.1109/icce-berlin.2018.8576165

Castillo-Villar F, Villasante-Arellano A (2020) Applying the multisensory sculpture technique to explore the role of brand usage on multisensory brand experiences. J Retail Consum Serv 57:102185. https://doi.org/10.1016/j.jretconser.2020.102185

Cheok A, Karunanayaka K (2018a) Discussion and conclusion. Human–Computer Interact Ser:119–124. https://doi.org/10.1007/978-3-319-73864-2_7

Cheok A, Karunanayaka K (2018b) Electric taste. Human–Computer Interact Ser:49–68. https://doi.org/10.1007/978-3-319-73864-2_4

Chianese A, Piccialli F (2016) A smart system to manage the context evolution in the Cultural Heritage domain. Comput Electr Eng 55:27–38. https://doi.org/10.1016/j.compeleceng.2016.02.008

Chylinski M, Heller J, Hilken T et al. (2020) Augmented reality marketing: a technology-enabled approach to situated customer experience. Australas Mark J (AMJ):1–11. https://doi.org/10.1016/j.ausmj.2020.04.004

Cirulis A, Ginters E (2013) Augmented reality in logistics. Procedia Comput Sci 26:14–20. https://doi.org/10.1016/j.procs.2013.12.003

Čopič Pucihar K, Kljun M (2018) ART for Art: Augmented reality taxonomy for art and cultural heritage. In: Geroimenko V (eds) Augmented reality art. Springer series on cultural computing, 73–94. https://doi.org/10.1007/978-3-319-69932-5_3

Debouzy J, Perrin A (2012) RFID. Electromagnetic fields, environment and health, pp 81–87. https://doi.org/10.1007/978-2-8178-0363-0_7

Dobrucka R (2013) The future of active and intelligent packaging industry. LogForum 9:103–110

Ducasse J, Kljun M, Čopič Pucihar K (2019) Playful ambient augmented reality systems to improve people's well-being. In: Geroimenko V (eds) Augmented Reality Games II, Springer, Cham, pp 125–157. https://doi.org/10.1007/978-3-030-15620-6_6

Đurđević S, Novaković D, Kašiković N et al (2018) NFC technology and augmented reality in smart packaging. Int Circ Graph Educ Res 11:52–65

Dutot V (2015) Factors influencing Near Field Communication (NFC) adoption: an extended TAM approach. J High Technol Manag Res 26:45–57. https://doi.org/10.1016/j.hitech.2015.04.005

Eve S (2012) Augmenting phenomenology: using augmented reality to aid archaeological phenomenology in the landscape. J Archaeol Method Theory 19:582–600. https://doi.org/10.1007/s10816-012-9142-7

Fazio F, Herrmann D, Duckworth D (2018) Capturing value from the smart packaging revolution. In: Deloitte Insights. https://www2.deloitte.com/us/en/insights/industry/retail-distribution/smart-packaging-how-to-create-and-capture-value.html. Accessed 19 Sep 2020

Genç R (2017) The impact of augmented reality (AR) technology on tourist satisfaction. Augment Rity Virtual Rity:109–116. https://doi.org/10.1007/978-3-319-64027-3_8

Gheorghiu D, Ştefan L (2019) Invisible settlements: discovering and reconstructing the ancient built Spaces through gaming. In: Geroimenko V (eds) Augmented Reality Games II, pp 83–102. Springer, Cham. https://doi.org/10.1007/978-3-030-15620-6_4

Girardet H (2008) Cities people planet: urban development and climate change, 2nd edn. Wiley, New York

Goshey M (2008) Radio Frequency Identification (RFID). Encyclopedia of GIS:943–949. https://doi.org/10.1007/978-0-387-35973-1_1071

Greer C, Burns M, Wollman D, Griffor E (2019) Cyber-physical systems and internet of things. https://doi.org/10.6028/nist.sp.1900-202

Gregor-Svetec D (2018) Intelligent Packaging. Nanomater Food Packag:203–247. https://doi.org/10.1016/b978-0-323-51271-8.00008-5

Gretzel U, Sigala M, Xiang Z, Koo C (2015) Smart tourism: foundations and developments. Electron Mark 25:179–188. https://doi.org/10.1007/s12525-015-0196-8

Gretzel U, Zhong L, Koo C (2016) Application of smart tourism to cities. Int J Tour Cities. https://doi.org/10.1108/ijtc-04-2016-0007

Gutiérrez M, Vexo F, Thalmann D (2008) Stepping into. Virtual Rity. https://doi.org/10.1007/978-1-84800-117-6

Han D, Jung T (2017) Identifying tourist requirements for mobile AR Tourism applications in urban heritage tourism. Augment Rity Virtual Rity:3–20. https://doi.org/10.1007/978-3-319-640 27-3_1

Han D, Jung T, Gibson A (2013) Dublin AR: implementing Augmented reality in tourism. Inf Commun Technol Tourism 2014:511–523. https://doi.org/10.1007/978-3-319-03973-2_37

Harrison C, Eckman B, Hamilton R et al (2010) Foundations for smarter cities. IBM J Res Dev 54:1–16. https://doi.org/10.1147/jrd.2010.2048257

Harrop P, Das R, Holland G (2020) Near Field Communication (NFC) 2014–2024. In: IDTechEx. http://www.idtechex.com/research/reports/near-field-communication-nfc-2014-2024-000363.asp. Accessed 8 Apr 2020

Hunter W, Chung N, Gretzel U, Koo C (2015) Constructivist research in smart tourism. Asia Pac J Inf Syst 25:105–120. http://dx.doi.org/10.14329/apjis.2015.25.1.105

Jansen M, Beaton P (2020) The best augmented reality apps for android and iOS | digital trends. In: Digital Trends. https://www.digitaltrends.com/mobile/best-augmented-reality-apps/. Accessed 19 Sep 2020

Javornik A (2016) 'It's an illusion, but it looks real!' Consumer affective, cognitive and behavioural responses to augmented reality applications. J Mark Manag 32:987–1011. https://doi.org/10.1080/0267257x.2016.1174726

Jia X, Feng Q, Fan T, Lei Q (2012) RFID technology and its applications in Internet of Things (IoT). In: 2012 2nd international conference on consumer electronics, communications and networks (CECNet). https://doi.org/10.1109/cecnet.2012.6201508

Joo H, Hong B, Kim S (2012) Smart-contents visualization of publishing big data using NFC technology. Commun Comput Inf Sci:118–123. https://doi.org/10.1007/978-3-642-35600-1_17

Joutsela M (2010) Multisensory persuasion and storytelling through packaging design. In: 17th IAPRI World Conference on Packaging, pp 225–229

Jurenka R, Cagáňová D, Horňáková N (2020) The smart logistics. Mobil Internet Things 2018:277–292. https://doi.org/10.1007/978-3-030-30911-4_20

Kasapakis V, Gavalas D, Dzardanova E (2018) Mixed reality. Encycl Comput Graph Games:1–4. https://doi.org/10.1007/978-3-319-08234-9_205-1

Khorov E, Lyakhov A, Krotov A, Guschin A (2015) A survey on IEEE 802.11ah: an enabling networking technology for smart cities. Comput Commun 58:53–69. https://doi.org/10.1016/j.comcom.2014.08.008

Kolb M, Blazek P, Streichsbier C (2014) Food customization: an analysis of product configurators in the food industry. Lect Notes Prod Eng:229–239. https://doi.org/10.1007/978-3-319-04271-8_20

Κωνσταντίνου Π (Konstantinou P) (2020) Η Έξυπνη Συσκευασία ως Ανταγωνιστικό Πλεονέκτημα (Smart Packaging as a Competitive Advantage). allpack hellas 96:36–37. https://www.allpackhellas.gr/arthra/i-exypni-syskeyasia-os-antagonistiko-pleonektima/. Accessed 2 Oct 2020

Κωνσταντίνου Π, Σταθάκης Γ, Νομικός Σ (Konstantinou P, Stathakis G, Nomikos S) (2018) Εφαρμογές Ευφυούς Συσκευασίας για Συστήματα Διαχείρισης Απορριμμάτων (Smart packaging applications for waste management systems). In: 5th conference intelligent packaging new forms of communication, pp 60–68. ISBN 978-618-84016-0-0

Konstantinou P, Nomikos S, Stathakis G (2019) Smart tourism prospects, International Conference on Business & Economics of the Hellenic Open University

Kuswandi B, Wicaksono Y, Jayus et al. (2011) Smart packaging: sensors for monitoring of food quality and safety. Sens Instrum Food Qual Saf 5:137–146. https://doi.org/10.1007/s11694-011-9120-x

Lee C, Kim M, Park J et al. (2010) Development of wireless RFID glove for various applications. Commun Comput Inf Sci:292–298. https://doi.org/10.1007/978-3-642-16444-6_38

Lee L, Kim M, Hwang W (2019) Potential of augmented reality and virtual reality technologies to promote wellbeing in older adults. Appl Sci 9:3556. https://doi.org/10.3390/app9173556

Li H, Si Z (2019) Application of augmented reality in product package with quick response code. Adv Graph Commun, Print Packag:335–342. https://doi.org/10.1007/978-981-13-3663-8_45

Liu T, Wei B (2015) Digital publishing to create "smart tourism". LISS 2014:1733–1738. https://doi.org/10.1007/978-3-662-43871-8_249

Loureiro S, Guerreiro J, Ali F (2020) 20 years of research on virtual reality and augmented reality in tourism context: a text-mining approach. Tour Manag 77:104028. https://doi.org/10.1016/j.tourman.2019.104028

Lovelace B (2016) 'Pokemon Go' now the biggest mobile game in US history. In: CNBC. https://www.cnbc.com/2016/07/13/pokemon-go-now-the-biggest-mobile-game-in-us-history.html. Accessed 3 Oct 2020

Lucio R (2018) Nespresso goes futuristic with chatbots and smart speakers. In: Inside FMCG. https://insidefmcg.com.au/2018/11/26/nespresso-goes-futuristic-with-chatbots-and-smart-speakers/. Accessed 3 Oct 2020

Lydekaityte J (2019) Smart interactive packaging as a cyber-physical agent in the interaction design theory: a novel user interface. Hum-Comput Interact—INTERACT 2019:687–695. https://doi.org/10.1007/978-3-030-29381-9_41

Mahmood A, Butler B, Jennings B (2018) Potential of augmented reality for intelligent transportation systems. Encyclopedia of Computer Graphics and Games:1–7. https://doi.org/10.1007/978-3-319-08234-9_274-1

Majid I, Ahmad Nayik G, Mohammad Dar S, Nanda V (2018) Novel food packaging technologies: innovations and future prospective. J Saudi Soc Agric Sci 17:454–462. https://doi.org/10.1016/j.jssas.2016.11.003

Martins J, Gonçalves R, Branco F et al (2017) A multisensory virtual experience model for thematic tourism: a Port wine tourism application proposal. J Destin Mark & Manag 6:103–109. https://doi.org/10.1016/j.jdmm.2017.02.002

Milovanovic D, Pantovic V, Bojkovic N, Bojkovic Z (2019) Advanced human centric 5G-IoT in a smart city: requirements and challenges. Hum CentEd Comput:285–296. https://doi.org/10.1007/978-3-030-37429-7_28

Mountzouri A, Papapostolou A, Nomikos S (2020) Intelligent packaging as a dynamic marketing tool for tourism. Strat Innov Mark Tour:31–40. https://doi.org/10.1007/978-3-030-36126-6_5

Muguira L, Vazquez J, Arruti A et al. (2009) RFIDGlove: a wearable RFID reader. In: 2009 IEEE international conference on e-Business engineering, pp 475–480. https://doi.org/10.1109/icebe.2009.75

Naik P (2016) Importance of artificial intelligence with their wider application and technologies in present trends. Int J Sci Res Comput Sci, Eng Inf Technol 1:57–65. ISSN: 2456-3307

Nguyen T, Camacho D, Jung J (2016) Identifying and ranking cultural heritage resources on geotagged social media for smart cultural tourism services. Pers Ubiquit Comput 21:267–279. https://doi.org/10.1007/s00779-016-0992-y

Νομικός Σ (Nomikos S) (2008) Νέες Τεχνολογίες Εκτύπωσης - Τυπωμένα Ηλεκτρονικά (New printing technologies—Printed electronics). Tsotras, Athens. ISBN 978–960-92682-1-9

Νομικός Σ (Nomikos S) (2019) Ευφυής Συσκευασία (Intelligent packaging). Tsotras, Athens. ISBN 978-618-5309-62-6

Nomikos S, Kordas A, Mountzouri A et al. (2014) Why RFID will become one of the biggest communicational system in the world? In: 13th flexible & printed electronics conference & exhibition (2014FLEX). Curran Associates, Inc, Phoenix, Arizona, USA, pp 460–472. ISBN 978-1-63439-625-7

Ortiz de Gortari A (2019) Characteristics of game transfer phenomena in location-based augmented reality games. Augment Rity Games I:15–32. https://doi.org/10.1007/978-3-030-15616-9_2

Panagiotakopoulos D (2020) Introducing intelligent ticket's dual role in degraded areas: electronic monitoring of crime and transmedia content presentation to users. In: Leoni G, Mirabile M, La Spina A, Cabras E (eds) Gentrification & crime: new configurations and challenges for the city. BK BOOKS (TU Delft), pp 52–78. ISBN 9789463663229. https://books.bk.tudelft.nl/index.php/press/catalog/book/771

Panagiotakopoulos D, Dimitrantzou K (2020) Intelligent ticket with augmented reality applications for Archaeological sites. Strat Innov Mark Tour:41–49. https://doi.org/10.1007/978-3-030-36126-6_6

Park M, Lim K, Seo M et al (2014) Spatial augmented reality for product appearance design evaluation. J Comput Des Eng 2:38–46. https://doi.org/10.1016/j.jcde.2014.11.004

Perret J, Poorten E (2018) Touching virtual reality: a review of haptic gloves. ACTUATOR

Pesonen J, Horster E (2012) Near field communication technology in tourism. Tour Manag Perspect 4:11–18. https://doi.org/10.1016/j.tmp.2012.04.001

Poghos N (2018) Augmented & virtual reality: experiential marketing tools for the catering industry. In: Medium. https://medium.com/@narpoghos5/augmented-virtual-reality-experiential-marketing-tools-for-the-catering-industry-ab3ca88d8b9. Accessed 19 Sep 2020

Ramakrishnan R, Gaur L (2016) Application of internet of things (IoT) for smart process manufacturing in Indian packaging industry. Adv Intell Syst Comput:339–346. https://doi.org/10.1007/978-81-322-2757-1_34

Roya A, Elham M (2016) Intelligent food packaging: concepts and innovations. Int J ChemTech Res 9:669–676. ISSN: 0974-4290

Schaefer D, Cheung W (2018) Smart packaging: opportunities and challenges. Procedia CIRP 72:1022–1027. https://doi.org/10.1016/j.procir.2018.03.240

Shirowzhan S, Tan W, Sepasgozar S (2020) Digital twin and CyberGIS for improving connectivity and measuring the impact of infrastructure construction planning in smart cities. ISPRS Int J Geo-Inf 9:240. https://doi.org/10.3390/ijgi9040240

Σιάκας Σ (Siakas S) (2018) Το 3d Animation ως Περιεχόμενο Επαυξημένης Πραγματικότητας (Augmented Reality) στην Συσκευασία (3d animation as augmented reality content in packaging). In: 5th conference intelligent packaging new forms of communication, pp 12–19. ISBN 978-618-84016-0-0

Spence C, Obrist M, Velasco C, Ranasinghe N (2017) Digitizing the chemical senses: possibilities & pitfalls. Int J Hum Comput Stud 107:62–74. https://doi.org/10.1016/j.ijhcs.2017.06.003

Sterling B (2011) Augmented reality: Blippar Qwak Smack snack. In: WIRED. https://www.wired.com/2011/08/augmented-reality-blippar-qwak-smack-snack/. Accessed 4 Oct 2020

Thai M, Hoang T, Phan P et al (2020) Soft microtubule muscle-driven 3-axis skin-stretch haptic devices. IEEE Access 8:157878–157891. https://doi.org/10.1109/access.2020.3019842

Thrasher M (2013) McDonald's Australia lets customers find out exactly where their burgers came from. In: Business Insider. https://www.businessinsider.com/mcdonalds-find-your-maccas-app-2013-6. Accessed 4 Oct 2020

Välkkynen P, Boyer A, Urhemaa T, Nieminen R (2011) Mobile augmented reality for retail environments

Vauclair M (2011) NFC. Encyclopedia of cryptography and security 840–842. https://doi.org/10.1007/978-1-4419-5906-5_295

Velasco C, Spence C (2018) Multisensory product packaging: an introduction. MultisensY Packag:1–18. https://doi.org/10.1007/978-3-319-94977-2_1

Vigneshwaran N, Kadam D, Patil S (2019) Nanomaterials for active and Smart packaging of food. Nanosci Sustain Agric:581–600. https://doi.org/10.1007/978-3-319-97852-9_22

Viswanathan S, Rajan R (2020) Digital scent technology—a critical overview. Int J Trend Sci Res Dev (IJTSRD) 4:218–221

Wang J, Erkoyuncu J, Roy R (2018) A conceptual design for smell based augmented reality: case study in maintenance diagnosis. Procedia CIRP 78:109–114. https://doi.org/10.1016/j.procir.2018.09.067

Wang Q, Spence C (2018) Sonic packaging: how packaging sounds influence multisensory product evaluation. MultisensY Packag:103–125. https://doi.org/10.1007/978-3-319-94977-2_5

Wang X, Li X, Zhen F, Zhang J (2016) How smart is your tourist attraction? Measuring tourist preferences of smart tourism attractions via a FCEM-AHP and IPA approach. Tour Manag 54:309–320. https://doi.org/10.1016/j.tourman.2015.12.003

Wei W, Lin Q (2020) Research on intelligent tourism town based on AI technology. J Phys: Conf Ser 1575:012039. https://doi.org/10.1088/1742-6596/1575/1/012039

Widiyanto A, Rifa A (2014) User manual with augmented reality to support packaging products. In: International conference on engineering technology and industrial application, pp 307–310

Yam K, Takhistov P, Miltz J (2005) Intelligent packaging: concepts and applications. J Food Sci 70:R1–R10. https://doi.org/10.1111/j.1365-2621.2005.tb09052.x

Yang L, Martin L, Staiculescu D et al (2008) Conformal magnetic composite RFID for wearable RF and bio-monitoring applications. IEEE Trans Microw Theory Tech 56:3223–3230. https://doi.org/10.1109/tmtt.2008.2006810

Yildirim S, Röcker B, Pettersen M et al (2017) Active packaging applications for food. Compr Rev Food Sci Food Saf 17:165–199. https://doi.org/10.1111/1541-4337.12322

Zaiţi I, Pentiuc Ş (2013) Glove-based input for reusing everyday objects as interfaces in smart environments. Distrib Comput Artif Intell:537–544. https://doi.org/10.1007/978-3-319-00551-5_64

Zhu W, Owen C, Li H, Lee J (2004) Personalized In-store E-Commerce with the PromoPad: an augmented reality shopping assistant. Electron J E-Commer Tools Appl 1:1–19

Chapter 5
The New Normal Tourism in Indonesia: The Expansion of the Wonosari AR Project to Enhance Holiday Experience

Ima Kusumawati Hidayat, Dimas Rifqi Novica, Dwi Nikmah Puspitasari, Denik Ristya Rini, and Khairul Azhar Bin Mat Daud

Abstract This chapter examines the expansion of Wonosari AR, an Augmented Reality (AR) application in Agrowisata Wonosari, Malang, Indonesia. Digital reality applications have been widely used in the tourism industry of developed countries. The advancement of Augmented Reality technology in the tourism field has helped to increase people's interest, however in developing countries, such as Indonesia, these approaches have not yet been used. During the COVID-19 pandemic, most tourist attractions were closed for a few months to prevent the spread of the virus, which caused a reduction in the number of tourists. This chapter comprises the introduction of the research problem, the previous Wonosari AR project, the Wonosari AR project during The New Normal Tourism, and the development of this new application. The authors designed three AR markers in playing cards, face masks, and tea packaging using the design thinking methodology. The combination of three different shapes of the AR marker fitted perfectly to promote future digital tourism. The chapter's discussion explores the prototyping and trial experiences, including the opportunity for future research in the use of AR for agrotourism.

I. K. Hidayat (✉) · D. R. Novica · D. N. Puspitasari · D. R. Rini
Faculty of Letters, Art and Design Department, Universitas Negeri Malang, Malang, Indonesia
e-mail: ima.hidayat.fs@um.ac.id

D. R. Novica
e-mail: dimas.novica.fs@um.ac.id

D. N. Puspitasari
e-mail: dwi.nikmah.fppsi@um.ac.id

D. R. Rini
e-mail: denik.ristya.fs@um.ac.id

D. N. Puspitasari
Faculty of Psychology Education, Universitas Negeri Malang, Malang, Indonesia

K. A. B. M. Daud
Fakulti Teknologi Kreatif Dan Warisan, Universiti Malaysia Kelantan, Kelantan, Malaysia
e-mail: azhar.md@umk.edu.my

© The Author(s), under exclusive license to Springer Nature Switzerland AG 2021
V. Geroimenko (ed.), *Augmented Reality in Tourism, Museums and Heritage*, Springer Series on Cultural Computing,
https://doi.org/10.1007/978-3-030-70198-7_5

5.1   Introduction

For most of 2020, people across the world were involved in the fight against COVID-19. The virus, most likely, started in China at the end of 2019 and was known as "Wuhan pneumonia." The virus, which is closely linked to the MERS-CoV and SARS (Severe Acute Respiratory Syndrome) viruses, then spread exponentially worldwide. During this difficult time, the Indonesian government encouraged the whole community to participate in preventing transmission of the virus with the Stay-at-Home rules. Schools, universities, malls, airports, and many public spaces were forced to temporarily close. As a result, the number of tourists arriving at tourist destinations dropped significantly. Some venues were forced to close permanently because the owner could not afford to pay the monthly bills. Many countries in the world banned local and international travel, which caused economic devastation. Both developed and developing countries have been, and continue to be, adversely affected by COVID-19 and the resulting financial crisis.

Nevertheless, during July–August 2020, governments and doctors worldwide introduced the term 'New Normal'. It was originally a term to mark the situation after the economic and business crisis in 2007–2008, but in 2020 it became to mean the new healthy daily life routine for humans. The return of regular tourism activity during the pandemic was called The New Normal Tourism (TNNT). The difference between the "before Corona" tourism and TNNT are new health protocols, namely, wearing a mask, washing/sanitizing your hands, social distancing, and restricting visitor numbers. It is hoped that this will significantly help to return tourism activity to normal conditions; thus, these small changes could make a huge contribution. It is expected that if tourists obey the health regulations in public spaces, the tourism industry will slowly return to its previous levels (Yeh 2020).

As one of the countries that relied on tourism as a major source of its income, Indonesia encountered a huge problem during the pandemic. For example, on Bali, the island of gods, the tourism sector has been struggling to survive because of the international travel restrictions. Although Bali has already reopened its landmarks for local travellers to help its tourism industry, the mounting number of Coronavirus patients in Indonesia greatly reduces the local tourist market as many Indonesians continue to stay at home. Several attempts have been made to preserve businesses, but the inconsistent rules during the pandemic have caused businesses to flag (Gössling et al. 2020). Wonosari Agrotourism in Malang, one of the natural tourist attractions, was also affected by travel restrictions. It closed to tourism during the pandemic but continues to maintain its tea production. The problem during the COVID-19 era is that not only is Wonosari Agrotourism facing a major reduction in the number of tourists, but it is also facing significant export/import trading issues due to the International lockdown.

Many tourist destinations offer different promotional approaches to attract business with price reductions or offering "bundle" packages. We found that Wonosari Agrotourism has not explored this opportunity and so we proposed an upscaling digital promotion through Augmented Reality (AR) because of its novel technology.

We believed that AR could contribute to promoting agrotourism as people would be able to experience virtual immersion in two realms, the digital world and the real world (Azuma 1997). In tea plantations like Wonosari Agrotourism, adding virtual elements could enhance the tourism experience. As a consequence, this initiative could lead to new forms of interaction and social dynamics. Furthermore, AR technology is relatively new in Indonesia and could be pioneering for other tourism areas.

5.2 Augmented Reality in Tourism

In the European Union, digital media applications in tourism began to be developed primarily when governments provided financial assistance to develop this research in 2018 (Interreg Europe 2019). The motivation was so that digital tourism in the European Union was not inferior to that in the United States. As the name suggests, Digitourism means applying digital elements to tourist attractions in the form of Augmented Reality (AR) or Virtual Reality (VR), both of which can be involved in various ways. Given that AR and VR have been widely used in education (Akçayır and Akçayır 2016), these studies examine how AR can be adapted as promotional tools in tourism. The implementation of digital reality in tourism is considered as new and understudied (Levski 2019; Tsai 2019). The use of AR in tourism is escalating due to the consideration of modern marketing (Kounavis et al. 2012). Therefore, the novelty of AR technology could potentially attract tourist's attention rapidly (Reichstein and Härting 2018). AR can generally be defined as enhancing real-world environments using computer-generated image layers through a device (Guttentag 2010; Jung et al. 2015). Guttentag (2010) argues that AR is a type of VR because these two digital realities are interrelated, and it is valid to consider both concepts simultaneously. According to Milgram et al. (1994), AR and VR should be viewed as distinct in the one end consists only of real-world objects, and the other end consists only of synthetic or computer-generated objects. In AR, most of what the user sees is still the real world, whereas, with VR, the user is completely immersed in the virtual environment. Recent advances in smartphone digital realities have led to the development and enhancement of AR applications in tourism (Cranmer et al. 2016), where mobile devices' geolocation capabilities translate well to provide users with context-sensitive information on their surroundings (Scholz and Smith 2015). Despite the many benefits of digital realities for the tourism industry, research and literature on AR in the context of tourism remains limited (Tausova 2016).

Indonesia, a large country with many natural and manmade tourist attractions, has also tried to integrate AR technology into tourist activities, such as AR in Jatim Park 1 Batu, Malang; Rumah Pintar, Yogyakarta; and Taman Mini Indonesia Indah, Jakarta. Several Indonesian scholars have designed AR-based media to be applied to cultural tourism sites, such as temples. The problems that underline the design of AR media in tourist attractions are almost the same, namely how the user responds to these new media innovations. The results showed a positive trend in increasing user curiosity about objects that appear in augmented reality. AR looks like a promising technological development in Indonesia. Most Indonesians are still unfamiliar with AR technology, which presents an excellent opportunity to take advantage of it.

5.3 The Previous Wonosari AR Project

Wonosari AR is a project partnership between lecturers from Universitas Negeri Malang (UM), Universiti Malaysia Kelantan, and Agrowisata Wonosari Tea Plantation. The idea originated from a study about the lack of using new digital media in tourism promotion in Malang, Indonesia. With the aim of promoting neglected tourism areas, the media has been addressed to be the novel AR agrotourism project in Indonesia (Hidayat et al. 2019). To achieve this goal, the research team did an in-depth interview with agrotourism management and AR experts to determine the user requirements. We adopted Borg and Gall's ten stages in the design process (Gall et al. 2003), namely, (1) research and information collecting, (2) planning, (3) development of an initial product, (4) preliminary field testing, (5) preliminary product revision, (6) primary field testing, (7) primary revision of the product, (8) functional field testing, (9) final product revision, and (10) dissemination and implementation. The aim of the project was to develop a mobile AR application to enhance the experience for the tourists.

The application offers information about ten landmarks in Agrowisata Wonosari using ten cards, called Interactive Holographic Augmented Reality Cards (IHARC), to navigate 3D AR objects. The ten landmarks are Wonosari Park, Wonosari Tea House, Wonosari Tea Factory, Wonosari Villa, Wonosari Playground, Wonosari Joglo Live Music, Wonosari Outbound, Wonosari Bridge, Wonosari Swimming Pool, and Wonosari Tea Plantation. The packaging is a map of the Wonosari Tea Plantation with a distribution of the 10 landmarks provided on the cards. The 3D modelling that pops up is provided with animation and sound effects to enhance the tourists' experience. Figure 5.1 shows the first design of IHARC with colourful backgrounds and a large number behind each object. From the preliminary testing (stage 4) with the experts, we concluded that the large number overshadowed the landmark pictures. The choice of background colour also was an issue. Furthermore, we did stage 5, the preliminary revision, and continued to stage 6–7 for primary testing and revision. Figure 5.2 shows the result from stage 7, which was the final IHARC design. The new playing cards inspired the design style with a fantasy sky background and smaller numbers than the initial design.

5.4 The New Normal Tourism Wonosari AR Project

During the pandemic, Wonosari tea production was relatively good. However, the number of Wonosari tea sales decreased significantly, because 70% of tea production

Fig. 5.1 The first IHARC design

Fig. 5.2 The second IHARC design with the tourism information behind

was usually exported to various countries in Europe and Asia. The management of the Wonosari Tea Plantation had never promoted its products on social media because their target market was exporters. Due to the global pandemic, the management was trying to find other tea buyers by sending tea samples to Indonesia's target markets because the local Wonosari tea markets were somewhat limited. Therefore, in relation to tea sales, the management needed to consider a new marketing approach.

When the World Travel & Tourism Council (WTTC) issued a protocol called The New Normal Tourism (TNNT) for the reopening of tourist attractions in various parts of the world, the Indonesian Ministry of Tourism and Creative Economy obeyed the TNNT measures by focusing on proper hygiene in public spaces, such as the cleanliness of common facilities, to tourism safety. Focusing on tourism during TNNT, the Indonesian government enforced the measures to all tourist destinations. Once the regulations were ready, Agrowisata Wonosari reopened in August 2020 with restrictions. We were permitted to continue our research during the pandemic, adjusting to the current situation. A series of AR markers were proposed in which Agrowisata Wonosari's management, designers, and researchers were co-designing the end product.

5.5   The Development of Three Wonosari AR Packages

The content of the new project was adapted to the pandemic condition that required the use of face masks and adhered to health protocols. We applied design thinking methodology in this design process, which had been through the "Empathize" stage in our previous research. More precisely, we "Define" the problem in Agrowisata Wonosari during the Covid-19 outbreak and followed with "Ideate" the Forum Group Discussion (FGD) session to answer all the questions during the pre-production design process. This phase was challenging, especially for the Agrowisata Wonosari management. They did not have a creative background and seemingly only wanted the designer to be the decision-maker. We asked them to use their smartphones to search for inspiration and new ideas while the designer guided them to broaden their views. The results of this stage were quite impressive. The series of new Wonosari AR markers were IHARC cards, face masks, and tea packaging.

We continued the "Prototyping" stage with the designer and research team. Instead of maintaining the same mobile application and IHARC design, we redesigned all the products due to the FGD outcome. The visual complexity and the similar colour gradation of the IHARC complicated the AR programming phase. Some cards projected the wrong AR object while the application did not support the iOS system. We simplified the former IHARC card's design with a new icon design style. The evaluation from previous beta testing showed that the AR object picture in the former IHARC reduced the user curiosity. We used Blender, Adobe Illustrator, Corel Draw, and Unity to produce these products, which were the same tools we used in the previous research. Figure 5.3 shows the IHARC's design transformation to gain the end-user appeal towards the AR technology. Meanwhile, the Wonosari mobile application's User Interface (UI) transition is shown in Fig. 5.4. The more dynamic UI in the novel design reduces the end-user's confusion, especially for the first-time AR user.

We designed the second marker, a face mask, with the intention of selling it at the ticket sales counter. This product aimed to increase Agrowisata Wonosari's income and support the mandatory use of a face mask to tourists in a fun way. This

Fig. 5.3 The transformation of IHARC for the AR marker

Fig. 5.4 The transformation of Wonosari AR mobile application's User Interface

is a wearable AR-based item for tourists, where technology becomes part of human activity (Tussyadiah et al. 2018). In creating the face mask project, we used the pattern of the tea leaf on one side to highlight its figure and to make it easier for the end-user to scan the AR object (Fig. 5.5). When the user scans the mask with the tea leaf pattern, a simple tea leaf and a flower animation will appear. In addition, the user could also add a frame to the screen, take a picture, and share it on their social media accounts. Another advantage of the Wonosari AR Mask is that it can be a souvenir for Agrowisata Wonosari, as this destination hasn't produced souvenirs before.

The third marker we developed was tea packaging for Agrowisata Wonosari. In the beginning, we intended to apply the AR technology to the packaging for Rollaas Tea (a well-known tea product from Agrowisata Wonosari, which is widely sold in supermarkets), but the Agrowisata Wonosari's management suggested using their

Fig. 5.5 The design of the Wonosari AR face mask and the AR visual from the application

brand-new product, Santoon Black Tea, as an AR marker. Santoon Black Tea is a limited product that initially was not for sale at the Agrowisata Wonosari's ticket entrance. Their intention was to acquaint the market to the new tea brand, instead of further promoting the already famous tea. We decided to implement four main health measures to the packaging, wear a mask, sanitize your hands, social distancing, and prevent crowding. To simplify the AR design complexity, like the IHARC card, we decided to mix 2D and 3D elements in this AR design. When the users scanned the tea packaging, they could see four buttons with health information inside. The four images are 2D computer graphics (see Fig. 5.6), but the tea leaf frame gives a 3D impression.

5.6 Results and Discussion

As a consequence of the COVID-19 pandemic, several obstacles hindered our project. First, during our two-year collaboration with the management of Agrowisata Wonosari, they unexpectedly substituted the person who helped us during the research. We had to introduce our concept again, since this person had not followed our initial research. Second, some unpredictable COVID-19 regulations changed repeatedly. Despite these setbacks, we managed to conduct the online part of the research. People (target audience) were willing to learn online meeting applications like Zoom or online surveys like Google Form because they did not have any other options. Almost 80% of our research activities shifted to the online mode.

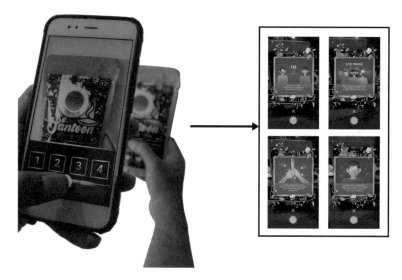

Fig. 5.6 Health protocol through AR in Santoon Black Tea's packaging

The first Wonosari AR maker, the novel IHARC card called Wonosari AR Card, was 6.35 × 8.89 cm and we used 150-g art paper. We applied the ergonomics principle (Elam 2017) according to which a product should be in proper proportion with the user's body. Our goal was to produce the Wonosari AR Card in a size suitable for adults and children (Fig. 5.7), as most of the tourists visiting Agrowisata Wonosari are families. The markers were differently coloured cards that represent ten landmarks at

Fig. 5.7 One group (G1) of father and son who tried Wonosari AR Card

Agrowisata Wonosari. Our sample testing consisted of five parents and children (age 4–7 years old). Three groups consisted of smartphone daily users (G1, G2, G3), while two groups (G4, G5) were non-daily users of smartphones. We explained how the programme worked and what was required for the mobile application. Every group had one and a half hours to explore the agrotourism site, and they were asked to save and upload the pictures of 10 landmarks from their smartphone. After a specific time, four groups (G1, G2, G3, G5) finished the task on time, whereas one group (G4) experienced difficulties to complete the mission because this was their first visit to Agrowisata Wonosari. Two other groups (G2 and G3) revealed that they worked together exploring the agrotourism site because they were also first-time visitors. The session's winner (G1) informed us that they had visited Agrowisata Wonosari before.

In terms of the Wonosari AR application's UI and UX, all the groups stated that the mobile application was easy to use. Compared to the non-daily users (G4 and G5), the smartphone daily users (G1, G2, G3) captured the 3D objects of ten landmarks more precisely (Fig. 5.8). All the groups could automatically save the pictures on their phones and upload them to their social media accounts, e.g., Instagram and Facebook, and also share the pictures with their friends via WhatsApp. However, one major issue in this trial was the poor Internet signal at Agrowisata Wonosari. Some groups had signal trouble during the task, especially when they wanted to share their picture in the Wonosari Pool, Wonosari Tea Factory, and Wonosari Tea House location.

The second marker we created for the Wonosari AR application, was the Wonosari Mask, which used polyester for the fabric and a Direct to Garment (DTG) printer to apply the ink. We decided to make a "scuba mask" using the DTG method for the

Fig. 5.8 The picture results from the sample groups

Wonosari Mask because the production time was relatively short and it provided high-quality results, even if the ink was not entirely absorbed into the fabric. During the mass production, the Indonesian government published a new regulation prohibiting the use of the "scuba mask". According to the regulations, the scuba mask's filtration capability was too low, with effectiveness of only around 5%. Also, the World Health Organization (WHO) claimed that people should wear three-ply-masks for better breathability, which also makes the filtration process more effective. We resolved this problem by continuing with our prototype production while planning for other options.

During the grand reopening of TNNT at Agrowisata Wonosari, the people who lived near the agrotourism site were selling masks with the tea plantation logo. It was a hand-made cloth mask with the Agrowisata Wonosari logo embroidered onto it. The masks were inexpensive and available in red, orange, and light brown, which often did not match with the embroidery's colour combination (for example, a red logo on orange fabric). According to the Agrowisata Wonosari management, these were not official products, it was a home-based-production business. We continued to introduce Wonosari Masks to the tourists and the mask sellers. The intention was not to generate competition between the masks; instead, we wanted to collaborate with them to expand our network. In fact, tourists wanted to buy both the Wonosari Masks and the hand-made masks because they believed that both were Agrowisata Wonosari souvenirs.

The third marker we created was for the Santoon Black Tea's packaging. The idea was to apply four basic health measures to the Agrowisata Wonosari tea product packaging. Instead of the usual information printed on paper, we implemented it as an AR application. There were three types of Santoon Black Tea packaging based on the net weight: 40 g, 80 g, and 120 g. All tea types had the same design packaging. For the smallest package, the management sells the product for Rp 5.000,—which seemed to be very affordable. The ticket itself was Rp 15.000,—on weekdays and Rp 20.000—at the weekend. Unfortunately, during the grand reopening of TNNT at Agrowisata Wonosari, the management only sold twenty packs of the tea because the packaging was very new and only a few tourists recognized the product.

We conducted two types of data sampling for the Wonosari Tea AR packaging. First, we performed a random sample at Agrowisata Wonosari. We interviewed five tourists with four questions to investigate their perception of AR technology: (1) What do you think about implementing AR in food packaging? (2) Will you buy a product because it has AR on it? (3) What do you like in this project? (4) What would you advise us for our next project in AR for tourism? The results of the four questions can be summarized as follows. The answers of the first two questions were similar. They were fascinated with the health protocol shown on their smartphone. All the tourists wanted to buy the product because of its price and its AR health protocol. Some tourists assumed that AR was only for children, just like cartoons and games. We explained that people might not be aware that Instagram's photo filter is an example of AR. The tourists particularly liked a new positive experience. Answering the third and fourth questions, the tourists stated that they believed that adding more information and animations about agrotourism would add to the value of the Wonosari App.

5.7   Conclusion

It can be summarized that the expansion of the Wonosari AR application could engage tourists to adhere to The New Normal Tourism regulations. Deriving from stage 7 of our research methodology (primary revision of the product), we unified the design analysis from designers, researchers, and stakeholders to continue to stage 8–10, functional field testing, final product revision, and dissemination and implementation, respectively. We used design thinking methodology throughout the design process. Firstly, this study has shown that tourists enjoy trying new digital media even if they have to learn the technology from the beginning. Most tourists were unaware that AR has been around for years. The tourists most appreciated the Wonosari AR Card because it allowed them to explore agrotourism while experimenting with AR. Secondly, our project has demonstrated that the implementation of AR in agrotourism has potential. AR has passed the hype stage and could now be implemented for practical purposes (Han et al. 2012). The augmented reality technology is able to enhance the holiday experience   and help the tourist destination maintain their business.

With respect to preserving the existence of agrotourism, this study has produced some recommendations for future research. Designing more entertaining and amusing AR applications could be an easy solution. Therefore, we suggest that tourists' participation, including their critical thinking during the design process, could help to deliver a well-designed product. Also, further research is needed to measure the effectiveness of visual aesthetics and to explore the potential of including games in AR applications for agrotourism.

Acknowledgements This activity has received funding from PNBP Universitas Negeri Malang, Indonesia and a collaboration research with Universiti Malaysia Kelantan and Agrowisata Wonosari Malang, Indonesia.

References

Akçayır M, Akçayır G (2016) Advantages and challenges associated with augmented reality for education: a systematic review of the literature. Educ Res Rev. https://doi.org/10.1016/j.edurev.2016.11.002

Azuma RT (1997) A survey of augmented reality. Presence: Teleoperators Virtual Environ 6(4):355–385

Cranmer E, Jung T, Miller A (2016) Implementing augmented reality to increase tourist attraction sustainability. Persperctive on Business Realities of AR and VR Conference, 27 April 2016, Dublin.

Elam L (2017) Ergonomic guidelines for designing handheld products: a case study of hand-held vacuum cleaners. KTH Royal Institute of Technology, Stockholm

Gall MD, Gall JP, Bord WR (2003) Educational research, 7th edn. Allyn and Bacon, Boston, MA

Gössling S, Scott D, Hall CM (2020) Pandemics, tourism and global change: a rapid assessment of COVID-19. J Sustain Tour 29(1):1–20. https://doi.org/10.1080/09669582.2020.1758708

Guttentag DA (2010) Virtual reality: applications and implications for tourism. Tour Manag 31(5):637–651. https://doi.org/10.1016/j.tourman.2009.07.003

Han D, Jung T, Gibson A (2012) Information and communication technologies in tourism. Inf Commun Technol Tour: 511–523. https://doi.org/10.1007/978-3-7091-7596-5

Hidayat IK, Rini DR, Novica DR, Daud KABM (2019) Implementing augmented reality and gamification in tourism. Int J Technol Manag Inf Syst 1(1):37–42

Interreg Europe (2019) Digitourism

Jung T, Chung N, Leue MC (2015) The determinants of recommendations to use augmented reality technologies: the case of a Korean theme park. Tour Manag 49:75–86. https://doi.org/10.1016/j.tourman.2015.02.013

Kounavis CD, Kasimati AE, Zamani ED (2012) Enhancing the tourism experience through mobile augmented reality: challenges and prospects. Int J Eng Bus Manag 4(1):1–6. https://doi.org/10.5772/51644

Levski Y (2019) Markerless vs. marker based augmented reality. https://appreal-vr.com/blog/markerless-vs-marker-based-augmented-reality. Accessed 25 August 2020

Milgram P, Takemura H, Utsumi A, Kishino F (1994) Augmented reality: a class of displays on the reality-virtuality continuum. Telemanipulator Telepresence Technol 2351:282–292

Reichstein C, Härting R (2018) Potentials of changing customer needs in a digital world—a conceptual model and recommendations for action in tourism. Procedia Comput Sci 126:1484–1494. https://doi.org/10.1016/j.procs.2018.08.120

Scholz J, Smith AN (2015) Augmented reality: designing immersive experiences that maximize consumer engagement. Bus Horiz. https://doi.org/10.1016/j.bushor.2015.10.003

Tausova M (2016) Information and communication technologies in tourism of Slovakia. 15th International Multidisciplinary Scientific GeoConference SGEM2015, www.sgem.org, SGEM2015 Conference Proceeding, book 2 vol 1, pp 131–138. https://doi.org/10.5593/sgem2015/b21/s7.018

Tsai S (2019) Augmented reality enhancing place satisfaction for heritage tourism marketing. Curr Issues Tour 23(9):1–6. https://doi.org/10.1080/13683500.2019.1598950

Tussyadiah IP, Jung TH, Tom Dieck MC (2018) Embodiment of wearable augmented reality technology in tourism experiences. J Travel Res 57(5):597–611. https://doi.org/10.1177/0047287517709090

Yeh S (2020) Tourism recovery strategy against COVID-19 pandemic. Tour Recreat Res: 1–7. https://doi.org/10.1080/02508281.2020.1805933

Chapter 6
Augmented Reality in Spain: Heritage Education, Cultural Tourism and Museums

Pilar Rivero, Silvia García-Ceballos, Borja Aso, and Iñaki Navarro-Neri

Abstract This chapter analyses how Spanish institutions, archaeological sites and publishers in the field of formal education are using Augmented Reality (AR) as an educational tool. After a decade since its arrival in the cultural world of Spain, augmented reality has undergone a process of implementation and settlement characterized by being in the background of activities, exhibitions and by apps with such short life cycles that only a few specific studies have been conducted. The use of AR in some Roman sites in Spain, the Sorolla museum in Madrid and the Alhambra in Granada are examples that are analysed in this chapter based on significant educational theories within the field of Heritage Education.

6.1 Introduction

The emergence and consolidation of the digital society in the twenty-first century has meant that the daily lives of citizens and institutions of any kind have been dominated by the systematic use of new technology.

Education, cultural tourism and museum spaces are not alien to the development of contemporary society, so they have turned to technology to generate new proposals adapted to a public accustomed to using mobile devices in their daily routines. In the case of education, this involves taking a new look at the teaching and learning processes, new possibilities to promote interest among students who

P. Rivero (✉) · S. García-Ceballos · B. Aso · I. Navarro-Neri
University Institute for Research in Environmental Sciences of Aragón (IUCA), University of Zaragoza, Zaragoza, Spain
e-mail: privero@unizar.es

S. García-Ceballos
e-mail: sgceballos@unizar.es

B. Aso
e-mail: basom@unizar.es

I. Navarro-Neri
e-mail: inakinavarro@unizar.es

are digital natives communicating with peers and with the world through screens. Augmented reality (AR) fosters active participation in learning and students can become intellectually, creatively, emotionally, socially and physically involved in the process (Ibáñez-Etxeberria et al. 2010). Cultural tourism has not been oblivious to the extraordinary development of Industry 4.0, and has found in it new tools and ways of interacting with the visitor in order to enhance and enrich the attractiveness of heritage sites and increase the market of potential visitors (Bernad 2020). This has meant that more and more tourist places are incorporating AR and virtual reality (VR) experiences in their cultural offer; although it is true that they continue to be a minority and the implementation of this type of technology is still in an initial phase.

During the last decade museums (as well as tourism at-large) have undergone an unprecedented technological revolution that, with greater or lesser success, has allowed them to acquire new resources through which they can extend their cultural content to a greater number of users through attractive and didactic experiences (Ruiz and Bellido 2014). The origins of the implementation of the digital world in museum spaces date back to the mid-1990s with the appearance of the World Wide Web and the creation of the first Web pages (Kargas et al. 2020). This first phase was followed by a second one characterized by the proliferation of social networks 2.0, digital tools used by museums to connect with their audience, without geographical barriers, and, in most cases, without cost. Kargas et al. (2020, p. 118) define the use of social networks by these spaces as "an alternative, faster, low cost and direct (user friendly) way to share content, to announce events and to extend 'potential' visitors' pool". Social networks, in addition to many other applications and digital environments, were favoured by the systematic use of smart mobile devices by the population (Luna et al. 2019). Parallel to the use of social networks by museums, over the last decade, two technologies have been developed (VR and AR), which represent a clear enrichment of the traditional visit to the museum's physical space and, therefore, improve the quality of the learning experience in visitors, participants or users (McGovern et al. 2019).

Among the various types of existing technology, AR is gaining strength within the museum field, although it is true that its use is limited to a small number of museums. Ruiz and Bellido (2014) point out that museums are not creating virtual spaces parallel to physical museums, but rather a virtual enrichment of real spaces is taking place, providing them with accessible digital content through applications and capable electronic devices to access AR. The use of this avant-garde technology allows the generation of new mediations between the visitor and the heritage asset, new forms of interaction and/or reconstruction of the spaces that are a plus to the traditional visit and mediation. Generally, to read these new languages, it is necessary to have only a smartphone, tablet or AR glasses, devices that are economically affordable for a large part of the population, which does not imply, however, that there are certain sectors that continue to be excluded because of the digital divide.

6.2 Research Areas

As Kargas et al. (2020) indicate, current research on virtual and augmented reality has been motivated by the first works published in this field, such as the analysis of interactive technologies in museums (Sparacino et al. 2000) or interactive exhibits using screens with augmented reality (Brown et al. 2003; Bowers et al. 2007). Later studies focus on the comparison between three close technologies: virtual reality, augmented reality and Web3D (Sylaiou et al. 2009; Santamaría and Mendoza 2014) and the development and application of augmented reality in archaeological sites (Angelopoulou et al. 2011; Esclapés et al. 2014; Gutierrez et al. 2015). Current research focuses on the evaluation of heritage education in virtual environments and augmented reality (Kortabitarte et al. 2017; Ibáñez-Etxeberria et al. 2010), and the analysis of the strengths and operational weaknesses of virtual and augmented reality in the field of museums (Loumos et al. 2018).

In 2020, museums continue their digitization and dissemination process based on three fundamental pillars: virtual reality, augmented reality and social networks. These three pillars are an insight into the interest of museums in meeting some of the objectives established in article 14 of the Faro Convention (Council of Europe 2005) regarding the use of digital technology to improve access to cultural heritage and some of the goals included in the Sustainable Development Goals adopted by the UN General Assembly as a plan of action in the 2030 agenda (UNESCO 2015; UNESCO et al. 2015). The current research aims to respond to these documents, focused on the appreciation of cultural diversity and on redoubling efforts to protect and safeguard the world's cultural and natural heritage.

This chapter analyses the implementation of AR and VR in cultural institutions that host heritage of diverse nature, from which unique practices and experiences that implement AR as an educational tool are collected.

6.3 Augmented Reality in Heritage, Tourism and Education

Heritage education can contribute in various ways to achieving a true awareness of people towards the cultural legacy. Currently, the relational method (Fontal et al. 2015), based on the links between people and assets (Fontal 2003, 2013) is one of the most valued for achieving quality meaningful experiences based on understanding and appreciation of the cultural legacy. In a certain sense, the intensity of the experiences, the emotions and the experience that we have with the patrimonial asset, will determine our link with it and, therefore, reinforce that relationship of understanding, valuation, care and transmission. The trigger in these relationships will predominantly occur through two lines of action, which respond to the main channels of approach of society to heritage environments: Education and Tourism—the fundamental pillars of this study.

The emergence of both tourism and education, as far as heritage is concerned, are almost a simile, since both tourism—a set of human interactions, a social and cultural phenomenon (Department of Economic and Social Affairs 2010)—and education—a social institution that develops the intellectual, moral and affective capacity of people in accordance with the culture and the rules of coexistence (Durkheim 1975; Sarramona 2000)—are the fundamental pillars for the achievement of the primary objective of heritage education and social awareness. Both forms of approach to heritage presuppose a social starting point based on the search for knowledge and enjoyment, which increasingly demands authenticity in experiences (Perea-Medina et al. 2018). For this reason, the context that is analysed in this chapter is a non-formal educative scenario, in particular apps with augmented reality related to tourism and the dissemination of heritage spaces to ascertain the extent to which experiences are enriched by their implementation in the visits. Not only are apps specifically aimed at the school public being studied, but they are also designed to expand cultural experiences, so that they can serve as an interactive complement or accompaniment to the visit, either individually or collectively, and for all ages.

Heritage education, in its most virtual and digitized aspect, turns its teaching–learning strategies towards a more real, subjective experience of heritage, enabling a greater approximation of the legacy to society. This experience is becoming increasingly important due to the incorporation of new technologies (Ibáñez-Etxeberria et al. 2018). A recent study by Ibáñez-Etxeberria et al. (2020) highlights the potentialities of the use of AR and VR in the teaching of heritage, pointing to this as one of the greatest impacts in mediation of assets. However, depending on the categories of heritage with which we are going to work, this potential will have more or less power and a surprising capacity linked to other social factors, such as the desire to know what the past was like. This is closely linked to archaeological heritage, and thus presents a large number of virtual educational initiatives. The archaeological remains and places linked to memory set us a strong challenge, since it implies an arduous task of reconstruction and cognitive interpretation of spaces by the visitor. A pathway of immersion into the spaces of the past is favoured. This enriches the experience and is the key to raising awareness. Archaeological heritage gives us more information about our past but requires a great effort of imagination for those who contemplate it, a practice that, when accompanied by AR or VR, can provide us with a more complete experience of the visit. AR allows us to enlarge the visible part of a vestige (Chang et al. 2014) or to show an entire context around a heritage element (Petrucco and Agostini 2016; Zhang et al. 2018). Likewise, its implementation can include a virtual guide to accompany us during the visit (Chatzidimitris et al. 2013), provide us with information superimposed in the context such as data, anecdotes or video recreations about places of interest (Furata et al. 2012), or propose an interactive game in which the virtual and the real overlap (Angelopoulou et al. 2011; Perra et al. 2019).

All these possibilities are an asset applicable to tourism, since at present it is also committed to an experiential and emotional tourism applying the same relational theoretical approach (Pérez-Martínez and Motis Dolader 2018). The promotion of heritage is increasingly based on the integration of narratives and the use of story-telling to move and captivate, as well as to awaken emotions in the visitor, providing a turn in tourism policy to maintain the "fascination for the past", legacy and memory (2018, p. 389). Some authors, such as Vinuesa and Torralba (2018), even speak of a dialectical relationship between territory, heritage and tourism. AR is established in tourism as a platform that provides new opportunities for the development of the sector, again, predominantly focused on virtual tours, preferably of historical places and their promotion. However, common limitations in both sectors are highlighted: arduous, slow and expensive processes of development of both manual and software (Templin and Popielarczyk 2020). Various studies agree that this new technology allows us to digitally preserve culture and favour sustainable development through the promotion of respect and care for heritage (González-Rodríguez et al. 2020; Little et al. 2020; Lv et al. 2020; Templin and Popielarczyk 2020). In addition, they speak of this technology as an asset for attracting tourism, as well as a more comprehensive and sensory learning experience with the integration of multifaceted information that is capable of providing data for a greater understanding of the space or for recreating events and places (Graziano and Privitera 2020).

Whether as a tourist asset or as an educational axis, museums and heritage spaces are at the forefront of new technologies. All these possibilities can be put into practice in situ or through virtual museums, although at the moment the latter is most used (Ibáñez-Etxeberría et al. 2020). This new way of approaching heritage without damaging or polluting it (Chang et al. 2014) allows us to increase motivation, interaction and knowledge of our cultural heritage. However, the integration of AR in culture is proving to be a slow and gradual process of progressive implementations. Each of the new AR applications implies high cost and laborious development to achieve the "magic" combination of the real space and the superposition of digital objects. In the tourism sector, the way of financing may be more pronounced through public–private partnerships, which promote tourism and guarantee the preservation and restoration of cultural assets (Medvedeva et al. 2018). So far, the search for AR-based heritage projects leads us to the conclusion that a high percentage is allocated to the documentation, reconstruction, restoration and dissemination of heritage. However, this gradual increase in AR-related education and tourism provides us with some unique and remarkable initiatives.

6.4 Emerging Practices: Spanish Institutions Committed to AR

The research group ARGOS, dedicated to the didactics of social sciences, is carrying out a continuous task of locating exemplary practices related to virtual environments, edu-communication in network and cutting-edge technologies. Hence, in this chapter, we seek to highlight some institutions that implement AR from their non-formal spaces and influence any of the axes addressed, be it tourism or heritage education.

Among the institutions studied, we found some museums that implement apps with AR to promote a more comprehensive and experiential experience of the visit, as is the case of the Carlos V Museum located in the town of Mojados (Castile and Leon), the first museum in Spain dedicated exclusively to the figure of King Charles V. The museum offers its visitors a free app for mobile devices, which is divided into two types of activities: a question-and-answer game type quiz where the visitor must answer questions about the monarch Carlos V. An AR tool provides access to different images and texts that allow the information received during the visit to be expanded (see Fig. 6.1). QR codes are represented in the form of different shields and these must be scanned with the rear camera of visitors' electronic devices.

Apps are at the forefront of attracting tourists to promote heritage and this is the case in the town of Fuendetodos (Zaragoza), which has its own app to promote the heritage of the area. The app is divided into two sections. The first section consists of a series of challenges to be met through gamification to obtain rewards; challenges related to different activities that can be carried out by visiting the municipality. The second section is dedicated to the various cultural itineraries that can be found in the town by visiting different points of interest during a town tour. It offers QR codes to access different AR content, for example, the painter Francisco de Goya's workshop

Fig. 6.1 A visitor using the app "Museo Carlos V" (Courtesy of Museo Carlos V. https://www.museocarlosv.es/es/interactua-aprende/juego-app-movil)

Fig. 6.2 Promotional image of the app "Fuendetodos" (Courtesy of Heraldo de Aragón. https://www.heraldo.es/noticias/aragon/zaragoza/2018/05/22/una-app-realidad-aumentada-invita-fotogr afiarse-con-goya-recrear-sus-caprichos-1245305-2261126.html)

(see Fig. 6.2). Finally, AR allows children to recreate in three-dimensioned colouring cards based on the works of Francisco de Goya.

Similarly, the town of Alcalá de Henares (Madrid) offers an app for visitors to access a virtual guide by scanning the codes of different points of interest. The AR-based impersonation of "Cardenal Cisneros" acts as a tourist guide offering explanations about the place (see Fig. 6.3). Finally, the app also allows visitors to take a selfie with a 3D reproduction of the character to share the image on Social Media Networks.

As we have mentioned previously, archaeological sites are one of the most profuse categories in the implementation of AR. This is the case of the "Open Air Museum Villa romana de l'Albir" in l'Alfàs del Pi (Alicante), where the Virtual Heritage team of the University of Alicante and the City Council of l'Alfàs del Pi have developed an app available on the iPad in four languages where, due to AR, visitors can access the virtual 3D visualization of the set of hot springs on the site. This allows tourists to visualize the original architecture on the archaeological remains; thus enriching the visit (see Fig. 6.4).

Another example is the "Yacimiento de Villaricos" in Almanzora (Almería), which offers an app for mobile devices that, in addition to giving users information about the hypogeum and the trousseau that it contain, allows a 3D in situ recreation of the Hypogeum of the Phoenician necropolis in two of its historical phases (sixth century B.C. and third century B.C.). This allows visitors a better visualization of the past (see Fig. 6.5).

Finally, the Phoenician archaeological site of Gadir (Cádiz) is a museum site in the heart of the city that shows the evolution of the city, from its beginnings as a

Fig. 6.3 An image of the app "Cisneros GO" (Courtesy of 6Dlab. https://apps.apple.com/es/app/cisneros-go/id1358631720)

Fig. 6.4 A visitor using the app during his visit to Museo al Aire Libre Villa romana de l'Albir (Courtesy of Patrimonio Virtual. https://www.patrimoniovirtual.com/proyecto-albir/)

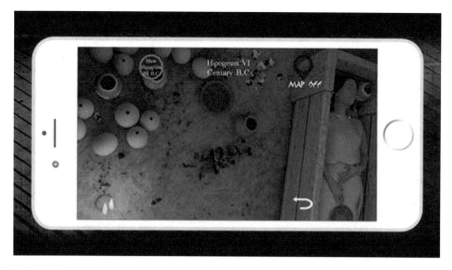

Fig. 6.5 Screenshot of the app "Villaricos Virtual" (Courtesy of App Store https://apps.apple.com/us/app/villaricos-virtual/id1434225495?l=es)

Phoenician settlement to its consolidation as a Roman city, among other features. The Vitelsa Group, in collaboration with the Institute of Promotion, Employment and Training (IFEF) of the Cadiz City Council, prepared the museum plan and a technological project for the implementation of AR. This project placed electronic devices where a 3D reconstruction of the compound archaeological remains can be observed in situ, among other things, by the intersection of two paved streets and eight houses of the ancient Phoenician settlement.

In addition to the examples mentioned above, we would like to examine some particularly striking cases, both for their success in terms of their dissemination and use and especially for their edu-communicative proposals.

6.4.1   Bilbilis: An AR Immersion into a Roman Site

The archaeological site of Bílbilis, located in the municipality of Calatayud (Zaragoza), was a site of Celtiberian origin (from the first century B.C.), which, due to the fertility of the lands and its important workshops, became a rich settlement which declined around the beginning of the second century and was abandoned in the late fourth or early fifth century A.D. Due to its richness, a free app "Augusta Bílbilis Guide" was developed to offer visitors a much more holistic experience of the place; to enhance their knowledge and enjoyment. This application, which offers its content in Spanish and English, was developed for ADRI Calatayud-Aranda by the company Prames S.A. The contents of the app were prepared by

Manuel Martín Bueno, Pilar Rivero and Carlos Saénz, specialists in history, archaeology, heritage education and didactics of the social sciences. The photographs and plans were provided by the Bílbilis excavation team and the modelling in 3D by the Advanced Graphic Computing Group (GIGA). In addition, the wide range of educational resources was completed by the virtual reconstructions carried out by the URBS research group and the GIGA of the University of Zaragoza, through the Government of Aragón project "Roman Heritage of Aragon: didactic application of images synthetics digital" (2007–2009) coordinated by Manuel Martín Bueno.

Through this app, users have access to: an archaeological itinerary, the history of the excavations, explanations of the main points of interest and the 3D reconstruction of different maps and buildings due to the use of Augmented Reality (see Fig. 6.6). The AR module activates the rear camera of the mobile device, offering a real image of the place that the device allows by combining with three-dimensional recreations, thus offering the user a mixed reality experience in real time. In this way, the images recreated in 3D appear incorporated into the different spaces of the site, adapting them according to the position and distance of the visitor to the archaeological remains.

In addition, in 2021, Bílbilis plans to enhance its AR resources with a new application called "Aragon Open Air Museum", a development from the University of Zaragoza with financing from the Government of Aragon and European Union (ERDF "building Europe from Aragon"). This app includes AR projected on archaeological remains. This initiative seeks to facilitate the understanding of the archaeological remains, which are often difficult to understand without prior archaeological knowledge. Compared to the usual virtual reconstruction, the placing of the digital model on the archaeological remains allows spontaneous association of each element with its reconstruction, so affording a much simpler interpretation process.

The app will allow users to add contents, comments and set customized routes that can be shared with other users. This constitutes an advance within the social

Fig. 6.6 Codes for using the app "Guía de Augusta Bílbilis" during the visit (Courtesy of Museo de Calatayud. https://museodecalatayud.blogspot.com/)

network or web 2.0 and is in line with the Sustainable Development Goals in terms of promoting participatory communities (Rivero et al. 2020b). This consequently promotes the creation of patrimonial cyber communities that grant the historical rest archaeological and symbolic-identity values (Rivero et al. 2018, 2020a).

6.4.2   Los Millares: AR Applied to a Copper Age Settlement

Continuing with the line of dissemination of archaeological heritage, we highlight the case of "Los Millares", an archaeological site from the European Chalcolithic, which was approximately occupied between 3200 and 2200 B.C. The site is made up of a town with four lines of concentric walls, a necropolis of collective tombs, comprising some 80 graves of different ceremonial structures distributed in small groups, and a set of 13 forts that complete a powerful defensive system which controlled the settlement and its surrounding territory. Like the previous example, this site has an application launched by the Ministry of Culture of the Junta de Andalucía and sponsored by Michelin, which allows, due to the use of AR, the interpretation of the archaeological remains preserved at the site. It is a visual recovery of the site made from an extensive documentation process complemented with more than 1,500 photographs that have made possible the virtual modelling of the three burial mounds located in the itinerary of the visit and of the first line of the town wall.

To access the AR, visitors stand in front of the information panels along the route through the archaeological site (see Fig. 6.7). This tool is an outstanding complement to the proposed educational itinerary and combines well with the materials offered at the site's interpretation centre.

6.4.3   Sorolla Museum: The Use of AR to Understand Pictorial Works

Another category within the non-formal settings is the Sorolla Museum. This museum, located in what was the residence and studio of the painter Joaquín Sorolla in Madrid, was created at the request of the artist's widow: Clotilde García del Castillo. In 1925 she made a will donating all her assets to the state to found a museum in memory of the painter. In 1932 the museum was inaugurated with Joaquín Sorolla García as director, the artist's only son, who bequeathed new funds to the museum, completing the collection with the purchase of more works by the painter. The free app for mobile devices "Museo Sorolla AR" is conceived as a pioneering project and in 2018 became the first free download cultural app (project led by the companies 6DLAB and ARS Viva).

This app allows users to discover details of the artist's work by pointing the rear camera of their electronic device at some of the works on display. The app integrates

Fig. 6.7 A visitor using the app "Los Millares" (Courtesy of Junta de Andalucía. https://www.jun
tadeandalucia.es/cultura/aaiicc/millares-virtual)

videos of actors characterized as the painter himself and other characters that appear
in the painting set to explain some significant data of the works (see Fig. 6.8). With this
video and image overlay obtained on the device screen, visitors can access a greater
amount of information about the artist's paintings in an attractive, dynamic and
unique way, thus replacing the cartouches attached to the wall that holds the works.
This app takes one more step in terms of accessibility for all audiences. Specifically,
the resource has been incorporated into its website so that it can be experienced
from home or the classroom, or elsewhere, by focusing the mobile device on the
photographs of the works hosted on the official website of the museum; taking the
viewer directly to the visualization of the videos.

Finally, as in some of the previous examples, the implementation of AR in the
museum also allows users to take a selfie with the painter Joaquín Sorolla and his
wife Clotilde García del Castillo, a feature that various institutions already promote
and that encourages users to share the image obtained on social networks, as so
enhancing their use.

Fig. 6.8 A visitor using the app "Museo Sorolla AR" (Courtesy of Jesús Jiménez. https://www. rtve.es/noticias/20180314/sorolla-guia-visitantes-su-museo-gracias-realidad-aumentada/1695701. shtml)

6.4.4 The Alhambra: The Use of AR in a Children's Audio Guide

Not a museum, but as one of the jewels of Hispano-Muslim Andalusian art in Spain, this monumental complex offers the app "La Alhambra, Castillo Rojo". It is a project financed by the Junta de Andalucía through the IDEA agency and put into practice by the tourist group Granavisión. It is presented as a motivating and gamification-based children's audio guide that invites you to visit the Alhambra in Granada through different features that integrate AR, games, audios and different challenges that users must overcome. This project, available in four languages, combines the free download of both the application and some content with other exclusive paid content to be unlocked during the visit.

In "La Alhambra. El Castillo Rojo", users must retrieve some hidden keys to ensure that the Alhambra does not disappear. To do this, they must look for the keys hidden around the monumental enclosure while interacting with different characters who will guide and explain not only characteristics of the rooms, but also part of the history of the area. The app provides information on the different rooms that make up the enclave, offering information adapted to children, which must be discovered through the codes distributed by the different rooms (see Fig. 6.9). These codes allow users to view on their electronic devices the explanations of four different characters (King Boabdil, Queen Morayma, the military Yusuf and King Carlos V) through photographs, stories, drawings and audios conceived for and adapted to children. Once again, the application allows selfies, in the end, with the characters that have accompanied the visitors.

Fig. 6.9 Visit using the app "La Alhambra. Castillo Rojo" (Courtesy of Alhambra on line. https://www.alhambraonline.org/audioguia-infantil-alhambra-castillo-rojo)

6.5   Conclusions

It is no coincidence that after almost ten years of experience, we have barely been able to collect cases where the implementation of AR has experienced a journey in time significant enough to allow us to analyse aspects such as the evolution in the use of AR as an educational tool or the perception of it by the public.

After observing the use of AR in Spain in the tourist, cultural and educational fields, it appears that the few specific, existing initiatives have either not developed into applications for electronic devices which last beyond a beta test, are already unusable today, or have not materialized due to a lack of funds.

A "magic formula" that would guarantee the success and durability of an AR application does not exist. Only if the content is sufficiently interesting and attractive, the parties involved in the financing, development and promotion of an AR app can manage to get good results.

Future research should investigate the student's perception of AR and its educational use in both formal and non-formal education. Initial technological problems such as excess battery consumption of the mobile device or the need to be connected to the Wi-Fi network in order not to consume excessive data are less and less significant due to the generalization of flat rates or the improvement of electronic devices. Now is the moment for public and private institutions to encourage and promote the use of AR for educational purposes.

In conclusion, public and private institutions should promote and enhance the use of AR for educational purposes. The design of heritage interpretation applications, from our point of view, should be in accordance with the concerns of our time and, consequently, be linked to the Sustainable Development Goals in at least two basic aspects: first, goal number 4 "education of quality", with applications designed from a didactic approach; and second, the creation of participatory communities, through applications to take advantage of the potential of web 2.0 or social web, in line with the promotion of heritage communities already included in the Faro Convention (Council of Europe 2005).

Acknowledgements This research was funded by the Government of Aragón and European Regional Development Fund (ERDF), grant number RISS3-LMP18_18 "Aragón open air museum" (2014-2020 Construyendo Europa desde Aragón) and by the Spanish Ministry of Science, Innovation and Universities/AEI and EU's ERDF grant number EDU2016-78163-R "Educomunicación web 2.0 del patrimonio". It was also funded by the Government of Aragón, the University Institute for Research in Environmental Sciences of Aragón (IUCA) and the Research Group ARGOS, grant number (S50_20R).

References

Angelopoulou A, Economou D, Bouki V et al (2011) Mobile augmented reality for cultural heritage. In: Venkatasubramanian N, Getov V, Steglich S (eds) Mobile wireless middleware, operating systems, and applications, Proceedings of the 4th International ICST Conference, Mobilware. London, UK, 2011, 1st ed. Springer, NewYork, NY, pp 15–22

Bernad MS (2020) Nuevas tecnologías y difusión del turismo cultural: descubriendo a Goya con realidad aumentada. ROTUR, Revista de Ocio y Turismo 14(1):81. https://doi.org/10.17979/rotur.2020.14.1.5945

Bowers J, Bannon L, Fraser M, Hindmarsh J, Bendford S, Heath C, Ciolfi L (2007) From the disappearing computer to living exhibitions: shaping interactivity in museum settings. Springer, pp 30–49

Brown B, MacColl I, Chalmers M, Galani A, Randell C, Steed A (2003) Lessons from the lighthouse: collaboration in a shared mixed reality system. Proceedings of the SIGCHI Conference on Human Factors in Computing Systems. AMC, New York, NY, pp 577–584

Chang K, Chang C, Hou H et al (2014) Development and behavioral pattern analysis of a mobile guide system with augmented reality for painting appreciation instruction in an art museum. Comput Educ 71:185–197

Chatzidimitris T et al (2013) Mobile Augmented Reality edutainment applications for cultural institutions. In: Proceedings of the 4th International Conference on Information, Intelligence, Systems and Applications, 2013—IISA2013, Mikrolimano, Greece, pp 10–12

Council of Europe (2005) Convention on the Value of Cultural Heritage for Society (Faro Convention). Retrieved from https://rm.coe.int/16806a18d3

Department of Economic and Social Affairs (2010) International recommendations for tourism statistics 2008. United Nations, New York

Durkheim E (1975) Educación y sociedad. Península, Barcelona

Esclapés J, Tejerina D, Bolufer J, Esquembre MA (2014) Augmented Reality System for the musealization of archaeological sites. VAR 4(9):42–47. https://doi.org/10.4995/var.2013.4246

Fontal O (2003) La educación patrimonial. Teoría y práctica en el aula, el museo e internet. Trea, Gijón

Fontal O (2013) La educación patrimonial, del patrimonio a las personas. Trea, Gijón

Fontal O, Marín S, García-Ceballos S (2015) Educación de las artes visuales y plásticas en Educación Primaria. Paraninfo, Madrid

Furata H, Takahashi K, Nakatsu K et al (2012) A mobile application system for sightseeing guidance using augmented reality. In: Proceedings of the 6th International Conference on Soft Computing and Intelligent Systems and the 13th International Symposium on Advanced Intelligence Systems, Kobe, Japan, 2012, pp 20–24

González-Rodríguez MR, Díaz-Fernández MC, Pino-Mejías MA (2020) The impact of virtual reality technology on tourists' experience: a textual data analysis. Soft Comput 24(18):13879–13892. https://doi.org/10.1007/s00500-020-04883-y

Graziano T, Privitera D (2020) Cultural heritage, tourist attractiveness and augmented reality: insights from Italy. J Herit Tour. https://doi.org/10.1080/1743873X.2020.1719116

Gutierrez JM, Molinero MA, Soto-Martin NO, Medina, CR (2015) Augmented reality technology spreads information about historical graffiti in temple of debod. Procedia Comput Sci 75:390–397

Ibáñez-Etxeberria A, Fontal O, Rivero P (2018) Educación Patrimonial y TIC en España: Marco normativo, variables estructurantes y programas referentes. Arbor 194(788):a448. https://doi.org/10.3989/arbor.2018.788n2008

Ibáñez-Etxeberria A, Gómez-Carrasco CJ, Fontal O, García-Ceballos S (2020) Virtual environments and augmented reality applied to heritage education. An evaluative study. Appl. Sci. 10(7):2352. https://doi.org/10.3390/app10072352

Kargas A, Karitsioti N, Loumos G (2020) Reinventing museums in 21st century: implementing augmented reality and virtual reality technologies alongside social media's logics. In: Guazzaroni G, Pillai AS (eds.) Virtual and augmented reality in education, art, and museums, pp 117–138

Kortabitarte A, Ibáñez-Etxeberria A, Luna U et al (2017) Dimensiones para la evaluación de aprendizajes en APPs sobre patrimonio. Pulso 40:17–33

Little C, Bec A, Moyle BD, Patterson D (2020) Innovative methods for heritage tourism experiences: creating windows into the past. J Herit Tour 15(1):1–13. https://doi.org/10.1080/1743873X.2018.1536709

Loumos G, Kargas A, Varoutas D (2018) Augmented and virtual reality technologies in cultural sector: exploring their usefulness and the perceived ease of use. J Media Crit 4(14):307. https://doi.org/10.17349/jmc118223

Luna U, Ibáñez-Etxeberria A, Rivero P (2019) El patrimonio aumentado. 8 apps de Realidad Aumentada para la enseñanza-aprendizaje del patrimonio. Revista Interuniversitaria de Formación del Profesorado 94(33.1):43–62. https://doi.org/10.47553/rifop.v33i1.72088

Lv M, Wang L, Yan K (2020) Research on cultural tourism experience design based on augmented reality. Culture and Computing, 8th International Conference, C&C 2020, Held as Part of the 22nd HCI International Conference, HCII 2020, Copenhagen, Denmark, July 19–24, 2020, Proceedings, 12215 LNCS, pp 172–183. https://doi.org/10.1007/978-3-030-50267-6_14

McGovern E, Moreira G, Luna-Nevarez C (2019) An application of virtual reality in education: Can this technology enhance the quality of students' learning experience? J Educ Bus:1–8. https://doi.org/10.1080/08832323.2019.17030

Medvedeva NV, Kabanova EE, Rogach OV et al (2018) Public-private partnership as a means of activating russian tourism potential. J Environ Manag Tour 9(4):832–840. https://doi.org/10.14505//jemt.9.4(28).17

Perra C, Grigoriou E, Liotta A et al (2019) Realidad aumentada para la educación del patrimonio cultural. In 2019 IEEE IX Conferencia Internacional de Electrónica de Consumo ICCE-Berlín, IEEE, 2019, pp 333–336

Perea-Medina MJ, Navarro-Jurado E, Luque-Gil AM (2018) Territorial intelligence: conceptualization and progress in the status of the issue. Possible links to tourist destinations. Cuadernos de Turismo 41:535–554. https://doi.org/10.6018/turismo.41.327141

Pérez-Martínez VM, Motis Dolader MÁ (2018) Narrativa transmedia y turismo experiencial: relatos sobre el patrimonio y la herencia judía en Aragón Sefarad. Church Commun Cult 3(3):389–407. https://doi.org/10.1080/23753234.2018.1535247

Petrucco C, Agostini D (2016) Teaching our cultural heritage using mobile augmented reality. J E-Learn Knowl Soc 12(3):115–128

Rivero P, Fontal O, García-Ceballos S, Martínez-Rodríguez M (2018) Heritage education in the archaeological sites. An identity approach in the Museum of Calatayud. Curator Mus J 61(2):315–326. https://doi.org/10.1111/cura.12258

Rivero P, Navarro-Neri I, Aso B (2020a) Educommunication Web 2.0 for heritage: A view from Spanish museums. In: Delgado-Algarra EJ, Cuenca-López JM, (eds) Handbook of research on citizenship and heritage education. IGI Global, Hershey, PA, pp 450–471

Rivero P, Navarro-Neri I, García-Ceballos S, Aso B (2020b) Spanish archaeological museums during COVID-19 (2020): an edu-communicative analysis of their activity on Twitter through the sustainable development goals. Sustainability 12(19):8224. https://doi.org/10.3390/su12198224

Ruiz D, Bellido ML (2014) La presencia de la realidad aumentada en los museos del siglo XXI: difusión y accesibilidad a través de lo virtual. In: Andrade V, Colorado A, Moreno I (eds), ArTecnología. Conocimiento aumentado y accesibilidad, pp 218–223

Santamaría L, Mendoza JF (2014) Construcción de mundos virtuales para el desarrollo de destrezas de lateralidad basado en Web3D. Revista Educación in Ingeniería 9(17):13–25. https://doi.org/10.26507/rei.v9n17.352

Sarramona J (2000) Teoría de la educación. Ariel, Barcelona

Sparacino F, Davenport G, Pentland, A (2000) Media in performance: interactive spaces for dance, theater, circus, and museum exhibits. IBM Syst J 39:479–510. https://doi.org/10.1147/sj.393.0479

Sylaiou S, Liarokapis F, Kotsakis K, Patias P (2009) Virtual museums, a survey and some issues for consideration. J Cult Heritage 10:520–528. https://doi.org/10.1016/j.culher.2009.03.003

Templin T, Popielarczyk D (2020) The use of low-cost unmanned aerial vehicles in the process of building models for cultural tourism, 3D web and augmented/mixed reality applications. Sensors 20(19), 5457:1–26. https://doi.org/10.3390/s20195457

UNESCO (2015) Policy document on world heritage and sustainable development. In The General Assembly of States Parties to the World Heritage Convention at Its 20th Session; France, 2015, pp 1–18. https://whc.unesco.org/en/sustainabledevelopment/

UNESCO, UNICEF, The World Bank, UNFPA, UNDP, UN Women, UNHCR (2015) Education 2030: Incheon Declaration and Framework for Action for the implementation of Sustainable Development Goal 4: ensure inclusive and equitable quality education and promote lifelong learning opportunities for all. ED-2016/WS/28 W. In: Proceedings of theWorld Education Forum 2015, Incheon, Korea, 19–22 May 2015. https://unesdoc.unesco.org/ark:/48223/pf0000245656

Vinuesa MÁT, Torralba LT (2018) Territorial view of heritage and tourism sustainability. Boletín de la Asociación de Geógrafos Españoles 78:212–244

Zhang Y, Han M, Chen W (2018) The strategy of digital scenic area planning from the perspective of intangible cultural heritage protection. J Image Video Proc 130. https://doi.org/10.1186/s13640-018-0366-7

Part II
Augmented Reality for Museums

Chapter 7
Immersive Installations in Museum Spaces: Staging the Past

Sebastian Pranz

Abstract This chapter reflects on museums' use of immersive media (IM) as a specific form of presentation. Augmented Reality and Virtual Reality have long since found their way into museums. Considering that the museum itself is effectively a stage on which objects are displayed to the public in a way intended to convey meaning, one can assume that immersive installations build on an already semiotically complex reality. By drawing on the concept of theatricality, as defined in cultural studies, as well as contributions made by micro-sociology, a conceptual framework is proposed to understand and analyze IM in the museum. Against this background, two theses are discussed: First, to create a meaningful experience, curators have to manage a specific form of perspectivity to integrate physical space, and the rules applied to it, into its augmentation. Second, like every form of media, IM must develop strategies to cope with technical imperfection by creating a sense of immediacy.

7.1 Introduction

When Germany celebrated the 30th anniversary of its peaceful revolution in 2019, its capital was divided by a virtual resurrection of the Berlin Wall: Through his AR-App *MauAR*, Berlin-based artist and developer Peter Kolski opened a window into the past and offered the user the opportunity to see tanks rolling through the city's streets and get an augmented view of a wired fence and reinforced concrete. *MauAR* used location-based data and 3D-modeling to create an augmented context of experiencing history. By choosing locations in the former East and West of Berlin, the user was presented with two opposing perspectives on the country's past. When Apple CEO Tim Cook was offered a sneak preview of the app, he was impressed: "Thank you

S. Pranz (✉)
Faculty of Media, Macromedia University of Applied Sciences, Munich, Germany
e-mail: sp@sebastianpranz.de

[…] for bringing the Berlin Wall's history to life through augmented reality—a new way to learn from the past."[1]

Immersive media (IM) has long been an integral part of museum presentation practice: XR technology is used to display contextual information about exhibits (Jung et al. 2016; Kolivand et al. 2019; Neuburger and Egger 2018) or replace them with virtual dioramas (Han et al. 2017; Haynes 2018); augmented guidance systems are being implemented in many museums' informational architecture (Chen et al. 2014), and entire monuments are being virtually reconstructed (Kolivand et al. 2019). The advantages are apparent: User studies indicate that immersive environments provide a higher level of information and affection (Caldera-Serrano and León-Moreno 2016) and specific gratification effects (Rauschnabel 2018). However, the museum's "mixed reality" is not as unconditional as it may seem at first glance. On the contrary, the physical and the virtual space don't merge seamlessly into each other: They create a complex figuration of conflicting social norms (Parker and Saker 2020), semiotic conventions (Pranz et al. 2020), and alter the way we perceive information in/through space in general (Saker and Frith 2020).

Considering that the museum itself is a stage on which objects are displayed to the public in a meaningful way, this chapter reflects on museums' use of immersive media as a specific form of staging. As we will see, the concept of theatricality, as discussed in cultural studies and sociology, offers a framework within which immersive installations can be analyzed. First, the following section introduces the term "immersive media" (IM) and its possibilities in the museum. Subsequently, two seminal concepts will be outlined: The use of space and perspective in theater, and the strategy of staging immediacy.

7.2 Immersive Media in Museum Exhibitions

The term immersive media was coined by various early researchers, including Ronald T. Azuma (1997) and Milgram et al. (1995), who described the technical possibilities of merging virtual with real environments. In contrast to virtual reality, which is conceptualized as a fully immersive scenario, Augmented Reality "supplements reality, rather than completely replacing it" (Azuma 1997, p. 2). The major contribution of Milgram et al. (1995) was to harmonize the different concepts by organizing them according to their degree of immersion: The "reality-virtuality continuum" allows for any number of gradations of mixed reality (Milgram et al. 1995) and, more importantly, releases the idea of immersion from a mere technical understanding of devices and channels. Today, the different forms of immersive media are usually summarized with the term XR, although there "is no agreement about whether the 'X' stands for 'extended', 'expanded' or only serves as a variable X for 'anything' about new and innovative forms of realities" (Dwivedi et al. 2020, p. 15). However,

---

[1] Cited from a tweet by Cook on October 21, 2018 (https://twitter.com/tim_cook/status/105409001 8455777280?lang=de, retrieved on December, 21, 2020).

this chapter does not focus on the technical channels or devices used to create immersion. Instead, it is informed by a broader understanding of *immersive media* (IM) as a "complex social, cultural and aesthetic practice rather than a mere technology" (Pranz et al. 2020).

Considering the early discussions in the mid-1990s, one may wonder why we still do not live in a world where "virtual and real objects coexist[ed] in the same space, similar to the effects achieved in the film 'Who Framed Roger Rabbit?'" (Azuma 1997, p. 2). Twenty-five years after the concept was defined, immersive media is still *the* next big thing (Belisle and Roquet 2020, p. 3), with global players like Google, Facebook, and Apple offering more and more everyday applications and 5G providing the technical framework for realizing immersive mobile media. While the first aspect may play an essential role in "educating" users on how IM can be applied to "real-world tasks" (Azuma 1997, p. 3), the latter opens the possibility of displaying augmented content on-location. This has attracted interest from archeologists, who increasingly use augmented and virtual content on-site: In their interdisciplinary approach, Brusaporci et al. (2021) document a virtual reconstruction of an Italian basilica that can be perceived as an additional layer of information through a mobile device. However, despite the potential immersive heritage sites might have for remembrance culture in the future, the technical process from registering to visualizing historic media on-site remains complex (Kolivand et al. 2019). That is why frictions between the augmented content and its real environment may reduce the experience of immersion (Han et al. 2017, p. 402).[2]

Besides understanding immersive content primarily by its technical boundaries, other scholars have focused on its communicative aspects. Wallis and Ross (2020) have examined the role indigenous creators have in pioneering virtual content by "reimagin[ing] traditional storytelling in new media forms" (Wallis and Ross 2020, p. 2). Projects like *Crow: The Legend*, released on *Oculus Rift* in 2017 (Wallis and Ross 2020, p. 10), demonstrate that IM as a media form still contains much unknown territory that is only now being explored by media practitioners and users. As an interactive medium, immersive environments enable non-linear forms of storytelling where sense-making is always co-created by the user—who is always at risk of becoming lost in the story world (Aitamurto 2019, p. 10). Against this background, Walden (2019) imagines immersive remembrance as a participatory process: By drawing on Deleuze's reading of the term "virtual" as a process of "re-actualization," she conceptualizes the practice of virtual Holocaust memories as an "attempt to involve the embodied visitor or user consciously in this reactualization process" (Walden 2019, p. 5).

It is important to note that IM has to be understood in the context of its cognitive appropriation by a user. Accordingly, virtual and augmented media have received increasing interest from interdisciplinary effect and user studies. Firstly, on the *affective* level, IM can lead to an increase in personal *involvement*. Studies have shown

---

[2]It is worth noting that virtual artifacts themselves have become a matter of archival preservation, as is the case for "digital ruins" (Miller and Garcia 2019) in online roleplaying games like *Blue Mars* and *Second Life* (Kim 2020).

that users of VR content feel more "present" (Pallavicini et al. 2019; van Berlo et al. 2020, p. 13), which may result in desired effects like physical well-being (Kruzan and Won 2019) or the feeling of empathy (Gabriels et al. 2014) as well as in sensory dissociations like physical nausea (Bollmer and Guinness 2020) or "cybersickness." Secondly, on a *cognitive* level, IM is considered to reduce complexity and facilitate the reception of information (Aitamurto 2019; Nielsen and Sheets 2019, p. 9) as well as increase the perceived level of education (Neuburger and Egger 2018, p. 73); thirdly, on a *conative* level, recent consumer studies indicated VR content increased the likelihood of taking action (Gibson and O'Rawe 2018; Jung et al. 2018).

It should be pointed out that the ability to extract meaning from an augmented environment might depend on the user's previous experience with this medium. In their study of immersive stories in journalism, Shin and Biocca (2018) differentiate between the user's traits: Users with a high tendency to immerse themselves were found to experience greater satisfaction, attributed higher credibility to the story and "found the (high immersion) VR more engaging and conducive to empathizing than the (low immersion) TV" (Shin and Biocca 2018, p. 2810). This is important as it illustrates that *immersion* must not be conceptualized merely within technical arrangement, but more in the context of an interactive *socio-technical* figuration (Lepa et al. 2014, p. 127) that includes the material form of the medium, the conditions of the spatial situation (Lepa et al. 2014, p. 127) as well as the user him- or herself, who interacts with the media by taking specific roles (Lepa et al. 2014, p. 127). Or to put it more simply: *Media figurations are theatrical arrangements.*

7.3 Staging Immersive Installations

Theater has a long tradition in social science and cultural studies (for an overview, see Willems 2012, pp. 320–327). While sociologists like Erving Goffman (1956, 1986) and many others (Dahrendorf 2006; Rapp 1973; Soeffner 2004) have used the theatrical figuration as a *form of comparison* to understand and describe the reality of social interactions, a second surge of studies emerged in the field of cultural studies in the late 1990s and early 2000s (Willems 2012, pp. 320–327) that has lasted until today (Hans 2017). Scholars like Erika Fischer-Lichte (2004b) and Herbert Willems (2009) take a more *diagnostic approach* when describing an everyday culture of staged experiences (Fischer-Lichte 2002, pp. 291–292). The concept of *theatricality* is closely linked to a "mediatized" society (Krotz 2007), with different kinds of media creating different kinds of stages and audiences. Drawing on both traditions, this chapter understands theater as a media reality per se, which helps us understand other media realities. *Us*, in this case, means both: the scholar, who applies the concept of theatricality in order to analyze immersive installations in the museum; as well as the everyday visitor, who asks the question "What is it that's going on here?" (Goffman 1986, p. 8). To discuss the potential of both concepts for analyzing immersive media, two basic concepts are proposed: The conception of space and perspective and the idea of immediacy.

7.3.1 Space and Perspective

The use of space in the museum is highly formalized. The semiotic conventions used to display objects in museum space form a social grammar applied by visitors and curators (Leahy 2016; Scholze 2010, 2015). Thus, the specific meaning of an exhibition has to be embedded in its spatial order: It is translated into a curational concept that unfolds along the exhibition tour; it is communicated by visual guiding systems and limitations of access marked with exhibition barriers; and it interacts with the architecture of the museum as a framework for social interactions.

From a theatrical standpoint, space is conceptualized as a duality of *visibility* and *concealment*: What becomes visible and what must remain invisible determines theatrical performance practice both in the selection of its materials (masks, costumes, scenery) (Pranz 2009, p. 63) as well as in its organization of space into *stage, backstage* and *audience space*. All these dimensions are interlinked—in order to create visibility, curators (as well as artistic directors) have to limit the viewer's access: Just as there is no open theater where audience members can walk from backstage onto the stage, the open museum remains an exception, which is why every canvas has its backside and every exhibit is taken from an archive that is not accessible to the everyday visitor. This specific form of sense-making is addressed with the term "perspectivity" (Rapp 1973, p. 183). While in traditional theater, perspectivity requires a fixed viewpoint by the audience, walking through an exhibition means a constant change of perspective (Leahy 2016): "Movement is a key element in the experience of spectatorship for which it is also an anchor. The visitor is the mobile spectator, 'seeing' the 'spectacle' from different viewpoints, angles, distances and so forth" (Christidou and Diamantopoulou 2017, p. 14).

The possibility of expanding the physical space with virtual augmentations is a far-reaching intervention into the museum's spatial figuration that may create all sorts of conflicts. First of all, from a technical standpoint, presenting a virtual exhibit requires the notion of the viewer's position in physical space to render a precise augmentation.[3] Interestingly, the physical object and its virtual representation both remain *intangible* in different ways: While the "real" object is usually separated by physical barriers as well as the convention of not touching exhibits, the virtual representation is, of course, intangible by its nature. In a recent study, Parker and Saker (2020) describe possible conflicts that visitors of mixed reality exhibitions might run into when navigating immersive environments. While some visitors ended up bumping into physical objects when focusing on the screen (Parker and Saker 2020, p. 6) it's noteworthy that some of the interviewees responded to an internalized set of rules when navigating virtual museum space: "You know that the table is not really there. You've seen the space you could walk straight through it, but you just obey the rules of the virtual space and walk around it" (Thomas, male, as cited in Parker and Saker 2020, p. 8). Pranz et al. (2020) describe further problems of visitors adapting to an immersive installation in city space: "Some of our visitors waited for an exhibit to

---

[3] In marker-based Augmented Reality this is usually achieved by a photographic registration of the physical object that is then compared with the image perceived by the Head Mounted Device.

appear while pointing the device in the wrong direction whereas others gazed at a three-dimensional model without even considering the possibility of changing the perspective by taking a step to one side. Just like the first generation of computer users had to adapt to the concept of drag and drop, our subjects had to develop a mode of orientation to cope with the concept of augmented space" (Pranz et al. 2020, p. 148).

In order to understand augmented space, our experiences in physical space are crucial. To create a meaningful experience, curators have to manage a certain form of perspectivity to integrate physical space and the rules applied to it into their augmentation. Besides thinking about visual "markers" to trigger Augmented Reality content, this could also mean providing "markings" in the physical space to guide the visitor through the exhibition and orient him/her toward augmented content (Pranz et al. 2020, p. 147).

7.3.2 Staging Immediacy

With the emergence of HMD (head-mounted devices) in the consumer market during the last few years, virtual environments have become more everyday experiments. Videos go viral of people trying to walk *Richie's Plank*, a VR plank sticking out over a void from the top floor of a virtual sky scraper (Ross 2018, p. 9): *Richie's Plank* "confirms my suspected acrophobia (…) but that's also an important VR experience because it really goes to show you your body and your brain are gonna be generating a good 70% percent of what's to gain from VR," said author and producer Dan Harmon after his self-experiment.[4] The user's effectual involvement might make up for some of the technical limitations like a limited visual field or the "ghost-like sensation of moving through space without seeing the body (or apparatus) that directs this movement" (Ross 2018, p. 10). Contrary to VR, Augmented Reality applications are usually considered less immersive as they blend the physical space with its virtual augmentation. Yet they offer great potential in creating immersive experiences on-site. Museums are at the forefront of implementing Augmented Reality into everyday experiences: Since 2017, the Smithsonian in Washington has offered its famous *Bone Hall* as a virtual collection. With the Augmented Reality app *Skin & Bone*, visitors can bring the museum's exhibits to life as three-dimensional models. The skeletons can also be covered by a virtual layer of feathers, fur, or scales on a smartphone screen.[5]

Marketers and scholars agree that Azuma's vision of a world where real objects and their augmentations become indistinguishable is still a dream for the future. Nevertheless, we interact with immersive content naturally when we stretch out our hand to release a virtual bat from its display case or become sick by stepping from

---

[4]Retrieved from https://www.youtube.com/watch?v=e8reAZ_GzFA (December 30, 2020).

[5]The effect can be seen in a YouTube video retrieved from https://www.youtube.com/watch?v=7ag Vb4IG16M (December 30, 2020).

a virtual plank. From a theatrical standpoint, immersion can be understood as the human's universal ability to extract meaning from contexts that are—semiotically speaking—'virtual' (Pranz 2009, p. 260). The theatergoer "collaborates in the unreality onstage. He sympathetically and vicariously participates in the unreal world generated by the dramatic interplay of the scripted characters. He gives himself over" (Goffman 1986, p. 130). By applying the theatrical "frame," we experience human characters when we see masks, costumes, and props, we accept a painted wooden wall as a rural landscape and freeze when Ferdinand and Luise take a poisoned drink (Pranz 2009, p. 36).

Every media form has to develop its own strategies for coping with technical imperfection by creating what Fischer-Lichte calls "immediacy" (Unmittelbarkeit) (Fischer-Lichte 2005, p. 24). Against this background, mediated experiences come with a complex set of framings that the user has to adapt and decipher in order to "understand what is going on": Building on video games' rich history of staging bodies and space (Pranz 2008; Álvarez and Duarte 2018), *Richie's Plank* gives us a feeling of height by making us take the elevator before we are presented with a virtual abyss (Ross 2018, p. 9). While the ability of a medium to create "seemingly unmediated–mediated experiences" (Saker and Frith 2020, p. 1434) might depend on its technical potential to simulate a realistic environment (Saker and Frith 2020, p. 1433), the user's ability to understand the media-specific "brackets" (Goffman 1986, pp. 251–269) that indicate a desired mode of experience must not be neglected.

7.4 Conclusion

This chapter discusses immersive installations from a theatrical perspective, starting from the thesis that immersive media has to be staged in a meaningful way to create a satisfying experience. By drawing on the concept of theatricality, as discussed in cultural studies, and contributions made by micro-sociology, this chapter proposes a conceptual framework to understand and analyze IM in the museum. For reasons of space, the theoretical concepts were reduced to two primary considerations: The concepts of perspectivity and immediacy. Considering the huge productivity of scholars in both fields, crucial concepts had to be omitted, i.e., the idea of "performance" and "embodiment" that might both offer great insights for understanding immersive realities (Fischer-Lichte 2002, 2004a; Fischer-Lichte et al. 2001). However, this chapter's aim was to demonstrate the potential for a theatrical perspective for analyzing IM in the museum. As shown above, museums have their own convention of staging objects and "framing" the visitor's experience, and immersive media adds another layer of meaning to an already semiotically complex reality. In a broader sense, we can assume that besides its technical realization, immersive content has to be presented in a meaningful way to engage the visitor. Like all media presentations, immersive media forms share some DNA with theater: They organize perception by showing and concealing, they translate space into a figuration of perspectives, and they evoke the viewer's ability to "immerse" him- or herself into a virtual environment.

Of course, the museum has a long tradition of contextualizing artifacts through media content—ranging from printed brochures to audio guides and interactive displays. Immersive media, on the one hand, offers a new contribution to the museum's educational resources. Interactive and immersive content can engage the visitor in ways video screens cannot, by taking him/her into Casanova's Venice[6] or—in reverse—merging an exhibition room with a prehistoric environment.[7] The "liveness" (Fischer-Lichte 2004b, p. 24) of a successful presentation creates a feeling of "being there" and the impression of immediacy, offering a new dimension to the museum experience. On the other hand, the possibility of staging virtual objects and creating mixed objects goes much further in challenging the definition of what the actual exhibit is. Why not consider the virtually reconstructed Baroque configuration of an Italian basilica (Brusaporci et al. 2021, p. 43, see above) as the latest contribution in a long history of the monument's reconfigurations? In this context, Brusaporci et al. speak of a "new kind of cultural heritage," a "further manifestation related to the tangible, which can play an important role in processes of interpretation, communication, conservation and enhancement of cultural heritage" (Brusaporci et al. 2021, p. 44).

Returning to Berlin in 2021, one can still visit a virtual Berlin Wall. But one day, once the markers in city space have faded, the virtual presentation itself will be the subject of preservation. How will we remember the virtual?

References

Aitamurto T (2019) Normative paradoxes in 360° journalism: contested accuracy and objectivity. New Media Soc 21(1):3–19. https://doi.org/10.1177/1461444818785153

Álvarez R, Duarte F (2018) Spatial design and placemaking: learning from video games. Space Cult 21(3):208–232. https://doi.org/10.1177/1206331217736746

Azuma RT (1997) A survey of augmented reality. Presence Teleoperators Virtual Environ 6(4):355–385. https://doi.org/10.1162/pres.1997.6.4.355

Belisle B, Roquet P (2020) Guest editors' introduction: virtual reality: immersion and empathy. J Vis Cult 19(1):3–10. https://doi.org/10.1177/1470412920906258

Bollmer G, Guinness K (2020) Empathy and nausea: virtual reality and Jordan Wolfson's *Real Violence*. J Vis Cult 19(1):28–46. https://doi.org/10.1177/1470412920906261

Brusaporci S, Graziosi F, Franchi F, Maiezza P, Tata A (2021) Mixed reality experiences for the historical storytelling of cultural heritage. In: Bolognesi C, Villa D (eds) From building information modelling to mixed reality. Springer, Cham, pp 33–46

Caldera-Serrano J, León-Moreno J-A (2016) Implications of augmented reality in the management of television audiovisual information. J Inf Sci 42(5):675–680. https://doi.org/10.1177/016555 1515608341

---

[6] As is possible in the Casanova Museum in Venice.

[7] As is possible in the above-mentioned Smithsonian in Washington.

Chen C-Y, Chang BR, Huang P-S (2014) Multimedia augmented reality information system for museum guidance. Pers Ubiquitous Comput 18(2):315–322. https://doi.org/10.1007/s00779-013-0647-1

Christidou D, Diamantopoulou S (2017) Seeing and being seen: the multimodality of museum spectatorship. Mus Soc 14(1):12–32. https://doi.org/10.29311/mas.v14i1.623

Dahrendorf R (2006) Homo Sociologicus: ein Versuch zur Geschichte, Bedeutung und Kritik der Kategorie der sozialen Rolle, Aufl 16. VS, Verl. für Sozialwiss, Wiesbaden

Dwivedi YK, Ismagilova E, Hughes DL, Carlson J, Filieri R, Jacobson J, Jain V, Karjaluoto H, Kefi H, Krishen AS, Kumar V, Rahman MM, Raman R, Rauschnabel PA, Rowley J, Salo J, Tran GA, Wang Y (2020) Setting the future of digital and social media marketing research: perspectives and research propositions. Int J Inf Manag. https://doi.org/10.1016/j.ijinfomgt.2020.102168

Fischer-Lichte E (2002) Grenzgänge und Tauschhandel. Auf dem Wege zu einer performativen Kultur. In: Wirth U (ed) Performanz Zwischen Sprachphilosophie und Kulturwissenschaften. Suhrkamp, Frankfurt, p 277–300

Fischer-Lichte E (2004a) Ästhetik des Performativen. Suhrkamp, Frankfurt

Fischer-Lichte E (ed) (2004b) Theatralität als Modell in den Kulturwissenschaften. Francke, Tübingen

Fischer-Lichte E (2005) Einleitung. In: Fischer-Lichte E, Umathum S, Warstart M (eds) Diskurse des Theatralen. A. Francke, Tübingen und Basel, pp 11–34

Fischer-Lichte E, Horn C, Warstat M (eds) (2001) Verkörperung. Francke, Tübingen

Gabriels K, Poels K, Braeckman J (2014) Morality and involvement in social virtual worlds: the intensity of moral emotions in response to virtual versus real life cheating. New Media Soc 16(3):451–469. https://doi.org/10.1177/1461444813487957

Gibson A, O'Rawe M (2018) Virtual reality as a travel promotional tool: insights from a consumer travel fair. In: Jung T, tom Dieck MC (eds) Augmented reality and virtual reality. Springer, Cham, pp 93–107

Goffman E (1956) The presentation of self in everyday life. University of Edinburgh Social Science Research Centre, Edinburgh

Goffman E (1986) Frame analysis. An essay on the organization of experience. Northeastern University Press, Boston, MA

Han D, Li X, Zhao T (2017) The application of augmented reality technology on museum exhibition—a museum display project in Mawangdui Han dynasty tombs. In: Lackey S, Chen J (eds) Virtual, augmented and mixed reality. Springer, Cham, pp 394–403

Hans B (2017) Inszenierung von Politik. Springer Fachmedien, Wiesbaden

Haynes R (2018) Eye of the Veholder: AR extending and blending of museum objects and virtual collections. In: Jung T, tom Dieck MC (eds) Augmented reality and virtual reality. Springer, Cham, pp 79–91

Jung T, tom Dieck MC, Lee H, Chung N (2016) Effects of virtual reality and augmented reality on visitor experiences in museum. In: Inversini A, Schegg R (eds) Information and communication technologies in tourism 2016. Springer, Cham, pp 621–635

Jung T, tom Dieck MC, Rauschnabel P, Ascenção M, Tuominen P, Moilanen T (2018) Functional, hedonic or social? Exploring antecedents and consequences of virtual reality rollercoaster usage. In: Jung T, tom Dieck MC (eds) Augmented reality and virtual reality. Springer, Cham, pp 247–258

Kim J (2020) The archive with a virtual museum: the (im)possibility of the digital archive in Chris Marker's *Ouvroir*. Mem Stud 13(1):90–106. https://doi.org/10.1177/1750698018766386

Kolivand H, El Rhalibi A, Tajdini M, Abdulazeez S, Praiwattana P (2019) Cultural heritage in marker-less augmented reality: a survey. In: Turcanu-Carutiu D, Ion R-M (eds) Advanced methods and new materials for cultural heritage preservation. IntechOpen

Krotz F (2007) Mediatisierung. VS Verlag für Sozialwissenschaften, Wiesbaden

Kruzan KP, Won AS (2019) Embodied well-being through two media technologies: virtual reality and social media. New Media Soc 21(8):1734–1749. https://doi.org/10.1177/1461444819829873

Leahy HR (2016) Museum bodies: the politics and practices of visiting and viewing. Routledge, London and New York

Lepa S, Krotz F, Hoklas A-K (2014) Vom ›Medium‹ zum ›Mediendispositiv‹. In: Krotz F, Despotović C, Kruse M-M (eds) Die Mediatisierung sozialer Welten. Springer Fachmedien Wiesbaden, Wiesbaden, pp 115–141

Milgram P, Takemura H, Utsumi A, Kishino F (1995) Augmented reality: a class of displays on the reality-virtuality continuum. In: Das H (ed). Boston, MA, pp 282–292

Miller V, Garcia GC (2019) Digital Ruins. Cult Geogr 26(4):435–454. https://doi.org/10.1177/147 4474019858705

Neuburger L, Egger R (2018) Augmented reality: providing a different dimension for museum visitors. In: Jung T, tom Dieck MC (eds) Augmented reality and virtual reality. Springer, Cham, pp 65–77

Nielsen SL, Sheets P (2019) Virtual hype meets reality: users' perception of immersive journalism. Journalism. https://doi.org/10.1177/1464884919869399

Pallavicini F, Pepe A, Minissi ME (2019) Gaming in virtual reality: what changes in terms of usability, emotional response and sense of presence compared to non-immersive video games? Simul Gaming 50(2):136–159. https://doi.org/10.1177/1046878119831420

Parker E, Saker M (2020) Art museums and the incorporation of virtual reality: examining the impact of VR on spatial and social norms. Converg Int J Res New Media Technol 26(5–6):1159–1173. https://doi.org/10.1177/1354856519897251

Pranz S (2008) Die Präsentation des Raumes im Videospiel. In: Willems H (ed) Weltweite Welten. VS Verlag für Sozialwissenschaften, Wiesbaden, pp 319–339

Pranz S (2009) Theatralität digitaler Medien. VS Verlag für Sozialwissenschaften, Wiesbaden

Pranz S, Nestler S, Neuburg K (2020) Digital topographies. Using AR to Represent archival material in urban space. In: Jung T, tom Dieck MC, Rauschnabel P (eds) Augmented reality and virtual reality—changing realities in a dynamic world. Springer, Wiesbaden

Rapp U (1973) Handeln und Zuschauen Untersuchungen über den theatersoziologischen Aspekt in der menschlichen Interaktion. Sammlung Luchterhand, Darmstadt und Neuwied

Rauschnabel PA (2018) A conceptual uses & gratification framework on the use of augmented reality smart glasses. In: Jung T, tom Dieck MC (eds) Augmented reality and virtual reality. Springer, Cham, pp 211–227

Ross M (2018) Virtual reality's new synesthetic possibilities. Telev New Media. https://doi.org/10. 1177/1527476418805240

Saker M, Frith J (2020) Coextensive space: virtual reality and the developing relationship between the body, the digital and physical space. Media Cult Soc 42(7–8):1427–1442. https://doi.org/10. 1177/0163443720932498

Scholze J (2010) Kultursemiotik: Zeichenlesen in Ausstellungen. In: Baur J (ed) Museumsanalyse. Transcript Verlag, Bielefeld, pp 121–148

Scholze J (2015) Medium Ausstellung Lektüren musealer Gestaltung in Oxford. Leipzig, Amsterdam und Berlin

Shin D, Biocca F (2018) Exploring immersive experience in journalism. New Media Soc 20(8):2800–2823. https://doi.org/10.1177/1461444817733133

Soeffner H-G (2004) Die Wirklichkeit der Theatralität. In: Fischer-Lichte E, Horn C, Umathum S, Warstart M (eds) Theatralität als Modell in den Kulturwissenschaften. Francke, Tübingen/Basel, pp 235–247

van Berlo ZMC, van Reijmersdal EA, Smit EG, van der Laan LN (2020) Inside advertising: the role of presence in the processing of branded VR content. In: Jung T, tom Dieck MC, Rauschnabel PA (eds) Augmented reality and virtual reality. Springer, Cham, pp 11–22

Walden VG (2019) What is 'virtual Holocaust memory'? Mem Stud. https://doi.org/10.1177/175 0698019888712

Wallis K, Ross M (2020) Fourth VR: indigenous virtual reality practice. Converg Int J Res New Media Technol. https://doi.org/10.1177/1354856520943083

Willems H (ed) (2009) Theatralisierung der Gesellschaft. VS Verlag für Sozialwissenschaften, Wiesbaden
Willems H (2012) Synthetische Soziologie. Idee, Entworf, Programm. VS Verlag, Wiesbaden

Chapter 8
The Use of Augmented Reality to Expand the Experience of Museum Visitors

Sandra Maria Correia Loureiro

Abstract This chapter is devoted to augmented reality in the museum context. Augmented reality has been regarded as a way to enhance the real-world environment using computer-generated perceptual information. It is a tool that museums should explore more to enhance the visitor experience. The aim of this chapter is to go further in understanding the use of augmented reality technology in museums. The objectives are (1) to give an overview of the meaning of augmented reality in tourism, (2) to provide examples of the use of augmented reality in museums, and (3) to offer suggestions for future research in the field. The results are the suggestions for future research and the contributions for academics and practitioners.

8.1 Introduction

Museums offer a way to occupy time through entertainment and learning (Benckendorff et al. 2014; Buhalis and Law 2008; Rhodes 2015; Loureiro and Sarmento 2018). A museum experience does not occur only during the visit but includes pre and post-visit and co-creation activities (Loureiro and Guerreiro 2018; Loureiro 2020). Social media platforms allow interaction and the exchange of ideas involving visitors, tourists, and managers (Kumar et al. 2013; Xiang and Gretzel 2010; Bimber and Raskar 2005; Boes et al. 2016). Museum managers and curators should be able to get closer to visitors and tourists, involving them in a relationship that extends beyond the visit (Loureiro 2019).

Technologies such as virtual (VR) and augmented reality (AR) can contribute to the experience and consequently the proximity among players (Cheong 1995; Stangl and Weismayer 2008; Arafa 2017; Ng and Wakenshaw 2017; Tussyadiah et al. 2018). Augmented reality can add an explanation to pieces in an exhibition (Jung et al. 2015; Kumar et al. 2016). An audio tour can be transformed in an immersive experience by creating a 3D audio environment so that the visitor can understand from where the sound is coming (Manojlovich et al. 2003). Combining augmented reality apps and

S. M. C. Loureiro (✉)
Business Research Unit (BRU), Intituto Universitário de Lisboa (ISCTE), Lisbon, Portugal
e-mail: sandramloureiro@netcabo.pt

© The Author(s), under exclusive license to Springer Nature Switzerland AG 2021
V. Geroimenko (ed.), *Augmented Reality in Tourism, Museums and Heritage*, Springer Series on Cultural Computing,
https://doi.org/10.1007/978-3-030-70198-7_8

a smart headset, museum visitors receive information from all the phone's sensors. GPS-based augmented reality platforms allow experiences outside museums. An example of these platforms is the Pokémon GO game. Augmented reality markers use AR apps which can overlap audio, image, video, and 3D models (Huang et al. 2013; Wang 2002; Loureiro et al. 2020b). The use of augmented reality in a museum context can enhance the experience. This chapter aims to go further in understanding the use of augmented reality technology in museums. Therefore, the objectives are (1) to give an overview of the meaning of AR in tourism, (2) provide examples of the use of augmented reality in museums, and (3) point out suggestions for future research in the field.

8.2 Overview of AR in Tourism

8.2.1 Augmented Reality Meaning and Evolution

Augmented reality is changing the way individuals live their experiences (Williams and Hobson 1995; Guttentag 2010). Augmented reality is an interactive process of a real-world environment where individuals can visualize the objects of the real-world "augmented" by computer-generated perceptual information, which can sometimes occur across multiple sensory modalities (e.g., visual or hearing) (Milgram et al. 1994; Loureiro et al. 2019; Loureiro et al. 2020a). Therefore, using augmented reality, one can experience both the real world and virtual objects overlaid, usually by wearing see-through displays (Buhalis and Yovcheva 2013; Buhalis and Amaranggana 2013; Loureiro and Guerreiro 2018; Loureiro et al. 2020a).

Augmented reality dates back to the 1960s, with the first head-mounted display (HMD) created by Ivan Sutherland (Carmigniani et al. 2011). This mechanism connected to a stereoscopic display from a computer program and showed virtual wireframe shapes, which changed perspective as the user moved their head. Thus, the superposition of artificial images on a real background can be regarded as the beginning of AR (Digital trends 2018; Carmigniani et al. 2011; Verhoef et al. 2017).

The commercial development process began in the 1990s (Javornik 2016). Augmented reality is reshaping the tourism industry (Guttentag 2010; Tussyadiah et al. 2017; Huang et al. 2017), because tourists can learn more about a museum or art gallery through smartphone applications and without a human guide (e.g., Skyline 2020).

8.2.2 Research on Augmented Reality

The first decade of twenty-first century sees the emergence of papers associated with conference proceedings, where new augmented reality technologies are presented

(Loureiro 2020). In the second decade, academics gradually publish more in scientific journals. Guttentag (2010, p. 638), for instance, is the first to establish a conceptualization of immersive technologies (e.g., virtual and augmented reality) in the tourism context, explaining that virtual reality is a more immersive "real-time simulation of one or more of the user's five senses," while augmented reality is the projection of computer-generated images onto a real-world view (Gutierrez et al. 2008).

Research in the second decade was supported by some specific theories: Technology Acceptance Model (TAM), Hedonic Theory, and S(stimuli)–O(organism)-R(response) framework. TAM and its extensions have been used to evaluate tourist experience (Huang et al. 2013), historic visitor attractions (Lagiewski and Kesgin 2017), golf (Han et al. 2014), wine tourism (Martins et al. 2017), or cultural heritage sites (tom Dieck and Jung 2017). Regarding S-O-R (Roschk et al. 2017), prior studies consider stimuli as drivers of cognitive and emotional states, which in turn result in behaviors. Tourist mobility studies are associated with the use of technology for geographical location (Hannam et al. 2014), and technology can avoid overcrowding and contribute to sustainable tourism.

8.3   Augmented Reality in Museums

According to Ding (2020), over 1% of US museums are providing augmented reality apps for visitors' mobile phones. Augmented reality apps can be used outside and inside the museum space. Chicago Project is an example of an app operating outside the Chicago History Museum, offering customized AR (Geroimenko 2014).

Augmented reality apps can be incorporated in mobile phones, which museums can lend, or visitors can use their own. Museums can use augmented reality to display digital versions of artists, called 3D personas, who can narrate their activity, and visitors show appreciation of these apps.

8.3.1   Seattle Art Museum

Several apps were developed in museums in the United States. For instance, the Seattle Art Museum used the Layar AR app for the "Kehinde Wiley: A New Republic" exhibition. ArtLens 2.0 was developed by the Cleveland Museum of Art and uses image-recognition software to recognize a selection of two-dimensional pieces of art. The "Skins and Bones" app conceived by the Smithsonian National Museum of Natural History serves as a good example of an educational tool. This app shares stories about the museum's iconic pieces. Users can see how the skin and muscle of animals would have looked over the bones. Visitors can also visualize, for example, a vampire bat in flight, or the pileated Woodpecker Skeleton Works augmented reality animation (see Fig. 8.1).

Fig. 8.1 Pileated Woodpecker Skeleton Works augmented reality animation (*Source* Skin and Bones app [2015])

8.3.2 Heroes and Legends Exhibit

The Heroes and Legends exhibit in the Kennedy Space Center uses an augmented reality experience to show a key moment in the history of America's space program, that is, the astronaut Gene Cernan performing the second spacewalk in history. The exhibition also employs augmented reality holograms giving faces and voices to those who worked on the space program (stories from NASA legends).

8.3.3 Pérez Art Museum

Invasive Species at the Pérez Art Museum can be seen through the PAMM App (Fig. 8.2) combining the architecture, spaces, and objects of the museum. University museums also use augmented reality technology in their gallery spaces. This is the case of Stanford University, which launched an augmented reality mobile application for the Anderson Collection.

Augmented reality apps have been used in museums outside the United States, such as the Latvian National Museum of Art. This app presents visitors with a story through several activities and levels of cognition. It provides four different routes (explore the museum building, highlights, full guided tour, and the current exhibition) complemented with interactive games and audio recordings. The section

Fig. 8.2 PAMM App in Pérez Art Museum (*Source* PAMM app [2020])

"getting to know the museum building" allows visitors to travel in time and space, letting visitors and potential visitors become involved, reflective, and analytical.

One important feature of augmented reality apps is the possibility to adapt the information to everyone, as some visitors may be seeking more information than others. Augmented reality can improve the use of guides, boosting the experience that a guide offers.

Museums tend to operate as niches and individuals tend to choose to visit a certain museum because they have a genuine interest in the exhibition. The augmented reality at Riga Motor Museum allows visitors to learn about how an old car works. In Tokyo's Sunshine Aquarium, augmented reality guides visitors through the busy streets to its premises. This app creates a journey or portal to the museum.

Magic mirrors is another device that allows interaction without the use of visitors' own mobile phones. Magic mirrors bring the museum experiences outside the museum, as in the case of the Jurassic Park Broadcast AR experience at Universal Studios. Another example is the HeroMirror, operating on a kiosk size footprint. HeroMirror creates instant snapshots for immediate sharing, via email or on-site printing.

8.3.4 Grand Palais

In Paris, the Grand Palais uses augmented reality in Robot Art Installation. Here, artists and robots operate together, with robots acting as creatives through their "artificial imagination." In the same city, in Palais Brongniart, the augmented reality app can scan photos of a renowned French singer to be displayed outside the Palais. In Vienna (Austria) the façade of the MUMOK transforms into a digital stage, revealing the related content and information about the exhibitions.

8.3.5   *National Portrait Gallery*

Another important contribution of augmented reality is the possibility to create compelling storylines. This process can enhance the experience at a museum, stopping it from becoming repetitive. The stories can be different from one visit to another and users can also create them outside the museum. Some examples are the Australian National Portrait Gallery, the National Museum Australia, Galeria Merida in Mexico, or Museu de Mataró in Spain.

8.4   Future Research

Museums have an important role in society in acquiring, conserving, and exhibiting human heritage to all who desire to learn, but also enjoy exploring and discovering the events of the past projecting the future. Museums are proving to be open to incorporating technologies into their public service. Augmented reality has been well incorporated in museums, but five aspects of research should be further explored. First, new models and frameworks should be developed instead of adapting and extending the previous models such as TAM or S-O-R. Therefore, what models and frameworks will arise specific to augmented reality in museums? How to understand and follow visitors' interests before, during, and after the visit?

Second, choosing and willingness to use augmented reality apps can depend on national culture and visitors' personal traits. For instance, open-minded visitors will be more interested in experiencing technologies. Societies that avoid uncertainty (Hofstede 2020) may be less open to the use new technologies than those that accept uncertainty.

Third, the relevance of augmented reality technology in creating value for visitors needs to be understood. How can managers and visitors work together to create value? What are the risks and benefits for visitors of using augmented reality and related technologies? How to personalize products/services in museums with the contribution of these technologies?

Fourth, the amount of data that can be collected and analyzed using these technologies can uncover issues connected to data access and protection (Bilal and Oyedele 2020). Thus, new laws dealing with such aspects must be developed by international organizations and governments.

Finally, augmented reality can be investigated and combined with other emerging technologies to increment the effects. Virtual reality (understood as the construction of a virtual world that can immerse users as if they were in the environment) can promote an increase in the visitor flow (e.g., Grewal et al. 2020). Nevertheless, most studies on virtual reality so far are not related with museums (Loureiro et al. 2019), but tend to focus on gaming, medicine, and education (e.g., Hainey et al. 2016; Howard 2017).

Virtual reality interfaces range from virtual reality headsets consisting of head-mounted glasses with a screen in front of the eyes to non-movable ones such as rooms with multiple large screens. The CAVE (Cave Automatic Virtual Environment) is a cubic room where stereoscopic images are projected on the walls around. The CAVE can be created in museums or the users may use Oculus or some other equipment associated with visitors' mobile phones to visualize the museum experience. Virtual reality can also be employed as a souvenir. Merchandize in the form of virtual reality films can be bought by visitors to recall the experience. These films may be personalized as the technology evolves and can even combine the interface with augmented reality apps.

Artificial intelligence robots are another form of technology often considered. Robots can assist visitors when they approach the museum, but also during the experience itself (Aiken and Sheng 1991). Artificially intelligent robots can learn from visitors and gradually become intellectually and emotionally closer to them (Cath 2018; Cath et al. 2018).

The key to artificial intelligence systems acting humanly is the roles they assume in relation to humans. By acting humanly, artificially intelligent systems can be considered as intelligent assistance or a replacement for humans. In business settings, the goals of artificial intelligence research have been to create machines capable of completing low-level processing, speeding up a task while freeing humans to do more creative work, and to create machines that augment human capacity to improve human performance by acting as knowledge amplifiers (Simmons and Chappell 1988). Researchers conceptualize artificially intelligent capacities based on human skills they can replicate. For example, in the service context, four different skills of artificial intelligence were suggested: mechanical artificial intelligence, analytical artificial intelligence, intuitive artificial intelligence, and empathetic artificial intelligence (Huang and Rust 2018). Mechanical artificial intelligence is the skill associated with repetitive tasks, allowing machines to provide extreme consistency and reliability. Analytical artificial intelligence is the skill associated with performing complex, yet systematic, consistent, and predictable tasks. This often involves processing a large amount of data and extracting patterns. Intuitive artificial intelligence is the skill associated with performing complex, creative, holistic, and contextual tasks that need intuitive intelligence. Empathetic artificial intelligence is the skill associated with providing psychological comfort for the well-being of humans (Huang and Rust 2018). Museums also provide a service to visitors and society and AI systems incorporated in robots can also contribute to the museum experience.

8.5   Conclusions

Augmented reality apps are becoming a particularly important tool to promote museums, enhance the experience of the visit, or even remember the visit. As a promotional tool, augmented reality can contribute to co-creating elements that will complement the experience and open the visitor's mind to what can be seen (e.g., Stangl and Weismayer 2008; Buhalis and Amaranggana 2015). During the visit, augmented reality gives educational information, but can also offer entertainment (games, quizzes). Augmented reality can even overlay images and information about what existed in the past at the same place (e.g., Buhalis and Amaranggana 2015; Tussyadiah et al. 2018). Augmented reality can help to create memories of the pieces on display and can be a good tool to lead visitors to encourage others to do the same.

Three words can characterize the use of augmented reality in museums: education, entertainment, and engagement. Education because it can provide valuable information about each exhibit and the space where it is physically on display. Entertainment represents learning with pleasure. Although entertainment elements can serve all types of visitors, these can be especially useful to capture the youngest. Engagement is crucial in developing the process of co-creating experiences (museum managers, curators, visitors, and all who are connected to the museum working together). Ultimately, this engagement process can develop a strong attraction and closeness.

Museums can become cool with the help of this technology. They can develop some of the 10 characteristics of a cool brand (Warren et al. 2019). A "cool" museum will enhance potential visitors' interest and be able to provide memorable experiences.

Acknowledgements   This work was supported by Fundação para a Ciência e a Tecnologia (Foundation for Science and Technology), grant UIDB/00315/2020. The author would like to thank Mr. Robert Costello and Mrs. Jennifer Inacio for allowing the use of their photos.

References

Aiken MW, Sheng ORL (1991) Artificial-intelligence based simulation in the design of a GDSS idea generation tool. Inf Manag 21(5):279–289

Arafa MN (2017) Achilles as a marketing tool for virtual heritage applications. ArchNet-IJAR. 11(3):109–118. https://doi.org/10.26687/archnet-ijar.v11i3.1385

Bimber O, Raskar R (2005) Spatial augmented reality merging real and virtual worlds, Cambridge. A K Peters, MA

Benckendorff P, Sheldon P, Fesenmaier DR (2014) Tourism information technology. CAB International, Oxford, UK

Bilal M, Oyedele LO (2020) Big data with deep learning for benchmarking profitability performance in project tendering. Expert Syst Appl 14:113194

Boes K, Buhalis D, Inversini A (2016) Smart tourism destinations: ecosystems for tourism destination competitiveness. Int J Tour Cities 2(2):108–124. https://doi.org/10.1108/IJTC-12-2015-
0032

Buhalis D, Yovcheva Z (2013) Augmented reality in tourism. 10 unique applications explained. In:
Digital tourism think thank—thinkdigital.travel. https://thinkdigital.travel/wp-content/uploads/
2013/04/10-AR-Best-Practices-in-Tourism.pdf. Accessed 3 September 2019

Buhalis D, Amarangganna A (2015) Smart tourism destinations enhancing tourism experience
through personalisation of services. In: Tussyadiah I, Inversini A (eds) Information and
communication technologies in tourism, Springer, Cham, pp 377–389

Buhalis D, Law R (2008) Progress in information technology and tourism management: 20 years
on and 10 years after the Internet—the state of eTourism research. Tour Manag 29(4):609–623.
https://doi.org/10.1016/j.tourman.2008.01.005

Carmigniani J, Carmigniani J, Furht B (2011) Handbook of augmented reality. Springer, New York,
NY

Cath C (2018) Governing artificial intelligence: ethical, legal and technical opportunities and challenges. Philos Trans R Soc A: Math, Phys Eng Sci 376(2133):20180080. http://https://doi.org/
10.1098/rsta.2018.0080

Cath C, Wachter S, Mittelstadt B, Taddeo M, Floridi L (2018) Artificial intelligence and the 'good
society': the US, EU, and UK approach. Sci Eng Ethics 24(2):505–528

Cheong R (1995) The virtual threat to travel and tourism. Tour Manag 16(6):417–422. https://doi.
org/10.1016/0261-5177(95)00049-T

Ding M (2020) Augmented reality in museums. https://amt-lab.org/blog/2017/5/augmented-reality-
in-museums. Accessed 12 August 2020

Geroimenko V (2014) Augmented reality art: from an emerging technology to a novel creative
medium. Springer International Publishing, Heidelberg

Grewal D, Noble SM, Roggeveen AL, Nordfält I (2020) The future of in-store technology. *Journal
of the Academy of Marketing Science* 48(2):96–113. https://doi.org/10.1007/s11747-019-00697-z

Gutierrez MA, Thalmann D, Vexo F (2008) Stepping into virtual reality: a practical approach.
Springer, London

Guttentag DA (2010) Virtual reality: applications and implications for tourism. Tour Manag
31(5):637–651. https://doi.org/10.1016/j.tourman.2009.07.003

Hainey T, Connolly TM, Boyle EA, Wilson A, Razak AA (2016) Systematic literature review
of games-based learning empirical evidence in primary education. Comput Educ 102:202–223.
https://doi.org/10.1016/j.compedu.2016.09.001

Han H, Hwang J, Woods DP (2014) Choosing virtual–rather than real–leisure activities: an examination of the decision-making process in screen-golf participants. Asia Pacific J Tour Res.
19(4):428–450. https://doi.org/10.1080/10941665.2013.764333

Hannam K, Butler G, Paris CM (2014) Developments and key issues in tourism mobilities. Ann
Tour Res 44:171–185. https://doi.org/10.1016/j.annals.2013.09.010

Hofstede (2020). Countries culture. Acessed on https://www.hofstede-insights.com/product/com
pare-countries/ (25 January 2021)

Howard MC (2017) A meta-analysis and systematic literature review of virtual reality rehabilitation
programs. Comput HumBehav 70:317–327. https://doi.org/ https://doi.org/10.1016/j.chb.2017.
01.013

Huang YC, Backman SJ, Backman KF (2013) Moore (2013) Exploring user acceptance of 3D
virtual worlds in travel and tourism marketing. Tour Manag 36:490–501. https://doi.org/10.1016/
j.tourman.2012.09.009

Huang CD, Goo J, NamK YooChW (2017) Smart tourism technologies in travel planning: the role
of exploration and exploitation. Inf Manag 54(6):757–770. https://doi.org/10.1016/j.im.2016.
11.010

Huang MH, Rust RT (2018) Artificial intelligence in service. J Serv Res 21(2):155–172

Javornik A (2016) Augmented reality: research agenda for studying the impact of its media characteristics on consumer behaviour. J Retail Consum Serv 30(May):252–261. https://doi.org/10.1016/j.jretconser.2016.02.004

JungT CN, Leue MC (2015) The determinants of recommendations to use augmented reality technologies: the case of a Korean theme park. Tour Manag 49:75–86

Kumar V, Dixit A, Javalgi A, Das M (2016) Research framework, strategies, and applications of intelligent agent technologies (IATs) in marketing. J Acad Mark Sci 44(1):24–45

Kumar V, BhaskaranV MR, Shah M (2013) Creating a Measurable Social Media Marketing Strategy: increasing the Value and ROI of intangibles and tangibles for hokey pokey. Mark Sci 32(2):194–212. https://doi.org/10.1287/mksc.1120.0768

Lagiewski R, Kesgin M (2017) Designing and implementing digital visitor experiences in New York state: the case of the Finger Lakes Interactive Play (FLIP) project. J Dest Mark Manage. 6(2):118–126. doi: https://doi.org/10.1016/j.jdmm.2017.03.005

Loureiro SMC, Guerreiro J (2018) Psychological behavior of generation Y: living between real and virtual reality. In: Gerhardt M, Peluchette JVE, (eds) *Millennials: characteristics, trends and perspectives* (chapter 3). New-York: NOVA science publishers, Inc. p. 67–90.

Loureiro SMC, Sarmento EM (2018) Engaging visitors in cultural and recreational experience at museums. ANATOLIA: Int J Cult Tour Hosp Res 29(4): 581–592. doi:https://doi.org/10.1080/13032917.2018.1484378

Loureiro SMC, Guerreiro J, Eloy S, Langaro D, Panchapakesan P (2019) Understanding the use of virtual reality in marketing: a text mining-based review. J Bus Res (Available online 9 November 2018). https://doi.org/10.1016/j.jbusres.2018.10.055

Loureiro SMC (2020) Virtual reality, augmented reality and tourism experience. In: Dixit SK (ed) *Handbook of Tourism Experience Management and Marketing,* chapter 38. Routledge, London, Oxford, pp 439–452. e-ISBN: 978–0–367–19678–3, p-ISBN: 978–0–429–20391–6

Loureiro SMC, Guerreiro J, Ali F (2020a) 20 years of research on virtual reality and augmented reality in tourism context: a text-mining approach. Tour Manag 77: 104028. https://doi.org/https://doi.org/10.1016/j.tourman.2019.104028

Loureiro SMC, Sarmento EM, Rosário EM (2020b) Incorporating VR, AR and related technologies in tourism industry: state of the art. In: Loureiro SMC (ed) Managerial challenges and social impacts of virtual and augmented reality (chapter 13). Hershey, PA, IGI Global, pp 211–233

Manojlovich J, Manojlovich JM, Chen J, Lewis M (2003) UTSAF: a multi-agent-based framework for supporting military-based distributed interactive simulations in 3D virtual environments. In: Chick S, Sánchez PJ, Ferrin D, Morrice DJ (eds) Proceedings of the international conference on machine learning and cybernetic. *North Bangkok: King Mongkut's University* of *Technology,* pp. 960–968. https://doi.org/10.1109/WSC.2003.1261517

Martins J, Gonçalves R, Branco F, Barbosa L, Melo M, Bessa M (2017) A multisensory virtual experience model for thematic tourism: a port wine tourism application proposal. J Dest Mark Manage 6(2):103–109. https://doi.org/10.1016/j.jdmm.2017.02.002

Milgram P, Takemura H, Utsumi A, Kishino F (1994) Augmented reality: a class of displays on the reality-virtuality continuum. Systems Research. In: Das H (ed) Telemanipulator and telepresence technologies, vol. 2351. Photonics for Industrial Applications, Boston, pp 282–292. https://doi.org/10.1117/12.197321

Ng I, Wakenshaw S (2017) The internet-of-things: review and research directions. Int J Res Mark 34(1):3–21

PAMM App (2020) https://www.pamm.org/blog/2019/04/pamm-teen-arts-council-accepts-grant-awarded-citizens-interested-arts. Accessed 10 Aug 2020.

Roschk H, Loureiro SMC, Breitsohl J (2017) Calibrating 30 years of experimental research: a meta-analysis of the atmospheric effects of music, scent, and color. J Retail 93(2):228–240. https://doi.org/10.1016/j.jretai.2016.10.001

Rhodes G (2015) Future museums now—augmented reality musings. Public Art Dialogue 5(1):59–79

Simmons AB, Chappell SG (1988) Artificial intelligence—definition and practice. IEEE J Ocean Eng 13(2):14–42

Skyline (2020) https://www.viewranger.com/en-US/premium/skyline. Accessed 12 January 2020

Skin and Bones app (2015) https://journals.openedition.org/midas/933?lang=pt. Accessed 10 August 2020

Stangl B, Weismayer C (2008) Websites and virtual realities: a useful marketing tool combination? an exploratory investigation. In: O'Connor P, Höpken W, Gretzel U (eds) Information and communication technologies in tourism. Springer, New York, pp 141–151

Tom Dieck MC, Jung TH (2017) Value of augmented reality at cultural heritage sites: a stakeholder approach. J Dest Mark Manage 6(2):110–117. https://doi.org/10.1016/j.jdmm.2017.03.002

Tussyadiah IP, Jung TH, Tom Dieck MC (2017) Embodiment of wearable augmented reality technology in tourism experiences. J Travel Res 57(5):597–611

Tussyadiah IP, Wang D, Jung TH, Tom Dieck MC (2018) Virtual reality, presence, and attitude change: empirical evidence from tourism. Tour Manag 66:140–154. https://doi.org/10.1016/j.tourman.2017.12.003

Verhoef PC, Stephen A, Kannan PK, Luo X et al (2017) Consumer connectivity in a complex, technology-enabled, and mobile-oriented world with smart products. J Interact Mark 40:1–8

Wang Y, Yu Q, Fesenmaier DR (2002) Defining the virtual tourist community: implications for tourism marketing. Tour Manag 23(4):407–417. https://doi.org/10.1016/S0261-5177(01)00093-0

Warren C, Batra R, Loureiro SMC, Bagozzi RP (2019) Brand coolness. J Mark 83(5):36–56. https://doi.org/10.1177/19857698

Williams P, Hobson JS (1995) Virtual reality and tourism: fact or fantasy? Tour Manag 16(6):423–427. https://doi.org/10.1016/0261-5177(95)00050-X

Xiang Z, Gretzel U (2010) Role of social media in online travel information search. Tour Manag 31(2):179–188. https://doi.org/10.1016/j.tourman.2009.02.016

Chapter 9
Gestures and Re-enactments in a Hybrid Museum of Archaeology: Animating Ancient Life

Dragoş Gheorghiu, Livia Ştefan, and Marius Hodea

Abstract The present chapter describes the interrelationship between a traditional archaeological museum and some digital ways of creating complex virtual cultural contexts. It is well known that the traditional archaeological museum has separated the objects from the viewer and has decontextualized them, thus greatly reducing the degree to which they can be understood. Lately, especially during a time of quarantine and lockdowns, museums are starting to become digital, and this renders possible a broad range of display options. However, the transformation is not a total one, the museums acting as hybrid organisms, with both real and virtual presences. This study describes the making of a virtual cultural context in which the shape of virtually reconstructed objects, gestures and re-enactments, positioned both in the real and virtual worlds, animate ancient life and create a museum of hybrid archaeology.

9.1 Introduction: The Digital Transformation of Museums

Digital culture and the IT advances are transforming museums in the twenty-first century (vom Lehn et al. 2001; Ciolfi and Bannon 2002; Tallon and Walker 2008; Styliani et al. 2009; Izzo 2017; Giannini and Bowen 2019; Clini et al. 2020) by changing how museums are creating exhibitions, communicate culture and engage visitors, either with physical or virtual presence, and also through a communitary space (Clifford 1997). Digital culture as a "digital states of being" (Giannini and Bowen 2019) resulted in an increased adoption of digital technologies by museum professionals, and also in how the visitors are perceiving museum visits. Among

D. Gheorghiu (✉)
Doctoral School, National University of Arts, Bucharest, Romania

Instituto Terra e Memória, Centro de Geociências de Universidade de Coimbra, Mação, Portugal

L. Ştefan
EasyDO Digital Technologies, Bucharest, Romania

M. Hodea
National University of Arts, Bucharest, Romania

the IT technologies that have significantly contributed to the transformation of the museums' offerings are the web and 3D, VR, AR technologies. These transformations have materialized in the development of new interfaces, new modes of interaction with the museum's objects and the development of multimodal interfaces in VR and AR (Styliani et al. 2009).

Digital culture is a complex process that consists of *digitization,* which refers to the production of digital content and virtual facsimiles, and *digitalization* is defined as "digital innovation in museum life" (Clini et al. 2020).

Digital culture has led to the emergence of a new type of museum, the virtual one, generally associated with web technologies and alternately labelled as online museum, hypermuseum, digital museum, cyber-museum or web museum (Hermon and Hazan 2013, 2014). Exhibitions are a museum's means of communication, and in the case of the virtual museum, these are the Virtual Galleries and the Cultural Objects (Styliani et al. 2009).

The idea of the virtual museum was first introduced by André Malraux in 1947 (Malraux 1996) as a museum without walls ("le musée imaginaire"). Scholars have been wondering whether virtual museums should be just a "digital surrogate" of the traditional museums, or whether they should be something completely different, or complementary to the latter (Hermon and Hazan 2013, 2014).

Initially, virtual museums were created using mostly 2D content, which, however, quickly evolved into 3D-based exhibitions. VRML and X3D technologies have allowed the creation of interactive museums based on the use of rich web browser interfaces and the ubiquitous access of desktop users (but not mobile devices' users). Currently, WebXR allows the VR or AR experience to be accessible via all the web browsers that support this technology, on desktops, mobile devices, VR or AR headsets (WEBXR website 2020). An advanced technological form is represented by haptics devices, which allow users to touch, feel and manipulate three-dimensional objects in virtual environments, or motion devices such as Microsoft Kinetics that provide motion capture, facial recognition and voice recognition capabilities (Microsoft Kinetics website 2020).

Recent virtual museums (Giannini and Bowen 2019) show a growing trend towards the use of VR/AR technologies alongside online exhibitions, to create hybrid museums and thus provide a different user experience. AR/VR technologies offer enhanced affordances, such as hyper-realistic image quality, dynamic application of content, contextualization, user interactivity and immersion.

Combining various IT technologies, including social media, hybrid museums mix the real and virtual with mobile devices and permanent internet connection (de Souza e Silva 2006). "Hybrid spaces" is considered a concept different from "mixed reality" as it is created by "the constant movement of users" and is the result of an interconnection of "connected spaces, mobile spaces, and social spaces" (de Souza e Silva 2006). This view emphasizes the user experience, viewed as a journey between the real and the virtual, which includes "sociability and communication", while the term mixed reality in the sense defined by Milgram and Kishino (1994) or Milgram and Colquhoun (1999) refers to intermediate experiences of Augmented Reality (AR) and Augmented Virtuality (AV) within the real-virtual continuum.

Regarding the museums with archaeological content, or archaeological sites and historic monuments, also included in the category of museums (Niccolucci 2007), these could be "intrinsically virtual", as the knowledge is constructed through "evidence, experience and intelligence" (Niccolucci 2007). That is why the implementation of virtual archaeology museums has fully benefited from web technologies, digitization, AR/VR. Thus, numerous 3D galleries have been created on the web, as well as through thematic AR applications, to quote only the "Augmented Reality companion applications for visitors" (Museum of Celtic Heritage), or "Augmented Reality app to digitally augment Terracotta Warrior exhibition" (Franklin Institute AR). In VR, uses refer to virtual tours on the web or with VR headsets, such as Oculus. The virtual archaeological museums have attracted visitors to see the collections but also to discover "sites remotely without physically visiting the museums" (Kang and Yang 2020).

Generally speaking, one can see a combined use of technology designed to meet the various needs of visitors or scholars (Giannini and Bowen 2019). An example is the "Keys to Rome" project (Keys to Rome 2014) that presents a new perspective on museums, demonstrating how these can be used to engage visitors in the future. The objects can be discovered through a digital itinerary supported by different technologies such as computer graphics movies, natural interaction installations, tangible interfaces, live projections, augmented reality, multimedia and mobile applications.

In this chapter, we propose an experiment to create a hybrid museum that increases the offer of a traditional museum by digitizing artefacts, by relating the shape of objects to that of human gestures and by introducing them in the virtual reconstruction of historical contexts.

9.2 The Pandemic, Social Distancing and Transferring Museums from Real to Virtual

The year 2020 was decisive in the decision to transform most traditional museums into hybrid museums, where, in addition to the classic system of narrative presentation of artefacts presented in display cases, one also encounters an online system, VR/AR installations or AR thematic applications.

According to a UNESCO Report of 2020 (UNESCO REPORT) based on 600 references to online sites or activities, 90% of the museums around the world have been affected by the pandemic, being forced to close their doors. All the digital initiatives and infrastructures implemented before the advent of COVID-19 (digitization of collections, creation of virtual museums) were widely used during the lockdown.

Other organizations such as the Network of European Museum Organisations (NEMO) surveyed 200 museum online sites (NEMO SURVEY) and discovered that 58% of the museums continued performing their online activities at the same rate, while 37% had increased them, and 23% had even started new online activities.

Recent events, which have imposed social distancing, or even the closure of museums, have favoured those museums that already had a digitized component in the form of online collections, such as Tate Online, digitized since 1998 (Stevens 2016), the Louvre Museum (Louvre Museum Paris) or the Smithsonian Institution (Smithsonian Natural History Museum), pan-European museum collections (Europeana website 2020) or online networks of museums (F-MU.S.EU.M [Merlini and Velichkov 2009]; V-MUST 2009). In addition, these events have prompted the museums that did not have an online presence to create one in order to retain their audience, while the museums with a pre-existing online presence, were stimulated to look for more advanced solutions, in the form of elaborate VR (Louvre VR) and AR (Smithsonian AR; Franklin Institute AR) applications.

The advantages of digitizing and virtualizing museums in online, AR or VR are:

- increased public exposure, audience access and promotion of the cultural heritage;
- remote access, from any location and anytime;
- the possibility to return at any time;
- the protection of the exhibits while providing visitors a degree of visual access impossible to achieve during on-site visits, due to the artefacts' encapsulation in glass showcases (Louvre VR);
- animation and the greater visitor engagement while studying the artefacts;
- integration with social-media communication (Kargas et al. 2020).

In particular, modern technologies such as AR/VR combined with online exposure can contribute to the continued activity of museums during and after the pandemic, due to advancements in current web browsers (WEBXR website 2020) or AR/VR versions for mobile devices.

9.3   The Current Problems of Traditional Museums of Archaeology

Many archaeology museums today are still dependent on old display methods and do not have the means to offer a technologically enhanced visitor experience, with the help of new AR/VR technologies.

Although museums are social "contact areas" (Clifford 1997), in traditional archaeological museums, contact with exposed cultural material is not possible, in these museums, the object remains distant from the visitor. The use of the digital form of visiting museums has not much changed the ways of displaying the exhibits, which have remained just as remote.

Given this context and taking into account the strategies proposed for contemporary museums, the following can be suggested as approaches to be taken by archaeology museums:

- prioritize the visitor (and the visitor's experience) rather than the object (Paddon 2014; Giannini and Bowen 2019);

- enhance the user's experiences (Li et al. 2012); for example, The Franklin Institute is using an AR application (Franklin Institute AR) to enhance their Terracotta Warrior exhibition and to teach visitors about the history behind the clay soldiers;
- facilitate understanding, learning and research through the diversification of the museum's cultural offerings (Styliani et al. 2009; Clini et al. 2020) and through an interactive experience with the museum's objects (Li et al. 2012).
- facilitate networking, playground and communications (Gheorghiu and Ştefan 2015; Varinlioglu and Halici 2019);
- establish metrics and the means to measure the visitor's preferences based on these metrics, and organize future exhibitions based on these preferences (Hermon and Hazan 2013, 2014).

In addition to the above, the enhancement of the pedagogical message (Time Maps www.timemaps.net; Gheorghiu and Ştefan 2019b) achieved by recreating the cultural-historical context of the exhibited object, is particularly important in the case of archaeological museums, for understanding its place in the daily life of the past. In the case of online archaeological museums, virtual contexts can be created to better understand the meaning of the objects, thus enabling an enhancement of the visitor's experientiality (Vlahakis et al. 2003).

9.4 Augmenting the Information Within the Virtual Space

Virtual and Augmented Reality are two technologies adopted by museums in search of alternative solutions to the offer of traditional museums both online and offline. Although both are derived from the real-virtual continuum defined by Milgram and Kishino (1994) and represent immersive technologies, the capabilities, as well as the user experience, are significantly different. VR completely immerses the user in a 3D context that re-creates reality, while AR brings in the same context the real environment, digital information and the user. AR also offers the adaptation of digital content to the geographical context and allows user mobility, which gives it greater versatility and attractiveness for archaeological museums and cultural institutions. This explains why the first uses of AR were for archaeological sites, such as Archeoguide (Vlahakis et al. 2003; Papagiannakis and Magnenat-Thalmann 2007).

Although in the case of AR technology, Azuma (2015) described the most accurate technical difficulties to overcome, from the point of view of the user experience, it highlighted the greater potential in relation to VR "in the long term", as well as the success factors in its acceptance by users.

AR applications cover many uses, including augmented objects, magazines, points-of-interest, educational games (Hughes et al. 2004, Naemura et al. 2010; Hammady et al. 2016; Gheorghiu and Ştefan 2019a, b; Banfia et al. 2019; Varinlioglu and Halici 2019). Recent implementations of AR based on the ARCore package (ARCORE website 2020) from Google have succeeded in 3D or semantic recognition of the environment, a process called environmental sensing.

For museum curators, AR is a creative and powerful IT tool, as it allows the overlaying of various and numerous layers of information (Kunjir and Patil 2020), as well as contextualization in a geographical space or cultural environment.

Mixed Reality is a term linked to both AR and VR (Milgram and Kishino 1994) which refers to the mix of digital and real-world content, and may make use of more advanced techniques and dedicated equipment (Hughes et al. 2014; Stapleton and Hughes 2006).

9.5 The Context as Information Augmentation

As already stated, traditional museums presented decontextualized artefacts, individually presented in display cases. Modest attempts to contextualize them were made early on by building dioramas (Dobres 2000, p. 27ff) or "explanatory images" that also maintained the distance between the object and the viewer. We could say that this type of museum belongs to a culture that generates places without identity (see Augé 1992).

What does context mean in the case of an archaeology museum? A definition, quite incomplete in rendering the "reality" of the past, would be that of representing the cultural experience of a certain place in a well-defined period of time, which means the experience of objects, i.e. technologies and the human behaviour conditioned by them, and of the relations between objects (Gheorghiu 2001), in order to be able to understand a part of the cultural experience of the people from that period. A context is, like a work of art, a cultural construct in which one can become immersed (Gheorghiu 2015), that is, in which one can experience a parallel reality. The role of new museums that are visitor centred (Paddon 2014) is to provide experimental contexts for the visitor, and thus allow him to discover the people behind the exhibits. One way to achieve this goal is re-enactment (Agnew 2004), an experiential practice of performing past actions that establishes kinetic empathy, sympathetic imagination or haptic communication (Daugbjerg et al. 2014, p. 282).

Within Time Maps, an international archaeology platform (TIMEMAPS website 2020), a first attempt was made starting in 2011 to relate the technological gestures of the construction of objects with those of their use, in order to better understand the cultures of the past (Mangalia Virtual Museum website 2020) (Fig. 9.1). Some of the experiments were done at the Callatis Archaeological Museum in Mangalia, Romania, which is also the case study presented here.

A second example of relating objects to gestures of use was made at the Archaeological Museum in Maçao, Portugal, during the exhibition "From Gesture to Art: Create, Make, Communicate" in 2015, where on the windows with prehistoric objects on display the gestures of producing or using these objects were drawn (Fig. 9.2).

The third example is that of the "Keys to Rome" exhibition (2014) which, through the use of the digital application Admotum, allows "a user's virtual hand re-collocating the object in its original virtual context" (Fanini et al. 2018, p. 4), thus, guiding the visitor's attention to the issues of scale or size of the objects in the virtual

Fig. 9.1 Mangalia Virtual Museum 2015 (3D reconstruction by M. Hodea)

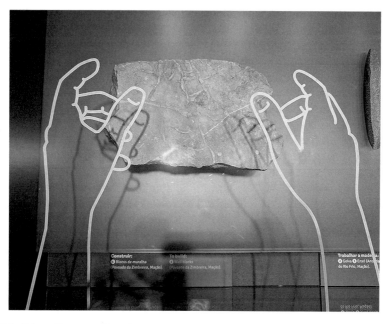

Fig. 9.2 "From Gesture to Art: Create, Make, Communicate" exhibition 2015, Archaeological Museum in Maçao, Portugal (Photo by D. Gheorghiu)

reconstruction. These examples show the importance of studying human gestures (SEMIOTICON website 2020) in order to understand the construction and ritual use of objects (Gheorghiu 2010) and also for a better understanding of archaeological artefacts through experiential learning (Loo 2002).

9.6   Case Study: Callatis Archaeologic Museum

The Callatis Archaeological Museum in Mangalia, a traditional museum (Mangalia Virtual Museum website 2020), was one of the research topics for the Time Maps project, with which the authors have been involved over the last decade (http://timemaps.net/timemap/mangalia/?page_id=2780). The museum exhibits Greek and Roman pieces excavated from the site of Callatis, one of the flourishing colonies of the city of Megara, established on the Black Sea coast.

Within the Time Maps project, a "thick description" (Geertz 1973), i.e. a detailed description of the context, was proposed to reproduce and explain the cultural context of objects from the Hellenistic period. It began with a 3D reproduction of the shape of the artefact, and then with a video presentation of its production technology, followed by a presentation of the use of the object in the form of re-enactments performed in contexts reconstructed in both real and virtual mediums.

In the current chapter, we propose a project centered on the reinvention of the local museum and the extension of the "museum experience" based on digital technology (Parry 2007, p. 319). For the creation of innovative experiences (Bannon et al. 2005) we propose the realization of an experiment with a hybrid museum by associating physical artefacts with digital resources, respectively, by mixing the current traditional artefact display system in the Callatis museum with a digital presentation of 3D reconstructed artefacts, their ergonomics, and finally with a virtual presentation of the cultural context, represented by the 3D reconstruction of the architectural spaces, and by the integration of the technical gestures (Dobres 2000, p. 152) within some re-enactments integrated in their turn in the architectural spaces reconstructed in 3D. The entire digitization part described represents an enhancement in the cultural information of the artefacts exhibited in the museum in the traditional manner.

We believe that the enhancement of museum information can be achieved in situ with the help of mobile devices, and online by visiting the digital version of the museum.

9.6.1   Augmenting the Museum Artefacts' Information

As much of the relatively recently collected archaeological material has not been restored, and consequently is not yet available to the public, we have proposed that there be at least one room dedicated to these discoveries. The showcases in which

Fig. 9.3 A shard on display
with QRs (Virtual
reconstruction by M. Hodea)

the fragments of objects are exposed will each have a series of QR codes that will allow a successive augmentation of the information (Fig. 9.3).

The visitor will scan the first code of the series, followed by the appearance of object fragment on the display of the phone or tablet. This 3D model can be rotated to be better understood (Fig. 9.4).

In this chapter, we will use as examples small Hellenistic vessels with black varnish and large fish-plates, whose ergonomic profiles and pedestals are always hidden from view by positioning the object in the glass box. The rotation of these objects will reveal their ergonomic shape and consequently the haptics of their design and the human gesture of almost two and a half millennia ago.

A second scan will bring on the screens the 3D reconstruction of the complete object (Fig. 9.5), which can be rotated to observe the hidden details by positioning it in the display case and to understand its use or manipulation. A short text will inform the visitor on some aspects (Martino 2020, p. 194) related to the shapes of Hellenistic vessels. This rhetorical action of transforming the fragment into a whole excites the visitor's imagination to reconstruct "wholes" from museum fragments (Burström 2016, p. 321).

The third scan of the third QR will show a series of hand gestures (scanned in 3D) of people using the previously reconstructed objects (Fig. 9.6). A short text urges the viewer to reproduce these gestures, keeping in mind the shape of the object.

These images will be replaced by other images in which the hands support the reconstructed objects (Fig. 9.7). By rotating them, the viewer can observe the location of the palms and fingers positioned around the vessel and thus can understand the

Fig. 9.4 3D model rotated (left) and original (right) (scanned in 3D by M. Hodea; photo by D. Gheorghiu)

Fig. 9.5 3D reconstruction of the complete object (Photo by D. Gheorghiu)

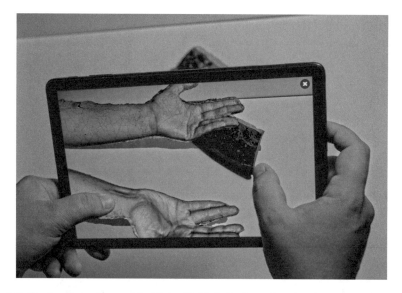

Fig. 9.6 Hand gestures (scanned in 3D by M. Hodea) of people using the reconstructed object (Photo by D. Gheorghiu)

Fig. 9.7 Ergonomic use and ritual manipulation of a reconstructed fishplate (3D scan by M. Hodea; photo by D. Gheorghiu)

relationship between shape and ergonomics, as well as the manner of use or ritual manipulation of these objects. At the end of this visual narrative, the whole character dressed in a period costume will appear (respectively, a real character scanned in 3D), which will enhance the information about the simple object displayed in the glass box and will bring before the eyes of the visitor the people of the Past (Fig. 9.8).

The fifth latest QR scan will lead to a panoramic virtual tour (panotour) by means of which the user is immersed in an interactive 3D reconstruction of a Hellenistic kitchen, with real 3D scanned characters performing various tasks in direct or indirect relationship with the scanned object. The panotour is hosted on the TimeMaps website (2020), on Mangalia's page, in the eLearning section, using the "Hybrid museum" dedicated link (http://timemaps.net/timemap/mangalia/panotour/panotour-kitchen/source/index.htm) (Fig. 9.9). Users can use the mouse or the keyboard arrows to navigate into the panoramic 3D view and explore the objects and the scene.

Fig. 9.8 Character dressed in ancient Greek costume carrying a fishplate (3D scan by M. Hodea; photo by D. Gheorghiu)

Fig. 9.9 3D reconstructed Hellenistic kitchen, with real 3D scanned characters (M. Hodea), TimeMaps website (2020)

This is the last level of augmented information about shards displayed in glass boxes. In this reconstruction in which people are present and interact with objects, the viewer can easily immerse himself and can recall the haptic experience he had on the occasion of repeating the gestures of holding the vessels, thus facilitating the embodiment into the digital environment. In the case of recent game proposals, "re-contextualization activities have been proposed which ask users to relocate virtual

Fig. 9.10 Study of natural and artificial lighting on the textures of materials (3D scan and virtual reconstruction by M. Hodea)

cultural objects to their former locations" (Fanini et al. 2018, p. 2), but it is an immersive action without good body memorization.

The feeling of reality of virtual 3D reconstruction will be achieved by taking into account several scenography principles, such as the correct use of natural or artificial light (Gheorghiu 2018), colours and textures of materials, many of which will be scanned (Fig. 9.10). The introduction in the virtual reconstruction of real characters, dressed in ancient Greek costumes and then scanned in 3D, as well as objects scanned in 3D, creates a blurred boundary between reality and virtuality, i.e. an Augmented Virtuality (see Eve 2014, p. 20).

Acoustics is an effective sensory contribution to augmenting the reality of the past. In the present case, sounds produced by all the technical actions of food preparation in the kitchen were collected, and combined with background sounds of some conversations or songs with instruments specific to the epoch. The acoustic augmentation of the context can produce a different perception of the objects and technologies, each material producing a specific sound.

This type of augmentation was introduced in the 3D virtual reconstruction of the cultural context; at this level, it is hoped that the sensory experience of the audience will produce an effect of synaesthesia or intersensoriality (Skeates 2010, p. 22), facilitated by the performative-ritual (Inomata and Coben 2006, p. 18) theatrical action (Pearson and Shanks 2001), of the characters interacting with the reconstructed objects.

9.6.2 Description of the 3D Scanning Solution and Virtual Reconstruction

For the creation of 3D models of the vessels, we used the technique of photogrammetry, or Structure from Motion (SfM), for generating 3D models from successive and overlapping photos, followed by post-processing and improving the models with specialized software applications, i.e. photogrammetry applications (Samaan et al. 2013).

Photogrammetry is "the art, science, and technology of obtaining reliable information about physical objects and the environment, through processes of recording, measuring, and interpreting imagery and digital representations of energy patterns derived from noncontact sensor systems" (DeWitt and Wolf 2000). In addition to its many years of use in aerial photogrammetry, cartography, documentation and remote sensing (DeWitt and Wolf 2000), photogrammetry is currently used on a large scale for the documentation of archaeological artefacts and buildings with 3D models.

The work started with a set of photographs taken from different angles with a professional DSLR camera (Kabadayi et al. 2020). As the objects to be photographed were small, macro photography was used (Gajski et al. 2016).

The photos were uploaded to AgiSoft (AGISOFT website 2020), one of the most popular photogrammetry applications, as it is a simple, low-cost tool, which also provides SfM algorithms (Kabadayi et al. 2020; Ulvi et al. 2019). The process of obtaining the 3D model from multiple photographs needs computational power, as several intermediate 3D structures such as "dense point cloud" and "mesh" are generated prior to obtaining the finally polished 3D model (Kabadayi et al. 2020).

In the case of the Callatis Museum where the photogrammetry was applied to the fragments of vases and to the gestures of the hands, over 50 images being taken for each object. To generate a 3D model for the reconstruction of the whole objects, 3Dmax (AUTODESK 3DMAX website 2020) was used, in which 3D models of the ceramic fragments to be reconstructed were imported, and on which approximations were made based on the geometry of the objects (like ellipses or edges).

9.6.3 The Description of the AR Solution

The 3D models were uploaded to the online platform Sketchfab (Sketchfab website 2020) which offers capabilities to host, expose and share 3D models, both publicly and privately. For the present research, the Sketchfab platform was chosen for the creation of the 3D model gallery, annotations of models, for its 3D model viewing capabilities in VR and AR views, both within web browsers and in the Sketchfab mobile application, due to its integration with advanced 3D technologies. Sketchfab is using WebGL and WebXR (WEBXR website 2020) based viewers that allow users to see 3D models on any desktop or mobile browsers or Virtual Reality headset.

Sketchfab mobile application, downloadable from iOS App Store or Android Google Play, offers an AR viewer based on Google ArCore plugin (ARCORE website 2020).

Another reason for the selection of the Sketchfab platform was its ability to share content through URL links. For each object, a link can be generated and further embedded in other applications or integrated into the QR codes. For the purpose of the present research, QR codes with web links to the 3D reconstructions were created. When scanned with a QR code reader, these QR codes will trigger the augmentation of the physical object, i.e. will redirect to a 3D reconstruction displayed within an AR viewer of the Sketchfab mobile application.

The QR-Code Generator application (QR-Code Generator website 2020) was used for the QR codes. This tool is simple to use and has the capabilities required by our research.

> *Accessing the Museum.* While in the museum, the user will scan the QR codes in front of the exhibit and will have a gradual augmentative experience, from the simple object to its cultural context.
>
> *Accessing the Online Virtual Museum.* The web page of the Callatis Museum will display 2D images of the fragmented objects, as well as all the QR codes. By scanning them with the mobile phone, the 3D model opens in the previously downloaded Sketchfab mobile application. The application interface offers two buttons for AR viewing, i.e. opening the camera and superimposing 3D objects over the real object, or in VR, with any Head-Mounted equipment.

By successively scanning the QR codes, the user will navigate through a sequence of augmentations, the last one being a virtual tour of the reconstructed cultural context, i.e. a Hellenistic kitchen. This virtual tour is also integrated in a web page of the Time Maps website (2020). To achieve this, the krpano application was used (KRPANO website 2020) which allows the creation of virtual tours (panotours) to be hosted on web pages.

9.7   Conclusions

The contemporary digital archaeology research has generated a trend towards a hyper-reality (Shanks and Webmoor 2013) of an "authentic" reconstruction of a "high fidelity" Past (McNamara et al. 1998; Roussos and Chalmers 2003). A more accurate reconstruction of reality creates an effective immersive environment that can be augmented by various methods, some involving the agency of the viewer.

In the case of museums, we believe that this immersive state can be achieved by using AR applications that may involve the use of gestures or hearing. Such an achievement transforms the simple display of information into a "constructed situation" of an artistic spectacle and consequently into a psychogeographic experience (Knabb 1995).

The experiment we proposed, involving the repetition of some gestures in relation to the exposed objects, and the enhancement of this experience with sounds, can help to create an immersive state in the final stage of augmenting an object, namely that of presenting the entire context of use. Also, the final augmentation allows first an experience of the ergonomic space of the technologies of using the objects, and then of the inhabited one. The second level of experience is that of the human behaviour, of the everyday secular or ritual performance, which takes place in an environment of Augmented Virtuality. In this case, the public's awareness of the gestures and haptics, as well as of the acoustics of the space, can create cross-sensory fusions in the audience.

The role of a twenty-first-century museum will be to bring back to life the humanity of the Past and not to continue to fetishize the objects decontextualized in their glass boxes.

We believe that some small institutions, such as the Callatis Museum, in the absence of funding to allow the use of Head-Mounted Display equipment and the existence of specialized spaces, can use a free application that can be accessed by phone, with which to experience cultural contexts from the Past, this being a first step towards creating an efficient hybrid museum.

The sensory relationship of people with objects, the immersive explanation of their use is the original digital insertion in the traditional collections of the Callatis Museum, which, in this way, will be able to continue existing in the contemporary world.

Acknowledgements The authors thank Professor Vladimir Geroimenko for the kind invitation to contribute to this book, M.Bogdan Căpruciu for the suggestions to improve the English text, and to Mrs Cornelia Cătuna for the editing. Many thanks also to the theatre students who played the Greek characters, and to Professor Paula Barbu for the ancient Greek costumes.

References

AGISOFT website (2020). www.agisoft.com. Accessed December 2020

Agnew V (2004) Introduction: what is reenactment? Criticism 46(3) Article 2. http://digitalco mmons.wayne.edu/criticism/vol46/iss3/2

ARCORE website (2020). https://developers.google.com/ar. Accessed December 2020

Augé M (1992) Non-lieux. Introduction a une anthropologie de la surmodernité. Seuil, Paris

AUTODESK 3DMAX website (2020). Accessed December 2020

Azuma RT (2015) Location-based mixed and augmented reality storytelling. In: Barfield W (ed) Fundamentals of wearable computers and augmented reality, vol 2. CRC Press, Boca Raton FL, pp 259–276

Banfia F, Brumanaa R, Stanga C (2019) Extended reality and informative models for the architectural heritage: from scan-to-bim process to virtual and augmented reality. Virtual Archaeol Rev 10(21):14–30

Bannon L, Benford S, Bowers J, Heath C (2005, March) Hybrid design creates innovative museum experiences. Communications of the ACM 48(3)

Burström M (2016) Fragments as something more: archaeological experience and reflection. In: Gonzáles-Ruibal A (ed) Reclaiming archaeology: beyond the tropes of Modernity. Routledge, London and New York, pp 311–322

Ciolfi L, Bannon L (2002) Designing interactive museum exhibits: Enhancing visitor curiosity through augmented artifacts. In: Proceedings of the European Conference on Cognitive Ergonomics, pp 311–317

Clini P, Quattrini R, Bonvini P, Nespeca R, Angeloni R, Mammoli R, Dragoni AF, Morbidoni C, Sernani P, Mengoni M, et al. (2020) Digit(al)isation in museums: Civitas Project—AR, VR, multisensorial and multiuser experiences at the Urbino's Ducal Palace. In: Virtual and augmented reality in education, art, and museums. IGI Global, Hershey PA, USA, pp 194–228, https://doi.org/10.4018/978-1-7998-1796-3.ch011

Clifford J (1997) Routes: Travel and translation in the late 20th century. Harvard University Press, Cambridge and London.

Daugbjerg M, Eisner RS, Knudsen BT (2014) Re-enacting the past: vivifying heritage 'again'. Int J Herit Stud 20(7–8):681–687. https://doi.org/10.1080/13527258.2014.939426

de Souza e Silva A (2006) Mobile technologies as interfaces of hybrid spaces. Space Cult 9(3):261–278

DeWitt BA, Wolf PR (2000). Elements of photogrammetry (with Applications in GIS) (3rd ed.). McGraw-Hill Higher Education

Dobres MA (2000) Technology and social agency. Blackwell, Oxford

Europeana website (2020). https://pro.europeana.eu/post/explore-hybrid-museum-experiences-at-europeana-2019. Accessed December 2020

Eve S (2014) Dead men's eyes: embodied GIS, mixed reality and landscape archaeology. Archaeopress, Oxford

Fanini B, Pagano A, Ferdani D (2018) A novel immersive VR game model for recontextualization in virtual environments: the mVRModel. Multimodal Technol Interact 2(20). https://doi.org/10.3390/mti2020020

Franklin Institute AR, Philadelphia. https://www.fi.edu/augmented-reality. Accessed December 2020

Gajski D, Solter A, Gašparovic M (2016) Applications of macro photogrammetry in archaeology. In: International Archives of the Photogrammetry, Remote Sensing and Spatial Information Sciences—ISPRS Archives 41:263–266. International Society for Photogrammetry and Remote Sensing

Geertz C (1973) The interpretation of cultures. Basic Books, New York

Gheorghiu D (2010) Ritual technology: an experimental approach to cucuteni-tripolye chalcolithic figurines. In: Gheorghiu D, Cyphers A (eds) Anthropomorphic and zoomorphic miniature figures in Eurasia, Africa and Meso-America: morphology, materiality, technology, function and context—BAR International Series 2138. Archaeopress, Oxford, pp 61–72

Gheorghiu D (2015) Sensing the past: the sensorial experience in experiential archaeology by augmenting the perception of materiality. In: Pellini JR, Zarankin A, Salerno MA (eds) Coming to senses: topics in sensory archaeology. Newcastle upon Tyne, Cambridge Scholars Publishing, pp 119–140

Gheorghiu D (2018) Lighting in reconstructed contexts: experiential archaeology with pyrotechnologies. In: Papadopoulos C, Moyes H (eds) The Oxford handbook of light in archaeology. Oxford Handbooks Online. https://doi.org/10.1093/oxfordhb/9780198788218.013.28

Gheorghiu D (ed) (2001) Material, virtual and temporal compositions: on the relationship between objects. British Archaeological Reports, Archaeopress, Oxford

Gheorghiu D, Ştefan L (2015) Augmenting immersion: the implementation of the real world in virtual reality. In: Börner W and Uhlirz S (eds) The 20th International Conference on Cultural Heritage and New Technologies CHNT 2015. Museen der Stadt Wien—Stadtarchäologie, Vienna

Gheorghiu D, Ştefan L (2019a) Virtual art in teaching and learning archaeology: an intermedia to augment the content of virtual spaces and the quality of immersion. In: Gheorghiu D, Barth T (eds) Artistic practices and archaeological research. Archaeopress Publishing, Oxford, pp 166–182

Gheorghiu D, Ştefan L (2019b) Invisible settlements: discovering and reconstructing the ancient built spaces through gaming. In: Geroimenko V (ed) Augmented reality games. Springer, Cham. https://doi.org/10.1007/978-3-030-15620-6_4

Giannini T, Bowen JP (2019) Rethinking museum exhibitions: merging physical and digital culture—present to future. In: Giannini T, Bowen JP (eds) Museums and digital culture: new perspectives and research. Springer Series on Cultural Computing, Cham, pp 195–214

Hammady R, Ma M, Temple N (2016) Augmented reality and gamification in heritage museums. In: Joint International Conference on Serious Games, pp 181–187 https://doi.org/10.1007/978-3-319-45841-0_17

Hermon S, Hazan S (2013) Rethinking the virtual museum. In: Digital Heritage International Congress 2013, Marseille, France, 28 Oct–1 Nov 2013, 2:625–632

Hermon S, Hazan S (2014) Virtual museums. a theoretical background, Florence. https://www.aca demia.edu/6131101/virtual_museums_a_theoretical_background. Accessed December 2020

Hughes CE, Smith E, Stapleton C, Hughes D (2004) Augmenting museum experiences with mixed reality. In: Proceedings of KSCE 2004

Hughes CE, Stapleton C, O'Connor MR (2014) The evolution of a framework for mixed reality experiences. https://doi.org/10.4018/978-1-59904-066-0.ch010

Inomata T, Coben LS (2006) Overture: an invitation to the archaeological theatre. In: Inomata T, Coben LS (eds) Archaeology performance: theatres of power, community, and politics. Altamira Press, Lanham, New York, Toronto, Oxford, pp 11–46

Izzo F (2017) Museum customer experience and virtual reality: H.Bosch exhibition case study. Mod Econ 8:531–536. https://doi.org/10.4236/me.2017.84040

Kabadayi A, Kaya Y, Yiğit A (2020) Comparison of documenting cultural artifacts using the 3D model in different software. Mersin Photogramm J 2(2):51–58. https://dergipark.org.tr/en/pub/mephoj/issue/58058/717483. Accessed December 2020

Kang Y, Yang KCC (2020) Employing digital reality technologies in art exhibitions and museums: a global survey of best practices and implications. In: Virtual and augmented reality in education, art, and museums. IGI Global, pp 139–161. https://doi.org/10.4018/978-1-7998-1796-3.ch008

Kargas A, Karitsioti N, Loumos G (2020) Reinventing museums in 21st century: implementing augmented reality and virtual reality technologies alongside social media's logics. In: Virtual and augmented reality in education, art, and museums. IGI Global, pp 117–138. https://doi.org/10.4018/978-1-7998-1796-3.ch007

Keys to Rome. Roman Culture, Virtual Museums (2014) Pescarin S (ed curatorship), Baker D, Palombini A, Ruggeri D (eds). Keys to Rome website: www.keys2rome.eu. Accessed December 2020

Knabb K (ed) (1995) Situationist international anthology, 3rd edn. Bureau of Public Secrets, Berkley, p 50

KRPANO website (2020). www.krpano.com. Accessed December 2020

Kunjir AR, Patil KR (2020) Challenges of mobile augmented reality in museums and art galleries for visitors suffering from vision, speech and learning disabilities. In: Virtual and augmented reality in education, art, and museums, Ch 9. IGI Global, pp 162–173. https://doi.org/10.4018/978-1-7998-1796-3.ch009

Li Y-C, Liew AW-C, Su W-P (2012) The digital museum: challenges and solution. In: 8th International Conference on Information Science and Digital Content Technology (ICIDT2012), Jeju, pp 646–649

Loo R (2002) A meta-analytic examination of Kolb's learning style preferences among business majors. J Educ Bus 77:252–256

Louvre Museum, Paris. https://www.louvre.fr/en/visites-en-ligne. Accessed December 2020

Louvre VR. https://arts.vive.com/us/articles/projects/art-photography/mona_lisa_beyond_the_glass/. Accessed December 2020

Malraux A (1996) La Musée immaginaire. Gallimard, Paris

Mangalia Museum, Mangalia. https://mangalia.ro/index.php/2012/10/04/muzeul-callatis/. Accessed December 2020

Mangalia Virtual Museum (2020). http://timemaps.net/timemap/mangalia/. Accessed December 2020

Martino S (2020) Vessel forms and functions. In: Durgun P (ed) An educator's handbook for teaching about the ancient world, vol 1. Archaeopress, Oxford, pp 193–195

McNamara A, Chalmers A, Troscianko T, Reinhard E (1998) Fidelity of graphics reconstructions: a psychophysical investigation. In: Drettakis G, Max N (eds) Rendering Techniques '98. EGSR 1998. Eurographics. Springer, Vienna, pp 237–246. https://doi.org/10.1007/978-3-7091-6453-2_22

Merlini M, Velichkov A (eds) (2009) Routes and itineraries from the Virtual Museum of the European Roots. F-MU.S.EU.M. Project. Published by Euro Innovanet Srl., Italy and Cultura Animi Foundation, Bulgaria

Microsoft Kinetics website (2020). https://developer.microsoft.com/en-us/windows/kinect/. Accessed December 2020

Milgram P, Colquhoun H Jr (1999) A taxonomy of real and virtual world display integration. In: Tamura H, Ohta Y (eds) Mixed reality: merging real and virtual worlds. Springer, New York, pp 5–28

Milgram P, Kishino F (1994) A taxonomy of mixed reality visual displays. IEICE Transactions on Information Systems E77-D(12):1321–1329

Museum of Celtic Heritage. https://heritageinmotion.eu/himentry/slug-4c385b0768f18d43ee862c5ae5db62b6. Accessed December 2020

Naemura T, Kakehi Y, Hashida T, ah Seong Y, Akatsuka D, Wada T, Nariya T, Nakashima T, Oshima R, Kuno T (2010) Mixed reality technologies for museum experience. In: Proceedings of the 9th ACM SIGGRAPH Conference on Virtual-Reality Continuum and its Applications in Industry (VRCAI '10). Association for Computing Machinery, New York, NY, USA, pp 17–20. https://doi.org/10.1145/1900179.1900182

NE-MO SURVEY. https://www.ne-mo.org/news/article/nemo/nemo-survey-on-museums-and-covid-19-museums-adapt-to-go-online.html

Niccolucci F (2007) Virtual museums and archaeology: an international perspective. In: Moscati P (ed) Virtual museums and archaeology, Archeologia e Calcolatori, Supplemento 1, pp 15–30

Paddon H (2014) Redisplaying museum collections: contemporary display and interpretation in British museums. Ashgate, Farnham

Papagiannakis G, Magnenat-Thalmann N (2007) Mobile augmented heritage: enabling human life in ancient Pompeii. Int J Arch Comput, Multi-Sci Publ 5(2):395–415

Parry R (2007) Recoding the museum: digital heritage and the technologies of change. Routledge, London

Pearson M, Shanks M (2001) Theatre/archaeology. Routledge, London

QR-CODE GENERATOR website (2020). https://www.qr-code-generator.com/. Accessed December 2020

Roussos I, Chalmers A (2003) High fidelity lighting of Knossos. In: Proceedings of the 4th International Conference on Virtual Reality, Archaeology and Intelligent Cultural Heritage (VAST'03). Eurographics Association, Goslar, pp 195–202

Samaan M, Héno R, Pierrot-Deseilligny M (2013). Close-range photogrammetric tools for small 3D archeological objects. In: International Archives of the Photogrammetry, Remote Sensing and Spatial Information Sciences, XL-5/W2, XXIV International CIPA Symposium, 2–6 September 2013, Strasbourg, France

SEMIOTICON website (2020). http://www.semioticon.com/virtuals/archaeology/arch.htm

Shanks M, Webmoor T (2013) A political economy of visual media in archaeology. In: Bonde S, Houston S (eds) Re-presenting the past: archaeology through text and image. Oxbow, Oxford, pp 85–108

Skeates R (2010) An archaeology of senses: Prehistoric Malta. Oxford University Press, Oxford

SKETCHFAB website (2020). https://sketchfab.com/. Accessed December 2020

Smithsonian Natural History Museum, Washington, DC. https://naturalhistory.si.edu/visit/virtual-tour. Accessed December 2020

Stapleton CB, Hughes CE (2006) Believing is seeing. IEEE Comput Graph Appl 27(1):88–93

Stevens M (2016) Touched from a distance: the practice of affective browsing. In: van den Akker C, Legêne S (eds) Museums in a digital culture: how art and heritage become meaningful. Amsterdam University Press, Amsterdam, pp 13–30

Styliani S, Fotis L, Kostas K, Petros P (2009) Virtual museums, a survey and some issues for consideration. Journal of Cultural Heritage 10(4):520–528

Tallon L, Walker K (2008) Digital technologies and the museum experience: handle guides and other media. Altamira Press, London

The Smithsonian AR. https://naturalhistory.si.edu/exhibits/bone-hall. Accessed December 2020

TIMEMAPS website (2020). www.timemaps.net. Accessed December 2020

Ulvi A, Yakar M, Yiğit A, Kaya Y (2019) The use of photogrammetric techniques in documenting cultural heritage: The Example of Aksaray Selime Sultan Tomb. Univers J Eng Sci 7(3):64–73

UNESCO REPORT. https://en.unesco.org/news/launch-unesco-report-museums-around-world-face-covid-19

Varinlioglu G, Halici SM (2019) Gamification of Heritage through augmented reality. In: Sousa JP, Xavier JP, Castro Henriques, G (eds) Architecture in the Age of the 4th Industrial Revolution—Proceedings of the 37th eCAADe and 23rd SIGraDi Conference—Volume 1. University of Porto, Porto, Portugal, 11–13 September, pp 513–518

Vlahakis, V., Pliakas T, Demiris A, Ioannidis N (2003) Design and application of an augmented reality system for continuous, context-sensitive guided tours of indoor and outdoor cultural sites and museums. In: VAST 2003, the 4th International Symposium on Virtual Reality, Archaeology and Intelligent Cultural Heritage, Brighton, UK, pp 155–164

vom Lehn D, Heath C, Hindmarsh J (2001) Exhibiting interaction: conduct and collaboration in museums and galleries. Symb Interact 24(2):189–216

WEBXR website (2020). https://www.w3.org/TR/webxr. Accessed December 2020

Chapter 10
Supporting Spontaneous Museum Visits by Deaf People: An Augmented Reality Application and a Case Study

Priscyla Barbosa, Patricia Amorim, Simone Bacellar Leal Ferreira, and Aline Castro

Abstract This chapter presents research that aims to identify accessibility characteristics necessary for a satisfactory interaction of prelingual deaf users with the contents of a museum exhibition. To achieve this goal an application was developed and a case study carried out at the UFRJ (Federal University of Rio de Janeiro) Geodiversity Museum. Augmented reality was chosen in order to provide different types of information about one of the museum's exhibition rooms. The application was submitted to an accessibility evaluation with experts and, subsequently, to tests with users, involving five prelingual deaf volunteers. The users' observations occurred in the real context and identified the demands of the deaf and the effects of providing accessibility with the help of augmented reality.

10.1 Introduction

The Brazilian Law for the Inclusion of Persons with Disabilities (BRASIL 2015) established important guidelines for the promotion of the rights of persons with disabilities aiming at their social inclusion, equal opportunities and good citizenship, highlighting the right to culture, sport, tourism, and leisure, and defining that access to cultural goods, monuments, and spaces offering services must be guaranteed in accessible formats.

P. Barbosa (✉) · P. Amorim · S. B. L. Ferreira
Graduate Program in Informatics (PPGI), Federal University of the State of Rio de Janeiro (UNIRIO), Rio de Janeiro, Brazil
e-mail: priscyla.ferreira@uniriotec.br

P. Amorim
e-mail: patricia.amorim@uniriotec.br

S. B. L. Ferreira
e-mail: simone@uniriotec.br

A. Castro
Museum of Geodiversity, Institute of Geosciences (IGEO), Federal University of the State of Rio de Janeiro (UNIRIO), Rio de Janeiro, Brazil
e-mail: alinecastro@igeo.ufrj.br

V. Geroimenko (ed.), *Augmented Reality in Tourism, Museums and Heritage*, Springer Series on Cultural Computing,
https://doi.org/10.1007/978-3-030-70198-7_10

A survey on the Living Conditions of People with Disabilities in Brazil (DATASE-NADO 2013) with 1007 participants indicated some figures regarding leisure activities. About 68.8% of respondents prefer activities integrated with others over activities specific for people with disabilities. As for the main needs in the leisure scene today, 44.4% indicated that it was important to adapt environments. Thus, the need to adapt environments for users must be considered, especially in public spaces.

According to the IBGE Census (IBGE 2010), 9.7 million Brazilians are hearing impaired, 2.1 million of whom are severely so. According to the National Health Survey—PNS/IBGE (IBGE 2013), 20.6% of the hearing impaired population had an intense or very intense degree of limitation or was unable to perform everyday activities. This shows that a considerable percentage of the Brazilian population with deafness may encounter barriers to information and actively participate in society.

Hearing impairment is defined as the "bilateral, partial or total loss, of forty-one decibels (dB) or more, as measured by an audiogram" (BRASIL 2014). Some people with hearing impairment may have difficulty hearing and may be able to use hearing aids in order to hear partially, others with profound deafness don't have the capabilities of amplifiers or hearing aids. According to Sacks (Alves 2012), deafness can also be classified according to the onset of hearing loss as prelingual; or post-lingual, when hearing loss happens after language acquisition.

The Brazilian Sign Language—Libras—is the language of visual-motor nature used by the deaf and has its own characteristics as it considers facial and body expressions, hand configuration and points of articulation to transmit the signals, as well as having its own grammar, being completely different than a literal translation from Portuguese. In view of this, bilingual pre-linguistic deaf users have difficulties understanding textual information in Portuguese (Alves 2012).

Accessibility is defined as the "possibility and condition of reach for the use, with security and autonomy, of spaces, furniture, urban equipment, buildings, transport, information and communication, including their systems and technologies, as well as other services and facilities open to the public, for public use or of private nature for collective use, both in urban and rural areas, by persons with disabilities or reduced mobility" (BRASIL 2015). An accessible information system should not have barriers that prevent access to different types of users. Barriers are obstacles that limit and prevent accessibility (Ferreira and Nunes 2008).

Several researchers explore the potential of using interactive augmented reality (Mendonça and Mustaro 2011) as a tool for digital simulation and dynamic visualization which could improve learning (Yoon et al. 2017) and the dissemination of information in cultural environments such as touristic sights and museums (Martins et al. 2015). Augmented Reality (AR) can be defined as the combination of the real world and virtual content where the interaction takes place in real time (Azuma 1997). As such, digital objects (images, videos, 3D shapes, sounds) and sensory experience (such as touch and smell) are brought to the user's physical environment. A recent example of the application of this technology was the game Pokémon GO, which inserted cartoon characters in the real world for everyone to hunt using cell phones. It enriches the real environment with virtual information that can assist in the performance of tasks. As a result, the use of this technology to support accessibility in museums can be explored as a way to enrich the visit of people with disabilities.

The access of visitors with disabilities to museums normally happens through guided tours that must be scheduled in advance so that a Libras mediator/interpreter can be available. It is unlikely that a cultural space such as a museum would be prepared to receive a spontaneous visit from a person with disabilities if it doesn't invest in resources such as a Libras mediator/interpreter who is available at all times or in communication technologies such as audio and/or video guides.

This research intended to identify the characteristics of usability and accessibility necessary to develop an assistive technology using augmented reality that supports the spontaneous visitation of deaf people to museums.

10.2 Methodology

Through an exploratory and qualitative approach, a case study was implemented in the context of the UFRJ (Federal University of Rio de Janeiro) Geodiversity Museum to identify aspects of the experience and perception of accessible content made available in a digital and interactive system using augmented reality. A mobile application prototype was developed for the museum environment. This research had the following nine stages:

1—**Choice of environment:** The Geodiversity Museum (MGeo) of the Geosciences Institute (IGEO/UFRJ) was selected for the case study, as it is an organization that has been concerned with reducing barriers and providing quality service to all types of audiences, taking into account accessibility and the promotion of access rights to culture and science (Castro 2014). One important factor is that its exhibition should be long-term, as it would offer sufficient time to carry out theoretical studies, develop the application prototype, produce accessible content and execute tests with users. It has shown to be ideal for meeting deadlines required for the stages of this study.

2—**Study of the selected environment:** For an in-depth look at the geodiversity museum and its actions, we reviewed its publications at www.museu.igeo.ufrj.br and academic works (Castro et al. 2011; Castro 2014; Castro et al. 2015); analysis of the content developed by the museum such as folders, audio description script, videos; visits to the space and supervision of a guided tour with a school group. We observed a group of 25 students, between 12 and 14 years old, who interacted with the educators and with elements of the exhibition.

3—**Selection and study of user profile:** In order to perform the case study, two groups were selected to compose units of analysis and comparison: pre-linguistic deaf and hearing users. It was necessary to get to know the deaf culture up close so one of the researchers participated in a guided tour at MGeo with a group of 22 eighth- and ninth-grade students with hearing impairment from the National

Institute of the Deaf (INES). The visit was done with two trained Libras interpreters/mediators who led the visit for the deaf public accompanied by two mediators from the museum for specific geology questions. In addition, unstructured interviews were conducted with accessibility specialists who pointed out: difficulties in translating concepts and specific questions into Libras in the classroom; caution in adapting the content to maintain quality when simplifying concepts; need for the interpreter to master the content to be translated; use of illustrations and images of different subjects to help understand the theme; consider time and amount of information in the development of video guides. The participation of events related to the theme of accessibility and deafness was also prioritized for the study of users, in addition to participation in meetings of the working group specializing in accessibility in museums of the Accessible and Inclusive UFRJ Permanent Forum.

4—Definition of the environment for the prototype: After a meeting with the participation of the director of the museum, the museologist, the coordinator of the educational area, mediators, and IT specialists, it was concluded that it would be interesting to select a room that could provide different types of information, textual, videos, and images; as well as information that needed describing during the guided tours in order to be understood. The "Mares do Passado" room, in addition to presenting a variety of information, has objects that can be touched, enabling enough interactivity for its visitors and, as such, was chosen for application of the interactive augmented reality system.

5—Study of accessibility recommendations for mobile devices: To meet the demands of the project's target audience, it was necessary to search the literature for accessibility recommendations typical of mobile devices.

6—Prototype development: The project has a multidisciplinary approach so it was necessary to gather knowledge from different areas of museology, pedagogy, software engineering, and design as well as the project's accessibility profile. For this reason, meetings were held with the museum and application development teams.

7—Definition of evaluation methods: It was defined that two types of evaluation would be done: a specialist evaluation (inspection) and later an user evaluation. The specialist evaluation was accomplished through an inspection based on recommendation guidelines, analyzed in the development of the research, to verify if the accessibility requirements were met by the prototype. In order to observe the effects and relationships that the prototype generated in the context of use, an evaluation was done with the participation of deaf users. This method was applied due to the spatial issues of the museum, which required user interaction at different points in the room. In order to understand user interaction, the SAM—Self-Assessment Manikin—assessment instrument was used, as it allows the identification of the satisfaction, motivation, and command of users regarding the use of technology.

8—Conducting the evaluation: As the selected method, the expert evaluation used inspection based on recommendation guidelines to verify that the accessibility recommendations on mobile devices had been followed in the project.

According to Nielsen (1995), using the average of three expert evaluators is satisfactory for identifying problems for practical purposes. As for the evaluators (Barbosa and Silva 2010), highlights the importance of evaluations being conducted by specialists who did not participate in the design of the solution, for the sake of impartiality. Given the above, three evaluators from the scholar's research group who have experience and knowledge in the accessibility area were invited to participate in this evaluation. These were based on the checklist technique adopted in the work of (Lacerda et al. 2013), who proposed an online checklist to evaluate the usability of applications for touchscreen phones, and the severity scale proposed by Nielsen (1995).

9—Analysis of the obtained results: The information from the case study accessibility assessments was obtained through direct observation of the user's interaction with the prototype and the researcher's simultaneous paper annotation and through the pre-test questionnaire, post-test interview, and the adapted emoti-SAM questionnaire.

10.3 Study of the Accessibility Recommendations for Mobile Devices

Attention must be paid to accessibility from the idealization to the last phase of a project so that adaptations and rework are avoided in the end. Therefore, it was necessary to study the accessibility recommendations which are typical of mobile devices to adapt the development of the prototype to the needs of the target audience.

W3C (2008, 2010, 2014) references dealing with this theme were reviewed. Schefer's work (Schefer 2016) was found in the literature, which outlines guidelines for the development of specific applications for the deaf audience. These works were gathered as references for the realization of a checklist for future evaluation of the prototype with specialists.

Due to the practical content of the project, we analyzed the general techniques of the document: "WCAG 2.0 Techniques Applicable to Mobile without Changes" (W3C 2015a) which deals with the techniques and failures that can be applied on mobile devices.

There was a need for specific instructions for the creation of accessible content for the hearing impaired and the following works with practical guidelines were suitable for this purpose: NBR 15290 (ABNT 2005), NBR 15599/2008 (ABNT 2008), and a research developed by the Ministry of Justice (BRASIL 2009). NBR 15290/2005 (ABNT 2005) establishes guidelines regarding communicational accessibility on television and deals with important aspects for closed captioning in text (alignment, characters, positioning, synchrony, and time) and for the Libras screen (studio, screen, clipping, interpretation, and visualization). NBR 15599/2008 (ABNT 2008) deals with accessibility in the provision of communication services, with emphasis on the guidelines for: redundancy when the same information must be covered with different forms of communication (visual and sound); availability of the description of environments, the routes of points of interest and the pieces in cultural environments; and the various requirements and attitudes of Libras interpreters. The work of the Ministry of Justice (BRASIL 2009) evaluated the parental rating messages on television vignettes in Libras. These recommendations were considered for the production of the Libras content of the prototype.

10.4 Development of the Assistive Technology

The application prototype focused on user-centered design. It was based on Garret's methodology (2003) which deals with elements of the user experience for software interfaces and the work of Doerr (2014) who adapted Garret's methodology for the development of mobile applications. The stages of the present work are illustrated in Fig. 10.1. In order to adapt to the needs of the target audience, the Content of Libras stage was added.

The activities at each stage were as follows:

Strategy Stage: A collaborative briefing was done in order to identify the objectives, information about the institution and responsible persons, target audience, application content, visual identity, and ideas to differentiate the application from other existing ones.

Scope Stage: To encourage discussion, we analyzed screens, resources, and functionality of apps that dealt with the themes: museum, accessibility, and augmented reality and we observed: different approaches given to the treatment of accessibility in applications (by type of disability or available features); identification of different multimedia and technological resources for the dissemination of information present in cultural environments.

Structure Stage: The information architecture and application navigation were defined. We thought through how to organize and arrange the information on the screen, define the forms of content interaction in augmented reality. A mental map of the application was made to organize ideas raised during meetings and configure the hierarchy and relationship of the information. The map helped visualize the complexity of the application both in its relationships and in its demand for content. Subsequently, we defined how the elements would be presented in the

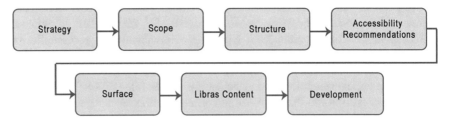

Fig. 10.1 Development stages adapted from Garrett (2003) and Doerr (2014) (*Source* The authors)

interface (screens, positioning, format, use of images, buttons, links), the forms of interaction (touch, screen scrolling) and the system behavior for each user action, consolidated in the wireframe.

Surface Stage: This stage involved the design of the application layout and the visual treatment of interface elements. Some aspects were considered to stimulate its use: combination of colors; use of names and icons that are easily understood; icon size; click area; spacing between shapes and typography. To assist in artistic creation, visual references related to the theme of the museum were made. To meet the accessibility recommendations, a color contrast validation tool—"The Accessible Color Evaluator—ACE" was used. Subsequently, to create the application screens, a template file "Android UI Design Kit" (Ling 2014) was used, which offered options for structure and visual components to help build a consistent layout for android applications. The necessary resources for the prototype were selected and adapted and the pages were developed: Opening, General Information, About the Modules, Help, and Augmented Reality. The icons representing the options available in augmented reality were designed to highlight the view of the augmented reality camera. Since the user can point it in different directions, we decided to use a white line with a black outline in order to establish greater contrast (see Fig. 10.2). A "target image" marker was developed, which can be scanned with the device's camera and provides programmed information.

Fig. 10.2 Image developed as a marker of augmented reality and the options menu (*Source* The authors)

Libras Content Stage: In order not to differentiate the content offered to hear and deaf visitors, short texts in Portuguese were developed for each selected piece, which were adapted for Libras. If necessary, during the recording, the interpreters could mention exhibited objects by pointing or including supporting images. The recordings were made in a studio with a Chroma Key screen (background clipping effect made by a standard background, usually green or blue). For the recordings, a notebook was positioned below the camera to display the annotated text and the online prompter tool (http://www.freeteleprompter.org/) to assist the interpreters in reading at the time of recording. It was necessary to have more than one interpreter in the recordings, one being responsible for checking the performance of the interpreter being filmed. Subsequently, an editing script was created to consolidate the sections of each piece. The editing of the videos cut the background to allow visitors to see the interpreter/mediator signaling in Libras and the object about which he was talking at the same time.

Development Stage: The prototype was developed with the integrated software development environment, Unity, and with the augmented reality development kit, Vuforia. To insert the videos of Libras interpreters in augmented reality, it was necessary to use a plugin, "Chroma Key Kit," to remove the background of videos recorded on Chroma Key (see Fig. 10.3).

Fig. 10.3 Libras video without the background in the environment (*Source* The authors)

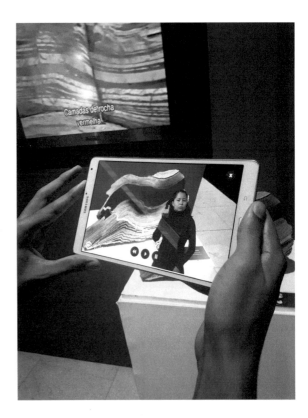

Each screen of the application was built within a Unity scene and is composed of layout images. The functions and commands of the application were adaptations of the codes which already existed in the development tools. In some cases, it was necessary to create functions in the C# programming language. The "information," "our rooms," and "help" screens were implemented with text and image resources, being relatively simple in both content and function. The augmented reality function, on the other hand, demanded more time due to the complexity of inserting different types of media, Chroma Key plugin, and marker registration. The augmented reality option was implemented to make the multimedia contents (text, Libras, images, some animation, and video) from the room available for the seven selected pieces by reading and recognizing their respective markers. To be used, the user must select the "augmented reality" button on the home page which activates the camera with instructions on how to proceed. By pointing the tablet's camera at any marker, the application will identify the piece and its available information. The menu with the available options will be displayed onscreen and the display of the environment through the camera remains active, giving the impression that the content is virtually inserted.

It was possible to observe the need for teams to be focused on fulfilling accessibility guidelines, from the planning stage to the development of assistive technology.

Content production included those responsible for geology content in Portuguese and later those were translated into Libras, being developed by specialists trained in different areas. It is interesting that the application structure is well outlined, especially when the same item has several presentation formats and are developed by different teams, as was the case with the pieces chosen to display contents of text, video in Libras, images, and animation. Visualization tools, such as a mental map, and cloud task tools, i.e., Google Drive, helped manage content and the project as a whole.

The surface and development stages took place simultaneously, since some elements built for the interface had to be adapted when the prototype was being programmed. The tests were performed constantly using the Unity "play" function to run the application locally on the machine. A webcam connected to the computer was used to simulate the tablet's camera and the marker was read through an image of the markers onscreen.

Another element that should be highlighted is the creation process of the Libras content, which included: translation of the Portuguese text, writing of the script with the identification of the inclusion of images and gestures, subsequent studio recording, videos editing, inclusion of dactylology captions, and review. The participation of more than one interpreter is always recommended to check the execution of the movements at the time of recording as well as the standardization of signals for specifics terms that may vary within the context of Libras.

10.5   User Evaluation

In order to observe users interacting with the prototype in the museum, the following activities were accomplished: preparation of tests; task selection; creation of the test material; selection of participants; pilot test execution and test execution.

In detail, the activities were as follows:

Preparation of tests: In order to understand the interaction problems in the application interface, users were asked to perform tasks that involved augmented reality, at various points in space of the room, during an interactive visit. Thus, when planning the test, it was necessary to take into account: the movement through space, lighting for positioning the markers, the positioning of the user and the interpreter for the recording of the tests, recording the application screen, positioning of the evaluator to observe in-app interaction.

Task selection: Four tasks were created in order to visualize the different formats: text, Libras, image gallery, and animation, with the visualization in different pieces being indicated so that the user had the experience of reading different markers. A printed document entitled "Test Instructions" was created, which, in addition to explaining the tasks, highlighted important points to make them comfortable: the lack of time limits or maximum duration of the test, the possibility of interruption at the participant's discretion, the appreciation of sincere opinion and the focus on evaluating the interface above the participant's performance. It emphasized that in addition to successes, mistakes would also help improve the application.

Creation of the test material: Based on the guidelines of the works of (Ferreira et al. 2012; Sarraf 2008) the free and informed consent form, pre-test questionnaire, and post-test interview were elaborated. In order to identify the user experience, the emoti-SAM questionnaire (Hayashi et al. 2016) was applied. The work of Hayashi et al. adapted the Self-Assessment Manikin (SAM) assessment tool in a pictographic format for use in research with low literacy people, children, and the elderly. Due to its visual configuration, it was applied in this research for deaf users. Thus, at the end of the tests, users were asked to indicate their experience according to the three levels: satisfaction, motivation, and feeling of control (see Fig. 10.4). In addition to the pictograms, the characteristic feelings at the ends of the figures were used as indicated in (Pagani 2013) to facilitate the understanding of these concepts by deaf users and the explanation of the Libras interpreter.

A checklist was created to verify the materials needed for the test as it would be necessary to transport equipment and materials to the museum. The markers were fixed with adhesive tape in the appropriate places and backup copies were made in case they were removed by any visitors to the museum.

Selection of participants: The study was done with five participants aged 29–48. In addition, all participants must be experienced in mobile devices such as smartphones or tablets; be deaf with severe hearing loss without the use of a hearing aid or profound hearing loss; and use Libras for communication.

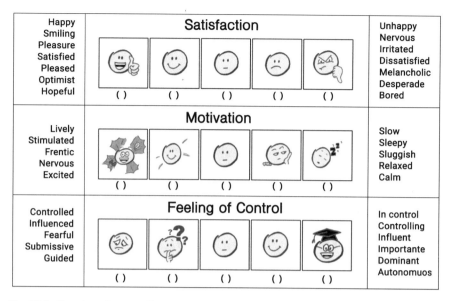

Fig. 10.4 Questionnaire to verify user experience (*Source* Adapted from Hayashi et al. [2016] and Pagani [2013])

Execution of the pilot test: The pilot test was performed with a 29-year-old user (pilot) with severe hearing loss and who does not use hearing aids. He is a pre-linguistic deaf person who learned Libras at age six. For the test, the museum's tablet was used, running the AZ Screen Recorder application (Google Play 2018) to record the onscreen interaction and also capture the audio. We opted for direct observation of the user's interaction with the prototype and taking notes on paper. When questions were asked to the user during the activities, he had to lay the tablet on furniture to communicate in Libras. Therefore, we realized that it would be necessary to use the consecutive verbalization protocol so that successive interruptions for clarifications and opinions did not occur (Ferreira et al. 2012). The pilot test contributed to the conclusion that the post-test interview, the "emoti-SAM" questionnaire and the users' considerations about the prototype would be done after the execution of the tasks instead of simultaneously. The pilot test was the first time when two applications were running at the same time: MGEO Interactive and AZ Screen Recorder. Due to the tablet's limited processing power, we chose not to record the screen in the following tests. To increase processing capacity, the tablet was restored to factory settings before reinstalling the museum app.

Execution of tests: Five other tests with users were done at the museum, based on the research developed by Nielsen (2000), who identified that the number of five participants is sufficient to detect and identify most problems. Thus usability tests with small units of analysis can avoid wasting resources such as time and budget, in addition to detecting 85% of the problems necessary for planning a new redesign (Nielsen 2000). To maintain anonymity, participants were labeled as P1, P2, P3, P4, and P5. The test was done with adults. Three volunteers work in administrative areas and two in the research area. Only one of them was not pre-linguistic deaf and learned Libras at age 29. Even though he had been oralized, the test was performed with the presence of the interpreter as he uses Libras as a form of communication. The other participants learned Libras as children. As for training, three participants were in higher education, one had started a master's degree (he objected that he did not have the option of an incomplete master's degree and checked a postgraduate, master's degree) and another had a doctorate (a volunteer who lost his hearing as an adult). Only one participant had severe hearing loss, did not use a hearing aid and also used Libras. All of them had smartphones and only one declared that his knowledge level of use was good. One of the participants informed in the questionnaire that he didn't know about the reading of markers and an explanation and demonstration were given. After that, he declared that he had not used it, but had seen it before.

10.6 The Results Obtained and Their Analyzes

The researcher started the MGEO Interactive app on the tablet and handed it to the participants so that they could have an initial interaction. Participants were taken to the museum room. The researcher gave a brief presentation of the site, showed them the markers and passed the test instructions. The four tasks were gradually informed so as not to burden the participants' memory. At the end of the four tasks, it was informed that the participants could feel free to explore other pieces and content. When they signaled that they were satisfied with the interaction in the environment, the post-test interview and the emoti-SAM were done.

10.6.1 Test with Participant P1

The participant showed a great deal of familiarity with the use of mobile smartphones and tablets. In the first task, he had no difficulty reading the marker, did not use the help and managed to trigger the video in Libras by reading the application instructions. When viewing the video with the interpreter, he did not point the camera at the object and remained pointing it at the floor. When instructed on the second task, the participant returned to the initial screen and clicked the option "Start your visit here," repeating this action for all tasks. He had no difficulty reading another marker and entering the image gallery. P1 understood that the frame next to the image was for viewing the object and pointed it to the piece in question. However, he did not notice that there were other images of this piece in the gallery. In the third task, the participant was asked to view the piece's description. He first viewed the video in Libras and continued to point the camera down. Then he was asked to read the text contained in the Description option. In the fourth task the reading of the marker and the selection of the animation icon was done correctly. P1 took some time to notice the video controls and first scanned the entire screen with his eyes before starting. After completing the tasks, P1 visualized just one more piece and started giving opinions and showing interest in finishing the activity, consequently beginning the post-test interview. P1 said it was interesting to have videos recorded in Libras by deaf people. According to him, the best thing was the research initiative, and that projects targeting the deaf need to be more publicized. As for suggestions for improvements, he declared that the animation needs content in Libras, otherwise some deaf people would not understand it. He suggested content in 3D format to make the description of the piece clearer as well as inserting images in the Portuguese descriptions, placing a short text, as Portuguese subtitles in the Libras videos help understand the message.

10.6.2 Test with Participant P2

As soon as entering the application, she read the room marker and chose to access the help, as she didn't notice the options menu. It took her a while to understand the help instructions, and she navigated to the end of the help by herself. Afterward, the instruction for the first task was given: viewing the video in Libras of the piece "Ferro Bandado." It took her a while to read the marker, as it was positioned in a location that cast a shadow on the tablet. First she accessed the image gallery and later, viewed the video as requested. In the second task, she went straight to the image gallery and, unlike the first time activating this option, she realized that she could scroll to other images. She positioned the object within the frame to be able to compare images. It is worth noting that P2, after viewing the videos in Libras and the image galleries that present the content in a horizontal position, started to use the tablet in that same position most of the time and turned her head to read the menu options that appeared upright. In the third task, she had difficulty noticing the title change, signaling the reading of another marker by the system. After some time, she visualized the title of the "Fossil Showcase" and went to the description without problems. In the fourth task, she also had no difficulty reading the marker, activating the Animation option, and playing the video, but initially did not continue pointing the tablet at the rock. In the post-test interview, P2 rated the Portuguese text as excellent and found navigation in the app to be easy. As an observation, she indicated that the title change that occurred between the readings of the markers was too subtle. P2 suggested placing the room marker next to its name or description, as it was isolated in its current location, in addition to emphasizing the positioning of the markers to avoid shadows. She suggested the participation of deaf people, both in recording and in the translation/interpretation of signs. She reported an interesting fact: within the same institution there may have different signs for the same term, so it would be interesting to create a specific glossary for the museum terms and make it available in the application, as, according to P2, too much dactylology is tiring. As for the augmented reality proposal, the camera activated in the background could distract and confuse users. Despite being a new technology, some deaf people may be uncomfortable with this form of content presentation. The inclusion of images and dactylology was very good, because it helps comprehend the video in Libras. However, the content could be divided into two windows with the interpreter positioned on single color background.

10.6.3   Test with Participant P3

This volunteer quickly went through the Help option for the interactive visit. In the instructions for the first task, she was able to read the marker and access the Libras option without problems. However, she waited for the video to start automatically and after a while pressed the play button. As soon as the video ended, P3 reported that the signaling in Libras was too fast. In the second task, she didn't notice that the system had not read the piece marker. The researcher had to intervene and ask her to point the tablet at the image again. P3 used the tablet tilted. In the third task, despite being asked to access the text description in Portuguese, P3 only accessed the video in Libras. After viewing all the video content, she did not understand what had been informed and rewinded the video to the beginning and asked: "What fell? Did the fossils stay there, did they remain there?" P3 expressed that the video message was very similar to "signaled Portuguese" (when the content is similar to a literal translation from Portuguese to Libras) and there could have been a little more expression from the video interpreter. In the fourth task, the participant again did not perform the requested task and first accessed the video in Libras. She understood the message of this video, as the interpreter used Libras classifiers. After that, the researcher asked P3 again to access the animation and the task was accomplished without difficulties. In the post-test interview, P3 characterized the project as laborious and the technology used was unusual. "This technology can be confusing at times, because there is a lot going on (dactylology, image and interpreter) and the background of the camera." The suggestions given by P3 were: Help in Libras option for people who are not used to Portuguese; Portuguese subtitles with a short text; include classifiers in videos in Libras. P3 informed that it is important for the deaf to follow the video recordings to identify possible speed variations in the signaling of the interpreters.

10.6.4   Test with Participant P4

When the first task was requested, P4 clicked the Description option (Portuguese text) and then saw the content in Libras. He had no trouble reading the markers and navigating through the options. In the second task, he observed the rock well and read the label description before using the tablet. He thought that the system had already recognized the next marker and was going to read the same content again. The researcher interrupted and asked P4 to read the marker again. He saw the video in Libras without pointing at the rock and commented that the location on the label was missing. Then he accessed the image gallery and found that they had other images, scrolled to see them and closed the window without framing it. In the third task, he saw the video in Libras before seeing the text description. He had no trouble reading the marker and navigating the app. In the fourth task, after accessing the Animation option, he made a horizontal sliding motion to play the video. Then he saw the controls and managed to play the video. After that, he accessed the other options Description and Libras. In the post-test interview, P4 found the idea of the research interesting. He mentioned that making the visit by themselves would give the deaf autonomy, but it would be necessary to have an explanation in Libras of how the system works for those who don't read Portuguese. As a suggestion he said that the content of the pieces' captions could be in the application as a summary of the pieces. He asked if the Portuguese texts on the walls of the rooms were in Libras in the application and were informed that this has been proposed for future stages.

10.6.5 Test with Participant P5

As soon as she started the interactive visit, P5 made a surprised expression when she saw the video in Libras with the interpreter without the background. P5 tried to fast forward and rewind the video with short taps on the screen, then noticed the control menu and returned to the beginning of the video and then closed it. She did not want to open the video again and signaled that it was good and she had liked it. Then she started using the tablet in a horizontal position to read the markers and tilted her head to read the menu options. Before accessing the option requested in the following tasks, P5 always started the video in Libras of each piece and then accessed the format indicated by the researcher. In the second task, when entering the gallery, she didn't understand what she had to do with the frame. The researcher explained it and P5 accomplished the task. In the third task, she had no trouble opening, scrolling, and closing the window with the description. She also had no problems opening the animation for the fourth task. After waiting for the animation to start, she noticed the play button and started the video. She realized that the drawing was referring to the piece and saw the animation pointing it at the object. In the post-test interview, she said she quite liked the app and the information found in it, although she expected more interactive content. P5 cited as an example: other animations, 3D objects, and content that popped out of the screen. According to P5, the animation helped understand the message and showed the explanation step by step. As a suggestion for improvement, she warned that at times, dactylology was performed too quickly and she did not have time to read it. She declared that it is important to have the content in Libras and that only few elements are missing to improve the prototype.

10.6.6   Results of the Emoti-SAM

At the end of the post-test interviews, participants were asked to complete the satisfaction form. To consolidate the responses, a scale of 1–5 was considered, representing the following states of each level:

Satisfaction: 1 for unhappy, dissatisfied, bored; 5 for happy, satisfied, hopeful.
Motivation: 1 for slow, sluggish, calm; 5 for lively, frantic, excited.
Feeling of Control: 1 for controlled, feared, guided; 5 for in control, influential, autonomous.

The level satisfaction averaged 4.6, indicating that users were satisfied with the experience. As for motivation, the average was 4.2, and it is understood that the participants identified more with the feelings of lively, frantic, excited. The feeling of control received lower ratings, with an average of 3.6. Therefore, it is believed that although they are satisfied and motivated to use the application, it is essential to promote improvements in the application prototype to leverage the feelings of dominance and control of the technology, so that deaf users can feel autonomous enough to visit the museum using the application (see Fig. 10.5).

After performing the evaluations, the following corrections identified to adapt the technology to promote better use and accessibility for the deaf audience were proposed:

Layout orientation: Tablet manipulation wasn't done as expected. The design was not responsive and readjustable according to the horizontal/vertical orientation of the tablet. When in use, it was necessary to turn the position of the tablet, as the

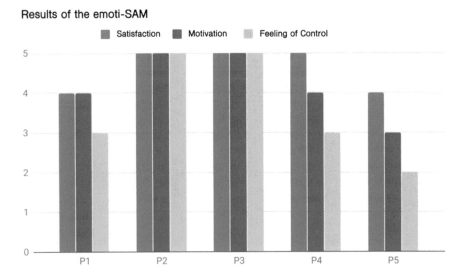

Fig. 10.5 Emoti-SAM responses (*Source* Data collection by the authors)

main screens were presented in vertical orientation and some content horizontally. In the test, some participants used the tablet tilted or kept it horizontal and tilted their heads to read the menu displayed vertically. As for orientation, one of the recommendations of (W3C 2015b), determines that both orientations (portrait and landscape) must be supported or facilitate the change of orientation to a point where it is supported. Another solution for this project would be to adapt the entire layout of the screens to the horizontal position since the presentation of interactive content such as videos and animations would then be displayed taking advantage of the entire screen space.

Feedback for the reading of the marker: Access to the marker of the pieces was done in different ways: some returned to the home screen to read a new marker, others continued on the page of the interactive visit and pointed the camera to read other markers (expected and recommended by the Help option). In this second case, it wasn't evident whether the reading of another marker was successful. The identification of the change from one marker to another was through the name of the piece in the page title and through the options available in the menu, which in some cases were similar. Other visual and even vibratory resources could be explored to emphasize the performance of the reading by the system. As the recommendations proposed by (W3C 2010) point out, the use of icons, patterns, or colors for each piece would help differentiate and assist recognition. The advantage of using vibrating features is the possibility of perception by different user profiles.

Redundancy and customization: (ABNT 2008) accessibility recommendations emphasize the availability of the same information in different ways. One of the users' requests was to include Portuguese subtitles in Libras videos and to include the Libras window in the animation. It is worth noting that this information must be provided in a customizable way. The customization flexibility according to the user's needs (Schefer 2016) is recommended, as there are variations within the same user profile.

Inclusion of PWD in projects: Adding hearing impaired or deaf people to the team was essential, but not possible. It became evident that bringing this perspective during development can help avoid problems, such as the Libras execution speed when recording videos, a recommendation found in the Ministry of Justice research (BRASIL 2009). In addition, participation in all phases of the project also emphasizes the role of people with disabilities in working on projects that are developed by and for them.

Help in Libras: Some users didn't choose to use the Help option, as it only presented Portuguese instructions. Having this content available in Libras is necessary for deaf people who have difficulty understanding Portuguese. Libras content that describes the application and its features should also be available. Although it is outside the scope of the project, this option would assist the deaf in the museum's reception. In the user profile surveying stage, experts observed the non-use of technologies in museums due to the reception staff's lack of knowledge of how to offer or explain them to deaf visitors.

10.7   Conclusions

The prototype developing methodology went through adaptations to suit the project's objectives. Although the proposal presented had a linear configuration of the stages, some occurred simultaneously during development. Due to the incremental and iterative characteristic of the prototype development, its activities gradually increased and its versions improved with each advance thanks to the profile of scientific research, which allows discoveries and experiments in technologies. It is worth mentioning the project's multidisciplinary nature, which involved the combination of several areas of knowledge through the different stages of the project: Museology, Pedagogy, Geosciences, Accessibility, Libras, Design, and Computer Science.

From the user evaluation it could be observed that the expected (projected) viewing of videos in Libras wasn't used by users. Most volunteers did not point the tablet at the object while observing the Libras interpreter. The videos in Libras were recorded with the interpreters simulating interaction with the objects, since the augmented reality would make it possible to view the content in Libras and the real object through the camera. To make the need to point at the object clear, it is necessary to use other mechanisms such as a Libras warning or to position the interpreter in front of the object in augmented reality. In this case, adjustments would be necessary to calibrate the marker distances and the positioning on the screen to fit the interpreter. Therefore, the augmented reality technology needs to be adjusted to evaluate the content in Libras being displayed in the real environment. Thus it would be possible to establish a comparison to determine whether this new form of display would provide a better experience and content comprehension.

The availability of content in Libras was highly praised by the volunteers, as they recognize that not all deaf people understand Portuguese well. The participants stated that this research initiative needs to be publicized so that more work can be done in this area. They were able to view the other contents (texts, images, animation) as designed and expressed the expectation of more visual and interactive content, such as animation or 3D objects. These contents are commonly used in virtual and augmented reality applications designed for entertainment.

The emoti-SAM questionnaire was applied to verify the user's experience. As a result, it was identified that although the satisfaction and motivation criteria have reached good levels, it is essential to promote enhancements in the prototype to improve the feeling of mastery and control of the technology, so that deaf users can feel autonomous enough to visit the museum and use the application without any mediation.

It is worth mentioning that the user evaluation should not be seen as the end of the process. In order to provide accessibility and inclusion, constant evaluations are necessary, considering timelines, new needs, social conditions, and technological resources, so that the benefits achieved do not become outdated (Sarraf 2008). It was possible to learn and understand the needs of the deaf audience and experience the augmented reality for displaying content in Libras, enabling new insights and solutions. As a technological contribution, the application prototype can be replicated for other contexts of use and support accessibility to the contents of other exhibition environments such as museums, historic centers, and touristic sights.

As future work, we envision offering content to other audiences, such as audio description for people with visual impairment; or even, due to the specificity of Libras, offer the option of selecting content according to age group (children and adults). Another development need is to expand to other rooms of the museum and check the requirements for an approach that contemplates the visit of the museum as a whole, including: Libras instructions for the application, room identification using GPS and location map, and customization of the visit itinerary as well as creation of mechanisms for user feedback regarding the visit and the effort to promote interaction through the application.

Storage means and availability of a greater number of media content should also be studied when the application is expanded to other rooms, in addition to studying the technical feasibility of making content available in a virtual environment, so as not to overload the storage of mobile devices. Other studies related to the use of technology for spontaneous visits could assess the issues of content comprehension and learning when compared to guided tours or other forms of augmented reality.

References

ABNT Associação Brasileira de Normas Técnicas (2005) NBR 15.290: Acessibilidade em Comunicação na Televisão. Rio de Janeiro, Brasil

ABNT Associação Brasileira de Normas Técnicas (2008) NBR 15.599: Acessibilidade - comunicação na prestação de serviços. Rio de Janeiro, Brasil

Alves AS (2012) Estudo do Uso de Diálogos de Mediação para Melhorar a Interação de Surdos Bilíngues na Web. Dissertação de Mestrado, Programa de Pós-Graduação em Informática da Universidade Federal do Estado do Rio de Janeiro (UNIRIO)

Azuma R (1997) A survey of augmented reality, presence: teleoperators and virtual environments 6:4

Barbosa SDJ, Silva BS (2010) Interação humano-computador. Editora Campus-Elsevier

BRASIL (2015) Lei 13.146/2015, de 06 de julho de 2015. Lei Brasileira de Inclusão, Brasília, DF

BRASIL (2014) Decreto 5.296, de 2 de dezembro de 2004. Lei Brasileira de Inclusão, Brasília, DF

BRASIL (2009) Secretaria Nacional de Justiça. A Classificação Indicativa na Língua Brasileira de Sinais. Secretaria Nacional de Justiça. Brasília: SNJ

Castro ARSF (2014) Caminhando em direção ao museu inclusivo: diagnóstico de acessibilidade da exposição Memórias da Terra (Museu da Geodiversidade – IGEO/UFRJ) com o mapeamento das intervenções necessárias. Monografia em Acessibilidade Cultural. Faculdade de Medicina. Universidade Federal do Rio de Janeiro, Rio de Janeiro

Castro ARSF, Aracri EMRP, Diogo MC, Greco PD, Mansur KL, Carvalho ISA (2015) Olimpíada Brasileira de Geociências: contribuição para a popularização das Ciências da Terra. Terra e Didática

Castro ARSF, Greco PD, Mansur KL, Romeiro EM, Diogo MC, Carvalho ISA (2011) A atuação do Museu da Geodiversidade (MGEO – IGEO/UFRJ) na proteção e divulgação do patrimônio geológico. Actas del I Simposio de Geoparques y Geoturismo en Chile. Santiago: Sociedad Geologica de Chile

DATASENADO (2013) Condições de Vida das Pessoas com Deficiência no Brasil. Secretaria de Transparência, Coordenação de Pesquisa e Opinião. https://www12.senado.leg.br/institucional/programas/senadoinclusivo/pdf/pesquisa-2013. Acessed 05 Mar 2017

Doerr MM (2014) DESIGNMOB: proposta metodológica para criação de interfaces digitais para dispositivos móveis. Monografia (Bacharelado em Design Digital). Universidade Federal de Pelotas

Ferreira SBL, Nunes R (2008) e-Usabilidade. Rio de Janeiro, LTC

Ferreira SBL, Silveira DS, Capra E (2012) Protocols for evaluation of site accessibility with the participation of blind users. Procedia Comput Sci 14:47–55

Garrett JJ (2003) The elements of user experience: user-centered design for the web. New Riders

Google Play (2018) AZ Gravador de Tela. https://play.google.com/store/apps/details?id=com.hec orat.screenrecorder.free. Acessed 10 Feb 2018

Hayashi ECS, Posada JEG, Maike VRML, Baranauskas MCC (2016) Exploring new formats of the Self-Assessment Manikin in the design with children. In: Simpósio Brasileiro sobre Fatores Humanos em Sistemas Computacionais, 15, 2016, São Paulo. Anais, 1–10

IBGE (2013) Pesquisa Nacional de Saúde - PNS. Ciclos de Vida. Brasil e Grandes Regiões. Ministério do Planejamento, Orçamento e Gestão, Instituto Brasileiro de Geografia e Estatística – IBGE, Diretoria de Pesquisas Coordenação de Trabalho e Rendimento. Rio de Janeiro, 2015

IBGE (2010) Censo Demográfico 2010: Características gerais da população, religião e pessoas com deficiência. http://www.ibge.gov.br/home/estatistica/populacao/censo2010/caracteristicas_religiao_deficienciadefault_caracteristicas_religiao_deficiencia.shtm

Lacerda TC; Nunes JV; Gresse von Wangenheim C (2013) Customização de Heurísticas de Usabilidade para Celulares. In: Encontro da Qualidade e Produtividade em Software - EQPS. http://www.gqs.ufsc.br/usability-engineering/match/. Acessed 15 Apr 2018

Ling T (2014) Android UI design kit for photoshop 4.4. https://androiduiux.com/2014/01/10/and roid-ui-design-kit-for-photoshop-4-4-free-download/. Acessed 11 Apr 2017

Martins ML, Malta C, Costa V (2015) Viseu Mobile: Um guia turístico para dispositivos móveis com recurso à Realidade Aumentada. Dos Algarves: A Multidisciplinary e-Journal 26(1):8–26

Mendonça RL, Mustaro PN (2011) Como tornar aplicações de realidade virtual e aumentada, ambientes virtuais e sistemas de realidade mista mais imersivos. XIII Symposium on Virtual and Augmented Reality. Realidade Virtual e Aumentada: Aplicações e Tendências, Editora SBC, MG

Nielsen J (1995) Severity ratings for usability problems. https://www.nngroup.com/articles/how-to-rate-the-severity-of-usability-problems/. Acessed 03 Fev 2018

Nielsen J (2000) Why you only need to test with five users. https://www.nngroup.com/articles/why-you-only-need-to-test-with-5-users/. Acessed 03 Fev 2018

Pagani T (2013) Perguntas a serem evitadas em pesquisa com usuários. https://uxdesign.blog.br/perguntas-a-evitar-em-pesquisascomusuarios-8ae93a205264. Acessed 03 Fev 2018

Sarraf VP (2008) Reabilitação do Museu: políticas de inclusão cultural por meio da acessibilidade. Dissertação (Mestrado em Ciência da Informação) Escola de Comunicação e Artes, Universidade de São Paulo, São Paulo

Schefer RP (2016) Diretrizes Mobideaf: uma abordagem para desenvolvimento de aplicações de redes sociais em dispositivos móveis para os surdos. Dissertação de mestrado da Universidade Federal de São Carlos

Yoon S, Anderson E, Lin J, Elinich K (2017) How augmented reality enables conceptual understanding of challenging science content. Educ Technol & Soc 20(1):156–168

W3C (2008). Mobile web best practices 1.0—Basic guidelines—W3C recommendation. https://www.w3.org/TR/mobile-bp/ Acessed 22 Mar 2017

W3C (2010). Mobile web application best practices—W3C recommendation. https://www.w3.org/TR/mwabp. Acessed 22 Mar 2017

W3C (2014) Mobile accessibility examples from UAAG 2.0 reference. https://www.w3.org/TR/IMPLEMENTING-UAAG20/mobile Acessed 22 Mar 2017

W3C (2015a) WCAG 2.0 techniques that apply to mobile. https://www.w3.org/WAI/GL/mobile-a11y-tf/MobileTechniques. Acessed 02 Jun 2017

W3C (2015b) Mobile accessibility: how WCAG 2.0 and other W3C/WAI guidelines apply to mobile. https://www.w3.org/TR/mobile-accessibility-mapping. Acessed 22 Mar 2017

Chapter 11
Ensuring Resilience Using Augmented Reality: How Museums Can Respond During and Post COVID-19?

Gek-Siang Tan, Kamarulzaman Ab. Aziz, and Zauwiyah Ahmad

Abstract This chapter explores how cultural and heritage sites such as museums can weather the unpredictable storm of the Covid-19 pandemic by quickly adapting to the unprecedented situation to continue serving their communities in new innovative ways. The museums are awakening to the need for proactive and innovative measures for mitigating the impacts of the pandemic in order to ensure survival. These include offering online educational resources, showcasing of museum collections and engaging its communities with art-related discussions on social media. Powered by the key enabling technologies of the Fourth Industrial Revolution, many popular museums create virtual tours using mixed reality technologies to improve visitors' discovery in an interactive, engaging and enjoyable way. This chapter also highlights the challenges of the innovative applications. What might be introduced as temporary measures to address the current situation, could become paradigm shifts that lead to higher and more impactful engagement between the museums and the society, ensuring museums' resilience and irreplaceable status in the people's minds. Also, during such times of high stress in society, culture can play an important healing role as it can offer rallying beacons of solidarity leading to emotional resilience and overall well-being.

11.1 Introduction

Being an enduring form of travel, cultural heritage tourism is growing steadily as a high-yielding sub-category of tourism which involves travelling to places of cultural

G.-S. Tan (✉) · Z. Ahmad
Faculty of Business, Multimedia University, Melaka, Malaysia
e-mail: gstan@mmu.edu.my

Z. Ahmad
e-mail: zau@mmu.edu.my

K. Ab. Aziz
Faculty of Management, Multimedia University, Cyberjaya, Selangor, Malaysia
e-mail: kamarulzaman@mmu.edu.my

and historical significance, experiencing the sites and events that truly reflect the people as well as stories (Jung and Han 2014; Tom Dieck and Jung 2015). The richness in culture, history and architectural components of cultural heritage sites has exerted strong influences on travellers' choice of holiday destination (Chung et al. 2017). To illustrate further, destinations that listed as the UNESCO World Heritage Sites would raise tourists' level of awareness and provide them with a good sense of visiting the cultural heritage site (Patuelli et al. 2013).

Regarded as one of the most iconic cultural and heritage tourist attractions, museums are seen as a social powerhouse to bridge world heritage sites to the local communities so that knowledge and skills can be transferred to promote local cultural assets, boost employment and enhance the overall societal well-being. While preserving local culture and heritage, museums play an important role in providing a common space to promote education, inspiration, creativity and dialogue, particularly in a culturally diverse and inclusive society. Museums which are strategically located at cultural heritage sites have exerted strong influences on travellers' choice of holiday destination (Chung et al. 2017), promoting cultural heritage tourism as one of the key drivers of sustainable economic development.

The Covid-19 pandemic which hit nearly all parts of the world in 2020 has severely impacted the global travel and tourism sector, putting it at a standstill due to the implementation of lockdown in many countries. Also, the closure of national borders has paused international tourism activities. Thus, international tourist arrivals are expected to contract by nearly 80%, according to the United Nations World Travel Organisation (UNWTO 2020). Many tourist destinations, including cultural and heritage institutions are forced to shut their door and some may never reopen, causing millions of tourism-related jobs at risk.

While travel and tourism is one of the sectors being heavily affected by the Covid-19 pandemic, the United Nations World Travel Organisation (UNWTO 2020) reported that the unprecedented global health crisis has put global economy and social development at an alarming state. It suspends the opening of many tourist destinations, including cultural and heritage sites. Museums, which rely on government funds and public donations to sustain its operations, are among those severely affected. Most are pessimistic or cautious at best, as they face a total lack of visitors as authorities place restrictions to avoid mass gatherings, crowds and proximity among the population in order to fight the spread of the disease. Furthermore, the forecast for posting the various lockdowns or movement control measures continues to be grimed as the population will still need to practice social distancing while the threat of the pandemic still persists.

11.1.1 Museum Closures During the Covid-19 Pandemic

In May 2020, the United Nation Educational, Scientific and Cultural Organisation (UNESCO) published a report entitled "Museums Around the World in the Face of Covid-19" on the challenges faced by the cultural and heritage institutions, as well as

Table 11.1 Distribution of museums across regions

Region	Estimated number of museums	Percentage (%)
Western Europe and Others	61,634	65.10
Eastern Europe	11,465	12.11
Latin America and the Caribbean	8,067	8.52
Asia Pacific	12,195	12.8
Africa	841	0.88
Arab States	473	0.50
Total: 195 Countries	94,675	100.00

Source UNESCO (2020)

the opportunities to seize and be resilient in the times of crisis. The report estimated that there are 95,000 museums worldwide, which is a leap of 60% of the total number recorded in 2012 (see Table 11.1).

Nevertheless, the museums are distributed unevenly across regions. Only 16 countries or approximately 8% of the 195 countries studied have more than 1,000 museums (more than 5,000 museums: Germany, Japan, Russian Federation and USA; 2,001 to 5,000 museums: France, Brazil, Italy, United Kingdom and Canada; 1,001 to 2,000 museums: Spain, Mexico, Poland, Switzerland, Republic of Korea, China and Argentina). Based on the estimation, as many as 104 countries (53.33%) have less than 50 establishments while 13 countries (6.67%) have no museums at all.

The Covid-19 pandemic which started during the first quarter of 2020 resulted in many countries having to take radical measures including the closure of museums. Specifically, 156 (80.00%) of the total 195 countries studied and reported that all museums were closed during the pandemic while 13 countries (6.67%) did not take any measures such as all museums in Benin were opened during the pandemic but reported having no visitors. Some countries shut their museums in the first quarter of 2020 but were able to welcome visitors sometime in April. In May, some were getting ready to reopen or had even begun to operate fully while others were still closed as most countries are still implementing containment measures including physical distancing which is not conducive in normal museum settings (see Table 11.2). This problem is even more significant among the popular museums that are highly visited with numbers reaching millions annually. In short, the report estimated more than 85,000 (>90.00%) of the cultural and heritage institutions worldwide being temporarily shut by the respective local government and authorities as one of the precautionary measures to combat Covid-19.

Table 11.2 Closure of museums across regions

Region	Estimated number of museums	Estimated number of museums temporarily closed	Estimated percentage (%) of museums temporarily closed
Western Europe and Others	61,634	58,281	94.60%
Eastern Europe	11,465	11,311	98.70%
Latin America & the Caribbean	8,067	8,061	99.90%
Asia Pacific	12,195	7,237	59.30%
Africa	841	738	87.80%
Arab States	473	473	100.00%
Total: 195 Countries	94,675	86,101	90.9%

Source UNESCO (2020)

11.1.2   The Impact of Covid-19 Pandemic on the Cultural and Heritage Institutions

While some museums are operated using public subsidies channelled from the government or relevant authorities, many museums are depending mainly on the income generated by visitors in the form of paid visits and purchases of merchandises, as well as donations or sponsorships. Although the suppressed economic conditions due to the pandemic do not immediately stop public subsidies from funding the cultural and heritage institutions (at least for the short-term), private museums might not be as fortunate. The closure of museums has had considerable economic consequences on the private museums, some might not be able to sustain their operations and close down. With national borders remain closed for some countries, cultural and heritage tourism can be badly affected especially cultural and heritage sites that are largely depending on international tourists. Furthermore, the economic aftermath of the pandemic also may lead to drastic contraction of public donations and sponsorships. According to the International Council of Museum, more than 10% of the museums may never reopen again.

In the times of crisis, museums around the world ought to be resilient and many have taken steps in staying connected with their patron credit to the Internet and social media. According to the United Nation Educational, Scientific and Cultural Organisation (UNESCO 2020) among museums in 86 countries reported approximately 826 evidences of online sites or activities initiated by museums' management. The digital readiness in responding to closure of museums was based on the earlier investments and continuous efforts made before the Covid-19 pandemic such as the creation of virtual tours and digitalising the museum collections (see Table 11.3) However, the digitalisation of museums during the Covid-19 pandemic across regions suggests significant disparities between states and regions. Some of the factors leading to such disparity are uneven distribution of stable Internet access around the world,

Table 11.3 Digitalisation of museums during covid-19 pandemic across regions

Region	Number of countries studied	Number of sites and activities being digitalised	Percentage of sites and activities being digitalised
Western Europe and Others	16	220	26.60%
Eastern Europe	12	137	16.60%
Latin America & the Caribbean	18	226	27.40%
Asia Pacific	19	168	20.30%
Africa	10	17	2.10%
Arab States	11	58	7.00%
Total: 195 Countries	86	826	100.00%

Source UNESCO (2020)

insufficient museum collections, lack of IT infrastructures, as well as lack of skills, knowledge and competencies of museum staff in embracing digitalisation of heritage and cultural institutions. Also, highly visited museums in developed nations with strong financial capability have responded timely and invested heavily in digitising their collections and engaged with their patrons on social media platform. As a result, these museums which were regarded as more agile to the unprecedented pandemic saw a substantial increase in the number of visitors to their online platforms even during the lockdown period when museums were closed.

11.1.3 Types of Digital Activities Developed During Museum Closures

Using previously digitised resources. In responding to the Covid-19 crisis worldwide, many cultural and heritage institutions have leveraged on the benefits of digitising existing museum collections and communication based on the digitisation policies developed by public authorities. These include online collections, online publications, digital exhibitions, 360° virtual tours and even virtual museums with gamification elements to stay connected and engaged with their patrons. For examples: the Bangabandhu Museum in Bangladesh, the National Costume Museum of Grand Bassam in Cote d'Ivoire and the online portal set up by the Department of Antiquities in Jordan.

Digitising of planned activities during the months of lockdown. Many earlier-scheduled events such as concerts, talks and exhibitions were migrated online during the lockdown in the form of interactive digital visits presented online mostly via social media platform. The online events are usually live or pre-recorded, allowing online visitors to download or available on digital platforms such as YouTube and

SoundCloud. For example: the Gallery of Modern and Contemporary Art located at the Bergamo, Italy created an online radio show while the Museum of Arts and Crafts in Zagreb, Croatia launched numerous online events.

Increasing activities on social media. In transforming and diversifying the digital media of cultural and heritage institutions, some museums increased their social media activities on Facebook. Twitter, Instagram or launched a YouTube or SoundCloud channel through the managers of the virtual community and museum management and staff who offer specific content adapted to the digital format.

Creating special activities during the lockdown. In contrast with the more traditional projects mentioned above, some cultural and heritage institutions were actively developed original projects during the lockdown by transforming deserted rooms or spaces in museums to present an offbeat view of the collections or virtual tours with a robot (e.g. Hastings Contemporary, United Kingdom). Many museums have also offered new forms of experience online such as inviting patrons to participate in a "cocktail with the curators" in the Frick Collection, New York; associating a work with a song in the Valence Museum, France or presenting the collections in the Anger-museum, Germany in the form of video game named "Animal Crossing". With an aim to involve patrons' participation through fun and instructive activities, museums organised photo-taking contests, education games such as children's stories telling, quizzes, video games, colouring activities and games involving parents and children.

Organising professional and scientific activities in the context of lockdown. Several museums singularly or collaborated with associations regularly initiated web conferences in the form of webinars or meetings and talks via various videoconfer-encing media. In a more strictly professional and scientific manner, the web conferences focused on topics related to the Covid-19 crisis but such a form of initiative is expected to continue in the future.

In short, in responding to the Covid-19 crisis worldwide, many museums have transformed many planned activities by means of digital using investments made before the pandemic, as well as using social networks to engage with visitors. On the other hand, large museum associations also organised webinars on a professional level, as well as special activities initiated to alleviate the challenges of confinement such as games, quizzes and many other educational activities being conducted virtually. However, there are many challenges in accessing culture and heritage through digital means as millions of people around the world, especially in developing countries are out of reach to virtual museums and online collections due to limited Internet access and gender equality, suggesting digital divide is now more evident than ever.

11.2 Augmented Reality Technology

First surveyed by Azuma (1997), Augmented Reality (AR) is a technology which permits users to see computer-generated objects being overlaid with the real environment instantaneously, using head-worn, handheld or projection displays. The Virtuality Continuum proposed by Milgram and Kishino (1994) (see Fig. 11.1) suggests

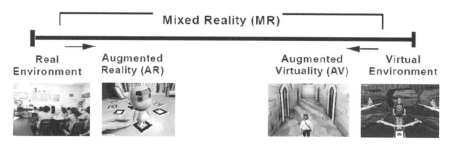

Fig. 11.1 Virtuality continuum (*Source* Milgram and Kishino [1994])

that mixed reality exists in between the real environment and virtual environment (commonly referred as Virtual Reality or VR). In a real environment, every object is real in nature whereas a virtual environment consists of computer-generated objects. Anything that lies between real environment and virtual environment is called mixed reality.

Gartner (2018)'s "Hype Cycle for Emerging Technologies, 2018" (see Fig. 11.2) predicted that AR is one of the emerging technologies which will remain relevant in the next five to ten years with increasing trends and investment prospects. The AR technology has seen massive applications in various industries which include medical, education, entertainment, robotics, as well as in the travel and tourism industry to enhance traveller experience. The market value of AR is forecasted to triple from USD 6.10 billion in 2016 to USD 18.8 billion in 2020 (Statista 2020).

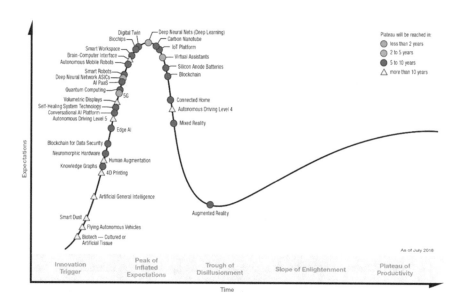

Fig. 11.2 Hype cycle for emerging technologies (*Source* Gartner [2018])

Lonely Planet (2018) named AR is one of the revolutionary trends that shapes the travel and tourism sector in 2019 and beyond, as well as significantly contributes to the growth of the tourism sector.

In view of tourism is now dominated by young travellers who are savvier in technological innovations, many tourism businesses have started to utilise cutting-edge digital technologies such as AR to offer tourists with value-added tourism products and services. With an increasing number of new AR applications emerged to make travel more interactive and enjoyable, past studies (Jung et al. 2015; Tom Dieck and Jung 2015) have recognised the potential of AR technology in enhancing the travel experience. More specifically, the increasing use of AR applications at cultural heritage sites (Chung et al. 2017; Jung et al. 2018) has made cultural heritage tourism to be among the economic sectors supplemented by mobile AR applications (Adhani and Rambli 2012; Jung et al. 2018; Portalés 2009; Tutenea 2013).

The provision of useful tour information makes AR application an ideal tool in guiding non-expert tourists to navigate and explore the surroundings of a tourist destination (Garau 2014). Also, AR application can help tourists in reminiscing significant events in history as historic properties can be restored and preserved by using three-dimensional objects through virtual reconstruction (Kourouthanassis et al. 2015). This would directly improve their knowledge and enhance their appreciation towards cultural heritage tourism (Jung et al. 2015). In short, AR application can enhance the overall travel experience (Tom Dieck and Jung 2015) because it creates a fun, interactive and meaningful learning environment for the tourists by stimulating their imagination and arousing their interest towards a cultural heritage site (Tom Dieck and Jung 2015). Remarkably, AR applications also give cultural heritage sites a competitive advantage in building a stronger destination branding which can attract more tourists (Kourouthanassis et al. 2015).

11.3 How Cultural and Heritage Institutions Use AR Applications in Response to the Covid-19 Pandemic?

Today, the cultural and heritage tourism sector such as museums are looking for innovative ways to engage with visitors by mean of cutting-edge digital technologies (Tscheu and Buhalis 2016). For instance, AR. The "World's Top 10 Most Visited Museums in 2018 and 2019" have integrated AR applications or similar virtual technologies for visitors to interact with museum exhibits and enhance their overall experience while visiting the museums, except the State Hermitage Museum in Saint Petersburg, Russia (The Art Newspaper 2019; Themed Entertainment Association 2019) (see Table 11.4). A study reported that visitors only spend an average of 2.31 s for each museum exhibit thus the use of AR applications in museums would grab their attention and explore the exhibits which lead to longer time spent in the museums (MuseumNext 2019). The section below discusses how the world's most visited museums responded to the Covid-19 pandemic with respect to the application

Table 11.4 World's top 10 most visited museums in 2018 and 2019

No	Name of museums	City	Visitors (in million)		Use of AR
			2018	2019	
1	Louvre	Paris, France	10.20	9.60	Yes
2	National Museum of China	Beijing, China	8.61	7.39	Yes
3	Vatican Museums	Vatican City, Italy	6.76	6.88	Yes
4	Metropolitan Museum of Art	New York City, United States	6.95	6.48	Yes
5	British Museum	London, United Kingdom	5.83	6.24	Yes
6	Tate Museum	London, United Kingdom	5.87	6.10	Yes
7	National Gallery	London, United Kingdom	5.74	6.01	Yes
8	Natural History Museum	London, United Kingdom	5.23	5.42	Yes
9	American Museum of Natural History	New York City, United States	5.00	5.00	Yes
10	State Hermitage Museum	Saint Petersburg, Russia	4.50	4.96	No

Source The Art Newspaper 2019; Themed Entertainment Association 2019

of virtual technologies such as AR to connect and engage with its visitors during the post Covid-19 world.

Louvre Museum, Paris, France. Housing approximately 38,000 objects from over an area of 72,735 square meters, the world's largest museum and historical monument is the world's mostly visited cultural and heritage institution with 9.60 million visitors recorded in 2019. Due to the Covid-19 pandemic hit on France starting 13 March, the museum has resumed its operation on 6 July after four months with strict safety measure such as the visitors are compulsory to wear masks, one-way system, online ticketing and controlled number of visitors by cutting-down 80% of its normal capacity, causing a 40-million-euro loss on its bottom line. During last fall, a distanced queuing system was introduced for visitors to view the Leonardo Da Vinci's famous Mona Lisa painting in such a way that each visitor will be allowed to get closer to the painting with social distancing in place a distance of about 10 feet between visitors. Collaborated with the HTC VIVE Arts, the "Mona Lisa: Beyond the Glass" project is the inaugural virtual experience to be held at the Louvre, giving the visitors the chance to immerse and interact with the painting within a recreated virtual space using optical visor. The visitors will get to know more about the painting with the augmented textual information. What's more? The virtual experience will also be available in a home version through digital subscription service. The public

Fig. 11.3 Mona Lisa beyond the glass

now can tour in the virtual museum right from their own homes during the pandemic. Figure 11.3 illustrates the Mona Lisa Beyond the Glass Project.

National Museum of China, Beijing, China. Housing approximately 1,050,000 collections, the museum is the second most visited cultural and heritage institution in the world with 7.39 million visitors recorded in 2019. After being closed for almost 100 days, the museum started to reopen on 1 May as the pandemic has eased in China While implementing strict standard operating procedures, the museum management caps a maximum of 3,000 visitors per day (a reduction of 90% of its normal capacity), introduces online ticket booking and enforcing social distancing and health measures. With an aim to stay connected with the museum goers, the museum on 6 September launched the "Treasure Hunt Relay: Global Museum Director's Choice" which is an online campaign to showcase cultures and heritage for the global community. The initiative is a collaborative project with other 15 museums across five continents of the world, including Argentina, South Africa and Russia. Today, the museum provides exhibitions enriched by virtual technologies such as immersive AR glasses to augment and display detailed information about the Archaeological Ruins of Liangzhu City when the visitors wear a special pair of glasses equipped with audio commentary. Many Chinese museums, such as the Sanxingdui Museum has also opened an online virtual exhibition hall where visitors can view the exhibits from their own home. Figure 11.4 illustrates the AR glass used in the National Museum of China and others.

Vatican Museum, Italy. Owning approximately 70,000 collections in which 20,000 are on display, the public art and sculpture museum in the Vatican City is the third mostly visited cultural and heritage institution in the world with 6.88 million visitors recorded in 2019. After being closed for nearly three months due to national lockdown, the museum resumed its operation on 1 June with strict standard operating procedures such as online ticket reservation, limited number of visitors

Fig. 11.4 AR glass in the Chinese museums

per hour and other health measures. In reconnecting and engaging the museum goers around the world, the museum launched 3D virtual tours to provide an extraordinary and innovative experience in touring the site online from anywhere around the world. The guided virtual tour showcases accurate 3D replicas of the Vatican institutions and sites such as the Sistine Chapel, St. Peter's Basilica and many others for online visitors to discover Rome during the pandemic. Figure 11.5 depicts the screenshots of the virtual tours on mobile device.

Metropolitan Museum of Art, New York City, United States. Colloquially "The Met", the cultural and heritage institution is the largest museum in the United States houses more than two million collections. Since national lockdown on 13 March when most of the cultural institutions in the New York City were shuttered, the Met

Fig. 11.5 Screenshots of the virtual tours on mobile device

had reopened on 29 August with some new safety protocols in place, including reduction of 75% in hosting capacity, time ticketing, more frequent sanitising especially at high-contact areas and frequent hand-washing with sanitising stations throughout the museum. Today, the Met via its Imaging Department is bringing the "zemí cohoba stand" (one of the most iconic sculptures that survives from the ancestral civilisations in the Americas) to life through AR mobile application. Figure 11.6 shows the development of the AR model and screenshot.

British Museum, London, United Kingdom. Houses approximately 8 million collections, the museum is dedicated to human history, art and culture is among the largest and most comprehensive in existence. In 2019, the museum recorded 6.24 million of visitors, placing the public institution the fifth most visited museum in the world. The pandemic and lockdown implemented nationwide, all museums shuttered its door to the public on 17 March and only resumed on 27 August with stricter safety and health measures. The British Museum and Samsung have collaborated to launch a new AR application called "A Gift for Athena" to enhance visitor's experience in the museum. The AR application allows visitors, especially the kids to learn history more fun and exciting using gamification features such as fixing puzzles. Figure 11.7 depicts the AR application—"A Gift for Athena".

Tate Museum, United Kingdom. Houses a network of four art museums with rich collection of British art, and international modern and contemporary art, the cultural and heritage institution is the sixth most visited museum in the world with 6.10 visitors recorded in 2019. In collaboration with an AR-powered design firm, Facebook Creative Shop and The Mill, eight collections in the museums are now transformed using Facebook's Spark AR camera effect platform. Called the "Untold Stories", it is a project that explores the hidden narrative of existing paintings and the artists behind them to give patrons a more in-depth context and background of the iconic artworks. Using the camera in the Instagram application, the users have to scan the museum's Instagram name tag and activate the exciting virtual experience. Then, the users will see a map, guiding them to all the eight paintings powered by AR technology. Such innovative feature can help the visitors to learn and connect to

Fig. 11.6 Development of the AR model of 'Zemí Cohoba Stand'

Fig. 11.7 The "A Gift for Athena" AR application

the world more meaningfully. Figure 11.8 shows the AR-enhanced paintings in the Tate Museum.

National Gallery, United Kingdom. The 196-year-old art museum located at the Central London houses a collection of over 2,300 paintings dating from the mid-thirteenth century to 1900 is the seventh most visited museum in the world with 6.01 million visitors recorded in 2019. Today, the National Gallery is becoming "an innovation lab" as many experiments of cutting-edge digital technologies including AR to be relevant in bringing arts to the new audiences, mainly the younger travellers who are savvier in technologies. Envisioned by the tagline of "Culture is digital", the museum pledges to bring culture and digital closer together while shaping the nation as a global leader where sustainability is the key of survival. The museum has used 3D printing technology to recreate an Italian renaissance chapel and it is now offering a virtual reality tour of its Sainsbury Wing allowing visitors to examine its 270 paintings in detail. In its five-year digital transformation journey would see the

Fig. 11.8 AR-enhanced paintings in the tate museum

Fig. 11.9 The "Skin and Bone" mobile application

embedding of innovation in immersive media in the gallery such as a hologram of Sir David Attenborough used at the Natural History Museum to educate visitors about fossils, and a virtual reality experience at the Science Museum where astronaut Tim Peake guides users through space.

Natural History Museum, United Kingdom. Jointly produced with the BBC Natural History unit, the museum in London has just opened an interactive film called "Who do you think you really are?" to produce AR element for the film by adding "virtual" graphics to TV. The end result is an innovative museum experience that uses camera tracking technology with specially designed handheld displays and rendering software to bring extinct creatures to life using AR technology.

Smithsonian National Museum of Natural History, Washington, D.C, United States. The 110-year-old world's most visited natural history museum received 6.24 million visitors in 2019. Today, the Smithsonian's oldest museum hall is officially enriched with AR technology in the Bone Hall in which it collects and showcases many of the original skeletons and skins. With muscles and skins being superimposed on the exhibited bones. Among the thirteen highlighted features include a vampire bat flies away from its mount, a sea cow grows flesh, an anhinga catches fish, all accessible in situ or from home of the visitors through mobile application called the "Skin and Bone". Figure 11.9 illustrates the use of "Skin and Bone" mobile application in the museum.

11.4 Conclusion

The global coronavirus pandemic facing cultural and heritage institutions today remains a great concern of its sustainability and survival. While serving as repositories of both works and artefacts, museums play a significant role as spaces for meeting people, sharing knowledge and building social ties. The global health crisis has closed the door of around 90% of the total number of museums worldwide and some may never reopen. Although such closure is temporary, the impacts that hit a nation's economic and social development could be in long term. Being resilient is one of the fundamental traits of museums and this has become even more profound since the beginning of the Covid-19 crisis. It is crucial for museums to be able to reinvent themselves and being agile to adapt to the societal changes. Thus, museums ought to redefine their operations and their relationship with the public in order to move forward and survive during post Covid-19.

The examples reviewed give insights to innovative new ways museum offers the public to enjoy and interact with their collections. The solutions may be started as new or trendy attractions to ensure relevance and attract new patrons. However, the pandemic has shown how such initiatives have become key modes for the museums to continue engaging with the public given the various restrictions that have arisen. As the pandemic rages on, what was seen as temporary measures to address the current situation, could become the main method of how we now experience the museums. This could be a paradigm shift that leads to higher and more impactful engagement between the museums and the society.

References

Adhani NI, Rambli DRA (2012) A survey of mobile augmented reality applications. In: 1st International conference on future trends in computing and communication technologies, 89–96

Azuma RT (1997) A survey of augmented reality. Presence: Teleoperators & Virtual Environ 6(4):355–385

Chung N et al (2017) The role of augmented reality for experience-influenced environments: the case of cultural heritage tourism in Korea. J Travel Res 57(5):627–643

Garau C (2014) From territory to smartphone: smart fruition of cultural heritage for dynamic tourism development. Plan Pract Res 29(3):238–255

Gartner (2018) Hype cycle for emerging technologies. https://www.gartner.com/en/documents/388 5468/hype-cycle-for-emerging-technologies-2018

Jung TH, Han DI (2014) Augmented Reality (AR) in urban heritage tourism. e-Review Tourism Res 5

Jung T et al (2015) The determinants of recommendations to use augmented reality technologies: the case of a Korean theme park. Tour Manag 49:75–86

Jung TH et al (2018) Cross-cultural differences in adopting mobile augmented reality at cultural heritage tourism sites. Int J Contemp Hosp Manag 30(3):1621–1645

Kourouthanassis P et al (2015) Tourists' responses to mobile augmented reality travel guides: the role of emotions on adoption behavior. Pervasive Mob Comput 18:71–87

Lonely Planet (2018) Travel trends for 2019 augmented attractions. https://www.lonelyplanet.com/articles/travel-trends-for-2019-augmented-attractions

Milgram P, Kishino F (1994) A taxonomy of mixed reality visual displays. IEICE Trans Inf Syst 77(12):1321–1329

MuseumNext (2019) How museums are using augmented reality. https://www.museumnext.com/2019/02/how-museums-are-using-augmented-reality/ (2019, June 14)

Patuelli R et al (2013) The effects of world heritage sites on domestic tourism: a spatial interaction model for Italy. J Geogr Syst 15(3):369–402

Portalés C et al (2009) Photogrammetry and augmented reality for cultural heritage applications. Photogram Rec 24(128):316–331

Statista (2020) Augmented reality (AR) market size worldwide in 2017, 2018 and 2025 (in billion U.S. dollars). https://www.statista.com/statistics/897587/world-augmented-reality-market-value/

The Art Newspaper (2019) Art's most popular exhibition and museum visitors 2018. https://www.museus.gov.br/wp-content/uploads/2019/04/The-Art-Newspaper-Ranking-2018.pdf

Themed Entertainment Association (2019) Theme index and museum index 2018: the global attractions attendance report. https://www.aecom.com/content/wp-content/uploads/2019/05/Theme-Index-2018-5-1.pdf

Tom Dieck MC, Jung T, (2015) A theoretical model of mobile augmented reality acceptance in urban heritage tourism. Curr Issues Tour 21(2):154–174

Tscheu F, Buhalis D (2016) Augmented reality at cultural heritage sites. Information and communication technologies in tourism 2016. Springer, Cham, pp 607–619

Tutunea MFS (2013) Augmented reality-state of knowledge, use and experimentation. USV Ann Econ Public Adm 13(2[18]):215–227

UNWTO (2020) International tourist numbers could fall 60–80% in 2020, UNWTO reports. Retrieved from https://www.unwto.org/news/covid-19-international-tourist-numbers-could-fall-60-80-in-2020

Part III
Augmented Reality and Cultural Heritage

Chapter 12
Augmented Reality and New Opportunities for Cultural Heritage

**Metehan Unal, Fatima Zehra Unal, Erkan Bostanci,
and Mehmet Serdar Guzel**

Abstract This chapter considers the potential for Augmented Reality (AR) in cultural heritage, based on a literature review and authors' previous work. Firstly, AR technology is briefly presented and explained. Then, the cultural heritage applications of AR are examined in both the Visualization and Gamification sections. Visualization includes applications that enhance the visitor's experience by blending it with text, sound, or 3D models in a museum or heritage site. Gamification engages AR games about cultural heritage and is aimed at attracting the visitor's attention to inform the visitor about the site in a more entertaining way. Finally, future work is discussed within the context of the Total Augmentation Paradigm.

12.1 Introduction

In the past 30 years, the field of computer graphics has developed rapidly and introduced ever more complex and realistic graphical tasks (Mutlu et al. 2014). Augmented Reality (AR) is one of the most sophisticated computer graphics areas and has become popular with the development of smart phones and other mobile devices.

AR offers extended vision to the user by overlaying real-world images with computer-generated objects or information. In the earliest days of this technology, a Head Mounted Display (HMD) and a portable computer were required to acquire the real-world imagery and combine it with virtual content. Now AR can be achieved with a smart phone or AR glasses.

M. Unal · F. Z. Unal · E. Bostanci · M. S. Guzel (✉)
Computer Engineering Department, Ankara University, Ankara, Turkey
e-mail: mguzel@ankara.edu.tr

M. Unal
e-mail: metehan.unal@ankara.edu.tr

F. Z. Unal
e-mail: fzkilic@ankara.edu.tr

E. Bostanci
e-mail: ebostanci@ankara.edu.tr

© The Author(s), under exclusive license to Springer Nature Switzerland AG 2021   213
V. Geroimenko (ed.), *Augmented Reality in Tourism, Museums and Heritage*, Springer
Series on Cultural Computing,
https://doi.org/10.1007/978-3-030-70198-7_12

AR has a wide range of application areas from education to personal health (Li et al. 2020). It also promises great potential for cultural heritage. The reconstruction of cultural heritage sites typically is a time consuming and costly process. In addition, the possibility of damage to the remains during construction needs to be considered. With AR technology, it is possible to place 3D models that are designed in accordance with the originals on top of the ruins in cultural heritage sites without physically reconstructing areas. Using this technology for cultural heritage sites will be a very advantageous process in order to protect the remains and to save the time and cost of reconstruction (Unal 2017).

This chapter mainly focuses on Augmented Reality and its applications for cultural heritage. Our aim is to show the studies in the literature and display the potential of AR technology in cultural heritage. This study also includes our previous works in a detailed manner.

The rest of the chapter is built as follows: First, AR technology is explained in detail with its application areas included, then the cultural heritage domain of AR is demonstrated and the motivation behind using AR in the heritage sites and museum is explained. Next, some of the literature on AR in cultural heritage has been presented in two sections, namely Visualization and Gamification, then future work and the Total Augmentation Paradigm are described. Finally, the last part of this chapter concludes the study.

12.2 Augmented Reality

Augmented Reality (AR) is a concept of binding real-world images and artificial assets and information in real time to enrich the human perception of environment. AR can sometimes be confused with Virtual Reality (VR). The difference between AR and VR is the use of background real-world images. In other words, VR can be achieved using only an artificial environment, while AR incorporates a level of reality.

According to Azuma (1997), an AR application should have the following features:

- combine the real and virtual worlds,
- be interactive in real-time,
- operate in 3 dimensions.

Within the boundaries of this definition, the concept of AR is not limited to Head Mounted Display (HMD) but can be suitable for new mobile systems. Presently, AR technology is usable and applicable for different devices, including mobile phones, tablets, and smart glasses.

AR has been implemented for very different devices. The earliest applications of AR used an HMD with a low range of motion which was developed by Suther-land (Sutherland 1968). These HMDs became more sophisticated with advancing technology and now, two types of HMD are available on the market which are video-see-through and optical-see-through (Carmigniani et al. 2011). As the respective names suggest, the video-see-though HMD stream the video to the user while the optical-see-through models use a half-silver technology to allow the user to see the vicinity and augment virtual information on the screen. Smart glasses, the successors of the HMDs, are providing a much more suitable environment for the use of AR technology.

State-of-the-art smart glasses like Google Glass or Epson Moverio promise great potential for AR technology, yet it seems likely that it will take some time to start using this technology in daily life (Ro et al. 2018). Also, notebooks (laptops) were used with a camera mounted on a user for AR (Stricker and Kettenbach 2001; Piekarski et al. 2004) in the 2000s. With the new millennium, Personal Digital Assistants (PDAs) were introduced as a new medium for AR technology which has a more practical usage than notebooks or HMDs (Wagner and Schmalstieg 2003).

After the PDA era, smart phones were introduced and become very popular in a relatively short period of time. These devices have much greater processing capability compared to PDAs and are more portable than notebooks. Consequently, smart phones have emerged as a much more suitable environment for AR (Azuma et al. 2011). Since then, a tremendous number of AR applications have been presented in the literature. One of the interesting implementations of AR applications is using drones as a capturing device (Unal et al. 2020a). Although, it requires sophisticated methods for precise tracking (Unal et al. 2020b), the results are promising for the future. Lastly, Microsoft Kinect, which is a motion detection sensor, was used for AR studies in the literature (Vera et al. 2011; Casas et al. 2012).

The type of virtual data to be superimposed on top of the real image also increases the variety in applications. If the data to be superimposed on the image is part of an interface, a marker or a text, a 2D virtuality is provided and depth is not required (Liou et al. 2016; Nuernberger et al. 2016). There are also 3D AR applications that are more interesting, popular, and perhaps more challenging than 2D applications (Mourtzis et al. 2017; Panou et al. 2018). Nowadays, photo and video sharing applications like Instagram and Snapchat for smart devices come with small 3D AR add-ons.

Different surveys in the literature present a very broad range of application areas for AR (Wang et al. 2016; Chatzopoulos et al. 2017; Kim et al. 2017). Accordingly, AR can be employed for entertainment, advertisement, education, assembly, and medical areas. Furthermore, the literature indicates that cultural heritage is one of the most promising areas for AR.

12.3 Augmented Reality in Cultural Heritage

Cultural heritage AR applications have been shown as an important area of AR by Azuma (1997) and Papagiannakis et al. (2008). With the developing technology, the cultural heritage applications of AR became a very important instrument to transfer historical knowledge and experience. Studies have shown that the interest is increasing when an AR application has been employed in a museum or historical site (Haugstvedt and Krogstie 2012). In this way, historical awareness and knowledge of societies can be increased (Kounavis et al. 2012).

Reconstruction models or virtual tours of archaeological sites provide an enjoyable learning tool. Applications of AR in cultural heritage can improve the visiting experience of a heritage site by in situ reconstruction that elevates it with 3D models of ancient buildings. While AR systems take considerable time to develop, another beneficial feature of such systems is that they can be implemented in situ with minimum physical damage to the remains or artifacts. AR reconstructions can be in different configurations, while some applications provide a roam-able environment around the heritage site, others can only present the reconstruction of old buildings from a fixed perspective as they are (Bostanci 2014).

12.3.1 Visualization

In this subsection, visualization-based applications of AR which include superimposed virtual objects on top of real-time cultural site images will be discussed.

Cultural heritage visits can be enhanced by showing 3D models of ruined ancient buildings on site. Historical structures built by ancient civilizations have often been destroyed or ruined by wars, earthquakes, and other disasters. Physical reconstruction is required to return these structures to their state when they were built. However, this is a very laborious and presumably costly process. Instead, it is much easier and presumably cheaper to superimpose virtual models designed in a computer environment on historical buildings or sites.

The literature presents different visualization applications for virtual reconstruction of historical sites since the beginning of the 2000s. Sticker and Kettenbach (2001), implemented an AR application where its location was determined with the help of reference photographs for open spaces. In this application, the computer-generated 3D model of the historical building was placed in the correct position with the help of reference photographs.

Vlahakis et al. (2001) developed ARCHEOGUIDE project which is a tour assistant and guide for the archaeological site of Olympia, Greece. Projects include real-time AR reconstruction of ancient buildings and a personalized guide for visitors.

Bruns et al. (2007) demonstrated one of the earliest mobile AR applications that can be used with a camera-equipped mobile phone. The application used object recognition to identify and track the historical artifacts at a museum. The detailed information and multimedia content about the tracked artifact were shown to the visitor. The application also provided location-based contents to the visitors of the museum.

Choudary et al. (2009) presented a mobile application (MARCH) to enhance the visiting experience of restricted prehistorical sites. The application is designed to augment the prehistoric drawings on caves on the French Pyrenees through the interpretations of experts. The system is designed to work without a marker.

Zoellner et al. (2009) proposed an approach to using AR to virtually reconnect an artifact on a museum with its excavation site. The paper emphasizes that the artifact that was excavated from its original site and placed into the museum loses its context. Thus, the study presented an AR system for museums to provide contextual awareness to the visitors. The application binds a large-scale image and virtual information (like text and videos) on top of the historical artifacts. Also, 3D reconstructions models of the artifact are superimposed to the historical structure. The system is designed to work on video see-through tablets.

Damala et al. (2012) developed a prototype of personalized AR guidance system for museum visitors. The project, titled as "ARtSENSE," uses data from three different sensors (visual, audio, and psychophysiological) to adapt the multimedia content according to the interests of the visitor.

A different approach has been developed using Microsoft Kinect by Bostanci et al. (2015). In this study, Kinect was used to calculate the camera pose and augment the 3D model of the columns by locating the rectangular features. Human tracking has been implemented to the project and a 3D model of clothes of roman soldiers is augmented to the human on the screen. Results of tracking and augmentation can be seen in Fig. 12.1.

A mobile AR application was presented by Galatis et al. (2016) to overcome the usability and acceptance problems of AR. The application, KnossosAR, is a mobile AR guide to support guided visits of students, designed for a historical site Knossos in Greece. The application superimposes the computer-generated content on top of actual historical site to enrich the visiting experience of the students. The study

Fig. 12.1 The augmentation results of a Kinect-based application (Bostanci et al. 2015)

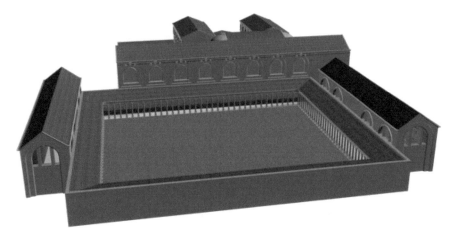

Fig. 12.2 Model of Roman Bath (Unal et al. 2018)

claims that using the mobile AR technology successfully increases the interest of the students and that AR is a usable technology in cultural heritage sites.

The literature presents many different visualization applications of AR for cultural heritage. In light of this, we designed and implemented an AR application which works in Android mobile devices, for Roman Baths of Ankara (Turkey) (Unal et al. 2020b). This project will be explained in the remainder of this subsection.

As the first step, we designed a 3D model of the Roman Baths using 3DS Max (Autodesk Inc 2020) according to the drawings of experts because the original baths have fallen into ruins. After the raw design, an optimization phase was employed to reduce the size of the 3D model which is important for mobile devices. The last step was assigning the texture to render a more realistic model. The final state of the model can be seen in Fig. 12.2.

The project was designed as a mobile AR application which can be run on smartphones and tablets. Nowadays, these gadgets are widespread and easily accessible, which provides access to AR technology for anyone who installs the application. The Unity 3D (Unity Tecnologies 2020) which is a widely used game engine and provides a suitable medium for AR has been chosen as the development environment.

The main challenge in an AR application is the tracking of the user (Bostanci et al. 2013). In this project, we used two different tracking techniques, namely: geo-location based and vision based.

The geo-location-based method depends on data from two sensors which are GPS (Global Positioning System) and gyroscope. These sensors are able to integrate with almost all mobile devices. GPS and gyroscope data are used to find the position and orientation of the user, respectively.

The vision-based technique has also been implemented. This method uses camera image and distinguishable objects around the site. Algorithms detect objects in the vicinity and calculate the position and orientation of the mobile device held by the visitor.

Fig. 12.3 *In-situ* augmentation result (Unal 2017)

After the implementation of the tracking phase, the augmentation phase which includes placing the 3D model of the bath on top of the camera image has been employed. The augmentation system uses both geo-location-based method and vision-based method separately. The result of the augmentation can be seen in Fig. 12.3. Please note that the case study has not been implemented on the actual site due to the risk of damage to the historical remains.

In the final phase of the project, a distant augmented reality system was developed. This system uses the same tracking methods mentioned above, to track a drone. The camera stream and location data of the drone are transmitted to the mobile device and a 3D model is then augmented on top of the stream. The result of the distant augmentation can be seen in Fig. 12.4.

12.3.2 Gamification

The AR-based games have been developed for many purposes, especially entertainment and education (Ozdamli 2017). With the widespread use of mobile devices, many AR games have been developed (Jang and Liu 2019). In 2016, Pokémon GO, a location-based AR game, was introduced and became the most popular game on Google Play (Rauschnabel et al. 2017). Interest in AR games has increased tremendously with this development (Flavián et al. 2019). The game also demonstrated the high potential of AR games (Paavilainen et al. 2017). This subsection presents game applications of AR in the cultural heritage in the literature.

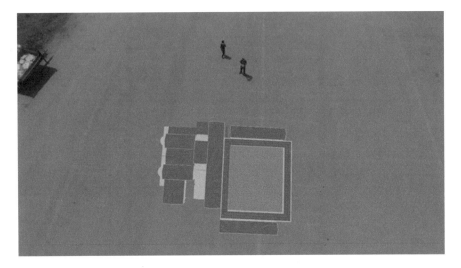

Fig. 12.4 Distant augmentation result (Unal et al. 2020b)

Historical places and buildings can become more interesting with AR games and it can especially appeal to the new generation. Also, visitors can learn more about the site history with location-based AR puzzles (Dieck and Jung 2018).

One of the earliest examples of a tourism-based AR game is the TimeWrap which is an interactive mobile location-based game used to explore the history of a city (Herbst et al. 2008). The aim of the game is to allow the visitor to discover the history of Cologne, a city largely destroyed in World War II. The game requires visitors to equip both an AR system which includes a laptop and head-worn optical see-through display, and a handheld device which provides an information page and interaction map. Visitors need to carry a laptop with an onboard graphic card. The final version of the game had problems with GPS jitter and registering.

Angelopoulou et al. (2011) introduced a multi-user AR application to use in the museum and historical site of Sutton Hoo which has both indoor and outdoor environments, to help inform the visitor about the site with an entertaining puzzle game. The application was designed with the ARToolkit to work with markers which are placed around the site.

Thon et al. (2013) designed an interactive game using drones to increase the number of visitors to the Arlaten Museum in France. This study aims to reduce the effects of stereotypes about museums, using a camera-equipped drone. The drone is used by the visitors to fly around the perimeter and then virtually shooting the stereotypes about the museums which are located in the vicinity. In this way, the museum became more popular and appealing for visitors of all ages.

Bostanci et al. (2013a) designed an AR game titled Treasure Hunt. The game uses Simultaneous Localization and Mapping (SLAM) to locate the user in the vicinity. The SLAM algorithm, which was originally used with robots, strengthened with robust data association to reduce tracking errors. The game was designed to work

Fig. 12.5   The Treasure Hunt game (Bostanci et al. 2013b)

on a simple system which includes camera mounted helmet and a laptop. The aim of the game is to collect the coins and treasures around the environment by walking and reaching the virtual objects. An in-game image can be seen in Fig. 12.5.

12.4   Future Work

Augmented Reality promises great potential and yet needs powerful mobile devices to render 3D models (Ar et al., 2018). Cultural heritage sites and museums can become more entertaining and informative with AR technology. Although current studies in the field of AR are generally still theory based, it has the potential more widespread in daily life in the near future.

The literature presents many different ways of enhancing user experiences in historical sites. The view of the visitor can be enriched with text and sound as basic augmentation. More sophisticated systems can provide an environment of augmented 3D models.

As future work, we aim to reach a Total Augmentation Paradigm which includes using not only mobile devices but also smart glasses and drones in a heritage site (Bostanci and Unal 2016)—see Fig. 12.6. In the system, the drones fly and capture the historical site and transmit the image to mobile devices or smart glasses. The augmentation is achieved on these smart devices in real time. The visitor can see other visitors with the era-appropriate clothes of the historical civilization. Also, a

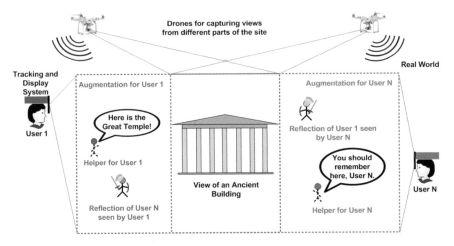

Fig. 12.6 The Total Augmentation System (Bostanci and Unal 2016)

virtual storyteller gives information as the visitors roam around the vicinity. This system can be implemented with powerful mobile devices and smart glasses in the future.

12.5 Conclusion

With advancing technology, the models designed in more detail will give more realistic results in more powerful devices, and the "reality" we know in the near future could begin to be insufficient for people.

In the early 2010s, with the increase of smart devices that are suitable for application development, the number of mobile applications developed has increased incredibly. Augmented Reality technology has also received its share from this increase. Many applications have been developed with this technology and the success of some of them has made a global impression. Many Augmented Reality applications have also been developed for cultural heritage sites with different tracking techniques including not only marker based but also vision based and location based.

The implementation of AR to cultural heritage has been an interesting matter of research, as it assists the conservation of original artifacts that have been exposed to aging for hundreds of years and offers a fun way to learn their history by viewing original artifacts in situ. Accurate user tracking is the most important part of developing and implementing an AR application for cultural heritage. In this study, we presented AR technology and its usage in cultural heritage in the literature. The AR studies in cultural heritage context have been demonstrated in the Visualization and Gamification subsections. As a result, the authors believe that AR technology has a promising and bright future and has the power to radically change the visiting experience of the cultural heritage sites.

Acknowledgements This study is funded by TUBITAK Grant no: (3001:215E156) for the project titled "Development of a Mobile and Distant Augmented Reality System for Cultural Heritage Sites".

References

Angelopoulou AE, Bouki V, Psarrou A, Jin L et al (2011) Mobile augmented reality for cultural heritage. In: International conference on mobile wireless middleware, operating systems, and applications, pp 15–22

Ar Y, Unal M, Sert SY, Bostanci E, et al (2018) Evolutionary fuzzy adaptive motion models for user tracking in augmented reality applications. In: 2018 2nd International Symposium on Multidisciplinary Studies and Innovative Technologies (ISMSIT). IEEE, pp 1–6

Autodesk Inc (2020) 3DS max. https://www.autodesk.com/products/3ds-max/overview

Azuma RT (1997) A survey of augmented reality. Teleoperators and virtual environments, Presence, pp 355–385

Azuma R, Billinghurst M, Klinker G (2011) Special section on mobile augmented reality. Computers & grafics

Bostanci E, Unal M (2016) Making visits to museums more fun with augmented reality using kinect, drones and games. In: The international conference on circuits, systems, signal processing, communications and computers, pp 7–10

Bostanci E, Clark AF, Kanwal N (2013a) Vision-based user tracking for outdoor augmented reality. In: 2012 IEEE symposium on computers and communications (ISCC), pp 566–568

Bostanci E, Kanwal N, Ehsan S, Clark AF (2013b) User tracking methods for augmented reality. Int J Comput Theory Eng

Bostanci GE (2014) User tracking methods for augmented reality applications in cultural heritage. Doctoral dissertation

Bostanci E, Kanwal N, Clark AF (2015) Augmented reality applications for cultural heritage using kinect. Hum-Centric Comput Inf Sci, pp 1–18

Bruns E, Brombach B, Zeidler T, Bimber O (2007) Enabling mobile phones to support large-scale museum guidance. IEEE multimedia, pp 16–25

Carmigniani J, Furht B, Anisetti M, Ceravolo P et al (2011) Augmented reality technologies, systems and applications. Multimedia tools and applications, pp 341–377

Casas X, Herrera G, Coma I, Fernández M (2012) A kinect-based augmented reality system for individuals with autism spectrum disorders. In Grapp/ivapp, pp 440–446

Chatzopoulos D, Bermejo C, Huang Z, Hui P (2017) Mobile augmented reality survey: from where we are to where we go. IEEE access, pp 6917–6950

Choudary O, Charvillat V, Grigoras R, Gurdjos P (2009) MARCH: mobile augmented reality for cultural heritage. In: Proceedings of the 17th ACM international conference on Multimedia, pp 1023–1024

Damala A, Stojanovic N, Schuchert T, Moragues J et al (2012) Adaptive augmented reality for cultural heritage: ARtSENSE project. In: Euro-Mediterranean conference, pp 746–755

Dieck TCM, Jung T (2018) A theoretical model of mobile augmented reality acceptance in urban heritage tourism. Tourism, pp 154–174.

Flavián C, Ibáñez-Sánchez S, Orús, C (2019) The impact of virtual, augmented and mixed reality technologies on the customer experience. J Bus Res, pp 547–560

Galatis P, Gavalas D, Kasapakis V, Pantziou GE et al (2016) Mobile augmented reality guides in cultural heritage. MobiCASE, pp 11–19

Haugstvedt AC, Krogstie J (2012) Mobile augmented reality for cultural heritage: a technology acceptance study. In: 2012 IEEE international symposium on mixed and augmented reality (ISMAR), pp 247–255

Herbst I, Braun AK, McCall R, Broll W (2008) TimeWarp: interactive time travel with a mobile mixed reality game. In: Proceedings of the 10th international conference on Human computer interaction with mobile devices and services, pp 235–244

Jang S, Liu Y (2019) Continuance use intention with mobile augmented reality games. Information technology and people

Kim SK, Kang SJ, Choi YJ, Choi MH et al (2017) Augmented-reality survey: from concept to application. KSII Trans Internet Inf Syst

Kounavis CD, Kasimati AE, Zamani ED (2012) Enhancing the tourism experience through mobile augmented reality: challenges and prospects. Int J Eng Bus Manag

Li H, Gupta A, Zhang J, Flor N (2020) Who will use augmented reality? an integrated approach based on text analytics and field survey. Eur J Oper Res, pp 502–526

Liou HH, Yang SJ, Chen SY, Tarng W (2016) The influences of the 2D image-based augmented reality and virtual reality on student learning. J Educ Technol Soc, pp 110–121

Mourtzis D, Zogopoulos V, Vlachou E (2017) Augmented reality application to support remote maintenance as a service in the robotics industry. Procedia Cirp, pp 46–51

Mutlu B, Haciomeroglu M, Guzel M, Dikmen M et al (2014) Silhouette extraction from street view images. Int J Adv Rob Syst 11(7):114

Nuernberger B, Lien KC, Höllerer T, Turk M (2016) Interpreting 2d gesture annotations in 3d augmented reality. In: 2016 IEEE symposium on 3D user interfaces (3DUI), pp 149–158

Ozdamli FH (2017) An emerging technology: augmented reality to promote learning. Int J Emerg Technol Learn (iJET), pp 121–137

Paavilainen J, Korhonen H, Alha K, Stenros J et al (2017) The Pokémon GO experience: a location-based augmented reality mobile game goes mainstream. In: Proceedings of the 2017 CHI conference on human factors in computing systems, pp 2493–2498

Panou C, Ragia L, Dimelli D, Mania K (2018) An architecture for mobile outdoors augmented reality for cultural heritage. ISPRS Int J Geo-Inf

Papagiannakis G, Singh G, Magnenat-Thalmann N (2008) A survey of mobile and wireless technologies for augmented reality systems. Comput Animat Virtual Worlds, pp 3–22

Piekarski W, Smith R, Thomas BH (2004) Designing backpacks for high fidelity mobile outdoor augmented reality. In: Third IEEE and ACM international symposium on mixed and augmented reality, pp 280–281

Rauschnabel PA, Rossmann A, Tom Dieck MC (2017) An adoption framework for mobile augmented reality games: the case of Pokémon Go. Comput Hum Behav, pp 276–286

Ro YK, Brem A, Rauschnabel PA (2018) Augmented reality smart glasses: definition, concepts and impact on firm value creation. Springer, In: Augmented reality and virtual reality, pp 169–181

Stricker D, Kettenbach T (2001) Real-time and markerless vision-based tracking for outdoor augmented reality applications. In: Proceedings IEEE and ACM international symposium on augmented reality, pp 189–190

Sutherland I E (1968) A head-mounted three dimensional display. Fall joint computer conference, part I, pp 757–764

Thon S, Serena-Allier D, Salvetat C, Lacotte F (2013) Flying a drone in a museum: an augmented-reality cultural serious game in Provence. In: 2013 digital heritage international congress (DigitalHeritage), pp 669–676

Unal M (2017) Kültürel Miras Alanları İçin Uzaktan Artırılmış Gerçeklik Sistemi. Master's thesis, Hacettepe University, Turkey

Unal M, Bostanci E, Sertalp E (2020a) Distant augmented reality: bringing a new dimension to user experience using drones. Digit Appl Archaeol Cult Herit

Unal M, Bostanci E, Guzel MS, Unal FZ et al (2020b) Evolutionary motion model transitions for tracking unmanned air vehicles. In: Smys S, Iliyasu AM, Balas VE, Tavares JMR (eds) New trends in computational vision and bio-inspired computing, pp 1193–1200. https://doi.org/10.1007/978-3-030-41862-5_120

Unal M, Bostanci E, Sertalp E, Guzel MS et al (2018) Geo-location based augmented reality application for cultural heritage using drones. In: 2018 2nd international symposium on multidisciplinary studies and innovative technologies (ISMSIT) IEEE, pp 1–4

Unity Tecnologies (2020) Unity 3d game engine. https://unity3d.com/. Accessed 9 September 2020

Vera L, Gimeno J, Coma, I, Fernández M (2011) Augmented mirror: interactive augmented reality system based on kinect. In: IFIP conference on human-computer interaction, pp 483–486

Vlahakis V, Karigiannis J, Tsotros M, Gounaris M et al (2001) Archeoguide: first results of an augmented reality, mobile computing system in cultural heritage sites. Virtual Rity, Archeol, Cult Herit, pp 584993–585015

Wagner D, Schmalstieg D (2003) First steps towards handheld augmented reality. In: Proceedings seventh ieee international symposium on wearable computers, pp 127–135

Wang X, Ong SK, Nee AY (2016) A comprehensive survey of augmented reality assembly research. Adv Manuf, pp 1–22

Zoellner M, Keil J, Wuest H, Pletinckx D (2009) An augmented reality presentation system for remote cultural heritage sites. In: Proceedings of the 10th international symposium on virtual reality, archaeology and cultural heritage VAST, pp 112–116

Chapter 13
User Experience and Engagement in Augmented Reality Systems for the Cultural Heritage Domain

Arvind Ramtohul and Kavi Kumar Khedo

Abstract This chapter reviews the different models of user experience (UX) and user engagement (UE) proposed for Augmented Reality (AR) systems and discusses their applicability to the Cultural Heritage (CH). Traditional models of UX and UE are not totally adaptable to the current trends in the AR continuum for the CH domain. Thus, an important HCI research area that requires investigation is the evaluation of UX and UE factors for AR systems in the CH field. This chapter proposes a conceptual framework model for assessing UX and UE in AR systems. Initially, the UX categories (such as instrumental, cognitive, emotional, sensory, social and motivational) are investigated thoroughly to have a deep understanding of all the related components. Further, the UE factors (such as aesthetics, interest, goal, novelty, interactivity, gamification and learning) are identified and categorised. Twenty AR systems in the CH domain (AR-CH) have been selected based on pre-defined criteria and evaluated against a list of derived AR characteristics. The gaps in current literature have been considered to formulate a comprehensive framework for the assessment of UX and UE factors in AR-CH systems. Metrics and methods are investigated and identified for the measurement of the UX and UE factors. This chapter lays a solid foundation for the assessment of UX and UE factors in AR-CH systems, which has the potential to help AR system developers with identifying and improving the most UX and UE influential factors in their systems.

13.1 Introduction

Cultural Heritage (CH) represents the ways of living developed by a community and passed on from generation, including customs, practices, places, objects, artistic expressions and values (Thompson 2016). CH can be expressed as Tangible or Intangible. Tangible CH is a physical property that can advocate the country's history and

A. Ramtohul (✉) · K. K. Khedo
University of Mauritius, Reduit, Mauritius

K. K. Khedo
e-mail: k.khedo@uom.ac.mu

© The Author(s), under exclusive license to Springer Nature Switzerland AG 2021
V. Geroimenko (ed.), *Augmented Reality in Tourism, Museums and Heritage*, Springer Series on Cultural Computing,
https://doi.org/10.1007/978-3-030-70198-7_13

culture, whereas Intangible CH refers to those aspects that cannot be touched or seen (Vecco 2010). Mauritius has known a vivid history in the past endorsing the CH sites as a reference to visualise the timelines of the different historical aspects. Those historical aspects have mapped all the events beginning with the discovery of Mauritius to its independence and denoting its importance in the development of Mauritius.

In most of the cases, Cultural Heritage sites do not have useful information, or they lack user guides which affect the visiting experience. Although CH sites have employed traditional mediums (such as dashboards, booklets and maps) for sharing of information, visitors find it uninteresting and not motivating enough (Pendit et al. 2014). In this context, CH sites can adopt the high-tech technologies to bring more liveliness to their static environment and also taking full advantage to showcase all the detailed heritage aspects to visitors. The World UNESCO centre has cited two CH sites in Mauritius as a World Heritage site in their records namely: Aapravasi Ghat and Le Morne Cultural Landscape (UNESCO 2020). Both sites are rich in cultures and they provide an automatic sense of unity to allow us to better understand previous generations and the history of where we came from.

Undoubtedly, the effervescence in new technologies has contributed various breakthrough in the worldly activities. In the same line, the apprehend-ability of artefacts can be enhanced using 3D modelling techniques through digital technologies. Augmented Reality (AR) has been a key focus lately in the CH industry, with more and more CH institutions implementing AR to give a competitive marketing edge to the heritage assets. Some examples include the Museum of London, the Netherlands Architecture and the Powerhouse Museum in Sydney (Lee et al. 2015). Augmented Reality is an emerging technology that is widely integrating into cross-dimensional activities across the globe through various forms (Chatzopoulos et al. 2017). The development of Augmented Reality is booming, and the adoption is fierce in several sectors including education, marketing, entertainment, tourism, retail and AECO (Architecture, Engineering, Construction and Owner) (Chatzopoulos et al. 2017; Chen et al. 2017). The concept of AR stems from virtual reality, except the information is mediated with more realness and naturalness (Azuma et al. 2001). The layer of information is contextualised and supplemented with readily available data (e.g. images, locations and sounds) that changes the perspective of the user perceptions (Van Kleef et al. 2010).

The wide-appealing of this technology is supported by the increasing demands of ubiquitous gadgets (smartphones, head-worn devices and projection displays) available in the market (Chatzopoulos et al. 2017). The maturity of AR is gradually outreaching the general public, therefore taking it to new heights of high-end products (Garzón et al. 2019). As a consequence, these systems have a certain attractiveness and they can activate emotional reactions. The emotional reactions may differ from user to user. This relation is sometimes complex to understand and very few works have investigated on Human–Computer Interaction (HCI). HCI is a predominant subject that still requires investigation to understand the user experience/engagement, its prerequisites and the situational/personal mediation. Lately, the sustainable progression of AR systems is taken for granted by designers and developers, as they often lacked focus on the HCI field (Datcu et al. 2015).

The HCI field, i.e. UX and UE is still an unexplored area in the AR-CH domain. More and more Cultural Heritage (CH) institutions are adopting AR to create the missing sparks from their static environment thus making it more energetic. Yet, the different mechanisms of visual information, interactions, interfaces and displays employed in AR application make this task even more challenging. Authors have used preliminary UX and UE frameworks to determine the enhancement aspects that could be used in the AR context. Nevertheless, the novelty of interactions with AR information has changed during the course and new types of AR, i.e. mobile AR (MAR) are surfacing and stimulating a unique experience (Chatzopoulos et al. 2017). In this lens, the previous UX and UE models are not adapted with the current trends that are ongoing in the AR-CH continuum. Though various AR applications have been available in the marketplace, very few researches have been carried out in this field of study. In addition, the user expectations are motivated by the prior experiences they had with the technology. A temporal model of the user expectations has been illustrated by Anu Kankainen that described the correlations between previous experience, present experience and more experiences (Kankainen 2003). Currently, there is a large interest in understanding the narrative aspects of AR-CH applications, but the focus on UX and UE is limited.

This chapter focussed on the application of the UX and UE enhancement models in the AR-CH field. A research methodology is employed to construct the chapter. At the initial stage, the generic UX and UE frameworks are enumerated, described and analysed to have an understanding on the technological aspects. Next, the frameworks are analysed in the AR-CH area and a classification of the influential factors affecting UX and UE is derived. The related metrics and methods to assess the UX and UE factors in AR-CH systems are identified.

13.2 Research Methodology

In this research, the objective is focussed on deriving the influential UX and UE factors in the AR-CH domain. This objective is derived based on the principles of UX and UE frameworks that were applied in the technology domain. In this vein, the general UX and UE frameworks in the technology perspectives are explored at the initial stage. The generic frameworks are filtered out based on the relevance to the field, citations, popularity and application area. The works have been categorised under the UX and UE frameworks. At the second fold, the UX and UE frameworks conceived for AR-CH systems are reviewed methodically. The next stage consists of a synthesis of the AR-CH design characteristics with the derived UX and UE factors. In this endeavour, a total of twenty works have been identified and reviewed methodically with the following conditions as described in subsections below. The methodology is depicted in Fig. 13.1.

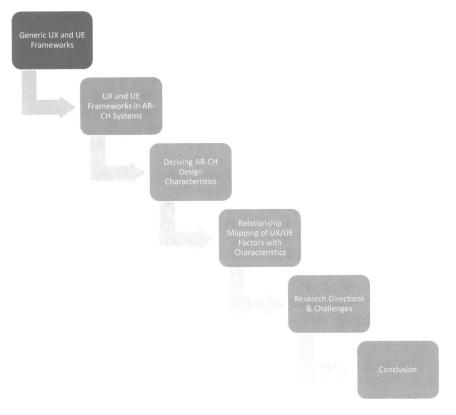

Fig. 13.1 Research methodology

13.2.1 Search Terms

The frameworks are selected by determining the most appropriate search strategy, the search items used were "Augmented Reality", "Mobile Augmented Reality", "Cultural Heritage", "Museum", "User Experience", "User Engagement", "Frameworks", "Models", "Metrics" and combination of them. The search was limited to the last 5 years from 2015 to 2020. The last update was on 10 August 2020.

13.2.2 Data Sources

With the recent technological advances in mobile systems, new positioning techniques have been developed. As such, there are some articles available on this subject. Initially, a general exploration is carried out on reputed scientific journals and conference proceedings to shortlist the relevant scientific databases. The highest relevance of indexed papers was found in IEEE Xplore, ACM Digital Library, Springer, Science Direct, Elsevier and ERIC.

13.3 UX Frameworks

Many UX frameworks have been conceived in the AR context, but they have been mostly conceptualised with the generic UX frameworks. The understanding of these universal frameworks is vital in this study, as they comprise of various components that have been plugged in on the UX-AR frameworks. To have a broader perspective of the different UX frameworks, this section describes, analyses and evaluates these generic frameworks, theories and methods. The generic frameworks are selected based on their popularity, relevance and application area. Given the wider spectrum of UX, the study focusses on UX-AR frameworks at a later stage in this study.

Hassenzahl (2004) presented a UX model based on two features of product quality: pragmatic and hedonic. Pragmatic quality is the product's ability to promote attainment of behavioural goals (product's usefulness, usability or appropriateness) whereas hedonic quality is widely associated with the social and emotional behaviours that are perceived based on the user's experience (or post-experience). Hedonic quality can be further broken into three subgroups: stimulation, identification and evocation. Stimulation enables personal growth, identification is related to express and build one's identity through the product and evocation is the memory and emotion revolved around the product. These outcomes can vary from user to user since the users construct their personal opinions based on the product features and characteristics. Figure 13.2 provides the graphical layout of the UX model proposed by Hassenzahl (2004).

Buccini and Padovani (2007) have reworked earlier UX models and proposed a consolidated model of product experience with six categories: (1) experiences related to the senses, (2) experiences related to feelings, (3) social experiences, (4) cognitive experiences, (5) use experiences and (6) motivational experiences. The "senses" experiential corresponds to the experience related to sensory factors through vision,

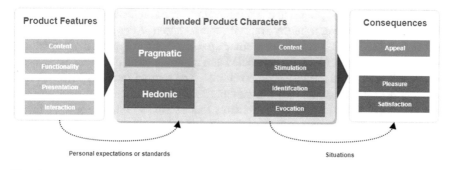

Fig. 13.2 UX model (Adapted from Hassenzahl [2004])

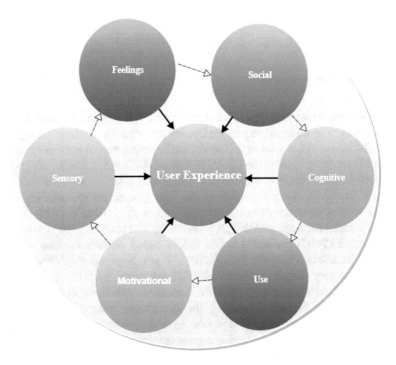

Fig. 13.3 Six categories of product experience (Adapted from Buccini and Padovani [2007])

hearing, touch, taste or smell. "Feeling" deals with emotional reactions originated from the use of the product. Social experience involves the behaviour patterns that lead to interaction and collaboration between individuals. Cognitive is related to the thought and interpretation by the user. Use experience is mainly associated with usability and functionality of the product. Motivational experience is related to the changes in human behaviour during or post usage of the product. Figure 13.3 depicts the different correlation between the six categories from the UX model proposed by Buccini and Padovani (2007).

Wright et al. (2008) proposed a UX framework based on Dewey's pragmatics and the relationship of user's interaction with the technology described by McCarthy and Wright (2004). The authors have come up with a holistic approach of experience with four main threads that are connected and common to all experiences: sensual, emotional, spatio-temporal and compositional. The sensual thread is involved with sensory, bodily engagement with a situation, i.e. the look and feel of a product. The emotional thread refers to "judgments that ascribe to other people or things of importance with respect to our needs and desire", i.e. frustration, desire, anger, joy or satisfaction is directed to another person or thing. The spatio-temporal thread underlines that experiences evolve to a particular situation ("place") at a particular time. Finally, the compositional thread is concerned with the narrative structure of

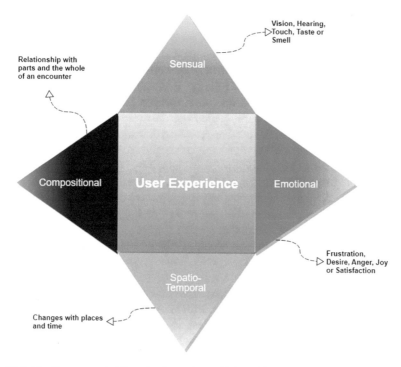

Fig. 13.4 The four connected threads of experience (Adapted from Wright et al. [2008])

an experience, how to make sense of the relationship between parts and the whole of an encounter. Figure 13.4 summarises the UX model presented by Wright et al. (2008).

13.4 UE Frameworks

The terminology "User Engagement" has been a buzzword in a variety of domain and application areas. This term as it is can be conflicting with "User Experience" as they both reveal certain aspects of a product that are deemed to provide comfort, immersion and motivation. Yet, UE has various differentiating factors with UX. As introduced earlier, UE is "a quality of interactive UX" thus highlighting a more qualitative dimension of a product. In some literature, it is often differentiated as a "non-passive consumer of information" that has a direct influence on engaging factors such as emotions, immersion, re-enactment, sharing, collaboration, endorsement, promotion, etc. (O'Brien 2016). In a more contrasting perspective, UE can be considered as the catalyst of the prior experiences that subsequently lead to a re-enactment of the same experience. For instance, the measurements of UE for a museum can be as follows: number of visits, number of activities, time spent per visit/activity, number of endorsements or promotions, etc. As discussed previously, the term "UE" has been interrelated with "UX" and it has not been deciphered properly in earlier studies. In this section, the granularities of UE are explained using related frameworks.

Pine and Gilmore (1998) introduced the Experience Economy to illustrate the four realms of consumer experience as follows: Entertainment, Educational, Escapist and Esthetic. The model is based on two dimensions: involvement, ranging from passive participation to active participation and the desire, ranging from absorption to immersion. For instance, the passive-active participation can be related to "those following a soccer game on TV versus those attending to the soccer game" whereas absorption-immersion connection can be explained by "those in a ground stand of a sports event versus those in the field". Figure 13.5 provides the classification of the four realms of experience classified by a spectrum of connection (immersion and absorption) along the vertical, and a spectrum of participation (active and passive) along the horizontal line of the model.

Positive Engagement Evaluation Model (PEEM) (Rutledge and Neal 2012) is a model that has been designed to incorporate holistic, qualitative experience in interactive and mobile applications. The model is based on several concepts from positive psychology, narrative transportation theory, psychological flow theory, cognitive psychology and perception theory. PEEM comprises of nine elements: goal, attention, concentration, interaction, content, identity, collaboration, enjoyment and satisfaction. The goal element addresses whether the goal of the applications is clear and aligned accordingly to the user needs and tasks. The attention investigates the

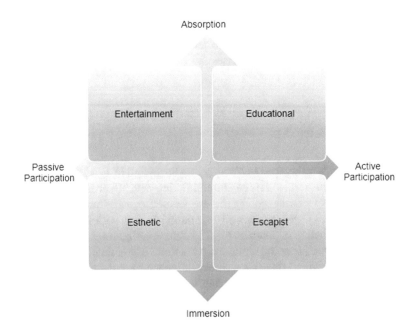

Fig. 13.5 The four realms of experience (Adapted from Pine and Gilmore [1998])

application tasks and their sequence. Concentration is accountable to keep the user attention on the application. The interaction investigates whether the application provides a clear progression from task to task. The content element addresses the media used in the application and whether the media used is seamless to execution. Identity focusses on the tasks of the application that should integrate the user into the experience. The collaboration encourages social aspects of the application. Finally, enjoyment and satisfaction is a mode of motivation or encouragement that users repeat their use of the application as well as sharing their experiences in the forms of ratings and comments. Figure 13.6 provides a graphical layout of the PEEM model.

O'Brien and Toms (2008) deconstruct the term engagement to reflect the people's experiences with technology. The authors carried out critical incident interviews with users of different types of technologies to model the process of UE. The results have indicated that engagement is a process comprised of four distinct stages: point of engagement, the period of sustained engagement, disengagement and re-engagement. The point of engagement may occur at any point during the interaction when the users delve beyond the mechanistic or routine level and invest themselves in the interaction. The period of sustained engagement is where users feel part of the interaction through an awareness of what the system is doing (feedback) and feeling connected to the technology. Disengagement is associated with positive emotions (user's needs and motivations are satisfied and they feel successful) or with negative feelings of frustration, uncertainty, being overwhelmed by challenges or information or loss of interest. Users may cycle through the stages of engagement several times during a single session, thus re-engagement is intrinsic to the model.

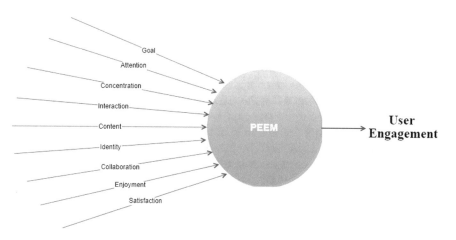

Fig. 13.6 The PEEM model (Adapted from Rutledge and Neal [2012])

13.5   UX and UE Frameworks for AR-CH Systems

The generic UX and UE frameworks have been elaborated and analysed in the previous sections. The terminologies have been described and differentiated to reach a common perspective on the nature of this study. The questions *(1) What UX and UE terminologies are? (2) What are the differences between the two terminologies? (3) What are the related frameworks? (4) How the related frameworks have improved tech-driven systems?* have been addressed in the previous sections. Yet, these questions have been answered without prior knowledge on the integration to AR-CH systems. This section concentrates solely on the UX and UE frameworks that have been modelled for AR-CH systems. The recent UX and UE frameworks in the AR-CH domain are enumerated, analysed and discussed in this section.

Han et al. (2018) presented a UX model for AR applications in urban heritage tourism through the identification of AR-related factors that influence users' satisfaction. This study extends the theoretical aspect of the UX model by Hassenzahl (2004) through the empirical confirmation of the work by Mahlke (2008). The initial stage consisted of data collection through a targeted number of groups. The data were analysed using thematic analysis to examine the alignment of the new themes and to investigate the emergent themes from the focus groups. The findings reveal that the UX is formed by the correlation of product features and the perceptions and experiences of tourists. Using the theories from Hassenzahl (2004), the formulated UX model has taken a similar shape. The UX model is depicted in Fig. 13.7. The authors have tackled each component independently to have a rationale perspective of all elements (characteristics) that are required. For instance, the attribute "content" has been associated with "personalised information", "information on local venues", etc. The product characters have been expanded with the pragmatic and hedonic attributes. Amidst all the attributes proposed in Fig. 13.7, the authors stressed that simplicity is a key driver for users next to accessibility and convenience. The hedonic aspect uncovered the emotional attachments that users can feel while using the system. The authors found that the visitors were very keen to accept the system since it supplemented their interest on the heritage aspect.

Figure 13.7 is an exploded UX map of the Hassenzahl 2004 UX theories. All the characteristics have been carefully identified in virtue of their functioning and output towards a user-centric approach. Moreover, the domain of the application is equally important in the derivation and selection of the correct characteristics. The environment on which the system should work is unequivocally central in moulding the UX model. In this way, designers and developers of such systems should be focussed on both these aspects. Though this model has been formulated with a smaller dataset, it certainly provides an initial starting point for researchers and practitioners in the field.

Tom Dieck et al. (2018a) carried out a study to examine the visitor engagement through AR at science festivals. The aim of the study is to investigate how educational, esthetics, escapist and entertainment experience using AR affect visitor satisfaction and memorable experience using the experience economy theory. At a preliminary

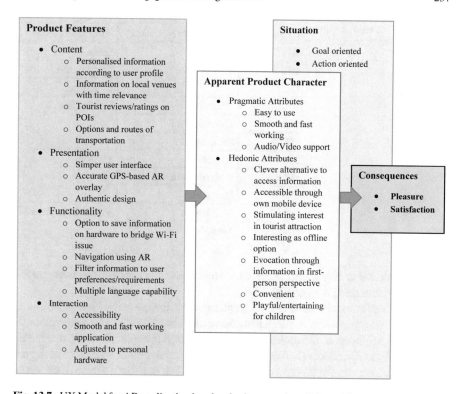

Fig. 13.7   UX Model for AR application in urban heritage tourism (Adapted from Han et al. [2018])

stage, a set of questionnaires was employed to identify and analyse the UE elements that have a greater influence on the human behaviours. From the findings, a basic theoretical framework of engagement has been conceptualised. Figure 13.8 depicts the model and relationships of the components. For instance, the authors concluded that aesthetics has a positive effect on education, entertainment and escapism. Similarly, the flow goes in the same trend (as per Fig. 13.8) until the "engagement" element is satisfied. In this study, the contributions were primarily to show a novel conceptualisation of experience economy and the links between memory and satisfaction

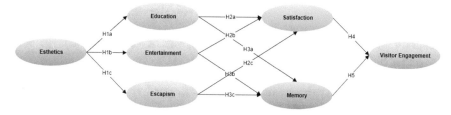

Fig. 13.8   Visitors' engagement model (Adapted from Tom Dieck et al. [2018a])

Table 13.1 The relationships between the antecedents

Hypothesis	Antecedents/experience	Positive effects on
H1a	Esthetics	Education
H1b		Entertainment
H1c		Escapism
H2a	Education	Satisfaction
H2b	Entertainment	
H2c	Escapism	
H3a	Education	Memory
H3b	Entertainment	
H3c	Escapism	
H4	Satisfaction	Visitor Engagement
H5	Memory	

leading to visitor engagement. Table 13.1 summarises the connections between the first, second and third tiers of Fig. 13.8.

The study of Tom Dieck et al. (2018a) extends the UE theories by Pine and Gilmore (1998). The engagement of visitors is theoretically conceptualised by the hypothesis in Table 13.1. However, the authors emphasised that AR experiences are originated with aesthetics rather than other elements. The authors have even evaluated the degree of positive effects on the aforementioned elements, but they have limited their study on four realms of experience (aesthetics, education, entertainment and escapism). In this context, more factors should have been identified to validate the determinants of visitor engagement.

Hammady et al. (2018) explore the UX of AR applications in museums in Leeds, UK and Cairo, Egypt. This paper delineated a clear framework of UX of AR applications in museums by emphasising on the UX theories. The authors have thus come up with an application called "MuseumEye" which encompasses a combination of multimedia content such as audio commentaries, video representations and a gallery of images. A UX design process model has been put forward in prior to develop the application. The model consists of three stages as follows: requirements, design for UX and evaluation. In the requirement phase, skills and data are required before starting to design and develop the system. The second phase "design for UX" determines the prerequisites of the application, e.g. museum context, visitors, technical information on AR. The third phase "Evaluation" assesses the UX experience of the AR application in the museum. This study contributes on synthesising a UX design model for AR application to reach the optimum levels of user interactions required that reflect ultimately on the entire museum experience.

The authors have evaluated the UX aspects based on the following parameters: immersion, useful, easy to use, interesting, intuitive and visuals. The assessments were carried out in both sites; Leeds, UK and Cairo, Egypt. The results show that the AR applications have been useful, as most of the respondents found it useful. In this study, the process of deriving the UX aspects has been supported by the three stages (requirements, design for UX and evaluation). They have not explored a UX framework in the first place to weigh on their prototype design model. As such, the UX factors in this work are limited to have an enhanced contribution on the museum experience.

13.6   Classification of UX and UE Factors in AR–CH Systems

The sections above have provided a comprehensive narrative of the UX and UE frameworks. At the preliminary stage, the generic UX and UE frameworks are reviewed that are conceived in the technological domains. Next, the chapter is focussed on the UX and UE frameworks on AR applications in the CH domain. The aforementioned sections have provided enough information to understand the underlying components of the UX and UE frameworks and create a virtual mapping of the requirements. In this endeavour, this section synthesises the UX and UE factors from the related frameworks discussed earlier. A classification of the factors is carried out methodically. At an initial level, the UX and UE factors are identified at a broader perspective, i.e. technological level. The second phase carries out a mapping of the requirements of the AR-CH applications (including MAR) with UX/UE factors. The third phase consists of evaluating the UX/UE factors in the CH domain.

The recent developments in AR (including MAR) have made the user-centred design process even more challenging since the users of emerging technologies find it difficult to express their needs because of their lack of knowledge in the technology's potential (Olsson 2013; Lee and Hannafin 2016). The concept has changed from a technological-driven perspective to a more user-centric perspective. The tangibility, interactivity and pervasiveness of AR have brought various instances of the initial perception of the technology.

13.6.1   UX Factors in AR Systems

In consideration of the literature in this field, Table 13.2 presents the expected UX elements. A new breadth of elements is included to adapt to the recent advancements of AR technology. In the same vein, the identified UX and UE elements will take into consideration the current users' expectations and the recent evolution of AR.

Table 13.2 presents a synthesis of characteristics of the desirable UX elements relevant for futuristic AR services. Twenty elements have been identified and categorised from the model proposed by Buccini and Padovani (2007). As a starting point, the model of Buccini and Padovani has been chosen for exploration since it comprises enough experiential categories. Each category has been expanded to retrieve the UX elements deem for AR context. Moreover, the models of Hassenzahl

Table 13.2 The identified UX elements for AR

#	Expected UX characteristics	Product features
1	Usefulness	Readily available context information for augmentation
2	Efficiency	Provides different layers of information
3	Accessibility	Device and environment free
4	Ease of Use	User-centric/Simple UI
5	Mobility	Navigating freely
6	Awareness & Knowledge	Real-time and Location-based enablement
7	Intuitiveness	Augmentation at the focal point
8	Personalisation	Personalised contents
9	Delightful	Showcasing hidden aspects
10	Liveliness	Novelty in the superimposition
11	Playfulness	Gamification element
12	Appealing	Multimodal interface
13	Immersive	360 degree panorama & 3D view
14	Connectedness	Connecting with other people
15	Sharing & Collaborating	Sharing and teaming with other people
16	Stimulation	Immersing on the experience
17	Evocation	Digital reconstruction of past events
18	Creativity	Storytelling
19	Dynamic	Contents are changed at regular intervals
20	Distinctive	AR contents change at the next encounter

(2004) and Wright et al. (2008) have also facilitated the inclusion of certain UX elements to cover up possible user expectations. Above all, the list of elements has been inspired from the work by Olsson (2013). Some of the elements have been tweaked to reflect the current user expectations and the changing dynamics of AR technologies. Some of the elements have been tweaked to reflect the current user expectations and the changing dynamics of AR technologies. For example, "usefulness" has substituted both "empowerment" and "meaningfulness" as characterised by Olsson (2013). The term "usefulness" in AR can be inferred as providing valuable information, therefore empowering the users at the same time. The characteristics "delightful" have consolidated both "amazement" and "surprise" since it implies "the experience has been enjoying and at the same time it provides some facets of revelations". In regards to the recent developments of AR, the term "immersive" is more appropriate to signify that the experiences should be engaging and arouse the users' senses that they are inside the experience. In another vein, "sharing and collaboration" instils more towards a sharing and learning cultures among the users thus creating certain bonds between them.

13.6.2 UE Factors in AR Systems

In this subsection, the discussion is oriented on the UE factors for AR services. As mentioned previously, very few works have focussed on the UE elements in the AR context. Many works have conflicted UX with UE or vice versa, and they have not provided a clear direction on the significance that they have in AR systems. In the context of the literature presented in this study, the differentiation between UX and UE is unequivocal. Recapitulating, UE is a quality of UX which can be attributed by the measurements of, but limited to: amount of time, number of activities, endorsements, promotions, suggestions, challenges-faced and solved and connecting/collaboration with users. Table 13.3 lists the UE elements from a conglomerate of existing models as follows: Experience Economy (Pine and Gilmore 1998), PEEM model (O'Brien 2016), Flow theory (Romero and Calvillo-Gámez 2011), UE theories by O'Brien and Toms (2008) and engagement model by Tom Dieck et al. (2018a). Existing UE elements have been identified from these models, and in turn they have been grouped as follows: initial point of engagement, the period of engagement and continued engagement. In addition, new elements have been included based on our own perception of engagement. For instance, exploration,

Table 13.3 The identified UE elements for AR

#	Expected UE factors	Engagement level
1	Aesthetics	Point of engagement
2	Interest	
3	Goal	
4	Novelty	
5	Interactivity	Period of engagement
6	Content	
7	Attention	
8	Exploration	
9	Awareness	
10	Feedback	
11	Concentration	
12	Learning	
13	Gamification	
14	Collaboration	
15	Sharing	
16	Immersion	Maximum engagement
17	Challenges	
18	Identity	
19	Satisfaction	Re-engagement/disengagement
20	Memorable	

gamification, sharing, immersion and challenges are the novel elements put forward in this study. Deciphering the proposed model, the initial start of engagement is often triggered by the following: (1) appearance/attractiveness of the product, (2) the user's interest (or things that captured their attention), (3) the users' goal that they want to achieve and (4) the new features proposed in the product.

Table 13.3 is a comprehensive list of the UE factors derived for the AR context. The factors have been further grouped in conjunction with their engagement propensity. For example, aesthetics is an important driver for interactivity, which dictates whether users accept or reject the technology (Pallud and Straub 2014; Limerick et al. 2019). User's interest is likely to incline on the amount of information available, a sense of exploring new places and being well-informed about new developments. Kim and Chan (2003), Cruz-Benito et al. (2015) and O'Brien (2016) demonstrate that interest and goal have an impact on content, exploration and awareness. In the same propensity, the novelty can be favoured by various antecedents such as interactivity, content, exploration and awareness (Zhuang et al. 2018). Thus, aesthetics, interest, goal and novelty are the four factors that are grouped in "point of. Interactivity can be the first precursor of engagement after the user has initially started using the AR system. Lindgren et al. (2016), Barrio et al. (2015) and Cruz-Benito et al. (2015) state that interactivity and attention have a positive influence on learning and gamification. Attention can arouse the user's consciousness towards more concentration and learning. In the same category, exploration can positively influence the following factors: learning, gamification, collaboration and sharing (Barrio et al. 2015; Lee and Hannafin 2016). Lee and Hannafin (2016) infer that both collaboration and sharing have a direct connection to identity. These factors characterise the likes and dislikes of the users, thus they play an important role in the identification of users' personalities. In this connection, interactivity, content, attention, exploration, awareness, feedback, concentration, learning, gamification, collaboration and sharing are the factors that are grouped in the "period of engagement" level. The final derivative of engagement can be entitled to satisfying experience and memories (Lee and Hannafin 2016; Kim and Lee 2015). Yet, immersion, challenges and identity are the three core factors which contribute to maximum engagement, thus reaching the ultimate step of satisfaction and memorable experiences (Lindgren et al. 2016; Ali et al. 2016).

13.6.3 Classification of AR–CH Systems

At first glance, AR-CH systems can have a wide range of characteristics that could differentiate among them. For example, the functioning of the system will vary in terms of the featured services, environment, technologies or any factors that could have direct link with the workability of the system. The subsections above have shed light on the key takings of the UX and UE frameworks in AR systems. Yet is imperative to have a holistic view on the characteristics of AR-CH systems and interrelate them with the UX and UE factors. In this perspective, AR-CH systems are evaluated against a derived list of AR-CH characteristics. Eventually, this subsection provides information on the potential UX and UE factors that can be drawn from the evaluation. Twenty works have been shortlisted based on the criteria defined in the research methodology earlier (see Fig. 13.1). Initially, an eccentric list of AR-CH characteristics is derived from the finding of Sırakaya and Sırakaya (2020), Akçayır and Akçayır (2017) and Wang et al. (2016). The reviewed works have provided additional novel types of characteristics that should be included. Table 13.4 presents a complete synthesis of the information on AR characteristics. Table 13.5 reviews the AR systems with the derived AR characteristics. Figure 13.9 formulates a relationship of the AR-CH characteristics versus the common UX and UE categories.

As shown in Table 13.5, all the related works have been reviewed thoroughly with the defined characteristics presented in Table 13.4. The assessment provides an indication of the area of focus for each system. For instance, "Real-time augmentation" is a prerequisite element for designing AR systems. The AR information should be accurate and precise to the users' field of view. In this perspective, this element should cater to all the underlying components such as data acquisition, user and device positioning, tracking and registration and superimposition. AR designers should imperatively focus on this element during the initial conception of such systems,

Table 13.4 Characteristics of AR-CH

Characteristics	Abbreviation	Description
Real-time Augmentation	RA	The perfect-inch augmentation at the right place and at right time
Fast interaction	FI	Simple UI that allows a quick interactivity between the user and system
Context-layering	CL	Augmentation of the surrounding environment
Object-layering	OL	Layered AR information is available for a particular object
Point of interest	POI	AR information is available in places of interest
Navigation	NA	Navigation map connecting the routes of the POI
Pervasive	PE	Continuously augmenting the physical world with respect to the context of the user
Storytelling	ST	3D/4D digital reconstruction of past events using AR
Gamification	GM	Inclusion of game elements to create a sense of playfulness
Sound and haptic feedback	SH	System carries out augmentation with sound and haptic mediums
Awareness and learning outcomes	AL	Increased insight into objects surrounding in a visually challenged environment

Table 13.5 Assessment of AR systems with defined characteristics

AR systems	Application area	AR characteristics										
		RA	FI	CL	OL	POI	NA	PE	ST	GM	SH	AL
LecceAR (Banterle et al. 2015)	Museum	•	•	–	•	–	–	•	–	–	–	•
AREAv2 (Geiger et al. 2013)	–	•	•	–	•	•	•	•	–	–	–	•
VisAge (Julier et al. 2016)	Town site	•	•	–	–	•	–	–	–	–	–	–
Svevo Tour (Fenu and Pittarello 2018)	Museum	•	•	–	–	–	–	•	•	–	•	•
Alleto et al. (2015)	Museum	•	•	•	•	–	–	–	•	–	–	•
Ramtohul and Khedo (2019)	Historic building	•	•	•	•	•	–	•	•	–	–	•
Han et al. (2018)	Archaeological site	–	•	•	–	–	–	–	–	–	–	–
Galatis et al. (2016)	Archaeological site	•	•	•	•	–	–	–	–	–	•	•
Gutierrez et al. (2015)	Historic building	–	–	–	•	–	–	–	–	–	–	•
New Philadelphia (Amakawa and Westin 2018)	Town site	•	•	•	–	–	–	•	•	–	–	–
Hammady et al. (2016)	Museum	•	•	•	–	–	–	•	–	•	–	–
Vecchio et al. (2015)	Town site	•	–	•	•	–	–	–	–	–	–	•
Cavallo et al. (2016)	Town site	•	•	•	•	–	–	–	•	–	–	•
Chin et al. (2017)	Historic building	–	–	–	–	–	–	–	–	–	–	•

(continued)

Table 13.5 (continued)

AR systems	Application area	AR characteristics										
		RA	FI	CL	OL	POI	NA	PE	ST	GM	SH	AL
Duguleana et al. (2016)	Historic building	•	•	•	•	–	–	–	•	–	–	–
Leach et al. (2018)	Cultural heritage	•	•	•	•	–	–	–	•	–	–	•
Tom Dieck et al. (2018b)	Art gallery	•	–	–	–	–	–	–	–	–	–	•
Pantille et al. (2018)	Museum	•	•	–	•	•	–	–	–	–	–	•
Pierdicca et al. (2015)	Archaeological site	•	•	•	•	•	–	–	•	–	–	•
Hammady et al. (2018)	Museum	•	•	•	•	•	–	–	–	–	–	•

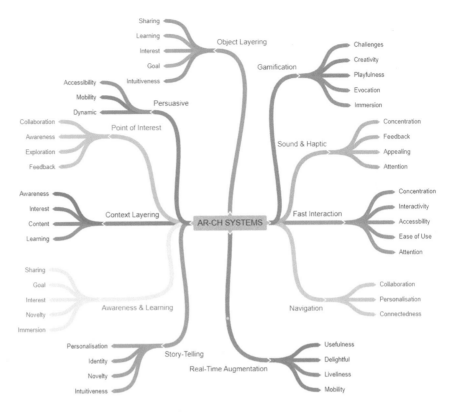

Fig. 13.9 AR-CH design characteristics

which explains the 100%-mark percentile. The next characteristic is "Awareness and Knowledge" which shares a large proportion of interest in AR systems. The works have focussed on providing a substantial amount of information which contributes to both the spatial and cognitive aspects of the users. Such systems comprise of multi-tiered interfaces which are interconnected to provide a real-time augmentation. In this endeavour, AR systems necessitate a quick intervention from users so that the augmentation can be carried out at a reasonable time delay. This process relies on having a user-centric UI that enables a smooth interaction and easy-to-go interface. Futuristic AR systems are implementing "storytelling" and "gamification" features to provide an edge over traditional AR systems. They have gained momentum during the recent years and can be perceived as the next-gen AR systems. This section has provided an insightful indication on the area of concentration in such systems. It is imperative to expose these characteristics in relations to the associated UX and UE factors. Figure 13.9 depicts a comprehensive mapping of the characteristics and the associated UX and UE factors.

The mapping on Fig. 13.9 provides the derivations of the UX and UE factors from the characteristics of AR systems. The information is insightful for developers and designers in the field as they can link the UX/UE factors to a specific characteristic. As mentioned above, the characteristics have been derived methodically with the recent findings carried out in this field. For instance, "Real-time Augmentation" is a prerequisite in the AR context because of the agility of the systems that make them very reactive and responsive. The speed of the augmentation should be in-line with the objects in the focus point. At the same time, such systems should provide accurate information for the particular context and should be transportable anywhere in the environment. "Awareness and Learning" have the most number of attributes associated with it. It is important because most of these systems have in focus to provide substantial information that would enhance both the spatial and cognitive aspects of the users. In the same vein, these systems can provide information that were never accessible before. The next section provides a classification of the UX and UE most influential factors in AR-CH.

13.7   Influential UX and UE Factors for Cultural Heritage AR Systems

AR technologies have been a breakthrough in the heritage industry. More and more CH institutions are adopting AR to create the missing sparks from their static environment thus making it more energetic. As this technology is maturing in the CH domains, UX and UE factors should always be in the limelight to provide an edge over the causal experiences. These factors are core aspects of the HCI that strengthens the relations among various stakeholders, e.g. visitors, products and exhibits. This section concentrates solely on the UX and UE factors of AR systems in the CH domain. Based on the identified UX and UE factors in this section, an assessment on each factor to see the most influential ones for the CH domain. Table 13.6 presents the impact assessment on the UX factors and Table 13.7 is the impact assessment on the UE factors.

The assessment from Table 13.6 provides an understanding on the importance of the different UX characteristics. The most impactful categories for the CH field are: instrumental, cognitive, emotional, sensory and motivational. The category "instrumental" revolved mostly around the practical usage of the AR system in the CH domain. For example, the composition of a museum is surrounded by several exhibits which are closely arranged to each other. Thus, the system should work effectively and flawlessly in order to present the AR information to the visitors at the right moment. Second, the interest of "learning" is certainly a priority when it comes to CH field. Visitors want to know the existence of these exhibits and the events associated with the same. In this vein, "cognitive" should be included as UX category for CH domain. The "emotional" construct is mostly related to the human behaviour while the visitors are engaging with the system. For example, an augmentation can highlight elements in a painting or artwork that are not visible to naked eyes. This can create a sense of excitement, joy or achievement, and it is important to emphasise

Table 13.6 Impact Assessment of UX factors for CH domain

Experience categories	Expected UX characteristics	Impact assessment (High—H, Medium—M, Low—L)	Rationale
Instrumental	Usefulness	H	All information should be available for a particular exhibit
	Efficiency	H	AR information should be displayed at every angle of the exhibits. Each users' action should correspond to feedback from the system
	Accessibility	H	AR should work irrespective of the device types and the environment
	Ease of Use	H	The users should be able to interact effortlessly and achieve the desired output without difficulties
	Mobility	H	System should be readily transportable anywhere on the site
Cognitive	Awareness and Knowledge	H	AR contents should be relevant to the subject and enhance the users' apprehend-ability on the exhibits
	Intuitiveness	M	The naturalness should be respected and kept within the users' context
	Personalisation	M	Personalised contents can be available at users' demand
Emotional	Delightful	H	The system should propose contents and features that make the experience enjoyable
	Liveliness	H	The AR context should be dynamic and propose new information

(continued)

Table 13.6 (continued)

Experience categories	Expected UX characteristics	Impact assessment (High—H, Medium—M, Low—L)	Rationale
	Playfulness	M	Game elements like a quiz to test the knowledge of the visitor
Sensory	Appealing	H	Interface should be attractive to capture the attention of visitors
	Immersive	H	Different layers of augmentation to captivate the users into the experience
Social	Connectedness	L	Users can connect with others at their wish
	Sharing and collaborating	L	Users can share and collaborate at their own demands
Motivational	Stimulation	M	The experiences should be exciting enough to arouse the interest of visitors
	Evocation	H	The experiences should be memorable to incite the users to come back again
	Creativity	M	The experiences should enable users to develop new skills
Spatio-Temporal	Dynamic	M	The contents should be changing at regular interval of times
	Distinctive	M	The content should be changing at the next experience

on these attributes for a working solution in a CH site. Third, the "sensory" aspect enables a flow of embodiment with the exhibits. Initially, the visitors can feel attracted by the looks and feels of the product, amplifying their sense of see, touch and taste. Furthermore, the augmentation should be carried out in such a way that visitors feel that they are inside the experience and their involvement is important. Last but not the least, "motivational" category inspires the visitors to discover new elements by themselves, develop or refine their skills and create a memorable event during their

Table 13.7 Impact assessment of UE factors for CH domain

UE factors	Impact assessment (High—H, Medium—M, Low—L)	Rationale
Aesthetics	H	The design and layout of the interfaces should be appealing
Interest	H	Users should show interest in the heritage industry before using the system
Goal	H	Users should have the aim to meet before starting the experience process
Novelty	H	The proposed contents and features should be original and innovative
Interactivity	H	The flow between users' actions should be spontaneous
Content	H	The contents on a particular exhibit should be readily available
Attention	H	The augmentation should be at the focal point
Exploration	M	The AR systems can propose users to make discovery of the exhibits by themselves
Awareness	H	Users should be aware of its surroundings and the system should push notification at regular times of interval
Feedback	H	The feedback from the system will keep the users focus on his/her user experience
Concentration	H	The system should maximise the concentration attribute to promote more learning and engagement from users
Learning	H	The augmentation should highlight elements that enhance learning on the users
Gamification	M	The system can have game elements to entertain the users in their engagement
Collaboration	M	Users can collaborate or create relationships with respect to their experience
Sharing	L	Users can share their experiences at their own demand
Immersion	H	The layers of augmentation should provide an immersive experience to the users. The users should be felt that they are inside the experience

(continued)

Table 13.7 (continued)

UE factors	Impact assessment (High—H, Medium—M, Low—L)	Rationale
Challenges	M	The AR should propose "challenges" at each level of their completed experience, making them more engaged in the completion of their activity
Identity	L	The proposed contents should have a positive influence on building oneself skills
Satisfaction	H	Globally, the experiences should be satisfying
Memorable	H	The experience should be mesmerising to engage users into more future experiences

experience. This factor influences the visitors to continue using the product for the long term.

Table 13.7 presents the impact assessment of the UE factors for the CH domain. Similarly, the assessment has been carried out taking into consideration the general requirements of an AR system and the functioning of a CH site.

From Table 13.7, it has been found that most of the factors are highly recommended for the CH domain. Fourteen attributes have been categorised as "highly influential" which represents around 70% of the total factors. Though the assessment has not been proven using statistical equations modelling, it provides some avenues on the contributing UE factors for a CH domain. For example, aesthetics and novelty are among the first factors that visitors will check before usage. During the period of engagement, factors such as interactivity, content, attention, concentration, learning and immersion play an important role. For instance, the content should be relevant to the field of view of the user, thus keeping the users attentive and concentrated on the focal objective of the exhibit. The learning interest would eventually be enhanced and users might be driven to know more on the particular object. The dimension of the experience can be augmented by immersion. Immersion can be triggered by the novelty of the features and contents proposed by the system. It can also be related to storytelling, 3D/4D, or even sound effects that render the experience more real and visitors can feel that they are inside the experience. In another perspective, gamification, collaboration and challenges have been rated as medium influencers. To the best of our knowledge, most visitors of a CH site have an objective goal when they visit a museum. The interest might be uncommon, but most of them want to enhance their cultural learning. These three attributes can provide a positive impetus on the total UE, but the features associated with these elements can be proposed at users' demand. Hence, all these attributes contribute to satisfaction and memorable factors. The re-engagement process occurs on how satisfied and memorable the previous experience was.

13.8   Research Challenges and Future Directions

This study has proposed new frameworks of UX and UE for the AR-CH systems. The frameworks have been conceived with the current literature in the field and with the consideration of the current trend happening in the AR field. First and foremost, this study has opened new research directions on the UX and UE aspects for AR-CH systems. The following existing gaps were derived from the findings of this research:

UE Literature
In the initial stage of the study, a general exploration of the UX and UE frameworks has been carried out to have a good understanding of all the stakeholders. Later, the frameworks have been narrowed down to tech-driven systems for the sake of this study. Due to very few works in this area, the frameworks have been selected based on their relevance in this field. Moreover, most of the UX frameworks covered the UE aspects in their models. In this study, UE frameworks have been declassified separately from the bias of our understanding on this topic because of the limited number of works in the area. The findings can be bias or generalised. As such, a clear delineation of UX and UE is required opening a research avenue for future works.

Conflicting UX and UE Terms
Though this study has attempted to decompose UX and UE terms individually, some factors can resonate to have the same meaning thus can be conflicting with each other. For instance, the derived UX characteristics: intuitive and liveliness can portray the same connotation at first glance. Another example of the UE factors can be attention and concentration, which have similar meanings. This conflict is mostly related to the limited number of works in deciphering the UX and UE factors. Again, this argument is widely associated with the above-mentioned point, where a critical assessment of UX and UE factors are required in the AR-CH field. In this perspective, a more granular characteristic can be derived to have a more explicit understanding of the UX and UE factors in the AR-CH domain.

Negative Experience
Most of the studies have concentrated on positive experiential elements and have not taken into consideration the negative ones. For example, "frustration" can part of the UX and it can be measured while the user is using the product. In another perspective, the disengagement factors in the UE model have not been studied. Interruptions in the systems can be one example of disengagement attributes. These negative factors can be further investigated to enhance the current models of UX and UE and eliminating the factors that are not necessary to be included. In this vein, this opens new avenues for research in this field.

13.9   Conclusion

This study has provided an extensive evaluation of the UX and UE factors that have direct influences on AR-CH systems. At the preliminary stage of the study, some general UX and UE factors are studied. The literature has been analysed thoroughly to identify the research gaps in the field of UX and UE for AR-CH systems. The study has proposed the model of UX and UE, respectively, for an AR system. The proposed UX framework has been inspired from the works of Olsson (2013). Novel elements such as accessibility, ease of use, mobility, personalisation, immersive, sharing and collaboration, dynamic and distinctive have been included in the proposed UX framework. These inclusions have taken into consideration the research gaps of existing literature. The conceptual model of UE has been put forward from the understanding of the topic and the few existing literature available on the topic. A comprehensive UE framework has been devised that demonstrates the following: a point of engagement, the period of engagement, maximum engagement and re-engagement. The model has emphasised on terms such as: aesthetics, novelty, learning, awareness, gamification and challenges which will contribute to a satisfying and memorable experience. Each UX and UE factor has been assessed qualitatively with the literature available in the field. Finally, this chapter identified the influential UX and UE factors for AR-CH systems and they are assessed qualitatively.

References

Akçayır M, Akçayır G (2017) Advantages and challenges associated with augmented reality for education: a systematic review of the literature. Educ Res Rev 20:1–11

Ali F, Ryu K, Hussain K (2016) Influence of experiences on memories, satisfaction and behavioral intentions: a study of creative tourism. J Travel & Tour Mark 33(1):85–100

Alletto S, Cucchiara R, Del Fiore G et al (2015) An indoor location-aware system for an IoT-based smart museum. IEEE Internet Things J 3(2):244–253

Amakawa J, Westin J (2018) New Philadelphia: using augmented reality to interpret slavery and reconstruction era historical sites. Int J Herit Stud 24(3):315–331

Azuma R, Baillot Y, Behringer R, Feiner S et al (2001) Recent advances in augmented reality. IEEE Comput Graphics Appl 21(6):34–47

Banterle F, Cardillo F, Malomo L et al (2015) LecceAR: an augmented reality app. In: Fifth international conference on digital presentation and preservation of cultural and scientific heritage (DiPP), Veliko Tarnovo, Bulgaria. CEEOL, pp 99–108

Barrio CM, Muñoz-Organero M, Soriano JS (2015) Can gamification improve the benefits of student response systems in learning? An experimental study. IEEE Trans Emerg Top Comput 4(3):429–438

Buccini M, Padovani S (2007) Typology of the experiences. In: Proceedings of the 2007 conference on designing pleasurable products and interfaces. ACM, New York, NY, USA, Aug, pp 495–504

Cavallo M, Rhodes GA, Forbes AG (2016) Riverwalk: incorporating historical photographs in public outdoor augmented reality experiences. In: 2016 IEEE international symposium on mixed and augmented reality (ISMAR-Adjunct). IEEE, Merida, Mexico, Sept, pp 160–165

Chatzopoulos D, Bermejo C, Huang Z et al (2017) Mobile augmented reality survey: From where we are to where we go. IEEE Access 5:6917–6950

Chen P, Liu X, Cheng W, Huang R (2017) A review of using Augmented Reality in Education from 2011 to 2016. Innovations in smart learning. Springer, Singapore, pp 13–18

Chin KY, Hou CX, Wang CS, et al (2017) Using Augmented Reality Technology for the Development of Historic Building Teaching Application: A Mackay Culture Course. In: 2017 IEEE 17th international conference on advanced learning technologies (ICALT). IEEE, Timisoara, Romania, pp 87–88

Cruz-Benito J, Therón R, García-Peñalvo FJ et al (2015) Discovering usage behaviors and engagement in an Educational Virtual World. Comput Hum Behav 47:18–25

Datcu D, Lukosch S, Brazier F (2015) On the usability and effectiveness of different interaction types in augmented reality. Int J Hum-Comput Interact 31(3):193–209

Duguleana M, Brodi R, Girbacia F et al (2016) Time-travelling with mobile augmented reality: a case study on the piazza dei miracoli. Euro-Mediterranean Conference. Springer, Cham, Nicosia, Cyprus, pp 902–912

Fenu C, Pittarello F (2018) Svevo tour: the design and the experimentation of an augmented reality application for engaging visitors of a literary museum. Int J Hum Comput Stud 114:20–35

Galatis P, Gavalas D, Kasapakis V et al (2016) Mobile augmented reality guides in cultural heritage. In: 8th EAI international conference on mobile computing, Applications and Services. ACM, Cambridge, Great Britain, pp 11–19

Garzón J, Pavón J, Baldiris S (2019) Systematic review and meta-analysis of augmented reality in educational settings. Virtual Reality 23(4):447–459

Geiger P, Pryss R, Schickler M et al (2013) Engineering an advanced location-based augmented reality engine for smart mobile devices. Technical Report UIB-2013–09; University of Ulm

Gutierrez JM, Molinero MA, Soto-Martín O et al (2015) Augmented reality technology spreads information about historical graffiti in temple of Debod. Procedia Computer Sci 75:390–397

Hammady R, Ma M, Temple N (2016) Augmented reality and gamification in heritage museums. In: Joint international conference on serious games. Springer, Cham, Brisbane, Australia pp 181–187

Hammady R, Ma M, Powell A (2018) User experience of markerless augmented Reality applications in cultural heritage museums: 'MuseumEye' as a case study. In: International conference on augmented reality, virtual reality and computer graphics. Springer, Cham, Otranto, Italy, pp 349–369

Han DI, Tom Dieck MC, Jung T (2018) User experience model for augmented reality applications in urban heritage tourism. J Herit Tour 13(1):46–61

Hassenzahl M (2004) The interplay of beauty, goodness, and usability in interactive products. Human-Comput Interact 19(4):319–349

Julier SJ, Blume P, Moutinho A et al (2016) VisAge: augmented reality for heritage. In: Proceedings of the 5th ACM international symposium on pervasive displays. ACM, Oulu, Finland pp 257–258

Kankainen A (2003) UCPCD: user-centered product concept design. In: Proceedings of the 2003 conference on designing for user experiences. ACM, San Francisco, California, pp 1–13

Kim HR, Chan PK (2003) Learning implicit user interest hierarchy for context in personalization. In: Proceedings of the 8th international conference on Intelligent user interfaces. ACM, Miami, Florida, USA, pp. 101–108

Kim JT, Lee WH (2015) Dynamical model for gamification of learning (DMGL). Multimed Tools Appl 74(19):8483–8493

Leach M, Maddock S, Hadley D et al (2018) Recreating Sheffield's medieval castle in situ using outdoor augmented reality. In: International conference on virtual reality and augmented reality. Springer, Cham, London, United Kingdom, pp. 213–229

Lee E, Hannafin MJ (2016) A design framework for enhancing engagement in student-centered learning: own it, learn it, and share it. Education Tech Research Dev 64(4):707–734

Lee H, Chung N, Jung T (2015) Examining the cultural differences in acceptance of mobile augmented reality: comparison of South Korea and Ireland. Information and communication technologies in tourism. Springer International Publishing, Lugano, Switzerland, pp 477–491

Limerick H, Hayden R, Beattie D, et al (2019) User engagement for mid-air haptic interactions with digital signage. In: Proceedings of the 8th ACM international symposium on pervasive displays. ACM Palermo Italy, pp 1–7

Lindgren R, Tscholl M, Wang S et al (2016) Enhancing learning and engagement through embodied interaction within a mixed reality simulation. Comput Educ 95:174–187

Mahlke S (2008) Visual aesthetics and the user experience. https://drops.dagstuhl.de/opus/vollte xte/2008/1624/pdf/08292.MahlkeSascha.Paper.1624.pdf. Accessed 10 Aug 2020

McCarthy J, Wright P (2004) Technology as experience, interactions. 11(5):42–43

O'Brien H (2016) Theoretical perspectives on user engagement. Why engagement matters. Springer, Cham, pp 1–26

O'Brien HL, Toms EG (2008) What is user engagement? A conceptual framework for defining user engagement with technology. J Am Soc Inform Sci Technol 59(6):938–955

Olsson T (2013) Concepts and subjective measures for evaluating user experience of mobile augmented reality services. Human factors in augmented reality environments. Springer, New York, NY, pp 203–232

Pallud J, Straub DW (2014) Effective website design for experience-influenced environments: the case of high culture museums. Inf & Manag 51(3):359–373

Pantile D, Frasca R, Mazzeo A et al (2016) New technologies and tools for immersive and engaging visitor experiences in museums: the evolution of the visit-actor in next-generation storytelling, through augmented and virtual reality, and immersive 3D projections. In: 2016 12th international conference on signal-image technology & internet-based systems (SITIS). IEEE, Naples, Italy, pp 463–467

Pendit UC, Zaibon SB, Bakar JAA (2014) Mobile augmented reality for enjoyable informal learning in cultural heritage site. Int J Comput Appl 92(14):19–26

Pierdicca R, Frontoni E, Zingaretti P et al (2015) Making visible the invisible. augmented reality visualization for 3D reconstructions of archaeological sites. In: International conference on augmented and virtual reality. Springer, Cham, Lecce, Italy, pp 25–37

Pine BJ, Gilmore JH (1998) Welcome to the experience economy. Harv Bus Rev 76:97–105

Ramtohul A, Khedo KK (2019) A prototype mobile augmented reality systems for cultural heritage sites. Information systems design and intelligent applications. Springer, Singapore, Mauritius, pp 175–185

Romero P, Calvillo-Gámez EH (2011) Towards an embodied view of flow. In: Proceedings of the 2nd international workshop on user models for motivational systems: the affective and the rational routes to persuasion (UMMS 2011), pp 100–105

Rutledge P, Neal M (2012) Positive engagement evaluation model for interactive and mobile technologies. In: The 2012 EEE international conference on e-Learning, e-Business, enterprise information systems, and e-Government, Las Vegas, NV, pp 1–12

Sırakaya M, Alsancak Sırakaya D (2020) Augmented reality in STEM education: a systematic review. Interactive Learning Environments, pp 1–14

Thompson S (2016) Cultural heritage and spectacle: painted and digital panoramic Re-presentations of versailles. Streetnotes, 25

Tom Dieck MC, Jung TH, Rauschnabel PA (2018a) Determining visitor engagement through augmented reality at science festivals: an experience economy perspective. Comput Hum Behav 82:44–53

Tom Dieck MC, Jung TH, Tom Dieck D (2018b) Enhancing art gallery visitors' learning experience using wearable augmented reality: generic learning outcomes perspective. Curr Issues Tour 21(17):2014–2034

Unesco (2020) Le Morne Cultural Landscape. https://whc.unesco.org/en/list/1259. Accessed 10 Sept 2020

Van Kleef N, Noltes J, van der Spoel S (2010) Success factors for augmented reality business models. Study tour Pixel, pp 1–36

Vecchio P, Mele F, De Paolis LT et al (2015) Cloud computing and augmented reality for cultural heritage. In: International conference on augmented and virtual reality. Springer, Cham, Lecce, Italy, pp 51–60

Vecco M (2010) A definition of cultural heritage: From the tangible to the intangible. J Cult Herit 11(3):321–324

Wang X, Ong SK, Nee AY (2016) A comprehensive survey of augmented reality assembly research. Adv Manuf 4(1):1–22

Wright P, Wallace J, McCarthy J (2008) Aesthetics and experience-centered design. ACM Trans Comput-Hum Interact (TOCHI) 15(4):1–21

Zhuang M, Toms EG, Demartini G (2018) Can user behaviour sequences reflect perceived novelty? In: Proceedings of the 27th ACM international conference on information and knowledge management. ACM, Torino Italy, pp 1507–1510

Chapter 14
The Transhuman Docent: Persistent Human Interaction in Digital Heritage Sites

Nathan Shafer

Abstract This chapter looks at the way mobile augmented reality has evolved since 2008, based on implementation, development, obsolescence and the persistent necessity of human docents to preserve its usage in heritage places such as museums and historical sites. Works examined include the various augmented reality festivals put on by members of the Manifest.AR group and others, including the Virtual Public Art Project and the (Un)Seen Sculptures in Australia. The usage of the term 'artist-as-docent' explores the intersections between various notions proffered from transhumanist philosophers from the twentieth century, such as Timothy Leary, FM 2030 and Buckminster Fuller. Concepts such as fifth circuitry, telespheres, info-space, psycho-geography and the infinitesimal are applied to the augmented reality artist as docent. Ultimately, the transhuman docents are necessary for mobile augmented reality to be used by a general audience in our contemporary setting. This is changing due to the new mediafication of all things due to the COVID-19 crisis, but ultimately the need for human interaction is what is driving the usage of augmented reality technology.

14.1 Layar, Junaio, Aurasma, Hoppala

In its brief history, mobile augmented reality (AR) has been kept in a permanent temporality brought on by third-party platforms, to which the bulk of mobile AR has been dependent. It has been dependent on these platforms for a variety of reasons, but the most significant has been user access. In the early days of smart phones, mobile applications took up a lot of memory and there was a hesitancy in users, to constantly be downloading applications for single usages. It is still an issue, especially with the increase of digital applications in the worldwide pedagogical phenomena brought on by quarantines from COVID-19, but devices are able to accommodate more memory than they did in 2009–2010. One of the less documented shortfalls of mobile AR apps

N. Shafer (✉)
Structured Learning Classrooms, Anchorage School District, Anchorage, AK, USA
e-mail: shafer_nathan@asdk12.org

N-Collective Media/Shared Universe, Anchorage, AK, USA

is that even after users had downloaded AR browsers, there needed to be a person present to explain and model the usage of the technology for their intended audience. This augmented reality docent played a vital role in early AR presentations, and far and wide still does to this day, when AR works are displayed in settings such as museums, heritage sites and art walks.

It wasn't long after the advent of the smart phones that AR tech started to appear. Artists, curators and exhibitors who were employing AR were at the mercy of these third-party apps as they would change their user interfaces, rewrite their business models or simply go out of business, rendering all content created on their platforms obsolete. No developers have created an archive for AR created on these platforms, and the documentation we have of them may be the only way to experience them now.

Very few mobile augmented reality artworks were unique works built on their own app or platform, for the most part they were pages on a third-party platform, such as Layar or Junaio. There were many others, back in the early days of mobile AR: Wikitude, Aurasma (later HP Reveal), Argon and others. Many creators on these platforms were looking for free access, or at least affordable access, with the addition of some sort of sustainability. But AR has not shown itself to be a sustainable practice in a manner similar to other artforms. This has been the issue with most new media genres for over a century, from the technologies employed in early cinema, moving into video and digital formats, to digital artworks created on floppy discs, CDs and even now defunct websites. Much of this could be summed up by the never-ending march of technology increasing its efficiency and computing power, but from a heritage stance, the archiving and preservation of these works has become a cottage industry, though early mobile augmented reality has not entered that phase of archival work as of the writing of this paper, though that would be a project worth undertaking at an international level. This would also require a standardization of mobile augmented reality that has also been rendered problematic by third-party platforms.

This leaves another problem in how we look at an archive of augmented reality works in a heritage format. Hal Foster, in his pre-mobile augmented reality work *An Archival Impulse* drew a distinction between the archive and the database. He posited that the Internet was a mega-archive and in 2005, was seen as a viable habitable zone for preserving and archiving works of art. But in reality, and practice, a more physical, i.e., 'recalcitrantly material' archive. They are "fragmentary rather than fungible, and as such they call out for human interpretation rather than machinic reprocessing" (Foster 2005). (This is in relation to notions offered by Lev Manovich.) It is this space where the role of the human to guide viewers through the augments comes into play, not just for interpretation, but also for navigation and access. The language used by these docents of augmented reality becomes crucial. For many, the role of the artist becomes necessary to dissect here, but the artist-as-curator, or artist-as-archivist notions create a refocus on the primacy of individual artists, and I am interested in positioning the artist-as-docent, who is bringing people to a more collective imagination, with many voices and many modalities.

A standardization, however, especially of language becomes important, and a standardization that does its best to work against what Timothy Leary called 'cyber-politics', "the use of language and linguistic-tech by the ruling classes in feudal and industrial societies to control children, the uneducated and the under classes…those who manipulate words and communication devices in order to control, to bolster authority" (Leary 1994). There is going to be much thinking placed on how the artist-as-docent engages with others, using third parties, by necessity.

This played out in real time with early augmented reality artmaking, as the terminology used in the early AR platforms varied in relation to what the augments were. Aurasma was very keen to have their language used in a more proprietary manner, for example, the term 'auras' was used in place of 'augment', which lead to a bit of confusion for users who would move across platforms. Layar and Junaio would use the term 'point-of-interest' for geolocated works, and the term 'target' for fiducial augments. Even the notion of artists working with AR was co-opted by the tech-linguistics of the opportunistic cyberpoliticians, wanting to refer to augmented reality artists as 'ARtists' making 'ARt'. Happily, that terminology did not continue with much fidelity.

Apart from the semiotics of augmented reality, artists were still creating works almost entirely on third-party platforms. Very few artists were creating and maintaining their own databases, servers and platforms for maintaining an augmented reality artistic practice. It was much more egalitarian. However, projects that were built on third-party platforms were at the whims of whether that particular app would survive, it could either go out of business altogether or be assumed by a larger company that was looking to remove competition from the market. For example, this happened to the Junaio/Metaio app in 2014, when Apple bought the company and simply took down the app never to replace it.

In tandem with the third-party mobile AR apps, there was a curious character, Marc René Gardeya. Gardeya was the CEO, founder and developer of a platform called Hoppala, which was a content platform for the three main augmented reality applications at that time: Layar, Junaio and Wikitude. Hoppala created a user interface that allowed augmented reality artists quick, easy and free access to the three AR applications, without having to code everything from scratch on one's own server. The convenience and reliability of the Hoppala platform created a major boon for early AR artists who could put augments up anywhere in the world in a matter of seconds. Gardeya himself created some interesting AR works, including a reconstruction of the Berlin Wall (Berlin Wall 3D) (Fig. 14.1). The reconstruction of the Berlin Wall, in situ as an AR heritage work is ambiguous. The accuracy of the work was impressive, even if tongue-in-cheek, and the historical significance of a no longer extant landmark is not just curious but logical in its inception.

The use of augmented reality technology to recreate or reimagine historical or heritage sites is one that may ultimately prove to be the most useful (and used) form of augmented reality artmaking, apart from videogaming. The general usage though of people creating original content on various platforms is dependent on the ease of access and usability of the platforms. This is another node for where the augmented docent appears, as an artist who provides access to other artists in augmented space.

Fig. 14.1 Berlin Wall 3D (Gardeya 2010). Augmented reality

This is ultimately what Hoppala was able to do, it created a usable space that artists and lay people could access and produce content in.

Manifest.AR was using the Hoppala platform for all of its major interventions and events, from the initial rogue intervention, *We AR MoMA*, to the somewhat final installment of *Manifest.AR at the Corcoran*. The two shows are strikingly dissimilar, in both their approaches, as well as their content and intentions. The earlier showing an intense thirst to insert itself into the contemporary art world and the later, an anxious guardianship of the legacy of augmented reality artmaking. Ultimately, Hoppala went out of business, and Manifest.AR did not stay functioning as a collective. Gardeya lost interest in maintaining the Hoppala platform, and Manifest.AR members each began walking alone.

But the walking is the important part. Psychogeography and the derive. The drifting into unknown worlds, a vestigial method from the Situationist International that would be one of the hallmarks of collective augmented reality artmaking.

14.2   Manifest.AR, Situationism, Transhumanism, Cyberpunks

The connection between augmented reality as an art form and the aesthetics derived from both the Lettrist and Situationist International art movements cannot be understated, specifically the usage of psychogeography and the deríve. The Manifest.AR group in early 2009 had started to employ methods of exhibiting augmented reality work outside of mainstream contexts, though with a serious interest in being invited into the more sacrosanct art spaces such as the MoMA or the Venice Biennial, for which the Manifest.AR group did produce some guerilla style interventions. Those invitations were never to properly come, but that did not stop the spread of mobile

AR as an international art phenomenon. It looked as if AR as a viable genre of new media art was going to move ahead, but the novelty value of the genre proved too much in the early days. For instance, Rhizome.org, which has since assimilated with the New Museum, held an annual contest for grants to produce new media works, and at one point they defined several different formats for augmented reality, which lasted one cycle and then were disregarded. Further compounding this, curators from several different organizations were actively not letting augmented reality into their spaces. If there were any professional new media artists who wanted to make a career with augmented reality, there were basically no avenues with which to do this.

Enter the notion of the 'cyberpunks' in connection to the usage of psychogeography in technology, who Timothy Leary describes as those who "use all available data-input to think for themselves…individuals who explore some future frontier, collect and bring back new information, and offer to guide the human gene pool to the next stage" (Leary 1994). Leary's usage of the term cyberpunk is a rather fluid one in his later writings, where he is pairing it very heavily with the notions of transhumanism with rugged individualism/anti-authoritarianism, but it works here when we are looking at the role of docent for augmented experiences. Leary notes that the term cyber means pilot in the original Latin and is the foundation for the term cybernetics. The AR docent is the 'pilot' here, one who steers and guides viewers through the new experience of augmented reality, which is fitting as well, since Leary also notes that a 'cyberperson' is "fascinated by navigational information—especially maps, charts, labels, guide, manuals that help pilot through life" (Leary 1994).

14.3 Infinitesimal Art, Island One, Cloud Nine, Dirigibles of Denali, Seawall

One of the other important concepts early makers of mobile augmented reality art would employ would be art infinitesimal (infinitesimal art), which simply stated is a work of art that can never exist in reality, and its theoretical existence, i.e., when one imagines the work in their mind is where its aesthetic value lies. There are other notions, such as metagraphics and hypergraphics, which were also useful in the way language became art in augmented spaces.

Returning to Foster's notion of the archive and database here, he noted that many artists working in this space are attracted to unfinished or unrealized heritage sites. Rather than focusing the works on reimagining what is no longer present, artists are simulating experiences that could have been. "(T)hese artists are often drawn to unfulfilled beginnings or incomplete projects – in art and in history alike – that might offer points of departure again" (Foster 2005). The locus of many of these types of augmented reality works can be based in situ, that is geolocated to inhabit spaces where the incomplete or unfulfilled can be simulated.

Pre-augmented reality examples of this can be found in several proposals and texts from Transhumanist philosophy from the twentieth century, instances such as *Island*

One (Fig. 14.2) from 1975 in Stanford where researcher Gerard K. O'Neill imagined the notion of Bernal Spheres, proposed by J. D. Bernal in his proto-transhumanist paper, *The World, the Flesh and the Devil* from 1929. Bernal spheres were proposed as space habitats, which O'Neill interpreted as living space for thousands of humans in an orbiting paradise. The visualizations of *Island One* and later, *Island Two* are rather famous examples of attempting to realize an infinitesimal work. Buckminster Fuller's proposal for a domed city built over top of Manhattan or his *Cloud Nine* (Fig. 14.3) proposal, of geodesic sphere habitats that are airborne on the Earth, that could be tethered to the Earth, or left to derive.

The *Dirigibles of Denali* project (Fig. 14.4) by Nathan Shafer offers an example of infinitesimal art as AR, in the form of unfulfilled cities. In the 1960s and 1970s there were several proposals for futuristic metropolitan cities to be built in Alaska. *Dirigibles of Denali* realized these using the Layar app, placing them in their proposed locations in Alaska.

Mark Skwarek's *Seawall Build.AR* project (Fig. 14.5) is another example of an incomplete project, built into the Layar app. *Seawall* is a wall that goes up around the coastal United States as a defensive measure against rising sea levels from dramatic climate change. It also is an ironic nod to the border wall that hyper-nationalistic thinking in American life has created an infinitesimal wall that surrounds the US, preventing 'illegal aliens' from entering American space.

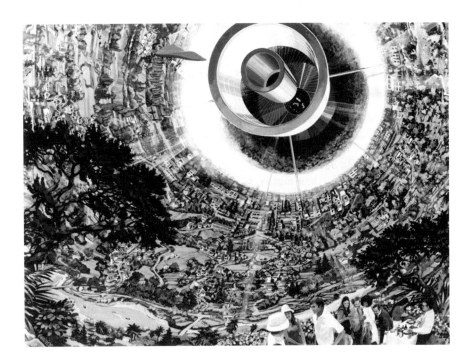

Fig. 14.2 Island One (O'Neill 1975). Illustration

Fig. 14.3 Cloud Nine (Fuller 1988). Illustration

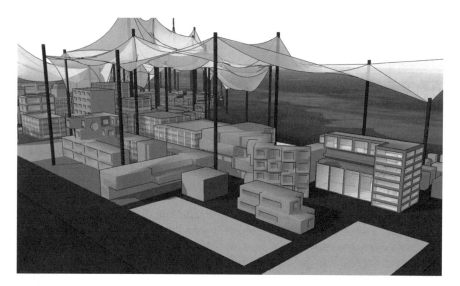

Fig. 14.4 Denali City (Shafer 2018). Augmented reality

While Situationist thinking was prevalent in Europe, Transhumanist philosophy, albeit way more of a contemporary philosophical movement than anything art related. As it is, in *Are You a Transhuman?* from 1989, the transhuman philosopher FM 2030 discusses the notion of National frontiers in a Transhuman worldview as being "nothing more than pissing borders created by dogs" (2030 1989). He views unlimited and unrestrained movement of people around the world as a fundamental right.

Fig. 14.5 Seawall (Skwarek 2011). Augmented reality

His thinking is also based on an optimistic, albeit aggressive futurism, he stated, "If governments do not do away with borders—modern technology will" (2030 1989). Again, reflected in Skwarek's *Seawall*, we see the contemporary usage of specula-tive technology (the border wall) being used as a protective measure to preserve the natural world to ensure a better future, rather than a national frontier weaponized against outsiders, to preserve an isolationist-superior way of life. FM 2030s philo-sophical notions as applied to Skwarek's work in a digital heritage framework also pulls out some of the fundamental structures at play, notably the idea of universal valuation. FM 2030 asserts that "(t)here are no constant or eternal values. The idea of constancy comes from an antiquated view of a stable or static world". Adding, "values change as the environment changes", and "values change roughly at the same rate as technological change" (2030 1989).

It should be noted here that *Seawall* as a work of art existed in several various iterations around the world in group shows organized by the Manifest.AR collective, and a few other outlier festivals put on by augmented reality artists. The role of the artist-as-docent here is as an interactive element of the various works of art. Much as a docent in a museological sense functions to bring viewers to the time, place and intention of the artists in a well-preserved archive of human achievement, the tran-shuman docent brings viewers to the intersections of time, place and historiography of the arcane and hidden augmented worlds all around them.

14.4   Christopher Manzione, Virtual Public Art Project, Activat.AR, Info-Space, Fifth Circuit

One of the first true instances of the transhuman docent was the *Virtual Public Art Project (VPAP)* (Fig. 14.6a, b, c), brainchild of Manifest.AR cofounder, Christopher Manzione. Manzione described the *Virtual Public Art Project* as "the first mobile AR outdoor art experience ever and maximizes public reception of AR art through compatibility with both iPhone 3GS and Android phones!" (Manzione 2009).

Of the founding members of Manifest.AR, Manzione is notable for his collaborative practice, one of the pioneers of the collective collaboration in AR spaces, where he functioned as the artist-as-docent. Though by nature all of the artists from Manifest.AR work collaboratively, Manzione's collaborations work well beyond curation and fabrication. When *VPAP* launched in 2009, psychogeography festivals were riding a wave of newfound popularity, during the recession, when artists were seeking practices that could accommodate the new economic realities. Augments placed in the Layar app would be located in individual 'channels'. These channels effectively functioned as sites for people or organizations. Inside of the channels, were maps, navigation and access points for geolocated augments. At one point, Layar also presented a function where users could search for augments around them, or search by theme for various works. By the time the Layar app sunset, there were no functions to check for augments in one's vicinity, or pages to search for augments, one had to have the exact channel or precise link to view a 'point of interest'.

One of the main differences in Manzione's artistic practice compared to the rest of the Manifest.AR group was that at least half of his practice was to make other artists' works be realized. He would often be the one 3D modeling or programming content, while working with the artist who conceived the work, and he would bring in artists who were not fluent in augmented reality coding. Collaboration at this level and quality is rare in the artworld at large, but not unheard of. Manzione is working in a space that simulates the infinitesimal, creating works that existed solely in the conceptual realm, and finding the methodologies of making them viable in one form of reality or another. As Leary would note in his *Musings on Human Metamorphosis* from 1988, "Whatever the mind can conceive, it tends to create. As soon as humans accept the notion of as-yet-activated circuits in the nervous system, a new philosophy of an evolving nervous system will emerge—human nature as seen from the vantage point of an older species" (Leary 1988).

Though many of the shows organized by Manzione for the *Virtual Public Art Project*, and later with his *Activat.AR* project, were curatorial enterprises, where he would put together a group show of augmented reality works revolving around a theme, notably with shows such as the *Albion AR Artwalk* and *Really Fake*. In these instances, the physical presence of Manzione in these spaces is where he would function as the docent, or ambassador to the various works included in the exhibition, ranging from curatorial decisions, to site-specific interventions. Viewers of these exhibitions would be guided through the works of art by Manzione as he walked them through a physical space. This is also the psychogeography of Manzione's

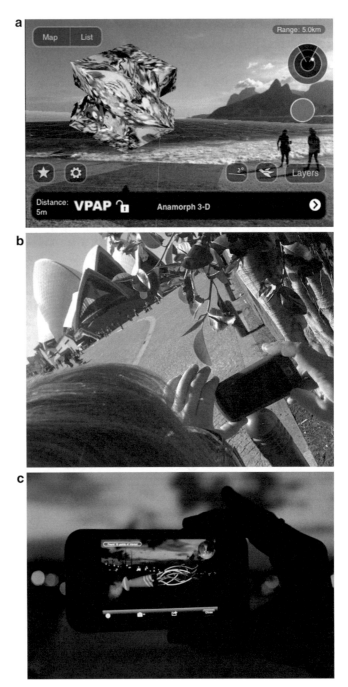

Fig. 14.6 **a** Anamorph 3D (Barata 2010). **b** Mirrored City (Meinhardt 2010). **c** Archie (Shafer 2010). Augmented reality

Period	Stage of Evolution
1. Bio-Survival (Marine) Stages	1) Invertebrate 2) Marine-vertebrate 3) Amphibian
2. The Terrestrial Mammalian Stages	4) Evasive Mammalian 5) Predator Mammalian 6) Hunter-Gatherer
3. The Symbolic Tool Stage	7) Tool User, Paleolithic 8) Tool Maker, Neolithic 9) Tribal, Metal Age
4. Industrial	10) Feudal 11) National, Low-Industrial 12) Multi-National, High-Industrial
5. Cyber-Somatic Piloting Sensory Info	13) Individual Consumer Hedonism 14) Individual Aesthetic Mastery 15) Hedonic-Aesthetic Linkage
6. Cyber-Electronic Piloting Quantum Electronic Info	16) Individual Consumer Access to Brain and Electronic Technology 17) Individual Mastery of Genetic Technology Information 18) Neuro-Electronic Networks
7. Cyber-Genetic Piloting DNA/RNA Data	19) Individual Brain Management through Genetic Technology 20) Individual Mastery of Genetic Technology Information 21) Electronic Networks – Linkage of Genetic Technology Information
8. Cyber-Nano-Tech Piloting Atomic Info	22) Individual Consumer Access to Nano-Tech (Atomic Information) 23) Individual Mastery of Nano-Tech (Atomic Information) 24) Nano Technological Linkage

Fig. 14.7 Periodic table of human evolution (Leary 1988). Microsoft Word Table

artmaking, more than a mere explainer or works, but a physical guide to bring the works to people as they are learning to navigate new neural networks. This body conscious, physical navigation, or cybernetic piloting of realities can be seen in terms of what Leary hypothesized as the Fifth Circuit of Human Evolution, that is the artist is a physical conduit bringing people into 'info-space'.

This is from Leary's *Info-Psychology*, and as it is far too much to digress into, a small explanation is necessary. Info-Psychology is the psychology of post-industrial society as it transitions into exo-psychology, or the psychology of a post-terrestrial existence, all described by eight circuits of human evolution. The fifth circuit on Leary's Periodic Table of Human Evolution (Fig. 14.7) is the first circuit beyond the terrestrial, as humans begin to enter into the 'cyber-quantum'. Fifth circuitry is extra-somatic, body conscious; moving from linear visual spatial thinking/perception to an aesthetic sensory space, the same space the artist-as-docent occupies in augmented reality. Fifth circuitry is also very much about pleasure, or rather rapture, "the response of the sense organs to natural stimulation, divorced from terrestrial conditioned meaning" (Leary 1987). Artist-as-docent here embodies the social aspect of art. "The origin of much social art is somebody's neurosomatic signal which has been socialized—imprinted and learned as "artistic" (Leary 1987). In the context of Info-Psychology, Info-Space is "our world, the galaxy, the universe defined and measured in terms of information. The quantum universe of signals, bits, digital elements, recorded by, stored in, processed, communicated by electronic language technology, the human brain and its electronic extensions" (Leary 1987).

The *Activat.AR* app (Fig. 14.8), which Manzione developed after the closing of the *Virtual Public Art Project* and as the Manifest.AR group was disbanding better

Fig. 14.8 Activat.AR (2018) Screenshot of landing pages from three months of programming

illustrates the trend in Manzione's work to the neurosomatic, by way of fifth circuitry. *Activat.AR* is a monthly curatorial/artist-as-docent project put on with Manzione as its facilitator. Each month there are three artists making new media works, usually one augmented reality work, one virtual reality work and one either video, interactive or videogame work. Some of the months revolve around a theme, and other times they are simply three collaborative projects that Manzione has helped bring into existence, i.e., info-space.

This extension into info-space is of course in direct reference to Marshall McLuhan's notion of all technology being extensions of the human body, clothing being an extension of human skin, electronics an extension of our nervous systems and the computer an extension of the human brain.

14.5   Regenerative Landscapes, Telespheres, Warren Armstrong, (Un)Seen Sculptures

As the Virtual Public Art Project was the first augmented reality format to bring the artist-as-docent into transhuman/cyberpunk inhabited info-space, several other artists began developing similar artistic practices that included this type of collaborative-collective process, manifesting in psychogeographic contexts. This is in relation to the info-space that sits above the natural world, in what Buckminster Fuller refers to as the 'regenerative landscape'. He also saw this regenerative landscape as the byproduct of future technologies, as they overcame the problems of the world, positing in his *Operation Manual for Spaceship Earth* from 1969, "you may very appropriately want to ask me how we are ever going to resolve the ever-accelerating dangerous impasse of world-opposed politicians and ideological dogmas. I answer, it will be resolved by the computer" (Fuller 1969). Looking back on this statement half-century after it was written, it is tempting to see this as a quaint observation by a twentieth-century futurist, trying to predict the future. There is a good bit of fantastical thinking on the part of Fuller as he envisioned the way computers would transform human life in the future. Look at the immediate example he gave for his reasoning here; he contends that all politicians, regardless of their political stripe, enthusiastically yield to the computer's safe "flight-controlling capabilities in bringing all of humanity in for a happy landing" (Fuller 1969).

Fuller, along with many of the futurists/transhumanist/cyber philosophers of the twentieth-century keenly looked towards a more globalized aesthetic, that would function on a more cooperative model, one where there did not need to be so much emphasis on individual authorship or meaning, rather a collective approach to making and ownerships of intellectual properties. In *Telespheres* from 1977, FM 2030 compiled a comparative list of things as conceived during 'primal/feudal/industrial' times to 'telespheres' (FM 2030s term for the age after the primal/feudal/industrial). His entries for 'art' and 'entertainment' are applicable here (Fig. 14.9):

Obviously predicting augmented reality as an art format of the future would have been a bit of a stretch, even for a futurist such as FM 2030, but some of his other predictions in this grouping are interesting 'sky illuminations via laser imagery or holograms' or 'total environmental holography' are pretty close to mixed reality applications.

Warren Armstrong's *(Un)Seen Sculpture* project is another example of the artist-as-docent, the fifth circuit, telespheric art. Similar to Manzione's approach to augmented reality artmaking, Armstrong would create geolocated works, where viewers would be physically, literally moved through a psychogeographic space,

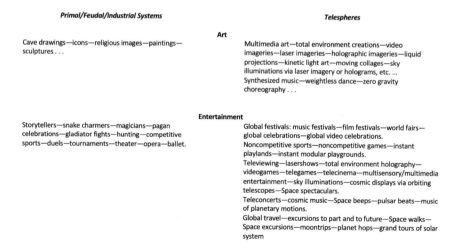

Primal/Feudal/Industrial Systems	Telespheres
Art	
Cave drawings—icons—religious images—paintings—sculptures . . .	Multimedia art—total environment creations—video imageries—laser imageries—holographic imageries—liquid projections—kinetic light art—moving collages—sky illuminations via laser imagery or holograms, etc. . . . Synthesized music—weightless dance—zero gravity choreography . . .
Entertainment	
Storytellers—snake charmers—magicians—pagan celebrations—gladiator fights—hunting—competitive sports—duels—tournaments—theater—opera—ballet.	Global festivals: music festivals—film festivals—world fairs—global celebrations—global video celebrations. Noncompetitive sports—noncompetitive games—instant playlands—instant modular playgrounds. Televiewing—lasershows—total environment holography—videogames—telegames—telecinema—multisensory/multimedia entertainment—sky illuminations—cosmic displays via orbiting telescopes—Space spectaculars. Teleconcerts—cosmic music—Space beeps—pulsar beats—music of planetary motions. Global travel—excursions to part and to future—Space walks—Space excursions—moontrips—planet hops—grand tours of solar system

Fig. 14.9 Chart from telespheres (Esfandiary 1977). Microsoft Word Table

then left to derivate their experiences on their own, once they have been shown access into the augmented spaces.

(Un)Seen Sculptures ran for around five years, starting in 2011, shortly after mobile AR became a reality. From its inception, *(Un)Seen Sculptures* was present in multiple locations, one of the realities of digital works is that they can inhabit more than one spot at a time. The first three cities to host *(Un)Seen Sculptures* was Sydney, Melbourne and Cairns, all in Australia. Like Manzione, Armstrong created a strong collaborative practice in his festivals, bringing many artists who were not AR artists to create works in this new neural network.

This method of artmaking that situates itself so firmly in the collaborative realm is significant in that it is a new paradigm of artistic practice in that it is moving beyond the age-old and rather dated notion of the auteur, positioning the artist as more of an ambassador for aesthetic experiences in the info-sphere. There are many artists who began producing AR works that were less concerned with content, rather negotiating the possibilities of the genre. While the potential for exciting new works in the genre of augmented reality are important, the need to produce works that transcend the genre are equally as important. Armstrong and Manzione both embody this transition from the artist-as-curator to artist-as-docent, in much the same way that how Fuller envisioned the regenerative landscape as nature being able to provide the roots for a new age to emerge, one that is more optimistic and inclusive than previous ages. This is illustrated best in how artists move through the notion of organizing an exhibition. Armstrong has been an example here of helping to guide new artists into the conception and execution of AR works, without exploiting them as content creators; they are allowed their own distinct voices included into the psychogeography of augmented spaces, rather than the stunted examples of his master plans.

Tiger Bay Flock (Fig. 14.10), from the 2015 iteration of *(Un)Seen Sculptures* exemplifies this new tendency. *Tiger Bay Flock* was produced in collaboration with Warren Central School in New South Wales, after a digital workshop was held teaching kids augmented reality artmaking. *Tiger Bay Flock* is a collection of birds from Tiger Bay, an artificial wetland outside of their town.

The regenerative landscape did not manifest the ways Fuller had predicted. For instance, Fuller (like others of the time) assumed that the rise of technological innovation was going to produce untold wealth the world over, that he was more concerned with aesthetics. Focusing on "living without spoiling the landscape, or the antiquities or the trails of humanity throughout the ages, or despoiling the integrity of romance, vision and harmonic creativity" (Fuller 1969). This is similarly reflected in how tools are discussed as extensions of man, Fuller breaks them down into craft tools (tools that individuals can make for themselves in the wilderness) and industrial tools (tools that are the culmination of a multitude of engineers, which no single person can produce on their own). From Fuller's point of view, collective industrial toolmaking was part of the evolution of man into Leary's Fifth circuit, a way humanity would be able to sustain itself metabolically on 'Spaceship Earth'. In this way, when the regenerative landscape and info-space intersect, there are mixed reality networks in play.

Fig. 14.10 Tiger Bay Flocks
(Warren Central School
2015). Augmented reality

Enter Armstrong's *The Information Virus (Notitiaviridae internets)* (Fig. 14.11) which treats the internet as a disease that has been keeping humanity from being able to process long-form data like novels and opera. (Note that FM 2030 places those artforms into the 'Primal/Feudal/Industrial' sphere.) Armstrong does not view the

Fig. 14.11 Armstrong W
(2011). The Information
Virus

Information Virus in eschatological terms, "a disease, but one, like latent toxoplasmosis, which may actually have positive side effects in certain cases (e.g., increased immediate connection with the knowledge and worlds of others)" (Armstrong 2011).

14.6   Digital Divide, Arcades, Sunsets

An element that is commonly overlooked when thinking back to early augmented reality artmaking and its evolution into more consumer-friendly environments such as museums and heritage sites, is the digital divide. While the new neural network of augmented reality was exciting, access to it was relegated to those who could afford to own a smart phone (which in 2010 was not near as universal as it is in 2021). It was here that the artist-as-docent originally bore its necessity. For viewers to experience the augments, the artist needed to be physically present, with the technology needed to access the work, and the appropriate software installed. In this way, the early augmented reality works had a user experience similar to VR in museuological spaces currently, a handheld, interactive cinematic experience. Viewers in these spaces do not own the technology they are using to access the work, separating it from other quotidian experience, but in a post-COVID world, the multi-use community VR headset in a heritage site may well end up as antiquated a notion as videogame arcades.

Since 2015, many of the third-party platforms augmented reality artists were using began to sunset. Hoppala, Junaio were some of the first to expire, and soon afterwards Layar went under. (Most of the artists connected to Manifest.AR were producing the bulk of their works in the Layar app.) Aurasma held on a little longer, changing into HP Reveal, sunsetting a few months later. In the apparent vacuum of third-party platforms, and with the membership of the Manifest.AR group being tenuous, there was a lull in AR artmaking which would resituate. Both Armstrong's and Manzione's practices were able to evolve from these sunset platforms into new venues. Manzione had already been producing AR works in spaces outside of Layar and Junaio, and Armstrong's connection to community, and in partnership with Susannah Langley, began working more directly in pedagogical models and with virtual reality systems, such as the *Keepsakery* at the Vrystaat Festival (Fig. 14.12).

14.7   The Post-Human Docent

As stated earlier in this paper, the artist-as-docent has been a necessary function of early augmented reality artmaking. It has persisted in necessity with the genre as it has evolved into new variations. As in transhuman theory, a transhuman is a person in transition from humanity, moving into a post-human reality. What that looks like varies from futurist to futurist, but it is agreed that they are not us and we are not them, but we are still connected to each other through the circuitry of our collective

Fig. 14.12   Keepsakery (Armstrong Langley 2018). Virtual reality

evolution. The same goes for the docent here. At present the human docent must be present to guide human viewers through the augmented reality info-space. We are transitioning to an extra-somatic, fifth circuit docent. In *Optimism One,* FM 2030 writes, "It is true that modern technology is growing more and more powerful. But the more powerful it becomes the more diversity it generates. Powerful communication satellites can reach every person on this planet. In so doing they also open up the world to every viewer" (Esfandiary 1970).

References

2030 FM (1989) *Are you transhuman? Monitoring and stimulating your personal rate of growth in a rapidly changing world.* Warner Books, New York
Armstrong W (2011) *(Un)Seen sculptures.* Accessed 15 Oct 2020. https://www.unseensculptures. com
Barata A (2010) Anamorph 3D. Augmented reality

Bernal HD (1928) The world, the flesh and the devil

Esfandiary F (1970) Optimism one. Norton and Company, New York

Esfandiary F (1977) Telespheres. Popular Library, New York

Foster H (2005) An archival impulse

Fuller B (1969) Operation manual for spaceship earth. Simon and Schuster, New York

Fuller B (1988) Cloud nine. Illustration

Gardeya M (2010) Berlin wall 3D. Augmented reality

Leary T (1987) *Info-psychology: a manual on the use of the human nervous system according to the instructions of the manufacturers.* Falcon Publications, Phoenix

Leary T (1988) Musings on human metamorphosis. Ronin Publishing, Berkley

Leary T (1994) Chaos and cyberculture. Ronin Publishing, New York

Leary T (2008) *Cyberpunks cyberfreedom: change your reality screen.* Ronin Publishing, Berkley

Manzione C (2010) *Virtual public art project.* Accessed 15 Oct 2020. https://virtualpublicartproject.com/Virtual_Public_Art_Project/The_Virtual_Public_Art_Project.html

McLuhan M (1964) Understanding media: extensions of man. Signet, New York

Meinhardt C (2010) Mirrored city. Augmented reality

O'Neill G (1975) Island one. Illustration

Shafer N (2010) Archie. Augmented reality

Shafer N (2018) Denali city. Augmented reality

Skwarek M (2011) Seawall. Augmented reality

Warren Center School (2015) Tiger bay flocks. Augmented reality

Chapter 15
Literature-Based Augmented Reality: Integrating Urban Novels with Context-Aware Augmented Environments

Dimitrios Makris and Maria Moira

Abstract This chapter investigates the ways in which the dialogism and unfinalizability of cultural heritage experiences redefine place attachment, so that inhabitants and visitors of cities can recognize and process the urban multivariate collective cultural and aesthetic distinctiveness. The suggested approach is founded on the amalgamation of novels with mobile/context-aware augmented reality. Urban novels play a threefold role. First, they reveal a multiplicity of embodied situations as spatiotemporal representations of the surrounding built environment. Second, they create socially mediated memories related to groups and places. Third, the reading of novels offers strong bodily enactment, opening up the minds of readers to the vivid collective, social and cultural potential, surprise and aesthetic awareness of the urban environment. Augmented Reality integrated with novels can render possible the exploration of such characteristics; as a result, a mutated, transformed urbanscape emerges as a multilayered experience capable of defining durable relationships with the city's hidden collective, cultural, and aesthetic memories.

15.1 Cultural Heritage Experiences

The perpetuation of urban cultural heritage (intangible and tangible sites and artifacts, intangible events, practices, and attributes of societies or communities through time) is a rapidly growing multidisciplinary field. A wide spectrum of information and communication technology-oriented theoretical schemes and applications provide numerous insights into Cultural Heritage (CH) experiences. The three-dimensional digitization of the various expressions of CH provides accurate new categories of

D. Makris (✉)
Faculty of Applied Arts and Culture, Department of Conservation of Antiquities and Works of Art, University of West Attica, Athens, Greece
e-mail: demak@uniwa.gr

M. Moira
Faculty of Applied Arts and Culture, Department of Interior Architecture, University of West Attica, Athens, Greece
e-mail: mmoira@uniwa.gr

objects and sites in the form of digital surrogates (Ioannides et al. 2017). Such digital surrogates have their own reference frame and their own intrinsic reality. Urban inhabitants' understanding and interpretation of multiple CH elements of various scales, as well as any three-dimensional digital surrogate, involve contemplation and study of the situational frame within which they occur and the context they reveal as digital substances (Lloyd 2016). A frame of reference can consist of historical and archaeological indications, geo-temporal references, collective cultural settings, roles, and functions. A set of information and knowledge about the city's intertwined dimensions is essential to make it accessible to scholars, experts, and the general public. The integration with dissemination and exhibition activities is made with the aid of digital technologies like virtual reality (VR) and/or augmented reality (AR), mixed reality, and extended reality (Papagiannakis et al. 2018). Ongoing work on this approach is oriented toward the urban CH integration and dissemination approaches based on AR.

15.1.1 Emergence of a New CH Experience Powered by Fiction-Informed AR

The introduction of AR in urban life could become a privileged immaterial shell/skin for enabling the numerous fragmented realities and imaginaries of the urban environment settings. Augmented Reality is a digital technology that can catalyze human perceptual, tangible, and sensory experience, collecting and contrasting multiple elements through the correlation of real and digital environment (Klopfer and Squire 2008). AR can achieve the reconstitution of unrecognized or invisible microcosms and macrocosms, allowing the emergence of sensory-motor and cognitive activities in a new space, under construction and constant negotiation (Azuma 2015; Jung and Tom Dieck 2018). Augmented Reality is a visual, cognitive, perceptual process that develops interactive and dynamic hybrid digital environments (Jung and Tom Dieck 2018; Azuma 2015). Such AR environments contribute to the creation of cognitive and physical models, which can transform the individual from a passive observer–receiver into an active participant, immersed in the palimpsest of the city. Powered by technological advances, it has become widely recognized that Augmented Reality creates more affluent and more stimulating content, resulting in improved experience, awareness, and understanding of real-world urban settings (Geroimenko 2014). Augmented Reality makes individuals' bodies dynamic interfaces, capable of developing new conditions of engagement with the collective dimensions of the body of Cultural Heritage. Inhabitants and visitors alike are able to discover the world by adding new stages to their perception of reality and space. As they are aware of moving in the immediate urban space and understanding its physical effect (MacIntyre et al. 2001), their sense of immersion is further enhanced. Consequently, AR's emerging knowledge profoundly alters the underlying and perceived entities and sites, as they offer new tangible and/or intangible substances into the everyday world (Liberati and Nagataki 2015).

Following the above, two main questions arise. First, in which ways are these digital surrogates consistent with their intrinsic reference context? Second, in which ways and procedures are they (if at all yet) integrated with the relative surrounding everyday urban reality? Their adaptation is technologically possible and applicable. However, the advent of another layer (whether augmented, digitally mixed, and/or extended) does not directly ensure the emergence of some new relationship/attachment and is in no way an extended everyday reality.

15.1.2 CH Experience and Place Attachment

In contemporary metropolises, both the current surrounding environment and any possible digitally overlaid content regarding absent, lost, and hidden former settings could pose the same degree of strangeness and unfamiliarly to both urban inhabitants and visitors. As shown by relevant research work (Moira and Makris 2018), the literature narrative, and particularly novels, can develop a sense of place and enforce locality as an approach toward the strange, unknown, unfamiliar urban environment (buildings, squares, monuments, streets, markets) from within a multivariate social and cultural framework. While the cities' pulsating environments are characterized by diverse and overlapping cultural and aesthetic fields, they also have a diasporic character through time and space. Everyday living in urban landscapes entails individuals living in a dense environment populated by trivial and repetitive actions, tangible and intangible remains from past epochs, and the imaginary creative currents that result in various imaginary-fictional universes. Urban cultural heritage landscapes are characterized by, and exist within, a particular context, which obviously can include the entire lifespan and relationships with every past epoch and location, as expressed by an interwoven field of relationships with past and current spatial continuities and discontinuities.

Seamon (2014) refers to place attachment as a complex, multifaceted, and dynamic experience that is based on a place's complex processes. Urban environments are creators and carriers of conventional and unconventional cultural heritage chronotopes (both spatial and temporal events, situations that have been inscribed and can be traced in the urban body in the form of buildings, squares, streets, and monuments). The framework proposed by Seamon assumes that site attachment is the result of the interaction between experiencing a place and the creation of meaning associated with that experience (Seamon 2014). A fruitful place attachment is a synthesis of diverse tangible and intangible CH elements, which could be brought together and amalgamated under the fictional expression of a novel. The main vehicle for engaging with the surrounding urban space is the body itself—the body moves in space and time, and at the same time uses language to propose/make meaning of its sensory experiences. Another important factor of localization is a person's ability to develop positive feelings about the surrounding urban environment. Attachment to urban places entails the inhabitants' positive emotional bond with specific places where they feel tranquil and safe from harm, places with which they wish to maintain a link (Low and Altman 1992). The body's position and situation in a place are fundamental for the two following capacities: first, for one's understanding of the medium of the AR and, second, for the medium's very capacity to offer something new to the relationship between human and the environment. The importance of novel-based integration features offered by AR is of paramount importance in understanding the involvement and participation of inhabitants and visitors in the urban landscape. The AR is suggested as a powerful instrument for the recording, expression, and visualization of the intrinsic complexity of the spatial and temporal dimensions of novels. In an AR system it is possible to define interconnected layers, which include the geography, temporal and topographical dimensions of a novel, the different scales of its evolving plot, the shades of the different emotions of its characters.

15.2   Collective Memory and the City's Cultural Heritage

> ...the city itself is the collective memory of its people, and like memory it is associated with objects and places. The city is the locus of the collective memory. (Rossi 1982, p. 130)

Roland Barthes indicates that the form of the literary message as defined by the author maintains a concrete connection with History and society, as the connotational factors inadvertently entailed in the text constitute the elements of a code, whose validity may be more or less long term but whose informative value is well grounded despite the divergence of interconnection between signs (Barthes 1975, p. 121). Sennett writes that a metropolis is functional because it streamlines the people's collective as well as subjective life (Sennett 1992). Literature, by representing the city through fiction, weaves the age-old past together with the present. It processes the inhabitant's personal experience, micro-history, and personal journey in parallel with the bigger picture of collective experiences and the echoes of broader sociopolitical and historical events. It constructs and constitutes a hypertextual diagram that traces the personal and collective expression of habitation through the embodied handling of urban space.

Novels create socially mediated memories (Halbwachs 1980) related to groups and places. In particular, Halbwachs underscored the pivotal importance of space in the formation of collective memory, noting that the recollection of spaces by members of a community is equally vital to social memory as the recollection of periods of time. Halbwachs emphasized the function of the familiar urban setting, the persistently unchanging character of a city, the "impassive stones," as a factor of continuity and stability (Halbwachs 1980, p. 158). The spatial focalizations of fictional texts contribute to the analysis of viewing and experiencing the city's habitation. Employment of disjunctive relationships and dipoles, and the mobilization of all the senses, serve to emphasize the contrast between current and past images of the city.

15.2.1   Dialogical Thinking and Cultural Heritage

The various different approaches to CH, as expressed by Muñoz-Viñas (2005), shifted from the one-dimensional focus of a materialistic framework toward a threefold scheme that interweaves individual narratives with collective social and cultural contexts. Bakhtin (1986) considers a principal qualitative force of contexts that of the spatiotemporal frame that they produce. He encapsulates the chronotope as a constitutive frame of the narrative (Bakhtin 1981). In the proposed approach, the concept of chronotopes is firstly framed as the internal biography and contextual reference of any CH item and site; secondly, all relevant novels' plots are seen as mutually interwoven chronotopes. Bakhtin considers of fundamental importance the quality of relations between individuals and events and their chronotopes (Bakhtin 1986). The spatialization of novels over the urban corpus is viewed as a dynamic emergence of diverse and parallel memory chronotopes. The urban cultural heritage context is uttered as a space that empowers the emergence of multidimensional cultural fragments, social overdeterminations, and historical layers (Friedman 2007). Based on Bakhtin's theoretical scheme, understanding and interpreting both the surrounding urban environment and CH is always accomplished through dialogical thinking, i.e. being open to relational processes. In the present approach, dialogical thinking is a privileged concept toward the discovery of the cultural heritage's unfinalizability, contrary to any established monological definitive (Holquist 2002).

The dialogic approach frames the identification and arrangement of relations between novels-based points of view. Such relations are at the core of the embodied simulation mechanism (Gallese and Gattara 2015). The emotional engagement and embodiment of a CH experience happen under a dialogical scheme that is founded on specific spatiotemporal contexts (Holquist 2002). Urban dwellers' activities and experiences are characterized as open dialogues under constant transformation and mutation. The proposed dialogic perpetuation is based on the establishment of a dialectic relationship between individuals and urban CH objects and sites, where values like culture, place, society, and cityscapes emerge as powerful reflection and experience connectors. A dialogical worldview encompasses that appreciation, interpretation, and absorption of CH urban experiences arise between individuals and the surrounding urban settings and places. The present approach adopts the dialogic experience paradigm where the urban environments (CH places, monuments, everyday sites) are experienced as spatiotemporal events and situations. The multiplicity of dwellers' and visitors' perceptions is mediated by means of the AR framework approach. The emergence of a new CH experience power by AR could reveal the dialogical character of urban CH experiences as a dynamic potential to immerse within a multivalent reality, where the various precedents and the present merge in a single moment. AR could define a spectrum of possible perspectives and, at the same time, it could provide and promote unique points of perception. AR may serve as the foundational media of the dialogical thinking approach (Bakhtin 1986), which in turn may enable an openness to any relational processes that could constitute/reconstitute the unfinalizability of urban CH. At the core of the urban

CH legibility lies the potential to digitally communicate through the lens of AR, in order to mediate the unfinalized relations between CH sites, anchor points (Couclelis et al. 1987), novels' chronotopes, and inhabitants' and visitors' personal chronotopes. These dialogic relationships that emerge, persistently and continually, between dwellers/visitors and urban places may be understood and interpreted through the concept of embodied simulation.

15.2.2 Embodied Simulation—Fiction and Memory

...to read fiction means to play a game by which we give sense to the immensity of things that have happened, are happening, or will happen in the actual world. (Eco 1994, p. 87).

Embodied simulation (ES) highlights that specific brain circuits are activated when seeing and imagining something, acting and imagining another person's action. In particular, direct action understanding of another individual articulating a particular emotional or bodily action, performing a movement or behavior, is possible to happen beyond the inference of any specific mentalization (Gallese et al. 2009). Action understanding is based on a mechanism of embodied simulation, a neural mechanism grounded on the activation of mirror neurons. Such concepts have been broadened to apply when individuals are reading narrative texts (Gallese and Wojciehowski 2011), when we behold a work of art (sculpture, painting, etc.), when watching a film in the movies (Gallese and Guerra 2019), or a theatrical performance. Research approaches in neuroaesthetics (Gallese 2017) reveal fundamental evidence that key element of ES are activated when we imagine doing something and when we recall a memory (Gallese et al. 2018). Aesthetic experiences are informed by particular characteristics generated through embodied simulation, whereas novels awake in the minds of individuals bodily memories and imaginative associations, which in turn are boosted by the potentiation of the mirroring mechanisms they activate (Gallese et al. 2018). Furthermore, brain-imaging studies provide evidence that ES is the basis for the fact that an individual's body senses, and acts in, the everyday surrounding environment in the same way that it senses the spatial environment of a literature narrative. The reading of novels offers strong bodily enactment (Gallese and Wojciehowski 2011), opening up the readers' minds to the vivid collective, social and cultural potential, surprise and aesthetic awareness of the reoffered surrounding environment. Novels can resonate in readers' bodies, as current research in neuroscience has noted and formulated as the concept of ES. Based on empirical and theoretical work (Gallese and Wojciehowski 2011), it has been proven that the content of novels can induce in the reader plentiful and diverse simulations that are experientially heightened and have a major effect. The narrative's intersubjectivity is possible to be translated as an experience of intercorporeality (Gallese 2020).

Following the embodied simulation paradigm (Gallese and Gattara 2015), the brain–body continuum is the vital element in engaging with the contemporary urban environments. The relations network that emerges by the location and stasis of the brain–body is of great importance to distinguish the AR medium and its abilities to propose a novel approach to the bonds between individuals and the built environment. AR is distinctively privileged as compared to other visual media, for the latter perpetuate the hegemony of vision in the representation of the CH urban setting. AR is uniquely positioned to allow inhabitants/visitors to experience CH objects and sites in an embodied simulation rather than merely visually conceive them. AR provides a setting and atmosphere where the revelation is offered as part of its development (Gould 2014). Thus, neither the digital content nor the relevant urban context (collective, social, cultural memory) dominates over one another. The imperceptible experience of CH values involves simultaneous perception of both media and memory. The various strands of contemporary CH theory redefine the individual's substance from a passive recipient of content as an emancipated actor (Ranciere 2011) in a multi-sensory dialogic context of approaching his or her immediate environment wherein he or she is entirely immersed.

15.2.3 Representation of Urban Places in Novels

The 'reality' that he tracks cannot be reduced to the immediate data of the sensory experience in which it is revealed; he aims not to offer (in)sight, or feeling, but to construct systems of intelligible relations capable of making sense of sentient data. (Bourdieu 1995, p. xviii)

Every novel enacts diverse dynamic, multi-layered and multi-fragmented chronotopes of the urban milieu. The specific and unique chronotopic frame of a novel is expressed through various chronological markers which situate the plot's events in various (historical, contemporary) times/epochs. In an interwoven manner, the plot's diverse and expressive spatial markers are located over the living canvas of the metropolis. Novels possess the inherent power to organize and synthesize the social, collective, cultural, emotional, and historical layers within the urban fabric. By following the fictional plot, the reader does not simply perceive the unequivocal voyeuristic image of a city-museum or a city-diorama, but the enriched picture of the ambulatory city–anti-museum of daily practices and performances of tasks carried out by its inhabitants, and of its continuously shifting semantic layer. According to Ricoeur, fictional narrative is an iconic augmentation of the world of human action, which consists of conjuring plots and constructing events in a rational manner. Speech, action, and integration into a storyline create new networks of reading an experience or producing it, precisely because they lend a dimension of denotation or notification rather than reduplication of reality. Fiction resorts to reality not to copy it but to propose a new approach to it of distinct cognitive value. The conceptual mental image created by the writer is marked by his or her characteristic intention to offer a model for a different perception of things, more specifically a paradigm of a new vision (Ricoeur 1985, pp. 66–70). Literature follows several different paths and devises several different starting points to represent space and paint a lucid picture of the spatial components and spatial qualities that lend it expression and substance as a creative reference. By tracing the lifecycles of the narrative's subjects, literature captures and attests to those discrete and selected elements which, by means of language's inherent capacity to reveal, fashion, i.e. render accurately and acutely, the distinctive features of space and its identity in the mind of the reader (Eco 2002, p. 245).

Kracauer speaks of the "experience of the city as a labyrinth of fragmented signals." In his article "Berlin Landscape" he makes a clear distinction between two types of images of the city: the cityscapes that are consciously fashioned and those that come about unintentionally. "The former spring from the artificial will that is realized in those squares, open vistas, building complexes and perspective effects that are generally marked with an asterisk in tourist guides. By contrast, the latter come into being without a prior plan" (Kracauer 1964, p. 40). According to Bourdieu, the "literary microcosm" is a relatively autonomous field that functions by means of a group of acting subjects, works, and phenomena, in which social forces are also present, since literary writing has the unique capacity "to concentrate and condense in the concrete singularity of a sensitive figure and an individual adventure, functioning both as metaphor and as metonymy, all the complexity of a [social] structure and a history" (Bourdieu 1995, p. 24). Urban sites offer today's visitors an equally fascinating field for exploration, new experiences, and knowledge (Stevenson 2003). Even during the brief time of their visit, modern-day visitors of historic cities of the twenty-first century inadvertently come across the complex nature of the city. The limited time they have at their disposal is an insurmountable obstacle in effectively "reading" the palimpsest of the living city. Thus, their perception of the city is largely based on viewing, more specifically, on hastily and haphazardly looking over the city, instead of living it, on mass-consuming a plethora of images instead of coming into contact with the substance and the spirit of the place. In this way, modern-day visitors tend to obtain a fleeting, voyeuristic spatial impression of the city, due to the inevitable inability to manage and interconnect the abundance of visual fragments and information they collect (De Certeau 1980).

15.3 Research Framework

The metropolis urbanscape is always in constant transformation and mutation. The metropolis urbanscape has numerous hidden collective, cultural, and aesthetic memories as part of its cultural heritage. If we consider an element of urban cultural heritage as an encrypted text, a hermetic palimpsest, the basic question that arises is: how can a resident or visitor communicate with multiple layers of fragments of historical memory and fragments of unrecognized topographies as a whole, in order to discover a city's special character? How to interpret its multifaceted spatial, syntactic, and sociopolitical reality? Inhabitants and visitors could barely recognize and process the urban multivariate collective, cultural, and aesthetic distinctiveness; understand, comprehend histories, reconfigurations, of urban life performance. The present approach attempts to address the question of the experience of urban (place-specific, contextual) memory (i.e. collective memory, cultural memory, historical, social, aesthetic context): In which ways can we enable the urbanscape to emerge as a multilayered experience, and promote the urban CH multifacetedness within the foregrounding everyday living environment? In which ways could we enhance the structures of imaginary being and living for urban dwellers and visitors? Following Scarry's notion that novels can be understood as a set of instructions for mental composition (Scarry 2001), the novel-based AR scenarios could act as a set of directions for how to re-synthesize contextual chronotopes within the vivid body of cities.

15.4 Perpetuation of the City's Myth

Everyday living in urban environments entails individuals living in a dense environment populated by trivial, repeated actions, tangible and intangible remains from past epochs, and the imaginary creative currents that result in various imaginary-fictional universes. According to Rossi, the city constitutes a palimpsest, a complex body of traces and a theater of memory, as "memory becomes the guiding thread of the entire complex urban structure" (Rossi 1982, 130). It is a combination between a structured environment and the individual and collective stories that are woven like a network of meeting places, a network of different pasts that are communicating with each other. In attempting to capture and render the "portrait" of a city and contribute to the art of urban imagery, literature brings to the fore the living city and its historicity as opposed to notional or idealized images of a city-theme park or a city-postcard. It recomposes the image of a "fragmented world" revealing contrasting parameters, indiscernible sociopolitical aspects, and overlooked qualities of the city's personality. As noted by Eco, "it is easy to understand why fiction fascinates us so. It offers us the opportunity to employ limitlessly our faculties for perceiving the world and reconstructing the past" (Eco 1994, p. 131).

Literary representations can serve as cultural intermediaries offering the source material for a substantial reading of the city. They prompt us to stimulating departures for the discovery of the city's idiosyncrasy, not by means of seduction, but by means of a critical perception of the city. With fiction as their tour guide, the inhabitants' and visitors' wandering through the city, through this garden of emotions, spares them from an emulative accession to a stereotypical image of the city. The walking navigation extracts them from the paralysis of "posing" in front of recognizable anchor points-fields, not because it provides them with clear instructions on how to "use" the space provided, but because it allows them to develop their own stimuli in discovering the identity of the place. The uncertainty inhabitants or visitors feel when faced with the unknown is not lifted by "taming" a place. The experience of heterogeneity is not conquered through luxury and comfort or by welcoming visitors into familiar surroundings that remind them of their own home country or places they know very well, such as multinational chains of hotels or restaurants; instead, it is conquered by offering visitors the opportunity to place themselves inside their surroundings and develop their own personal compass to roam about the city. Where, then, does one set out to get to know a city? How does one infiltrate the "body urban"? This question has concerned many writers over time, as each of them had to choose his or her own starting point when setting out to "draw the portrait" of the city; to create their individual spatial representations in order to render the city readable and comprehensible to the reader.

Inhabitants and visitors are in the surrounding urban space at the present moment, they live in the present time, they move along the paths indicated by the narrative, they draw different and varied sensory experiences according to the plot mapping, they receive messages and communicate with the other attendees. Inhabitants and visitors locate anchor points and tour different urban cultural monuments under the guidance of multiple literary currents and flows. Nevertheless, at the same time, they become able to inhabit earlier spatiotemporal epochs by reliving moments and recalling images and scenes of the past through different levels. The inhabitant or visitor, based on the digital medium of AR, has the ability to visualize and restore various anchor points (buildings, monuments, squares, statues, markets) that no longer exist, to look for the form and function of spaces in important historical, political, and economic periods, under the guidance of various archival sources and with the superimposition of multiple layers, in order to have a multi-collective, holistic experience of the spatiotemporal deepness of the city and the continuity of the sociopolitical and cultural becoming (Moira and Makris 2018). Within a set of novels, the symbiosis of their spatiotemporal formations affords room for the dialogic inter-illumination of contrasting biosphere views of the same urban environment.

15.4.1 Scales of Spatial Proximity and AR Storytelling Typology

Augmented Reality can improve and expand the everyday urbanscape, allowing inhabitants and visitors to draw conclusions about the assignment and configuration of sites, or to better understand what they are sensing. Three-dimensional digital models can be positioned in real life to re-erect remains of destroyed buildings or landscapes, or even ancient characters as they used to be. At the same time, the digitally enhanced environment will motivate and highlight qualitative physiognomies of the frame of reference, such as atmosphere, psychogeography, emotional horizons, etc., in different spatial scales.

The typical four categories of spatial proximity scales—figural, vista, environmental, and geographical space (Montello 1993)—could host augmented reality. The figural space is projectively smaller than the body; in that space, the objects' perception does not involve any extensive body movement. It could resemble a larger peripersonal space map where individuals could approach objects with limited bodily movements (eyes, arms, head). The vista space can be detected physically from a single spatial point lacking any prior movement of the individual. Such space is projectively close to the body volume and concerns spaces like interiors, urban squares, and closed sites. The environmental space fully involves the individual's body and it could be experienced through the individual's movement within sites like large edifices and urban or landscape surroundings. Although not plainly perceptible within a brief period of time, this spatial scale is still perceptible with modest access. On a greater scale, the fourth category of geographical space is not perceptible by direct personal experience or navigation. Such a scale can only be understood through representational illustrations, such as multilayered models based on multiple stratigraphies that help reduce a vast topographical scale to a geometric and semantic space.

Following the aforementioned scheme, the present approach proposes a foundational AR storytelling typology that interweaves with novels based on four strategies: reinforcement, re-contextualization, remembrance, and reembodiment (Moira and Makris 2018). The reinforcement strategy concerns the overlapping of digital spatial anchor objects that appear as real to the individual during the particular chronotopic frame. For example, augmentations comprise three-dimensional digital representations of absent monuments, sculptures, fragmented restorations or partly damaged or destroyed edifices, and artworks, which display the corrupted or vanishing part of a city. The re-contextualization strategy transmutes the physical and semantic framework of urbanscapes, which acquires new meaning and sense in the context of a chronotope-based narrative. The focal intention is to disclose the diverse facets of urban CH milieus. The reality reenactment consists of synthesizing, on an intertextual level, a story that allows dissimilar signs to appear. Based on the novel's plot, the related anchor places are expressed and digitally recreated. The related cultural heritage context timeline registers the narrative arrangements to the adjacent physical and digitally three-dimensional reshaped urban milieu. The augmented intertextual narration is digitally overlaid in such a way that collective, historical, and cultural contextual interrelations can be experienced in conjunction with the plot's evolving chronotope. Consequently, the urban image varies according to the narrative ambient and historical epoch of the contextual CH. In this way, inhabitants and visitors understand the overall urban site's character as blended within its historical, social, and cultural parameters.

The remembrance strategy supports the concurrent attendance of various mnemonic fragments from the same urban location (Azuma 2015). Certain temporal narratives afford mnemonic content from the specific urbanscape reference frame since they have different plot and ideological pointing. Thus, inhabitants and visitors may possibly independently discover the varied collective, cultural, aesthetic content of the urban sites through a similar set pathway. The emotional context provided by the novel's characters prompts inhabitants and visitors to approach relevant urban locations through CH narratives, with which they engage bodily and mentally. Based on their personal interests, inhabitants and visitors may take note of their distinct emotional states, their personal involvements with, and remembrances from, the urban surrounding locations they visit, and how these compare and contrast with those of the novel's fiction. The reembodiment strategy enables inhabitants and visitors to engage with hitherto unfamiliar urban surrounding milieus, which they desire to understand as they make their way through a socially distorted or strange place. Hence, individuals can discover the richness of a city's stratification of matter and meaning, as they reintroduce awareness and growth involvement. Following such a series of processes, inhabitants and visitors can obtain a deeper spatial, emotional, and bodily experience and comprehend the discriminations and transformations of urban places and events, to finally reconnect with the place's hidden spirit, of which they were previously unaware but which is now reemerging (Forte 2016). They are able to gradually engage with, rather than superficially observe, local societies and become aware of the collective and cultural memory of the place.

15.4.2 Omonoia (Concord) Square: A Symbolic Urban Anchor Point in Athens

Historic European cities, such as Athens, constitute a complex, open, and extremely interesting field for the development of alternative experimental models in the form of a customized AR-based navigation through the urban landscape and historic time; a journey, guided by literature, that shall be based on empirical and experiential rather than just visual perception. In an age of flux, mobility, and perpetual acceleration, there is ample room for identifying and employing a multitude of different types of approaches to the characteristic idiosyncrasy of a metropolis on the part of its inhabitant or casual visitor. Literary narrative is particularly apposite to constituting a guide for a multidimensional urban touring-reading of the city, as it provides a synthesis of urbanscapes made up of a multitude of different angles of observation. It identifies significant urban anchor points and fields, indicates sites worth stopping at, and suggests alternative routes. Making use of both literary spatial representations and AR, the "transient strangers" (either dwellers or visitors) are in a position to actively and vigorously manage a series of distinct narratives and, thus, briefly inhabit not the stereotypical image of a postcard-city but the "lived" city, tracing the footprints of lived time on the palimpsest of the city's material surface.

Current ongoing research by the authors proposes the historic Omonoia (Concord) Square as a starting line and point of departure for a series of alternative augmented journeys in search of the polysemous nature of Athens. Using prominent texts of Greek literature as guides, the urban citizen or sightseer is prompted to experience the "dialogic motion" that may be obtained from the experiential perception and personal interpretation of the distinct identity of the place. Anchor points, such as urban squares, function as condensers and capacitors of urban experience. They are popular public spaces of social interaction, focal points of urban life and identity, memory spaces representing the urban historicity and capturing the cultural transformations and mutations occurring over time. Unfolding in the space delineated by squares, almost as if in the form of a theatrical act, is the metropolis's network of meetings, relations, events, and incidents. This is where the inspection of urban life is enacted and new ideas and trends are tried out, where the conformations of morals and the popularity of novelties are being put to the test (Moira 2018, p. 340).

Omonoia (Concord) Square, the second most recognizable square in Athens after Syntagma (Constitution) Square, is an important urban anchor point; a place both central and liminal at the same time, both timeless and ephemeral, both flexible and yet stable and unchanged over time; a junction and a crossroads, a starting point and a point of convergence for six transport routes (even after its latest overhauls, which suspended the circular flow of pedestrians and vehicles). The square is graced with significant historic buildings of various periods and architectural styles affording the area a diverse, multimodal, and, more importantly, un-museum-like character. Over the course of the metropolis's long history, Omonoia Square has witnessed a variety of spatial configurations and deviations as reflecting relevant social and cultural influences. First it was simply an open space covered with scrub and gravel, on the rim of the inhabited parts of the urban milieu, the wider vicinity almost a wilderness featuring streams and vineyards and fig trees and pens for sheep and cows. In the urban plan designed by S. Kleanthis and E. Schaubert (which was never implemented), the square was vested with a monumental character, intended to become the city center, as the plan situated the Palace and other public buildings at the site. In subsequent plans, following the relocation of the Palace, the square became smaller, yet maintained its focal position insofar as it evolved into a space for walks, entertainment, and meetings. During the early decades of the twentieth century, Omonoia Square was completely linked to the changes in the city brought about by modernity. Bustling with the cultural pulse of several cafés, music clubs, hotels and theaters, hangouts for night-owls, journalists, actors, and writers, it was the most vibrant part of the capital, attracting all the cosmopolitans of the time. Up until World War II, the square had a middle-class air, an attribute about to change once and for all after the war, as the district became a working-class, blue-collar neighborhood (Giochalas and Kafetzaki 2012, p. 536). To this day, the square maintains its lively multicultural character and a prominent position in the public sphere and the political scene, constituting a meeting point, a destination, but also a point of departure for all sectors of the city, for residents and visitors alike. The novels-based AR framework reveals the voyage and explorations of the novels' characters, motivated by the provocation of surprise or desire, focusing on the emergence of bipolar contrasts which indicate the intersections and folds of the urban landscape and the collective, social, and cultural space: interior vs. exterior, familiar vs. unfamiliar, public vs. private.

Demarcating the boundaries of Omonoia Square is rather hard because the surrounding building blocks in all directions are considered an integral part of it. As a result, the boundaries of its perceived reach essentially meld into the urban fabric. In its territory, distinct pieces of the urban fabric meet and intertwine, this encounter and fermentation producing an atmosphere particularly dense in meaning and sensations. The traditional oriental city of rich sensory stimuli, polysemous and unpredictable, vibrant and multifaceted, bustling and colorful, featuring the Central Market of Athens (fruit and vegetable market, meat and fish market), the smells and the sounds, the small shops, the handicrafts and the haunts of various ethnic groups,

meets the capital of nineteenth-century modernity with its broad avenues, the prominent neoclassical buildings, and the western-type rationalist urban planning. A case
in point are the historic twin hotels Bageion and Megas Alexandros, which form
a peculiar gateway at the beginning of Athinas Street toward Monastiraki and the
Acropolis: "…a kind of gateway that is not marked by the presence of a gate or
tollbooths, but by the change of atmosphere" (Ioannou 1980, p. 100). A fact is also
noticeable on the city's urban planning map, where a triangle can be drawn with
Omonoia Square at its peak. The square is not only buzzing with the rhythmic ebb
and flow of crowds moving in intersecting trajectories as they walk in all directions,
but is also a site where people stop to look at shop windows, a rendezvous, and, generally, a site of communication and interaction among people from all social strata.
The boulevards fanning out from the square, a typical element of modernist urban
planning, are long and wide, highlighting the extravaganza of stores and noteworthy
public and private buildings. Thanks to their plotting and geometry, these urban
axes offer the public a view and a spectacle, while also allowing for the staging of
multitudinous political rallies and demonstrations, public exposure, and theatricality
of movement (Spyropoulou 2010, p. 125). To this day, Omonoia Square is packed
with cafés and restaurants, some big and renowned and others not so much, nestled
in secluded alcoves or hidden nooks, along the surrounding boulevards and popu-
lous arcades, mostly men's hangouts and watering holes, as well as refuges where
internal or external migrants can meet with their peers from the same village, town,
or country. Thus, the visitor who follows the routes fanning out from the square
can gain a comprehensive and thorough picture of Athens's collective and cultural
memories, seeing as the sense of the urban condition, according to Lynch, is directly
linked to "the apparent clarity or 'legibility' of the cityscape" (Lynch 1960, p. 2).

Omonoia Square is an iconic anchor point of Athens and, at the same time, a place
combining a multitude of stimuli laden with high emotional charge. A multifarious
hub that can serve as a starting point for the modern traveler who wishes to get to know
the city's particular personality following in the footsteps etched by literary narrative.
Setting out from Omonoia Square, the inhabitant or sightseer can recompose the
chronotopes of twenty-first-century Athens, not as a passive receiver of information,
but as an active subject exerting his or her choices, desires, and actions.

15.5 Conclusions

The AR medium engenders a remarkable shift in the perception of surrounding
urban anchor points by inhabitants and visitors alike, one that leaves the digitized
screen behind and moves forward toward a performance place, where people could
enact different roles inspired by the local urban tangible and intangible scenes, the
city's social, collective, and creative values. Through their spatiotemporal movement, a variety of multi-sensuous connections are defined between literature/novels
and various urban sites, constituting an influential intervention for dwellers and visitors toward place attachment and their engagement with the explicit and implicit

values of metropolises (hidden, disappeared and/or remaining, collective, cultural, and aesthetic memories). Urban Cultural Heritage experiences could be inspired by a fragmented multi-imaginative stratification of symbiotic interpretations, as a dialogic engagement with the variety of tangible and intangible urban anchor points and fields.

Augmenting the real world through digital data can actually create new urban constituents, with their own characteristics and their own dynamics. The AR of literary representations is not intended to coincide with a typical prevailing cartographic logic, which records objectively, measurably, and consistently consolidated spatial relations, a geography of indisputable points. On the contrary, it aims to highlight the possibility of continuous (re)negotiation of the spatial cultural and collective memories and meanings, which the literary representations bring forward and highlight through the various, often conflicting and contradictory, descriptions and markings of the urban space. The augmented relations frame an attempt to show the constant intertwining of spaces and human actions; to connect the significant elements of the syntactic structure with the human movements and practices, which make the perpetual reassembly of the urbanscape possible; to identify correlations and articulations of places that occur through the literary overview precisely because the places do not represent an established and unambiguously socially recognizable urban "reality" but a field of constant claims. As a result, novels-based AR localizes the important urban chronotopes in order to depict them as carriers of multiple meanings.

The integration of Augmented Reality focuses on the support of the symbolic and semantic dialogical transference between the various coexisting chronotopes in the form of contextual chronotopes of the Cultural Heritage object and site, the dialogism between the various frames of reference of novels, the inner chronotopes of inhabitants and visitors. Literary narratives and novels are extremely communicative for both city dwellers and visitors. Literary texts make the body of the urban environment's palimpsest bodily and psychologically accessible; they make it convenient. Therefore, literature allows the emergence of expectations for a wider participation and involvement in the urban landscape. The past epochs and collective memories of urban milieus are dialogically intertwined with the novels-based AR through the bonds of augmented relationships. Experiencing the urban environment through augmented relationships could invite both inhabitants and visitors to creatively select diverse places, while also proposing multiple ways of experiencing and interpreting the various vivid aspects of urban squares, streets, monuments, parks, and buildings.

The proposed AR conceptual framework is based on the discourse analysis of a series of novels and the intertextual fusion of their spatial representations. It provides a polyphonic perpetuation of the city as it emerges from complementary testimonies, utilizing the bodily experience and everyday practices that unfold within the boundaries of urbanscapes. The novels' indications identify the disobedient, stubborn, dark places, they collect the echoes of the struggle between tradition and modernity, the discontinuities of time, the unexpected, the important economic, social, cultural, and urban transformations (mobility of racial and ethnic groups, restructuring of social strata). They monitor traces and imprints of processes that take place in specific historical and sociopolitical turning points and make the metropolis change before the viewers' eyes and around their bodies. Through alternative descriptions, mixtures of urban aspects and events, the correlation of past and present chronotopes, and, mainly, through the very ability of language to communicate the essence of things and to reveal the visible and the invisible, urban places with their imprinted duration and stability of syntactic structure and historical origins are imbued with the actions of the people and the dynamics of renegotiating the dominant meanings they carry.

Augmented Reality enhances a constantly becoming, vivid, vibrant canvas, which expresses some precise characteristics, such as the fact that the urban fabric is not definitive, but continuously redefined. An AR dialogic framework is not simply offering established views and consolidated correlations between urbanscape and individual, urbanscape and Cultural Heritage, novel and urbanscape, novel and Cultural Heritage, novel and individual. Augmented Reality augments the relationships between Cultural Heritage and novels, between Cultural Heritage and individuals. The augmented relations (beyond augmenting realities) between the inhabitants' culture of everyday life and the Cultural Heritage chronotopes reveal a deeper view into the urban character that remains unknown to most individuals. The proposed novels-based AR media can be a path to uncovering hidden tangible and intangible CH values. The sensorial and bodily engagement engendered through the synthesis of the tangible and the intangible, the un-observable and the observable, the external and the internal, is an alluring call to inhabitants and visitors alike to participate in a variety of AR-based experiences.

References

Azuma R (2015) Location-based mixed and augmented reality storytelling. In: Barfield W (ed) Fundamentals of wearable computers and augmented reality, 2nd edn. CRC Press, Boca Raton, pp 259–276

Bakhtin M (1981) The dialogic imagination (ed: Holquist M; trans: Emerson C and Holquist M). University of Texas Press, Austin

Bakhtin M (1986) Speech genres and other late essays. University of Texas Press, Austin

Barthes R (1975) The pleasure of text. Hill and Wang, New York

Bourdieu P (1995) The rules of art: genesis and structure of the literary field (trans: Emanuel S). Stanford University Press, Stanford, California

Couclelis H, Golledge RG, Gale N, Tobler W (1987) Exploring the anchor-point hypothesis of spatial cognition. J Environ Psychol 7(2):99–122

De Certeau M (1980) L'Invention du quotidian, t. I: Arts de faire. Gallimard, Paris

Eco U (1994) Six walks in the fictional woods. Harvard University Press, Cambridge, MA

Eco U (2002) On literature. Mariner Books, New York

Forte M (2016) Cyber archaeology: 3D sensing and digital embodiment. In: Forte M, Campana S (eds) Digital methods and remote sensing in archaeology: quantitative methods in the humanities and social sciences. Springer, Cham. https://doi.org/10.1007/978-3-319-40658-9_12

Friedman S (2007) Cultural Parataxis and transnational landscapes of reading: toward a locational modernist studies. In: Eysteinsson A, Liska V (eds) Modernism, vol 1. John Benjamins Publishing Company, Amsterdam and Philadelphia, pp 35–52

Gallese V (2017) Visions of the body: embodied simulation and aesthetic experience. Aisthesis 1(1):41–50

Gallese V (2020) A bodily take on aesthetics: performativity and embodied simulation. In: Pennisi A, Falzone A (eds) The extended theory of cognitive creativity: perspectives in pragmatics, philosophy & psychology, vol 23. Springer, Cham. https://doi.org/10.1007/978-3-030-22090-7_9

Gallese V, Wojciehowski H (2011) How stories make us feel: toward an embodied narratology. California Italian Studies 2(1). https://escholarship.org/uc/item/3jg726c2. Accessed 31 May 2019

Gallese V, Gattara A (2015) Embodied simulation, aesthetics and architecture: an experimental aesthetic approach. In: Robinsons S, Pallasmaa J (eds) Mind in architecture: neuroscience, embodiment, and the future of design. MIT Press, Boston, MA, pp 161–180

Gallese V, Guerra M (2019) The empathic screen: cinema and neuroscience. Oxford University Press

Gallese V, Rochat M, Cossu G, Sinigaglia C (2009) Motor cognition and its role in the phylogeny and ontogeny of intentional understanding. Dev Psychol 45:103–113

Gallese V, Wojciehowski HC, Hogan PC (2018) Embodiment and universals. University of Connecticut. Available on https://literary-universals.uconn.edu/2018/09/25/embodiment-and-universals/#. Accessed 11 Dec 2020

Geroimenko V (ed) (2014) Augmented reality art: from an emerging technology to a novel creative medium. Springer International Publishing, Cham

Giochalas T, Kafetzaki T (2012) Athina: Ichnilatontas tin poli me odigo tin istoria kai ti logotechnia [Athens: Tracing the city with history and literature as guides]. Hestia Publishers & Booksellers, Athens

Gould A (2014) Invisible visualities: augmented reality art and the contemporary media ecology. Convergence: The International Journal of Research into New Media Technologies, special issue: Cultural Expression in Mixed and Augmented Reality, 20(1):25–32

Halbwachs M (1980) The collective memory. Harper & Row, New York

Holquist M (2002) Dialogism: Bakhtin and his world. Routledge, London and New York

Ioannides M, Magnenat-Thalmann N, Papagiannakis G (eds) (2017) Mixed reality and gamification for cultural heritage. Springer, Cham. https://doi.org/10.1007/978-3-319-49607-8

Ioannou G (1980) Omonoia 1980 (photography by Andreas Belias). Odysseas, Athens

Jung T, Tom Dieck MC (eds) (2018) Augmented reality and virtual reality: empowering human place and business. Springer International Publishing, Cham

Klopfer E, Squire K (2008) Environmental detectives: the development of an augmented reality platform for environmental simulations. Education Tech Research Dev 56(2):203–228

Kracauer S (1964) Strassen in Berlin und anderswo (Streets in Berlin and elsewhere). Suhrkamp Verlag, Frankfurt am Main

Liberati N, Nagataki S (2015) The AR glasses' "non-neutrality": their knock-on effects on the subject and on the giveness of the object. Ethics Inf Technol 17(2):125–137

Lloyd J (2016) Contextualizing 3D cultural heritage. In: Digital heritage. Progress in cultural heritage: documentation, preservation, and protection. Lecture Notes in Computer Science, vol 10058, Springer, Cham, pp 859–868. https://doi.org/10.1007/978-3-319-48496-9_69

Low S, Altman I (eds) (1992) Introduction. In: Place attachment. Human behavior and environment (Advances in theory and research). Plenum Press, New York 1992, pp 1–12. https://doi.org/10.1007/978-1-4684-8753-4_1

Lynch K (1960) The image of the city. The MIT Press, Cambridge, MA and London

MacIntyre B, Bolter JD, Moreno E, Hannigan B (2001) Augmented reality as a new media experience. In: Proceedings IEEE and ACM International Symposium on Augmented Reality, New York, Oct 2001, pp 197–206

Moira M (2018) The indiscernible city of Herakleion: Literary representations of the city during periods of reconstruction. Vikelaia Library, Heraklion

Moira M, Makris D (2018) Cultural memory in its spatio-narrative augmented reality. Int J Media & Cult Polit 14(2):151–169. https://doi.org/10.1386/macp.14.2.153_1

Montello D (1993) Scale and multiple psychologies of space. In: Frank AU, Campari I (eds) Spatial information theory: A theoretical basis for GIS. COSIT 1993. Lecture Notes in Computer Science, vol 716. Springer, Berlin, Heidelberg, pp 312–321. https://doi.org/10.1007/3-540-57207-4_21

Muñoz-Viñas S (2005) Contemporary theory of conservation. Routledge, London. https://doi.org/10.4324/9780080476834

Papagiannakis G, Geronikolakis E, Pateraki M et al (2018) Mixed reality, gamified presence, and storytelling for virtual museums. In: Lee N (ed) Encyclopedia of computer graphics and games. Springer, Cham, pp 1–13. https://doi.org/10.1007/978-3-319-08234-9_249-1

Ranciere J (2011) The emancipated spectator. Verso, London and New York

Ricoeur P (1985) Time and narrative, vol 1–3. University of Chicago Press

Rossi A (1982) The architecture of the city (trans: Ghirardo D, Ockman J). The MIT Press, Cambridge, MA

Scarry E (2001) Dreaming by the book. Princeton University Press

Seamon D (2014) Place attachment in phenomenology: the synergistic dynamism of place. In: Manzo LC, Devine-Wright P (eds) Place attachment: advances in theory, methods and application. Routledge, New York, pp 11–22

Sennett R (1992) The conscience of the eye: the design and social life of cities. Norton, New York

Spyropoulou A (2010) Morfes katoikisis stin Athina kata ta teli tou 19ou aiona: Architektonikos choros kai logotechnia [Forms of habitation in Athens around the end of the 19th century: Architectural space and literature]. Nissos Publications, Athens

Stevenson D (2003) Cities and urban cultures. Open University Press, Maidenhead and Philadelphia

Chapter 16
Applying Augmented Reality in the Italian Food and Dining Industry: Cultural Heritage Perspectives

Federica Caboni, Roberto Bruni, and Annarita Colamatteo

Abstract This chapter explores the intention to use Augmented Reality (AR) technology within dining experiences and activities in the Italian food and dining industry by focusing on cultural heritage perspectives. Six case studies are presented drawing on state of art within the industry, catching insights and highlighting limits and opportunities for the future. From the results, it emerges that AR is considered as a potential means able to increase opportunities for the food and dining industry. At the same time, the industry is not quite culturally ready for the technology improvement of customer contacts. From the analysis emerges the intention of entrepreneurs to consider AR as a potential element of business improvement to enhance the connection between food value proposition and cultural heritage.

16.1 Introduction

The digital transformation (Hagberg et al. 2016, 2017) is a phenomenon affecting people's daily life. In particular, the increasing use of Augmented Reality (AR) among other interactive technologies (Ukwuani and Bashir 2017), even though first applied in the military, industrial and medical sectors (Hwangbo et al. 2017), has created a technological enrichment in the daily lives of people. Several kinds of AR applications—in-store, online web-based and mobile apps—(Caboni and Hagberg 2019) were developed over recent years thanks to the increasing use of smartphones (Fuentes et al. 2017; Grewal et al. 2018). This shows huge potential in renovating user experiences into more exciting and wholly immersive ones (Kanak et al. 2018).

F. Caboni (✉)
Department of Economic and Business Science, University of Cagliari, Cagliari, Italy
e-mail: federica.caboni@unica.it

R. Bruni · A. Colamatteo
Department of Economic and Law, University of Cassino and Southern Lazio, Cassino, Italy
e-mail: r.bruni@unicas.it

A. Colamatteo
e-mail: a.colamatteo@unicas.it

© The Author(s), under exclusive license to Springer Nature Switzerland AG 2021
V. Geroimenko (ed.), *Augmented Reality in Tourism, Museums and Heritage*, Springer Series on Cultural Computing,
https://doi.org/10.1007/978-3-030-70198-7_16

Nowadays, people want to enrich their experience, and in particular the food experience, through food consumption (Quan and Wang 2004) and transforming it into an immersive, memorable, cultural and interactive experience. By following this perspective, food can be considered as a means of helping people perceive and evaluate local traditions and cultural heritage (Di Giovine and Brulotte 2016; Batat et al. 2019) in the place in which they experience them (Cresswell and Hoskins 2008), for instance, during a touristic journey (Yuan 2018).

The relevance to living, an amazing food journey could be considered as an experiential pleasure, as stated by Batat et al. (2019). By considering the actual scenario where people want to live an experience anywhere anytime (Caboni 2020), a food journey is contemplated as a cultural journey by tasting several and different recipes, even using interactive technologies (Ukwuani and Bashir 2017). Augmented Reality (Azuma 1997; Caboni and Hagberg 2019) could allow people to explore places, traditions and cultures. In particular, traditional food gives a sense of quality to the choice of meals during the dining experience. Also, a memorable experiential pleasure of food (Batat et al. 2019), enriches the experience of people that want to get as much information and knowledge as possible about the food they are about to consume and about the links with the culture behind. It is necessary to take into consideration the importance of cultural heritage to understand how cultural elements transform and enrich a food journey. Particularly, an experiential food journey involves people from different perspectives, both emotional and cognitive (Batat et al. 2019), by enjoying the multisensory and cultural meanings encased in a food experience. In this respect, the food journey is based on three phases as pointed out by Batat et al. (2019), such as contemplation of the food; connection with the food by tasting it; and creation of memories.

To increase the levels of the food experience enclosed in these phases such as: sensorial (Spence 2017), sharing, social and cultural (Hall 2013; Cruwys et al. 2015) and storytelling (Bublitz et al. 2013), AR could be considered as the fourth level of a food journey, presented in this chapter. In the dining experience context, AR permits people to become protagonists of their dining experience by using only mobile devices (Fuentes et al. 2017; Pu et al. 2017) and, for example, seeing on their table the value of the nutrition in their food while creating imaginary dining experiences. Hence, users see augmented food as 3D models before tasting it (Kanak et al. 2018). Taking the above contributions into consideration, this chapter will offer different definitions of AR applied to the food context as a digital technology that permits people to match cultural and food elements by experiencing a new "Augmented Food Experience" (AFEX).

The digital technologies are becoming interactive tools able to transform the dining experience in a "cultural dining experience". The use of technology in the food consumption has threefold consequences (Margetis et al. 2013): it increases the socialization between people during the food journey, develops the communication with the actors involved in the selection and preparation of food, including the connection between food and traditions and enhances the entertainment that can be provided to enhance dining activities.

Not considering the atypical market dynamics caused by COVID-19 (Cowling et al. 2020), the Italian dining market is considered to be in the third place of a European ranking of dining markets, and it represents 35.7% of the whole Italian food consumption (Ristorazione 2019—Annual Report). Restaurants, bars and other activities are, for the majority, based on family business organizations (Corbetta 1995; Colli 2003; Yanagisako 2020) and the use of technology is not fully exploited. Only 40% of Italian restaurants and dining activities use digital tools to manage business processes. However, almost everyone reads reviews on social media (Report on Dining Activities—Fipe 2017–2019). More specifically, the positive effects of Internet use could be evident for sales growth (Davis and Harveston 2000) but at the same time, the investments in the technology are not so evident (Davis and Harveston 2000; Wang and Ahmed 2009).

Explorative research about the use of AR experience in the dining context seems to be useful even considering the research questions that follow:

What could be the role of AR in food dining context in Italy?

How could AR enhance cultural heritage through food value proposition in the food dining industry?

The chapter explores the intention to use Augmented Reality technology within dining experiences and activities in the Italian food and dining industry, focusing on cultural heritage perspectives.

16.2 Literature Background

In the last decades, the use of interactive technologies (Ukwuani and Bashir 2017) has significantly permeated the people's daily life and, it has changed the way people interact with reality (Poushneh 2018). The digital transformation (Hagberg et al. 2016, 2017) has affected society, and people ask to live memorable experiences during their daily activity even in the dining context. For this reason, it is necessary to introduce new interactive features able to enrich the food experience where cultural and social elements are matched with the food one. The use of smartphones is increasing globally, modifying the approach to shopping (Hagberg et al. 2016; Fuentes et al. 2017; Grewal et al. 2018) and, in some cases, the approach to dining too. Use of a smartphone while dining varies. Some users may check news and current information, some write reviews,and some take photographs of their meal. Among these, Augmented Reality is an interactive technology that could be integrated with smartphone use. It combines the real environment with virtual contents by permitting the interaction between people and contents in real-time with reproduced objects (items) in three dimensions (Azuma 1997). Several definitions of Augmented Reality were developed (Carmignani and Furth 2011; Sood 2012; Olsson et al. 2013; Scholz and Smith 2016; Javornik 2016a, b; Grewal et al. 2017; Hwangbo et al. 2017; Pantano et al. 2017; Poushneh and Vasquez-Parraga 2017; Rese et al. 2017; Ukwuani and Bashir 2017; Brengman et al. 2018; Lee and Leonas 2018; Watson et al. 2018;

Caboni and Hagberg 2019; Caboni 2020) by identifying predominant elements. The integration of a real-world dining environment and augmented content (food information, nutrition values, heritage and traditional identity content in addition to place offering) allows people to enrich their reality (Poushneh and Vasquez-Parraga 2017) and, in a dining environment, enhance their dining experience (Batat et al. 2019). Through AR, people can experience overlap and interaction with virtual objects, leaving their real-life contexts (Ramadan and Farah 2017; Carmignani et al. 2011). The development of an immersive dining experience through AR tools is a recent strategy developed in the food context to attract people (Kanak et al. 2018). In this way, during the dining experience, people have the opportunity to overlap physical and virtual worlds, enriching their food experiences (Quan and Wang 2004) with new interactive elements and/or content. In this perspective, it would be interesting to deepen the research into limits and opportunities when introducing AR technology in the dining sector.

16.3   Methodology

The interpretivist paradigm, based on constructivism, is at the base of the research methodology for this chapter; following the cited paradigm, the interaction and the interpretation of phenomena create the perceived reality for the observer/researcher. Primary and secondary data in this work have been managed to attend the interpretivist paradigm to consider that people interact with the context they create, and they associate subjective meanings to phenomena.

This work is based on a multiple case study approach (6 Italian restaurants involved in the research), with an analysis of secondary and primary data of companies (restaurants) managed by key informants with the role of provincial representative for FIPE (Federazione Italiana Pubblici Esercizi)—a leading trade association in the food service, entertainment and tourism sector (more than 300.000 companies associated). Multiple case studies (Eisenhardt and Graebner 2007; Yin 2003) are commonly used in qualitative research, in particular, merged with interpretivist approach. The secondary data has been collected analysing the restaurants' websites, and semi-structured interviews generated the primary data exploring limits and opportunities in applying AR in the food context; further, the semi-structured interviews allow comparison across the companies (Massingham 2004). Entrepreneurs interviewed are responsible for companies' strategies, and they have the leadership to decide for the business model and approach of the firm. Because the key informants involved (entrepreneurs) have the role of representatives for FIPE, they can draw the sentiment of other food entrepreneurs' active in their province. For this reason, data can even contribute to show explorative results in the context of the food and dining industry.

16.4 Analysing AR Concept and Its Contextualization with the Dining Industry

To build the questions useful for the interviews, it has been possible to consider Augmented Reality as an interactive technology able to create an *"Augmented Food Experience"* (AFEX) between augmented contents in an actual dining environment and real-time. Identifying the characteristics of an *Augmented Food Experience* and their differences with the Traditional Food Experience (TFEX) (Table 16.1) it is possible to underline multiple meanings of technological experiences. AR in the dining context offers the possibility to increase the *level of experience* for consumers with a high level of *interaction and integration* between real environment, cultural elements and virtual contents. The *technology* in an AFEX is a predominant element of the entire experience differently from a TDEX. The amount of *information* people could acquire through the use of Augmented Reality is integrated with an assortment of updatable digital contents and with the web and, in particular, in the dining context, AR allows users to *see the food* in terms of shape, representation and organization, before ordering it.

With TDEX people can traditionally acquire information, and the relevant information could only come from people working inside the dining activities and by the physical context.

In AFEX, users can experience new ways in which real and virtual (augmented) elements coexist within the same context, and they can live deep levels of their experience. For this reason, guests in a restaurant can discover a story, social connection, territories, producers, nutritional information and cultural heritage (Di Giovine and Brulotte 2016; Batat et al. 2019) going beyond the simple eating of food. People's experiences during food consumption could be enriched thanks to the combination of a real environment and digital elements in three dimensions (Azuma 1997; Azuma et al. 2001; Reinwald et al. 2014; Jung and tom Dieck 2017) such as a reproduction of menu in an augmented version or any other kind of information related to the food.

Table 16.1 Differences between AFEX and TDEX

	AFEX	TDEX
Level of experience	Profound	Shallow
Interaction	High level	Low level
Technology	Present	Partially absent
Memory	High level of memory	Medium level of memory
Deep food information	High level	Medium or low level
View food before eating	Yes	No

Source Authors' data elaboration

16.5   Case Studies Description

Case studies analysed are being divided into three parts by considering all the Italian territory: North, Middle and South. In that way, it has been possible to collect contributions coming from different Italian geographical areas, to take information about the personal approach about AR of the interviewed entrepreneurs and, at the same time, acquiring information about the colleagues in their provinces. That is useful to understand the approach of restaurant entrepreneurs in the eventual use of AR as a potential element of business improvement and, at the same time, to discover if AR could be a useful means to enhance the connection between restaurants' food value proposition and cultural heritage (Bruni and Caboni 2017).

From the website analysis, the following table (Table 16.2) has been made, drawing the relevant information coming from available secondary data.

Table 16.2 presents an overview of the companies involved in terms of the name of the company, geographical area of activity, foundation's year and some brief information about the positioning of activity and main strategy. The last column presents the relevant information about the actual use of technology (particularly the use of communication technologies useful to increase the customer relationship, company communication and management effectiveness). Through these data, it is possible to understand how is important for all the interviewed entrepreneurs to handle traditional elements, such as culinary tradition or elements deriving from the cultural heritage, innovatively. All the cases express their will to interact with customers using the social media sites and, in general, Internet communication even through a simple website, eventually helping the customer to recognize signals to enjoy the food experience and enhancing sentiments like joy and pleasure. The connection and interaction are one of the main important elements inside the strategy developed by the entrepreneurs. This information is useful to have a clear scenario of the technology adoption by the companies and, of course, in terms of defined strategies.

16.6   Results

The results of the research are presented in this section by interpreting the answers coming from the interviews.

By considering the subjects involved in the survey as representatives for the Italian trade association in the food and dining industry, the answers' interpretation could be useful to explain the sentiment of their represented colleagues. The latter are sharing the same economic, political and territorial conditions.

The main considerations coming from the responses in terms of technology situation in the food and dining industry and the future perspectives for AR applications are presented below.

1.   The results show that many entrepreneurs within the food sector are considering the technology as a possible threat to traditions, cultural heritage and values

Table 16.2 Secondary data from companies' websites

	Company	Place area	Foundation's year	Company strategy	Interviewed position	Actual use of digital technology
1	THE COOK RESTAURANT AL CAVO	North (Genoa)	Not received	– Strong Communication strategy through social media – High attention to the cultural heritage both in the food and in the architecture of the restaurant – Inclination to the possible implementation of AR technology	OWNER	– FACEBOOK – INSTAGRAM – LINKEDIN – WEBSITE – ONLINE BOOKING – SPECIAL EVENTS PROMOTED ON THE INTERNET
2	ANTICA TRATTORIA STEFANI "DA BENEDETTO"	NORTH (Lucca)	1888	– Strong attitudes in the usage of innovation by considering the traditional roots and cultural heritage – Inclination to the possible implementation of AR technology	OWNER	– WEBSITE – THE GUIDE OF LUCCA APP – ONLINE BOOKING
3	DA UMBERTO	SOUTH (Napoli)	1916	– Attention to the quality and tradition – Innovation meets cultural heritage of Neapolitan culture – Inclination to the possible implementation of AR technology	OWNER	– FACEBOOK – INSTAGRAM – TWITTER – WEBSITE – ONLINE BOOKING – CULTURE EVENTS

(continued)

Table 16.2 (continued)

	Company	Place area	Foundation's year	Company strategy	Interviewed position	Actual use of digital technology
4	VILLA PATRIZIA	CENTRE (Latina)	1999	– High level of service and specialization on events and ceremonies – Family business restaurant – Italian traditional recipes – Opened to the innovation	OWNER	– WEBSITE – FACEBOOK
5	OSTERIA DA PIETRO	NORTH (Mantova)		A place to spend moments of tranquillity enjoying typical menus of the area accompanied by a particular selection of wines from Italy and the world	OWNER	– WEBSITE – PINTEREST – FACEBOOK – INSTAGRAM – TWITTER – THEFORK – DISHCOVERY
6	APELLE	NORTH (Ferrara)	2015	– Contemporary restaurant and cocktail bar – Mission is to propose "something different" – The claim is "Smart Food, Drink Good" – No traditional dishes – Every four months, both the restaurant menu and the drink list are changed to always offer customers something new	OWNER	– WEBSITE – FACEBOOK – INSTAGRAM – ONLINE BOOKING

Source Authors' data elaborations

of the place because they think that in some ways it can decrease the role of tangible aspects linked to physical structures, location and food. However, some entrepreneurs consider that it is possible to merge a technological approach with tradition in food dining context, adopting specific attention in the application phase.

2. The results also show that in some territories the situation of inadequate infrastructures and technology (lack of fast internet connection, the structure of communication, lack of advanced electronic infrastructures)—even poorly supported by the strategies of policymakers—negatively affect the use of both companies and users. For instance, companies that do not invest in technology also lack the knowledge and skills to manage and use the innovative technology. However, some companies are working a lot in technology integration, with much interest in social media management. The majority of interviewees are active on the main social media platforms in managing customer relationships. For instance, it is possible to consider internal activity management through devices to take orders, or software to manage a warehouse, or the use of social network sites to read consumer comments, respond and provide information.

3. It is possible to understand by the answers, entrepreneurs know the power of the web and the need of customers to share emotions and situations in and out of restaurants. Customer use of technology is increasing every day, and the use of mobile applications and the Internet is growing as well, as shown by the secondary data (Eurostat 2017).

4. The companies involved in the food sector consider the application of AR as a useful option for their regular activities. At present, AR does not seem to be a priority for the development of dining activities but being connected to the place value network is considered a useful opportunity to improve the communication about food value and production, entertain the users during the meal consumption and stimulate the interest in the food context.

5. As the interviewees, AR could create opportunities to improve the connection between place, tourism, producers and food industry, showing opportunities and contents in a fast and direct way of communication. Furthermore, AR could be good support for cultural heritage. Of course, at the same time AR could reduce human contact with the narrative of the restaurant/organization because the contents could be quickly presented attractively. Still, the solution is always in the correct balance between human and digital experience.

16.7 Discussion

People all over the world are enhancing their interests continuously to the technology by increasing the use of mobile devices to sharing information and experiences anywhere, anytime. The difference between what people want and what they manifest during a food experience originates from a lack of information provided to the users. The perspective of the interviewees explains the offerings (companies and place actors) that are tasked with stimulating users to be confident with technological updates in their food experiences, especially with AR projects.

The interviewees' answers show that AR could stimulate the final user to participate in sharing content, emotions and information and developing an Augmented Food Experience (AFEX). This interaction could be considered a tool that is useful for diffusing knowledge and the culture of the food during a food journey by also improving the knowledge and sharing of traditional elements related to the food context. Involving each actor in the creation of an emotional food experience can enhance user participation in the co-creation of the final dining experience. The meals' taste, information and sensations could be experienced through the AR by stimulating the user mind to recognize the place and the cultural heritage. The significant core of the perception of AR in dining activities remains centred on the opportunity of being able to find new ways to improve performance during the meal experience by producing an Augmented Food Experience (AFEX).

One demand for AR seems to be addressed by content and supported by customers/users sharing information during the food experience, addressing concerns about traceability of products, production or food quality characteristics, companies/people/subjects involved in the place network process up to the point of meal production. Simultaneously, it creates entertainment for customers/users. Nowadays, consumers are searching for new opportunities to learn about food production and transformation, cultural information, searching for new entertainment experiences and connections between reality and the virtual world, eventually integrating the AR experience with social network activities. Augmented Reality permits food peculiarities to be explained, eventually highlighting the significant anchors of the place, combining a food offering with the culture, tradition and heritage of the place. Its capability to contribute to place-making activities (Daramola-Martin 2009; Warnaby and Medway 2013) expresses place meanings.

16.8   Conclusions

Augmented Reality could have multiple applications in every sector, and the customization of the applications could affect tests and results. This study, without presenting a specific AR tool, shows the reaction of entrepreneurs in food dining industry, stimulating them to express themselves around the possible use of AR technology in improving the opportunity of communication with the customers, increasing and expanding the real-time experience with food, place and cultural heritage and, at the same time, able to give an innovative impression to the customer/user.

With respect to AR application, the food dining industry emerges as a complex system of value providers able to generate exclusive and particular service provisions where each entrepreneur has its own solution, and he/she competes in the market thanks to its "creative business models". The individualism of Italian food entrepreneurs emerges, and each one is ready to generate its own system of elements of differentiation that is a mix made by innovation, tradition, political influences, society interpretation and fantasy. As highlighted by the research, AR is considered a *"positive add on"* with specific *limits in the application on the classical dining experience management*, particularly in Italy where the food dining industry is characterized for the majority by small companies and family businesses.

16.8.1 AR as *"Positive Add On"*

The lack of diffusion of advanced technology and the delay in technology infrastructures diffusion, generate distrust in learning how to use and applying new technological means. For this reason, even if the entrepreneurs perceive the potentiality of the tool, they consider that this is not a need for its activity until the strong diffusion of technology within the industry. It has been the same thinking about social media management; only a couple of years ago, not many restaurants considered the need to work on social media management. Today, with the strong diffusion of this way to communicate, every restaurant is connected with the social network sites.

For this reason, the intuition of opportunities concerning to the AR is present, and entrepreneurs perceive the potentiality of this technology but, it is not the priority for the development of restaurants' business model and for this reason it should be an "add on". Indeed, probably the improvement of technological infrastructures and the increasing of its diffusion will bring much more opportunity in using AR. Its role will be much more focused on customer relationship and cultural heritage diffusion, in particular, explaining the connection between restaurant activities and place traditions. The pillars of restaurants' business activity will remain on the dining competencies of the entrepreneur.

About the customer relationship, entrepreneurs say that customers are asking for more opportunity to have technological contact with the restaurants and the improvement of these means could encourage the flexibility of the business model, the improvement of the service and the integration between online and offline activity (for example, AR could improve the online experience and the takeaway service for some restaurants). That is confirmed, for instance, by some answers that underlined the desire of customers who are visiting customers to be involved in having a clear vision about plates and recipes before ordering (online and offline) and, at the same time, they could be really interested in having thought-provoking information about the relationship between food, restaurant interpretation of recipes and cultural heritage, even in terms of place and relative culture.

16.8.2   Limits in AR Application on the Classical Dining Experience Management

Specific limits are highlighted about the AR application in everyday restaurant management in Italy. In particular, considering that limited dimensions characterize most of the restaurants integrated with the tradition and cultural heritage in terms of capitals, available space for guests, management and employees that, eventually, could manage AR application for the restaurant. More than a social network webpage, AR tools need to be improved and updated in information periodically; it is relevant to create contents tuned and integrated with the social network website. That causes the necessity to invest time in training, changing the classic way to work, managing the right personal/impersonal contact with the customer or, eventually, it is necessary to engage an external professional able to manage this activity externally, but that causes the need of specific investment. First investment in technology is not a real problem even for small restaurants and small company. The limit could be in the maintenance of the structure, creation of updated contents, training of the human resources in integrating the offline and online relationships (internal and external—including the customer) and cooperating with external professionals. That is a hard task to manage in particular for small companies that have the tradition, place attachment and reduced flexibility as key pillars in their business model strategies.

Certain research perspectives can be selected from this work. The first is to repeat the analysis using a specific AR tool tested and analysed and involving a greater number of companies, even segmenting the government. Another is to assert that from the data side, it could be useful to understand how AR data can connect with various business intelligence points (if present) of the various food providers. It is interesting to study how the pillars of the place actor network find satisfaction in being involved with difficulties in the implementation and maintenance of content. In particular, it would be interesting to understand how to generate "nudges" to stimulate several actors around the restaurants (within the supply chain but even integrating municipalities and cultural organizations) with the aim to integrate concretely cultural heritage with food and dining provision developing specific AR projects useful for business and cultural goals. In general, the entire AR tool must be studied to evaluate the AR system as a communication tool, integrating it with business research strategies.

References

Azuma RT (1997) A survey of augmented reality. Presence: Teleoperators and Virtual Environments 6(4):355–385. https://doi.org/10.1162/pres.1997.6.4.355
Azuma R, Baillot Y, Behringer R, Feiner S, Julier S, Macintyre B (2001) Recent advances in augmented reality. IEEE Comput Graphics and Applications. 21(6):34–47. https://doi.org/10.1109/38.963459

Batat W, Peter PC, Moscato EM, Castro IA, Chan S, Chugani S, Muldrow A (2019) The experiential pleasure of food: A savoring journey to food well-being. J Bus Res 100:392–399

Brengman M, Willems K, Van Kerrebroeck H (2018) Can't touch this: the impact of augmented reality versus touch and non-touch interfaces on perceived ownership. Virtual Reality, 1–12. https://doi.org/10.1007/s10055-018-0335-6

Bruni R, Caboni F (2017) Place as value proposition: the marketing perspective. Franco Angeli.

Bublitz MG, Peracchio LA, Andreasen AR, Kees J, Kidwell B, Miller EG, Vallen B (2013) Promoting positive change: advancing the food well-being paradigm. J Bus Res 66:1211–1218

Caboni F (2020) La tecnologia nell'evoluzione del retail. Creazione e definizione del retail esprienziale. Milan. FrancoAngeli

Caboni F, Hagberg J (2019) Augmented reality in retailing: a review of features, applications and value. International Journal of Retail and Distribution Management. Earlycite.

Carmignani J, Furht B (2011) Augmented reality: an overview. In B. Furht (ed) Handbook of augmented reality. Springer Verlag, Heidelberg, Dortrecht, London, and New York, pp 3–46. https://doi.org/10.1007/978-1-4614-0064-6_1

Carmignani J, Furht B, Anisetti M, Ceravolo P, Damiani E, Ivkovic M (2011) Augmented reality technologies, systems and applications. Multimedia Tools and Application, 51(1):341–377.

Colli A (2003) The history of family business, 47: 1850–2000. Cambridge University Press

Corbetta G (1995) Patterns of development of family businesses in Italy. Fam Bus Rev 8(4):255–265

Cowling BJ, Ali ST, Ng TW, Tsang TK, Li, JC, Fong MW, Wu JT (2020) Impact assessment of non-pharmaceutical interventions against coronavirus disease 2019 and influenza in Hong Kong: an observational study. The Lancet Public Health.

Cresswell T, Hoskins G (2008) Place, persistence, and practice: evaluating historical significance at Angel Island, San Francisco, and Maxwell Street, Chicago. Ann Assoc Am Geogr 98(2):392–413. https://doi.org/10.1080/00045600701879409

Cruwys T, Bevelander KE, Hermans RC (2015) Social modeling of eating: a review of when and why social influence affects food intake and choice. Appetite 86:3–18

Daramola-Martin A (2009) Liverpool One and the transformation of a city: place branding, marketing and the catalytic effects of regeneration and culture on repositioning Liverpool. Place Brand Public Dipl 5(4):301–311

Davis PS, Harveston PD (2000) Internationalization and organizational growth: the impact of internet usage and technology involvement among entrepreneur-led family businesses. Fam Bus Rev 13(2):107–120

Di Giovine M, Brulotte RL (2016) Introduction food and foodways as cultural heritage. In: Edible identities: food as cultural heritage. Routledge, pp 1–27

Eisenhardt KM, Graebner ME (2007) Theory building from cases: Opportunities and challenges. Acad Manag J 50(1):25–32

Eurostat (2017) Integration of Digital Technology. Europe's Digital Progress Report. EDPR 2017, European Commission

FIPE Centro Studi (2017) Ristorazione—Report on dining Activities 2017, https://www.fipe.it/centro-studi/2017.html. Accessed 20 Sept 2020

FIPE Centro studi (2019) Ristorazione—Annual Report 2019, https://www.fipe.it/centro-studi/2019.html. Accessed 20 Sept 2020

Fuentes C, Bäckström K, Svingstedt A (2017) Smartphones and the reconfiguration of retailscapes: stores, shopping, and digitalization. J Retail Consum Serv 39:270–278

Grewal D, Ahlbom CP, Beitelspacherv L, Noble SM, Nordfält J (2018) In-store mobile phone use and customer shopping behavior: evidence from the field. Journal of Marketing

Grewal D, Roggeveen AL, Nordfält J (2017) The future of retailing. Journal of Retailing 93(1):1–6

Hall CM (2013) Why forage when you don't have to? Personal and cultural meaning in recreational foraging: A New Zealand study. J Herit Tour 8(2–3):224–233

Hagberg J, Jonsson A, Egels-Zandén N (2017) Retail digitalization: implications for physical stores. J Retail Consum Serv 9:264–269

Hagberg J, Sundstrom M, Egels-Zandé N (2016) The digitalization of retailing: an exploratory framework. Int J Retail Distrib Manag 44(7):694–712

Hwangbo H, Kim YS, Cha KJ (2017) Use of the smart store for persuasive marketing and immersive customer experiences: a case study of Korean apparel enterprise. Mobile Information System. https://doi.org/10.1155/2017/4738340

Javornik A (2016a) Augmented reality: research agenda for studying the impact of its media characteristics on consumer behaviour. J Retail Consum Serv 30:252–261. https://doi.org/10.1016/j.jretconser.2016.02.004

Javornik A (2016b) It's an illusion, but it looks real! Consumer affective, cognitive and behavioural responses to augmented reality applications. Journal of Marketing Management. 32(9–10):987–1011

Jung TH, tom Dieck MC (2017) Augmented reality, virtual reality and 3D printing for the co-creation of value for the visitor experience at cultural heritage places. J Place Manag Dev 10(2):140–151. https://doi.org/10.1108/jpmd-07-2016-0045

Kanak A, Özlü A, Polat SO, Ergün ÖÖ (2018) An intelligent dining scene experience. In 2018 26th Signal Processing and Communications Applications Conference (SIU), pp 1–3, IEEE. https://doi.org/10.1109/siu.2018.8404549

Lee H, Leonas K (2018) Consumer experiences, the key to survive in an omni-channel environment: use of virtual technology. J Text Appar Technol Manag 10(3):1–23

Margetis G, Grammenos D, Zabulis X, Stephanidis C (2013) iEat: an interactive table for restaurant customers' experience enhancement. In International Conference on Human-Computer Interaction Springer, Berlin, Heidelberg, pp 666–670. https://doi.org/10.1007/978-3-642-39476-8_134

Massingham P (2004) Linking business level strategy with activities and knowledge resources. J Knowl Manag

Olsson T, Lagerstam E, Kärkkäinen T, Väänänen-Vainio-Mattila K (2013) Expected user experience of mobile augmented reality services: a user study in the context of shopping centres. Pers Ubiquitous Comput 17(2):287–304

Pantano E, Rese A, Baier D (2017) Enhancing the online decision-making process by using augmented reality: a two country comparison of youth markets. J Retail Consum Serv 38:81–95. https://doi.org/10.1016/j.jretconser.2017.05.011

Poushneh A, Vasquez-Parraga AZ (2017) Discernible impact of augmented reality on retail customer's experience, satisfaction and willingness to buy. J Retail Consum Serv 34:229–234. https://doi.org/10.1016/j.jretconser.2016.10.005

Poushneh A (2018) Augmented reality in retail: a trade-off between user's control of access to personal information and augmentation quality. J Retail Consum Serv 41:169–176. https://doi.org/10.1016/j.jretconser.2017.12.0100

Pu M, Abd Majid NA, Idrus B (2017) Framework based on mobile augmented reality for translating food menu in Thai language to Malay language. Int J Adv Sci, Eng Inf Technol 7(1):153–159. https://doi.org/10.18517/ijaseit.7.1.1797

Quan S, Wang N (2004) Towards a structural model of the tourist experience: an illustration from food experiences in tourism. Tour Manag 25(3):297–305. https://doi.org/10.1016/s0261-5177(03)00130-4

Ramadan ZB, Farah MF (2017) The Pokémonisation of the first moment of truth. Int J Web Based Communities 13(2):262–277. https://doi.org/10.1504/ijwbc.2017.084417

Reinwald F, Berger M, Stoik C, Platzer M, Damyanovic D (2014) Augmented reality at the service of participatory urban planning and community informatics—a case study from Vienna. J Community Inform 10(3)

Rese A, Baier D, Geyer-Schulz A, Schreiber S (2017) How augmented reality apps are accepted by consumers: a comparative analysis using scales and opinions. Technol Forecast Soc Chang 124:306–319. https://doi.org/10.1016/j.techfore.2016.10.010

Scholz J, Smith AN (2016) Augmented reality: designing immersive experiences that maximize consumer engagement. Bus Horiz 59(2):149–161

Sood S (2012) The death of social media in start-up companies and the rise of s-commerce: convergence of e-commerce, complexity and social media. J Electron Commer Organ 10(2):1–15

Spence C (2017) Gastrophysics: The new science of eating. Penguin UK.

Ukwuani N, Bashir E (2017) Emerging technologies: an exploration of novel interactive technologies. Int J Inf Syst Serv Sect 9(4):30–43

Wang Y, Ahmed PK (2009) The moderating effect of the business strategic orientation on eCommerce adoption: evidence from UK family run SMEs. J Strateg Inf Syst 18(1):16–30

Warnaby G, Medway D (2013) What about the 'place' in place marketing? Marketing Theory. 13(3):345–363

Watson A, Alexander B, Salavati L (2018) The impact of experiential augmented reality applications on fashion purchase intention. Int J Retail & Distrib Manag. https://doi.org/10.1108/IJRDM-06-2017-0117

Yanagisako SJ (2020) Producing culture and capital: family firms in Italy. Princeton University Press.

Yin RK (2003) Case study research: Design and methods, 3rd edn. Sage, Thousand Oaks, CA

Yuan Y (2018, July) Augmenting food experience while traveling abroad by using mobile augmented reality application. In International conference on cross-cultural design. Springer, Cham, pp 259–268

Chapter 17
Reintroducing Indonesian Folk Songs to Children Using Augmented Reality Books

Dimas Rifqi Novica, Dhia Asfa Awliya, and Ima Kusumawati Hidayat

Abstract This chapter explores a new approach to reintroduce Indonesian folk songs to children using Augmented Reality (AR) children's books. Indonesian folk song's existence as intangible cultural heritage is declining nowadays because children prefer popular music with exciting visuals and presentations. At the same time, augmented reality technology assimilation to conventional media has started to emerge. Previous studies show the great potential of AR-based books for children and indicate that this technology enhances their learning experience. This project adapts Bruce Archer's design methodology, including programming, data collection, analysis, synthesis, development, and communication. There were two phases for testing the AR book: the alpha testing phase used a digital book as a marker, then a printed book was used for the beta testing phase. The AR book is expected to provide a tangible experience for children to enjoy and preserve Indonesian folk songs.

17.1 Introduction

Many forms of Indonesia's cultural heritages reflect its diverse regions, knowledges, and local languages. Countless generations have passed down Indonesian cultural heritages orally. Indonesian folk songs provide an excellent example of this transmission. Although the Indonesian minister of Education and Culture (Indonesia Ministry of Education and Culture 2015) has stipulated that children should sing Indonesian folk songs in schools, their implementation has not been successful. Indeed, Indonesian children's participation and knowledge of folk songs have diminished over time. Indonesian children prefer popular music that comes in many exciting visuals and presentations.

D. R. Novica (✉) · D. A. Awliya · I. K. Hidayat
Faculty of Letters, Art and Design Department, Universitas Negeri Malang, Malang, Indonesia
e-mail: dimas.novica.fs@um.ac.id

I. K. Hidayat
e-mail: ima.hidayat.fs@um.ac.id

© The Author(s), under exclusive license to Springer Nature Switzerland AG 2021   309
V. Geroimenko (ed.), *Augmented Reality in Tourism, Museums and Heritage*, Springer Series on Cultural Computing,
https://doi.org/10.1007/978-3-030-70198-7_17

The decline of folksong's popularity in children is due to the lack of information in tangible media such as books. The ones that available in stores are those with musical notes and lyrics. As these books lack proper illustration and content, they are not very popular among young audiences. The children's book should contain illustrations to delight, capture attention, teach, amplify the story, and develop appreciation and awareness in children (Fang 1996). In addition, Brookshire et al. (2002) and Tursun-murotovich (2020) agree that illustration helps children with story comprehension and knowledge enrichment.

In an attempt to reintroduce Indonesian folk songs, scholars have been exploring various media, including smartphone applications (Purnomo et al. 2016), educative dolls (Soewardi and Maulidyawati 2018), and video games (Harahap and Hasibuan 2020). However, explorations into the use of children's books as media remain scarce. Nowadays, Augmented Reality (AR) has enhanced many children's books to improve attention and attractiveness by providing a more tangible reading experience to children. Also, multimedia content in an AR book will enhance reading comprehension in children (Danaei et al. 2020). Moreover, children can achieve higher levels of cognitive attainment by explaining what they have seen and/or heard (Cheng and Tsai 2014). In this study, we explored the design and development of AR technology in a book intended to reintroduce Indonesian folk songs to children.

17.2   Indonesian Folk Songs

Indonesian folk songs derive from particular regions of Indonesia. The folk song is an intangible form of heritage that reflects and generates the richness of contrasting Indonesian cultures. These folk songs usually employ simple melodies and are sung by people in their region's language (Prasetyo et al. 2020). They are taught initially to children for communicating the way of life. The songs have didactic elements such as moral values, religions, lives, and environmental concerns (Wibowo et al. 2018).

There are more than 400 Indonesian folk songs (Hakim 2020). However, we only explored folk songs in the provinces of Java. There are six folk songs in the AR Children's book that represent each of the provinces. The titles are "Gundhul-Gundhul Pacul," "Suwe Ora Jamu," "Rek Ayo Rek," "Kicir-Kicir," "Tokecang." and "Dayung Sampan." Each song has a distinct meaning that communicates moral knowledge to the children. The meaning is as follows: Gundhul-Gundhul Pacul teaches about leadership, trust, and responsibility. Suwe Ora Jamu teaches about patience. Rek Ayo Rek teaches about friendship and equality. Kicir-Kicir teaches about happiness in life. Tokecang teaches about moderation. Finally, Dayung Sampan teaches about hardworking.

Children need to participate directly in order to experience and comprehend the moral knowledge provided through folk songs. Through folk songs, children can express themselves in singing and playing while moral knowledge is inculcated through the song's lyrics (Widjanarko et al. 2018). This experience will help children develop their attitudes and behavior, as the early childhood cognitive-developmental period is the most crucial stage of their development. From a cultural perspective, it is critical to introduce folk songs to children at a young age.

17.3   Augmented Reality Children's Books

Augmented Reality is increasingly reaching children as it is becoming more known to their parents and teachers. Several practical learning effects of AR have shown the impacts on children, such as increased content understanding, long-term memory retention, increased student motivation, and improved collaboration (Radu 2012). Similarly, Cheng and Tsai (2014) mention that children are more successful at explaining and describing the content of a book that has AR integrated into it. Moreover, AR books not only shown that it has positive effects on cognitive domains but also affective domains such as engagement, presence, interactivity, and affordance (Lim and Park 2013). Hence, AR technology on children's books is suitable for reintroducing Indonesian folk songs to the children.

Even though there are several evidences that AR books can provide better learning experiences, Oranç and Küntay (2019) suggest that AR needs social interactions to make it work. Through parent and child social scaffolding, children can differentiate between realistic and non-realistic objects. Furthermore, working together with their peers contributes to children's engagement and learning, since it encourages them to discuss, collaborate, and reflect upon the content. In the case of younger children, a parent's and/or teacher's guidance is crucial to keep their concentration on the story while reading or helping them with the internet connection since AR depends on it (Chanlin 2018).

To design an AR application for children's books, Vanderschantz et al. (2018) suggest that there are five considerations to enhance the experience: focusing on objects that mentioned in the story text; determining objects to be visible or animated; using a unique marker; using different types of interaction; and adjusting camera level and distance. These considerations add to the print book's design quality that already draws children's attention through fonts, paper quality, dimensions, page layout, cover pages, and visuals (Çer and Şahin 2016). In this study, we will combine the guidelines for designing and developing the AR children's book.

17.4   Design Method

We adapted Bruce Archer's design methodology (Rowe 1991). The methodology has several stages, including programming, data collection, analysis, synthesis, development, and communication. The programming stage, as already mentioned in the introduction, explores the problem of Indonesian folk songs. The AR children's books design and development process combines the data collected through interviews, questionnaires, and observations. We interviewed two teachers, pre-school and primary school teachers, using the online platforms WhatsApp and Quora. The interviews were meant to collect data about Indonesian folk songs teaching in schools. We conducted the interviews on 25–26 February 2020, and 22 May 2020. To collect data about Indonesian folk songs teaching in the home environment, we conducted an online survey through Google Forms from December 2019 to February 2020. The results came from 41 respondents, all of whom were parents of children whose ages range from 5 to 8. We also observed the type of children's books available on the market on 18 and 19 February 2020 to investigate children's book types and visual styles. Then, we analyzed and synthesized the data into the design concept for the AR children's book. The development process revolves around the prototyping process of the AR children's book from the sketch to the final design, including testing the AR content and its marker. Finally, the communication process is to evaluate the book with the sample audiences.

17.5 Design Results and Discussion

According to the interviews, we could find several things that justified our hypothesis that children at the age of 4–8 love to listen and copy the songs they hear every day. In the case of Indonesian children, their first choice of media is YouTube. They listen to English or Islamic songs at schools because it is on the curriculum. The pre-school teacher mentioned that songs are an effective way to direct children's attention in the class and improve their interest in the subject. However, the advanced learning material, media, and pre-school tools that can teach moral knowledge and nationalism are still scarce. In addition to that, the respondents from primary schools claimed not to learn much about Indonesian folk songs. They explored only a portion of it in the art and cultural education class, which also focused on other traditional arts such as dance and fine arts. Obviously, the Indonesian folk songs need to have a more significant portion in the primary schools to sustain their existence.

From the questionnaire, we know that most children did not know about Indonesian folk songs except the ones they teach at the schools. Many children are more familiar with popular songs for adults because they hear them every day in their home environment, whether on television, radio, or smartphones. However, we know that all of the 41 parents agreed with the importance of teaching their children about Indonesian folk songs. The majority of them mentioned that the reason for this is to preserve local traditional cultures. Only two parents suggested that the Indonesian folk song is important because it communicates moral knowledge.

By observing two bookstores in Malang, East Java, Indonesia, on 18–19 February 2020, it can be deduced that most children's books available on the market involve characters that are intended to serve as role models for the children. The stories are mostly about fairy tales, myths, and the legends of Indonesia. There are also translated children's books from abroad. These books use vibrant colors and cute character designs on the cover to attract potential reader's attention. We found a few children's books that teach music, but there were none which included the Indonesian traditional folk songs.

These findings suggest that children's books about Indonesian folk songs are yet to be explored. We suggest that introducing AR to children's books about Indonesian folk songs could be of critical importance. We hope to tell a story with AR technology through exciting visuals and audios to reintroduce Indonesian folk songs to the children. It also builds interaction between adults and children to provide a better learning experience.

Print books are easy to carry and read. The reading experience of print books is irreplaceable by other form of books. Etta (2019) suggests that interactive print books are more commonly used for social purposes and serve more entertaining purposes than digital books. This AR children's book overall concept would serve as light reading for parents and children quality time. There are six Indonesian folk songs in this book that represent the Java region. They all have a playful tone and are replete with moral values to strengthen children's social development. The AR technology in the book helps to direct attention to the book and entertain the children. It will also enhance content comprehension and develop their imagination. The Android smartphone application will accompany the children's book to display the AR content if the camera scans the markers. This book aims to provides tangible experience using visual storytelling for children about Indonesian folk songs originally from the Java region. The page that has song lyrics is the marker for the AR technology. The scanned marker will displays simple animation and plays the audio of the Indonesian folk songs. Children will be able to know the melody, which will help them to recite the songs.

The design and development process revolves around children's preferences, such as the book's size, the title, the story, the vibrant color palette, the cute character design, and the fun typography. Tian (2018) suggests that children's book design should adapt to children's innocent, lively character traits and integrate them into their lives. Our book has a square shape with 22 × 22 cm in size. We consider this measurement appropriate after comparing it to many children's books available in the market. At this size, the book seems too big in the hands of 4–8 years old. Nevertheless, we would like to pursue the Big Book functionalities as it provides a sense of intimacy and safety between the children and their peers.

We chose the book title with brainstorming method. The word Pertiwi came up several times in the process. Therefore, we decided that the book's title should be "Lagu untuk Pertiwi" ("The Songs for Mother Earth"). The words "Pertiwi" in the title have a double meaning. Firstly, in Bahasa Indonesia, the word comes from Sanskrit "Pṛthvī," one of the gods in Hindu. The word has a personified meaning—like "mother" in "mother earth" or "mother nature." Secondly, the word is often used as a girl's name in Indonesia, which later become the name of the story's main character. Hence, there is a double meaning to the title: the folk songs represent Indonesia's (mother earth) intangible cultural heritage, and the folk songs are the birthday present for Pertiwi as the main character in the story.

The story revolves around Pertiwi as the main character. Pertiwi is a girl who loves to sing and dance. When it is Pertiwi's birthday, she is given a recorder rhinoceros doll from her mother. The doll can imitate her voice and sing it in melody. She loves it very much. However, Pertiwi is sad because she only knows one song. The mother then tells her about many Indonesian folk songs from the Javanese region. Late that night, Pertiwi has an adventurous dream of getting known one song after another with the help of her doll and other stuffed animal. There are six Indonesian folk songs in the book. Consecutively, these are Dayung Sampan, Suwe Ora Jamu, Rek Ayo Rek, Gundhul-Ghundul Pacul, Tokecang, and Kicir-Kicir.

This AR children's book used vibrant colors. We used warm color combinations with red and orange because these colors complement children's playful and energetic nature (Thompson and Schultz 2003). The illustration was created by a digital painting technique that emphasizes the brush stroke to create texture on the color. We applied a crayon texture because children start using colorful crayons at this age to aim for the closeness of the media. The drawing style is influenced by three children's book illustrators, namely Margarita Kukhtina, Hana Agustine, and Arief A. Putra. The books contain a spread that discusses the origins of the Indonesian folk songs and the lyrics of these songs. An example of the spread is shown in Fig. 17.1.

We used a circular shapes as it make the characters fun and approachable. Such shapes create soft and friendly vibes. We tried to define the concept of cute character by several physical characteristics, such as smallness, indulgence, and simplicity (Gn 2017). For example, for the character of Pertiwi, we use a relatively small nose in accordance with her head, eyes, and ears. This scale deformation makes the character appear cuter. Her joy and happiness as a girl reflect the character's indulgence. We could see that simplicity comes from the overall design of Pertiwi as we do not use excessive ornament on the character. The character design of Pertiwi is shown in Fig. 17.2.

Fig. 17.1 The illustration on the spread page of the book

Fig. 17.2   The cute character design of Pertiwi

For the book's typography, we used two different themes for the cover and content. The cover uses more fonts that have a thick and round shape to emphasize the title. The font on the cover uses orange color to attract the attention of children. As for the content, we still used round fonts, but with a slightly thinner shape to increase readability. We also use curly font for the song lyrics, so it differentiates from the story content. We use classic black on white color for the typography of the story content.

After the illustrations and page layouts were completed, we started to animate the image and integrate it to create the AR database. We separated the full image into moveable assets for animation. For example, we cut the boat and the trees in order to create a level later in the AR. In the smartphone app's alpha version, we tested the AR content using a digital book from a laptop screen. The animations and audios already played well at this stage. Then, we integrated the AR content into the remaining page spreads.

We used the same spread layout throughout the book to display the Indonesian folk songs, which is the left page for illustrations and the right page for lyrics. We printed the book in full color with two art paper types, 210 gr for the hardcover and 150 gr for the content for the prototyping and evaluation purpose. The example display of AR feature can be seen in Fig. 17.3. On the left side, we use signboard illustration for the word "Banten." This text inform about the song's origin, Banten

Fig. 17.3 The AR feature display on the spread page

Province of Java. On the right side, there are the lyrics of the song. In the example, there are Dayung Sampan lyrics. These spread pages has AR built into them. The AR content on this page will display an animation of Pratiwi's boat and audio from the Dayung Sampan song.

For this page to display the AR content, the recognition image is first scanned by the smartphone camera and transmitted to the online server to match the stored image. If the matching is successful, the smartphone will play the animation and audio of each spread page. If not successful, the smartphone will not play anything. The image we used for the marker is the whole two pages of the spread layout. The reason for this is because we want to differentiate the marker by the unique illustration and text. We used a simple structure for the AR system, as Yang et al. (2019) suggest, a smartphone with a camera and apps, recognition image/marker, and server for storing animation and the audio. In the beta phases, we had already tried three brands of mostly used smartphones with an android system in Indonesia.

For the evaluation session, we have three pair of participants, first, a male child (5 years old) and his mother (CP1); second, a male child (4 years old) and his mother (CP2), and a female child (5 years old) and her mother (CP3). The three pairs read the book while occasionally scanned for the AR content on spread pages. When the activities finished, each pair was interviewed to reflect on their experience while using AR technology on the spread pages. The primary objective was to investigate and discuss whether this application was fun and useful for 4–8 years olds.

While the three pairs of participants were exploring the books and the application, they mostly showed positive reactions to the book's content. The three children agreed that the illustration was excellent. They loved the characters and the backgrounds. Especially, CP3 mentioned that the background was splendid. However, there was slight disappointment regarding the AR application. CP2 and CP3 were experiencing a black glitch while the animation is playing. Our first assumption was that this had happened because of the big size of the animation's PNG image. Regarding that problem, the mother of CP2 also mentioned that the application was too big for their phone. CP1, CP2, CP3 mentioned that sometimes the song's audio was playing first, about 3 second before the animation starts. We still do not know what caused this glitch. Overall, all respondents stated that it was a new and positive learning and bonding experience. They are very interested to see how the final product will be delivered.

We suggest that having an initial page to explain how to use the AR in the book is crucial. We always felt the necessity to explain verbally to the participants on how to use the book in each beginning of evaluation sessions. Moreover, we believe that having a sign for each image marker on the page spreads will let the audience know when to hold their smartphone for scanning the AR content. The AR content is considered new in Indonesia; this may contribute to children's engagement and learning process since it enables the opportunity to discuss, collaborate, and reflect upon the story. Despite comprehending the story very well, the children still needed more than one read through to memorize the songs. Despite the fact that this AR children's book is meant to be read together with their peers, they also wanted to explore the book by themselves the second time. Figure 17.4 shows a participant using the AR application by himself after his parents have taught him.

Fig. 17.4 One of the children who explore the AR content by himself

17.6 Conclusion

Indonesian folk songs are an intangible cultural heritage that is declining in children's popularity due to a lack of exciting information and presentation. On the other hand, the integration of AR in children's books is emerging. AR technology has the potential to enhance attention and increase comprehension. The present project aims to develop an AR children's book with tangible experience as a media to reintroduce Indonesian folk songs to the children. Our book combines exciting visual and AR technology to increase children's engagement with the songs. It is important to create exciting visual images through the character and background as it will be the book's primary focus. Animation on the AR content keeps the children's attention to the books and intrigues them to read the rest of the story. Also, audio on the AR content complements them with information about how to sing Indonesian folk songs. We believe that adding merchandise for the children to improve the book's tangible experience further is mandatory. We also suggest that, while the children will want to explore the books themselves, the parent's presence is essential to mediate a discussion and/or to provide more information regarding the subject matter. Further exploration of the AR book's potential at various levels is expected to include more interactive and diverse user studies.

References

Brookshire J, Scharff LFV, Moses LE (2002) The influence of illustrations on children's book preferences and comprehension. Read Psychol 23(4):323–339. https://doi.org/10.1080/713775287

Çer E, Şahin E (2016) Validity of a checklist for the design, content, and instructional qualities of children's books. Hearne & Stevenson 7(24):128–137

Chanlin LJ (2018) Bridging children's reading with an augmented reality story library. Libri 68(3):219–229. https://doi.org/10.1515/libri-2018-0017

Cheng KH, Tsai CC (2014) Children and parents' reading of an augmented reality picture book: Analyses of behavioral patterns and cognitive attainment. Comput Educ 72:302–312. https://doi.org/10.1016/j.compedu.2013.12.003

Danaei D, Jamali HR, Mansourian Y, Rastegarpour H (2020) Comparing reading comprehension between children reading augmented reality and print storybooks. Comput Educ 153(April):103900. https://doi.org/10.1016/j.compedu.2020.103900

Etta RA (2019) Parent preferences: e-books versus print books. In: Literacy S (ed) Reading in the digital age: young children's experience with e-books. Springer, p 296. https://doi.org/10.1007/978-3-030-20077-0_6

Fang Z (1996) Illustrations, text, and the child reader: what are pictures in children's storybooks for? Read Horizons: J Lit Lang Arts 37(2):130–142. https://scholarworks.wmich.edu/reading_horizons/vol37/iss2/3

Gn J (2017) Designing affection: on the curious case of machine cuteness. In: Negra D (ed) The aesthetics and affects of cuteness. Routledge, New York

Hakim I (2020) Lagu Daerah Indonesia beserta Asalnya Lengkap! Dari Sabang Sampai Merauke - Insan Pelajar. https://insanpelajar.com/lagu-daerah-indonesia/. Accessed 13 October 2020

Harahap AA, Hasibuan NA (2020) Implementation of LCM (Linear Congruent Method) method in region song game. Int J Inform Comput Sci 4(2):57–62. https://doi.org/10.30865/ijics.v4i2.2118

Indonesia Ministry of Education and Culture (2015) Penumbuhan Budi Pekerti (No. 23). Indonesia Ministry of Education and Culture, Jakarta

Lim C, Park T (2013) Exploring the educational use of an augmented reality books. ProQuest LLC, pp 172–182

Oranç C, Küntay AC (2019) Learning from the real and the virtual worlds: educational use of augmented reality in early childhood. Int J Child-Comput Interact 21:104–111. https://doi.org/10.1016/j.ijcci.2019.06.002

Prasetyo A, Batubulan KS, Sujudi A Z (2020) Rancang Bangun Runner game 2d dengan Tema Pengenalan Kembali Lirik Lagu Daerah Menggunakan Algoritma Fisher-Yates Shuffle. In Sentia, vol 12. Politeknik Negeri Malang, Malang. https://prosiding.polinema.ac.id/sentia/index.php/SENTIA2020/article/view/364/310

Purnomo A, Hartono R, Hartatik H, Riasti BK, Hidayah IN (2016) Pengembangan Aplikasi info Lagu Nusantara Berbasis Android Untuk Melestarikan Warisan Budaya Indonesia. Simetris: Jurnal Teknik Mesin, Elektro dan Ilmu Komputer 7(2):527–536. https://doi.org/10.24176/simet.v7i2.764

Radu I (2012) Why should my students use AR? A comparative review of the educational impacts of augmented-reality. ISMAR 2012—11th IEEE International Symposium on Mixed and Augmented Reality 2012, Science and Technology Papers, pp 313–314. https://doi.org/10.1109/ISMAR.2012.6402590

Soewardi H, Maulidyawati SB (2018) Educative doll design as media for learning indonesian traditional folk song using affective design approach. Int J Inf Educ Technol 8(12):874–879. https://doi.org/10.18178/ijiet.2018.8.12.1156

Thompson M, Schultz K (2003) The psychological experiences of students of color. Indep Sch 62(4):42–48

Tian Z (2018) On the Illustration Design of Children's Books. 2018 2nd International Conference on Social Science, Arts and Humanities (SSAH 2018), pp 153–156

Tursunmurotovich SS (2020) Importance of illustrations for perception of content of the book. Eur J Res Reflect Educ Sci 8(4):98–101

Vanderschantz N, Hinze A, Al-Hashami A (2018) Multiple level enhancement of children's picture books with augmented reality. Lecture Notes in Computer Science (including subseries Lecture Notes in Artificial Intelligence and Lecture Notes in Bioinformatics) (Vol. 11279 LNCS). Springer International Publishing. https://doi.org/10.1007/978-3-030-04257-8_26

Wibowo A, Warto W, Sariyatun S (2018) Reinterpretation of values in the Folksong Ilir-Ilir by Raden Sahid. Int J Multicult Multireligious Underst 5(4):204–212. https://doi.org/10.18415/ijmmu.v5i4.263

Widjanarko P, Paud PG, Selamet U, Eka R, Andaryani T, Semarang UN (2018) The nationalism cultivation through the folk songs in Sandhy Putra, pp 305–309

Yang W, Liu L, Wang Y, Zhong Y (2019) Design and development of alcohol packaging anti-counterfeiting system based on augmented reality technology. Advances in Graphic Communication, Printing and Packaging, vol 543. https://doi.org/10.1007/978-981-13-3663-85

Concluding Remarks

This book presents to the reader with wide-ranging research into the use of augmented reality (AR) technology in the three interconnected and overlapping fields of the tourism industry, museum exhibitions, and cultural heritage, covering a great number of topics, areas, and applications: from the opportunities and challenges of augmented reality applications to their current status and future trends, from immersive installations to shared visitors' experience, from digital heritage sites to local dining industry, urban novels, and folk songs, from visitors with special needs to issues caused by COVID-19.

Augmented reality is revolutionising and reshaping the tourism and travel industry, museum and exhibition spaces, cultural and physical heritage sites. It has become increasingly popular thanks to spectacular advances in smartphone and tablet technology. The impact augmented reality is having on tourism, museums, and heritage can be explained by its ability to alter a person's perception of their physical surroundings, when viewed through a smartphone or tablet.

Augmented reality is a perfect tool for tourism, and it has limitless potential. Some of the most effective and innovative uses of AR apps include enhancing physical locations and tourist attractions, improving the overall experience by providing tourists with more information on demand and introducing an element of fun to their physical environment, including extra knowledge about the local places of interest, serving as a novel tourist information tool and a real-life digital tour guide. Augmented reality allows a tourist to point their smartphone at a historic landmark and learn more about it, be presented with information about its history in real time and on the go. AR apps are able to open a window into the past, tell the amazing story of a ruined building and show on top of the real-world scenery what it used to be hundreds of years ago. This ability may greatly enhance the entire travel experience, add new values and open new opportunities by both educating and entertaining the tourist.

There are many exciting possibilities for augmented reality technology in the museum space. AR apps can bring displays and exhibits to life, making museums no longer a boring place, especially for young visitors. Augmented reality invites visitors

V. Geroimenko (ed.), *Augmented Reality in Tourism, Museums and Heritage*, Springer Series on Cultural Computing,
https://doi.org/10.1007/978-3-030-70198-7

to find out more about exhibitions in an engaging manner, search for different objects using a third dimension, bring objects or scenes that existed thousands of years ago to life, contextualise history by blending the physical and the digital. AR apps can add more information and greater fun to existing collections and provide museums with new ways of engaging their visitors, attracting wider audiences, improving people's experience and their understanding of key concepts, capturing visitors' attention, and keeping their focus on exhibitions for longer.

In the same way, augmented reality heritage sites are able to support or even replace the traditional tour or re-enactment by bringing forward relevant information and showing areas and artefacts in the context of visually exciting and interactively engaging digital presentations integrated with real-world settings and surroundings.

In this light, augmented reality technology, thoroughly considered in this book, appears central to the future of the three interrelated and intersecting areas of tourism, museums, and heritage, taking them to the next level by building on demand visitor experiences that are both informative and fun to gain.

Printed in the United States
by Baker & Taylor Publisher Services